Turning
200

Turning 200

THE BICENTENNIAL
OF THE U.S. CONSTITUTION

Jane Nevins

RICHARDSON & STEIRMAN

This book is dedicated with love and gratitude
to my mother, Elizabeth A. Nevins

Contents

CONTENTS

Acknowledgements

FOR INSPIRING THIS BOOK, credit goes to the genius of Gouverneur Morris, who is my favorite Enlightenment man. I also owe a real debt of gratitude to the contemporary genius of Dr. William B. Allen of Harvey Mudd College, Claremont, California, who reviewed the manuscript and offered generous criticisms of all kinds, but especially guided me on the political principles of the Founding Era, which Dr. Allen understands in detail. Professor Paul Zall, of the Henry E. Huntington Library in San Marino, California, allowed me to refer to his work in progress, biographical studies of all the Framers deliciously flavored with human insights and foibles, which added happy impetus to the writing. At the National Park Service in Philadelphia, David Kimball, Chief Historian, not only made it 1787 again for me, but also reviewed the manuscript and gave me valuable suggestions. Additionally, I drew often upon the exciting "Bicentennial Daybook" prepared by Kimball and his staff—more than a thousand pages of information about the Convention and delegates, Philadelphia, and the American Confederation for the entire year 1787.

ACNOWLEDGEMENTS

Those who love this era tend to be unstinting in their willingness to help, and so were Ellen and Forrest McDonald, whose biography of Hamilton is without peer; Dr. Robert Goldwin of the American Enterprise Institute; Dr. Phillip Lyons; the people at the Bicentennial Commission, especially former Chief Justice Warren Burger, Dr. Mark Cannon, and Tish Avery.

Thanks, too, to Sheila Mulvihill for the thoughtful questions she asked.

Finally, to my publisher, Sandy Richardson, count me in the front ranks of your grateful authors.

Introductory Note

DURING THE FIVE YEARS after the Declaration of Independence, the thirteen new American states ratified an agreement, the Articles of Confederation and Perpetual Union, by which the states agreed to act in unison for certain purposes, such as the common defense. By 1787, however, it had become clear that the Articles were inadequate to guard against domestic rebellion, to provide economic stability, to prevent the states from acting against each other's interests, or to preserve the reputation and credit of the new Union in the eyes of the world.

Serious signs that the states would fragment into thirteen small, warring countries or realign themselves into three or four rival confederations persuaded the states' legislatures to appoint delegates to a general convention for the purpose of proposing revisions to the Articles of Confederation. The convention assembled in Philadelphia in late May, 1787. The result of their work was the Constitution of the United States, signed two hundred years ago this September 17, 1987.

The official Bicentennial period runs from 1987 to 1991, closing with the ratification of the Bill of Rights. This book tells *what* is "turning two hundred," the principles, problems, actions, and characters of the Americans who foresaw that a great nation could rise if a good beginning were made—but, most importantly, the remarkable framework constructed to meet the daunting challenge of providing for a people to govern itself.

1

Valley Forge

AT DAYBREAK ON TUESDAY, July 31, 1787, a fashionable open carriage pulled away from the house of Mrs. Jane Moore about twenty miles west of Philadelphia, Pennsylvania. The two men it carried wore casual attire; fishing gear rattled in the back of the phaeton as they turned it in a southeasterly direction over a rough path cut by farm wagons in the rolling countryside. The day was cloudy and cool, their destination just three miles away.

The fishermen did not have much to say to each other as they bounced along: the older was by lifelong habit an early riser, but taciturn; the other, though loquacious, was a city man who preferred late nights and was not overfond of the dawn.

Given the fame of the political convention underway in Philadelphia, a bystander spying the pair would have recognized—or guessed he was seeing—George Washington, who was presiding over the meeting. At fifty-five, Washington still bore himself with a dignity that caught people's attention. His six-foot-three-inch frame was lean, graceful, erect; his large bony hands manipulated the reins of the two gray horses with ease. Most striking was his massive head, with its high, broad forehead and heavy brow, and deep—very deep—set gray eyes. Prominent cheekbones and thick hair, now graying and tied back in a club, completed the picture of strength. Though the handsome face was somewhat disfigured by false teeth that did not fit well, Washington's jaw still looked capable of jutting the big chin into a hard tilt of determination. For almost a decade Washington had been called the Father of His Country, and everything in his appearance justified it.

The bystander might have decided that the large, good-looking man twenty years younger seated beside Washington was a military veteran because of his wooden leg, but Gouverneur Morris had not served in the Revolutionary Army. Nor was he the governor of anything; his first name (pronounced *goov-er-nure*) was simply his mother's family name. Even so, Morris was a revolutionary veteran in the political sense. He had served in the Continental Congress and as deputy financier of the Revolution. Now a delegate to the convention, Morris was a brilliant member of a fervent band of nationalists fighting for reform of the American confederation.

Washington and Morris made a natural pair, albeit one that puzzled people, because of their surface differences. Morris was quick of tongue, if not always consistent, gifted in intellect, and full of wit. Urbane and cynical, often far beyond other men's taste, the Tall Boy, as his friends called him, appeared to care deeply for no one and nothing. He disdained the pretensions of statesmanship, but abandoned himself to the great actions of his time; he catered to no other man's opinion, but scattered his gifts where he thought best, not stopping to see if or how they were picked up. And far from being the haunted soul those traits sometimes mark, he was entirely as he described himself when young: "I am . . . constitutionally one of the happiest among men."

For George Washington, who was an uncanny judge of character, friendship with Morris was almost inevitable. His own surface deliberation and remoteness masked an appetite for life that equaled, if it did not surpass, the younger man's. No one on the continent, for certain, had a greater capacity for good

2

company, good entertainment, and all the civilized pursuits of his time. Though Washington paid anxious attention to his own reputation, he regarded the ability to ignore other men's opinions as a useful talent in its proper place. In a few years, Morris's enemies would unsuccessfully challenge Washington's decision to appoint him ambassador to France. Without hiding his unhappiness about it, Washington would write Morris to report the criticism leveled at his glibness and sarcasm. The tone of their exchange on the subject speaks volumes about the candor and mutual warmth that supported their friendship.

". . . The promptitude with which your brilliant imagination is displayed," Washington told Morris, "allows too little time for deliberation and correction and is the primary cause of those sallies which too often offend, and of that ridicule of characters which begets enmity . . . but which might easily be avoided if it was under the control of more caution and prudence."

"I now promise you," Morris replied, "that circumspection of conduct which has hitherto, I acknowledge, formed no part of my character."

On this day in 1787, however, they could not be sure that the government in which they both would serve would be brought into existence. Their fishing trip had been possible because the Philadelphia convention had taken a ten-day break to let a small committee of its delegates compile a draft constitution. The draft would collect two months' debate and decisions into a plan that would have to be debated and revised again. Getting only that far had been harrowing, and at one point the convention had been, as one delegate said, "held together by the strength of a hair." If Morris and Washington were wrapped in silent thought as they drove along, their meditations could not have been too different: America was halfway between securing its future and losing its hardwon liberty, but even the boldest gambler would be slow to place a bet either way.

Washington loved fishing, and no record shows that Morris did. But when they reached their destination, it was Morris who fished—while Washington left his friend to ride about. Their hour's journey had brought them to Valley Forge, where Washington had not set foot since the Revolution had reached its lowest point in the bitter winter of 1777–78, nine years ago.

Today, Washington knew, the name Valley Forge stood for bloody footprints in the snow and death by starvation and freezing. He had not forgotten how deeply it had cut him. Seldom in Washington's closely watched career was he reported to have shed tears, even though men of his time cried easily. But at Valley Forge, the soldiers in review noted that their general wept as he walked along the line.

Behind that awful physical suffering had been a revolution mired in crisis, both political and military. The firebrands in the Continental Congress wanted victories, but when Washington had led his eleven thousand men into Valley Forge December 19, 1777, almost every battle that he had commanded had been lost. Philadelphia, the capital, had fallen. Congress, in refuge at York, Pennsylvania, was humiliated, but unable to face the fact that it was a victim of its own principles. A league of friendship among thirteen separate and sovereign states, merely a military alliance, the United States "government" could compel nothing—not men, money, or supplies from the states—and it was venal and clumsy in exercising the powers it did have. A political cabal aimed at replacing Washington was flourishing in the wake of the biggest American victory at Saratoga, New York, where the whole British army in the north had surrendered to General Horatio Gates. Near Valley Forge, British foraging parties stripped the countryside of food and supplies the American army needed, while the impunity with which the king's troops moved undermined civilian support for the fight.

If Washington wondered how much the starving men understood of their peril, he did not dwell on it. While laying down a steady barrage of complaints to Congress, he set the troops to building rows of cramped log barracks along the ridges overlooking Valley Forge, installing abatis (spiked stakes) in strategic positions where the area's defenses were weak, throwing up shops to repair the muskets, wagons, cannon, and other equipment, and constructing a provisions storehouse, a bridge to convey supplies across the Schuykill River, and fences for horse pens. Despite sickness from unsanitary conditions, wounds from skirmishing with enemy foragers, resentment, desertions, and officer resignations, the revolutionaries were still there when spring came.

But it was a different army. Not only were the men hardened by their trial, but they were vastly better prepared to fight. A foreign officer, Baron von Steuben, had presented himself to Washington at mid-winter bearing a commission from Congress for his services. He had proven to be a genius in military drill, combining curses and encouragement in three languages to teach the amateur soldiers the procedures and disciplines of combat—and the army was devoted to him for the confidence he inspired and the faith he showed them as fighters. In the four years of battle that still lay ahead, never again did the army face the kind of humiliation that had preceded Steuben's arrival.

As Washington rode slowly over the six square miles of the old camp, he had at least one piece of irrefutable evidence that his countrymen had lost sight of the real meaning of Valley Forge: although Congress had agreed to pay Steuben for his services, the old general was living on the generosity of Washington's former aide, Alexander Hamilton, in New York while appeal after appeal for Steuben's pension went ignored in the national legislature.

Not that Congress had totally failed to grasp the implications of Valley Forge at the time. After giving the cabal against Washington brief hope and then letting it wither, Congress had yielded to Washington's pleas for a reorganization of the army and sent him a committee to help. Morris, now busy with his fishing lines at Valley Creek, had been part of that committee. For three months, he had labored with Washington at Valley Forge, their friendship developing as they untangled the morass that splintered political leadership had created in all the military departments.

Then just four years ago, in March of 1783, Washington and Morris had separately faced another, more dreadful crisis—a near coup d'état by the army. Morris was then deputy financier of the United States, and Washington remained commander in chief, awaiting the peace treaty ending the war.

With the confederation almost penniless and the army still

unpaid, a committee of officers had gone to Congress to demand that something be done. The national financier, Robert Morris (no relation to Gouverneur), had laid his resignation before Congress, too, in an effort to force a solution. It had fallen to Gouverneur to work with a congressional committee to construct a plan that would do justice to the angry soldiers. But despite the combined genius of Gouverneur and the committee's two young leaders, a Virginian named James Madison and Washington's former aide, Hamilton, their labors failed. When four states voted against accepting the plan, anonymous circulars inciting the men to arms had been distributed at the army's headquarters camp.

Washington had faced mutinies before, but they had always been in the lines, the ranks of the enlisted men. These were his officers, the best men of the land, the exemplars of the Continental army. In his general orders, he canceled the meeting called by the unknown agitator and ordered another held in its place under his authority and with the ranking officers in charge. Although he gave no hint that he would attend, he dramatically appeared to speak to the officers himself. He had brought his remarks in writing and his demeanor full of mighty indignation.

"Gentlemen," he addressed the glowering faces, "by an anonymous summons, an attempt has been made to convene you together—how inconsistent with the rules of propriety!—how unmilitary!—and how subversive of all order and discipline let the good sense of the army decide—"

There, abruptly, he had stopped. A watching captain wrote later, "His Excellency, after reading the first paragraph, made a short pause, took out his spectacles, and begged the indulgence of his audience while he put them on, observing at the same time, that he had grown gray in their service, and now found himself growing blind. There was something so natural, so unaffected, in this appeal, as rendered it superior to the most studied oratory. It forced its way to the heart, and you might see sensibility moisten every eye."

Though Washington finished his denunciation of the "most insidious purposes" and "blackest designs" of inciting "this dreadful alternative of either deserting our country in the extremest hour of her distress or turning our arms against it," human affection had done its work. By the time he turned and left the meeting, the anger had been replaced by shame.

Never before had dissatisfaction been so complete, and when Washington had appeared at the meeting "in this he stood single and alone," an officer later said. "He appeared not at the head of his troops, but as it were in opposition to them, and for a dreadful moment the interests of the army and its general seemed to be in competition! He spoke. Every doubt was dispelled, and the tide of patriotism rolled again in its wonted course."

The officers voted to condemn the anonymous circulars and passed a resolution asking Washington to write to Congress on their behalf "earnestly entreating the more speedy decision of that honorable body."

Washington ached that the crisis should have arisen at all. He could not understand the petty blindness that seemed to corrupt everything—everything—that the Continental Congress tried to do. America had the rarest opportunity in the history of man to fulfill the dream of liberty. Yet in the most basic requirements of decency and honor, the confederation failed again and again.

Memories of pain vanish so quickly: How often those failures had been cited in the ten weeks of the convention, and how stubbornly unpersuaded so many delegates seemed! Washington must have sometimes wondered if he were a fanatic, so long had he begged for reform.

He had started soon after the arrival of the peace treaty, which came on the heels of the officers' unrest. Washington had been preparing to end his eight years of command—arranging with his British counterpart the return of New York and getting his own army ready to disband—but the anxiety would not leave his mind. So in early June, he sat down to compose what he called his "last legacy"—a letter more than four thousand words in length to the governors of all thirteen states. Into it he poured all the urgency he could summon.

He was giving his final blessing to the country in whose

7

service he had spent the prime of his life, Washington wrote, and he wished to step out of his military character and speak of the future of the union.

"The citizens of America," he said, "placed in the most enviable condition, as the sole lords and proprietors of a vast tract of continent, comprehending all the various soils and climates of the world, and abounding with all the necessaries and conveniencies of life, are now . . . acknowledged to be possessed of absolute freedom and independency. They are from this period to be considered as the actors on a most conspicuous theatre, which seems to be peculiarly designated by Providence for the display of human greatness and felicity."

Not only were Americans free upon a new and unspoiled land, but centuries of philosophy and political science lay at their fingertips for guidance, Washington said. Every conceivable advantage thus belonged to the United States, and "if their citizens should not be completely free and happy, the fault will be entirely their own . . . This is the time of their political probation. This is the moment when the eyes of the whole world are turned upon them. This is the moment to establish or ruin their national character forever . . . with our fate will the destiny of unborn millions be involved."

According to the policies the states would now adopt, he said, America would either stand or fall. In his opinion, the continued existence of the United States depended upon four things.

First, the states must give the Congress "a supreme power to regulate and govern the general concerns of the confederated republic" or else "every thing must very rapidly tend to anarchy and confusion." Second, they were duty-bound to honor the war debt, contribute to the support of the federal government, and do justice to the unpaid army. Third, the states must put their militias, "the palladium of our security," on a peacetime footing "absolutely uniform" so that the disarray of the Revolution would not be repeated if new hostilities broke out. And finally, the people must forget their local prejudices and politics and make concessions in favor of the general interest.

He concluded with a request that the governors pass on his message to their state legislatures "as the legacy of one who has ardently wished on all occasions to be useful to his country and who, even in the shade of retirement, will not fail to implore the divine benediction upon it."

In four short years, his worst fears seemed to have been realized, and his plea appeared to have failed.

Washington rode back to collect Morris, and the two made their way back to Mrs. Moore's house, stopping to talk with some farmers about buckwheat and fodder. That night, Washington jotted in his diary a note about his visit to Valley Forge:

"Whilst Mr. Morris was fishing, I rid over the whole old Cantonment of the American Army of the Winter, 1777 and 8, visited all the Works, wch. were in Ruins; and the Incampments in woods where the grounds had not been cultivated."

Would the constitutional convention at Philadelphia be able to create a government worthy of the sacrifice that had been made? Or would the idea of America prove also to be "in Ruins"?

2

The Men in the Empty Chairs

THE CONVENTION IN PHILADELPHIA was meeting without two of the Revolution's most distinguished figures—Thomas Jefferson, the author of the Declaration of Independence, and John Adams, one of the earliest, and considered by many the greatest, of the political leaders of the revolutionary confederation. Both men now were thousands of miles away in Europe, representing the United States as ambassadors.

Jefferson and Adams knew well the crisis of the confederation that had led to the convention. It had followed them overseas where it hampered their work and raised fears in both their minds for the fate of the American "experiment." Yet the nature of their fears was completely different—rising from principles that had strenuous adherents in the convention and were to echo long after.

JEFFERSON

Thomas Jefferson loved Paris—the charm and worldliness of the salons; the congenial conversation of diplomats, military officers and aristocrats; the promenades and the shops; the handsome residence he occupied at the edge of the city, just off the Champs-Élysées near the Bois de Boulogne. He loved giving the small, lavish dinner parties for which he had become famous; he loved leading the witty, gossipy table talk. "I do love this *people* with all my heart," he had written to Abigail Adams, John's wife, and he meant it. Success in the wake of Benjamin Franklin, the first American ambassador to France, was no small feat, but after three years here, Jefferson was entirely at home.

The Virginian's tall, lanky frame and wiry, reddish hair were a familiar sight to the booksellers and shopkeepers—and a welcome one, too. The big topaz ring he wore flashed as he examined their wares, always looking for treasures to be shipped back to Virginia. He had sent more than two hundred volumes to his friends and protégés, James Madison and James Monroe, and to his law teacher in Williamsburg, George Wythe. Numerous objects of art or novelties that struck his fancy had been packed off to still other friends, while scientific researches and reports had been scoured up and posted to his fellow members of the American Philosophical Society in Philadelphia and elsewhere.

It was as if Jefferson had been reborn, and in truth, it could be said that his appointment to Paris had saved his sanity. Madison had pressed the Continental Congress to add his mentor to the American peace commission negotiating with the British in Paris late in 1782, a few weeks after Jefferson had plunged into a deep and seemingly permanent depression upon the death of Martha, his wife of only ten years. Jefferson had been devoted to Martha and had spent the four months of her final illness personally nursing her, rarely leaving her bedside. Her passing had come just a year after the death of a baby daughter, the third infant they had lost in less than six years, and before his spirit had healed from the worst humiliation of his political career—a resolution of censure introduced in the Virginia legislature accusing him of failing to prepare the state's defenses and of flight when the British invaded during his governorship in the summer of 1781. Although the resolution had failed, his friends had never seen him so bitter.

While Jefferson waited to embark, word arrived that the peace treaty had been signed, so after a year-long interval, his appointment was changed to place him on a commission to negotiate trade alliances instead. He had finally arrived in Paris in the summer of 1784, was appointed the following spring to replace Franklin as United States minister. Since then he had found his days filled with satisfaction, both political and personal.

After first lodging at pensions, Jefferson had moved to the house he occupied now—nothing like Monticello, but with extensive gardens done in an informal English style and a courtyard. A two-story mansion, with a basement and mezzanine, the *Hôtel de Langeac (hôtel* meant "royal residence") had been designed by the architect whom Napoleon would one day commission to build the Arc de Triomphe. It was a warmly elegant place; everyone admired its oval room with a brilliant and ornate painting of the rising sun on the high ceiling. Jefferson had spent the equivalent of his annual salary on furnishings and alterations and was soon happily raising a small plot of Indian corn in the garden for his own table.

From this headquarters, the ambassador sought to lower trade barriers between France and America, cement the American-French relationship that had begun with their alliance against England in the Revolution, forestall French demands for repayment of America's war loans, and offer advice to the nobles, who were trying to take steps of their own toward political reform.

Though he had never expected to be happy again, the forty-three-year-old widower had fallen surprisingly in love*—with Maria Cosway, twenty-seven, a talented English artist and coquette. She was wed in a marriage of convenience to Richard Cosway, a successful miniaturist, described once as "a well-

---

*Benjamin Franklin, at age seventy, had fallen in love in Paris, too, with a wealthy widow, Madame Helvetius, who was then sixty. She was so beautiful in middle age that a compliment paid her by a French statesman had become legend: "Ah, Madame, if I were only eighty again!" Franklin had written a mutual friend referring to himself in the third person describing his devotion to her: "As he has already given her many of his days, although he has so few of them left to give, it seems ungrateful in her that she has never given him a single one of her nights." He apparently proposed to her in the early 1780s, but she refused, explaining that she had vowed to be faithful to the memory of her husband. Not one to brood, Franklin kept up his flirtation as always.

made little man, very like a monkey in the face," who left his pretty wife entirely to her own devices.

The day Jefferson had set eyes on Maria's small figure, dark blue eyes and clouds of curly blond hair, he sent a "lying messenger" to break his official engagements and, together with their companions, they had whiled away an afternoon going to St. Cloud to dine and finishing the evening with a visit to a well-known harpist and composer on the way back to Paris.

Born of English parents in Italy (James Boswell called her "serenissima Principessa"), Maria possessed all the attributes Jefferson admired. Besides her talent as a painter, she was a student of music; she spoke several languages, but liked Italian best; she sang, played the harp and pianoforte, and composed music. She was free of the things he disliked in females—she had no interest in politics or intrigue—and she often seemed more child than woman. Day after day in the autumn of 1786, the Virginian had kept company with her, visiting the Port de Reuilly, the hills along the Seine, the rainbows of the machine that drove water to the fountains of Marly, the terrace of St. Germains, the chateaux, the gardens, the statues of Marly, the pavillion of Lucienne. Their idyll had been marred only when he dislocated his right wrist while showing off for Maria by jumping over a fence during one of their walks. Then she and her husband had gone back to England.

Now it was the end of July, 1787, and if ever there was a time for Tom Jefferson to be dissatisfied in Paris, this was it.

Maria's return, scheduled for spring, had been postponed until summer but she still was not there, though Jefferson had written coaxingly a month earlier, "Come then, my dear Madam, and we will breakfast every day à l'Angloise, hie away to the Desert, dine under the bowers of Marly and forget that we are ever to part again."

He was in physical pain as well. His wrist had not healed, and the trip he had taken to have it treated had been useless. Now he feared that his writing hand was crippled forever, though he had taught himself to scratch legibly with his left. A flood of nostalgia for Monticello had been unleashed by the arrival in mid-July of his young daughter, Polly, nine, with her sixteen-

13

year-old attendant, the slave Sally Hemings. And Jefferson was still trying to absorb the news that his best American friends abroad, John and Abigail Adams, would soon terminate their embassy in London and return to America. They had cushioned his arrival in Paris, where John had been part of the trade commission, and the few days it took for their letters to cross from London made it seem almost as if they had hardly left Paris at all.

Most of all, however, Jefferson was uneasy about the federal convention now under way in Philadelphia from which he had gotten almost no information. He was upset that they had begun their deliberations "by so abominable a precedent as that of tying up the tongues of their members," which he thought showed "the innocence of their intentions and ignorance of the value of public discussion."

He trusted the men gathered there—thought them "really an assembly of demigods"—and expected their proposals to be "good and wise." But he hoped they would not go too far in their attempts at reform. His own opinion was that, imperfect as the federal system of the Revolution was, "it is without comparison the best existing or that ever did exist" and "a wonderfully perfect instrument considering the circumstances under which it was formed."

Jefferson's personal experience with the confederation, his service in the Continental Congress, had been brief, just over a year, but he had seen it both vigorous and debilitated. He had announced the birth of "the Thirteen United States of America in General Congress Assembled" by drafting the Declaration of Independence in the 1775–76 session, but then quit the Congress in late August, 1776, to go home to Virginia, his "own country," and serve in its legislature and as governor. He had reentered Congress for the first and only other time at Annapolis, Maryland, in mid-December, 1783, serving until his departure for Paris.

He promptly discovered for himself how weakened Congress had become—he had been unable to find it when he arrived in Philadelphia. It had gone to Princeton after the Pennsylvania state council refused to use the militia to protect it from Continental Army mutineers who briefly held it hostage for their unpaid wages.

The day Jefferson reached Princeton, Congress adjourned for Annapolis, where it settled in. The peace treaty with England had arrived to be ratified, but without nine states in attendance it could not be done. At first Jefferson was "sorry to say" that the required nine seemed unlikely to appear, but, when one of the waiting seven made ready to depart, he became alarmed that a missed deadline would furnish England with an excuse to extort changes. As chairman of the congressional committee on the treaty, it had been up to him to try to get everyone there and prepare instructions for the peace commission in Paris if the members did not come. He sent out new summonses and made a contingency plan to take the Congress to the bedside of an ailing delegate if need be. Finally, though, they came, after a harrowing two-and-a-half month wait.

The problem was that the states did not care. Like Jefferson, the great leaders of 1776 had gone home, taking their energy and political influence with them, and by 1783 their successors were, as a Boston newspaper sneered, *"inferior* luminaries, or *wandering* comets."* The loss of prestige had been swiftly followed by loss of support and impotence in persuading the states to act in concert for the good of the whole. They were concentrating on developing themselves.

Though in Paris Jefferson was necessarily five or six weeks behind in the news, he had received constant reports on the continuing problems of the federation. Madison, who was in his fourth term in Congress, had written every few weeks and at great length to keep him current, and Monroe too, though less often and less fully. Other correspondents and travelers combined to give Jefferson an accurate picture.

He knew that the federal treasury remained as empty as it had been at the time of his departure. The Congress's revenue plan for a five-percent import duty, drawn up in 1783, had been blocked—first by Rhode Island, then by New York—and remained a dead issue.

That was bad news for Jefferson. Over a year ago he had complained, "American reputation in Europe is not such as to be flattering to its citizens. Two circumstances are particularly objected to us—the non-payment of our debts and the want of energy in our government."

But Eliza House Trist, a friend of both Madison and Jefferson, had confirmed to him that Congress was paralyzed. "Every now and then we hear of an Honble. Gentleman getting a wife, or else we should not know there existed such a body as Congress," she wrote.

And singly, the states were no more kindly to each other than they were to the federation as a whole. In one three-thousand-word epistle, Madison had lamented the states indulging a "rage for paper money."* The stuff not only was depreciating as much as thirty percent in some states, he said, but it was creating "warfare and retaliation" as citizens of one state tried to use it to cover debts in other states.

The same sort of conflicts had erupted in taxation as states tried to squeeze cash from each other. New York was making New Jersey boats go through customs clearance "like any other foreign vessel" and New Jersey had struck back with a tax on a New York City lighthouse that stood on New Jersey land. Virginia, by Madison's estimate, was paying a thirty- to forty-percent markup on goods entering through the ports of Philadelphia and Baltimore.

Jefferson had enthusiastically welcomed the news that serious moves were afoot to give the Continental Congress greater power in the regulation of commerce. Until word had crossed the Atlantic of possible reform, he had been unable "to discover the smallest token of respect towards the United States in any part of Europe," he told Madison, even though "there was an enthusiasm towards us all over Europe at the moment of the peace.

". . . With respect to everything external, we should be one nation only, firmly hooped together," he urged. "And it should ever be held in mind that insult and war are the consequences of a want of respectability in the national character."

"My general plan would be," he told another correspondent,

*not always currency, but state certificates or loans, issued as legal tender only for certain obligations in the absence of hard money such as gold or silver.

"to make the states one as to everything connected with foreign nations, and several as to everything purely domestic."

In domestic matters, Jefferson counseled tolerance for the federation's "imperfections." He had a preference for weak systems, and, unlike Washington, he was not transported by a muscular dream of a great American "empire."

"You ask," he wrote one European friend, "what I think on the expediency of encouraging our states to be commercial? Were I to indulge my own theory, I should wish them to practice neither commerce nor navigation, but to stand with respect to Europe precisely on the footing of China. We should thus avoid wars and all our citizens would be husbandmen."

Societies came in three distinct forms, he had told Madison early in 1787, of which the first was "without government, as among our Indians . . . It is a problem, not clear in my mind, that the first condition is not the best. But I believe it to be inconsistent with any great degree of population."

A long letter from Madison several weeks before the convention opened had contributed to Jefferson's impatience for news. In it, Madison had described what he thought necessary to cure "the mortal diseases of the existing constitution."

Madison wanted to organize the federal powers so that they would not be blended where they ought to be separate. Jefferson agreed with that. Separating the executive business from Congress "in some degree," he had replied, "is just and necessary." In Congress in 1784, he himself had called for a resolution establishing an executive committee, but he supposed that Congress lacked the capacity for "self-denial" that it would take to surrender executive matters. Passing a federal law to separate the functions would be "much better," he said.

As to another of Madison's ideas, though, he told his protégé without mincing words, "I do not like it." In addition to trade and other areas where uniformity was needed, Madison had proposed "to arm the federal head with a negative *in all cases whatsoever* [he had underscored it] on the local legislatures." He had become convinced, he told Jefferson, that no matter how powerful the federal government was made and how clearly its jurisdiction defined, "they will be easily and continually baffled by the legislative sovereignties of the states."

This, Jefferson answered tartly, violates an essential maxim: "that the hole and the patch should be commensurate . . . this proposes to mend a small hole by covering the whole garment."

Where Jefferson differed from his correspondent in America was on whether the "hole" was small or large, whether Congress's inability to manage either its own business or its international responsibilities meant that the confederation was fatally defective.

While he recognized that the states were negligent toward the union, Jefferson did not think it necessary to make vast changes in the Articles of Confederation—the constitution of the union, which all the states had ratified—to achieve local compliance with federal authority. In his view, the union implicitly had as much power as it needed.

"When any one state in the American Union refuses obedience to the Confederation," he had said more than once, "the rest have a natural right to compel them to obedience. Congress would probably exercise long patience before they would recur to force; but if the case ultimately required it, they would use that recurrence."

Jefferson most definitely did not believe what Washington had written him from the convention on May 30: "The general government, if it can be called a government, is shaken to its foundation and liable to be overturned by every blast." Nor was he impressed with what Madison had called "symptoms which are truly alarming, which have tainted the faith of the most orthodox republicans"—the rebellion of Daniel Shays and the Massachusetts farmers. That was the most nagging point of unease: those sensible men seemed gripped, like his friend John Adams's wife, Abigail, with something very near hysteria, even when the danger had passed.

"With regard to the tumults in my native state which you inquire about," Abigail Adams had written in late January from London, "I wish I could say that report had exaggerated them. It is too true, Sir . . .

"Ignorant, restless desperadoes, without conscience or principles, have led a deluded multitude to follow their standard,

18

under pretense of grievances which have no existence but in their imaginations . . . Instead of that laudable spirit which you approve, which makes a people watchful over their liberties and alert in the defense of them, these mobbish insurgents are for sapping the foundation and destroying the whole fabric at once."

Mrs. Adams's jab at Jefferson's philosophy had not ruffled him. "I hope they pardoned them," he riposted without sympathy. "The spirit of resistance to government is so valuable on certain occasions, that I wish it to be always kept alive. It will often be exercised when wrong, but better so than not to be exercised at all. I like a little rebellion now and then."

Neither of them could be sure they knew all the facts in January, but what they did know by then was that disturbances had spread through western and central Massachusetts since August, 1786, and the authorities were only barely containing them.

The rebels were farmers and small landholders at the bottom of the pile of debt that the postwar depression had spawned. Violence had erupted in several states where small debtors were afflicted, but it had been worst in Massachusetts, where the legislature spurned the debtors' petitions for paper money, while at the same time approving a tax for additional contributions to the Continental Congress. The new tax burden, predictably, escalated foreclosures, imprisonments for debt—and outrage directed at the courts.

The Boston newspapers Abigail had been receiving reported that, under different leaders in different counties, armed farmers had descended on local courts to close them down. At Northampton, fifteen hundred surrounded the courthouse; in Worcester, several hundred confronted the presiding judge, the revolutionary hero Artemus Ward, who cursed them, declaring he "did not give a damn for their bayonets. They might, if they liked, plunge them into his heart." At Concord, the judges met at a tavern to avoid the farmers barricading their court, but the rebels searched out the jurists and surrounded the tavern until they were sure that no attempt to hold court would be made. In Berkshire County, eight hundred farmers closed the court and freed all the inmates of the debtors' prison.

"Some of them were crying out for a paper currency," Abigail raved, "some for an equal distribution of property, some were for annihilating all debts, others complaining that the senate was a useless branch of government, that the Court of Common Pleas was unnecessary, and that the sitting of the General Court in Boston was a grievance. By this list you will see the materials which compose this rebellion."

Most frightening was the mob of five hundred farmers that moved against the state supreme court in Springfield: the way they marched and deployed suggested they had been practicing military drills. This time, the local militia stood ready, but bloodshed had been averted by negotiations between the general in charge of the militia and the rebel leader, Daniel Shays, a former revolutionary captain. That had been in September.

Not until spring was it known in London and Paris that things had taken their worst turn late in January, when Shays led eleven hundred men in an assault on the Springfield arsenal. The militia had repulsed them, then gave pursuit in a blinding snowstorm. Fourteen of the rebel leaders had been captured; Shays had fled to the territory of Vermont.

ADAMS

To Jefferson, popular uprisings served a valuable purpose—checking the excesses of government. John Adams saw a positive side, too, but one exactly opposite. "The Massachusetts Assembly had, in its zeal to get the better of their debt, laid on a tax rather heavier than the people could bear," he informed Jefferson. "But all will be well, and this commotion will terminate in additional strength to government."

Jefferson's eyes darkened at his friend's conclusion. It was still bothering him thirty years later when he wrote that Adams had "originally been a republican" but "the glare of royalty and nobility during his mission to England had made him believe their fascination a necessary ingredient in government, and Shays's Rebellion, not sufficiently understood where he then was, seemed to prove that the absence of want and oppression was not a sufficient guarantee of order."

That was untrue: Adams was still a republican—a believer in elective government—but he believed, and always had, in strong government. In 1776, in his widely circulated *Thoughts on Government* (copies of which Jefferson's own state delegation requested of Adams while writing the Virginia constitution) Adams had observed that "the very definition of a republic is 'an empire of laws, and not of men.' " Even earlier he had written, "there must be a decency, and respect and veneration introduced for persons in authority of every rank, or we are undone. In a popular government, this is the only way of supporting order." And in 1787, the constitution most admired for firmness as well as republicanism was Massachusetts's. It was the instrument that allowed the state to move against Shays, and it had been written almost singlehandedly by Adams.

What Jefferson was likely remembering more than any change in Adams was his shock at the humiliation he suffered in the "glare of royalty and nobility"—a humiliation that John Adams perhaps could have spared him.

Eager that his luminous, intimate friend, the American minister to France, be presented to the British King, Adams invited Jefferson to accompany him to the Court of St. James during Jefferson's first visit to London. But court etiquette did not require the king to receive him and, according to Adams family tradition, George III turned his back on both men while his courtiers snickered. As Jefferson wrote decades later without giving the details, "it was impossible for anything to be more ungracious." He was less restrained eighteen months after the incident. The British, "of all the nations on earth," he said, "require to be kicked into common good manners."

If the king's gesture was crude, his reasons were at least obvious: not only had the Declaration of Independence fiercely indicted George III personally, but Jefferson, in talking with Europeans, invariably blamed British "lies" for the widespread belief that the American union was in chaos. George III knew Jefferson's attitude, and Adams should have suspected he knew it. Moreover, the British monarch knew that Jefferson was enamored of France, England's worst enemy on the globe, just as he had known—and told Adams he knew—that Adams was not. It had been naive of Adams to try to present Jefferson at court.

Adams's mistake was of the heart—his vanity and irascibility were matched by an equal measure of innocence and love. He had made a good start in his assignment and, until then, had been enjoying his duties at the Court of St. James. But it was not just the "glare of royalty and nobility." The core of Adams's attitude was his joy at representing the new nation, *his* homeland, as a power on equal footing with every other in the most important court in the world. And he had not forgotten the words of the French foreign minister, Count Vergennes, who had congratulated him: "Permit me to say, it is a great thing to be the first ambassador from your country to the country you sprung from. It is a mark."

Adams proudly recorded in his diary his reply to a Dutch diplomat who insisted that, with the name Adams, he must have English blood: "Neither my father or mother, grandfather or grandmother, great-grandfather or great-grandmother, nor any other relation that I know of or care a farthing for, has been in England these one hundred and fifty years. So that you see, I have not one drop of blood in my veins but what is American."

He had even let the pride slip in when he was first presented to the queen and included in his formal compliments the comment that "another Europe, madam, is rising in America . . . It will in future ages be the glory of these kingdoms to have first planted that country . . ."

The pain of the king's snub was probably made worse by the fact that Adams had liked the former tyrant, His Britannic Majesty, George III, ever since the day, nine months earlier, when he was first presented to him. On that day, chubby form decked out in a new coat, black silk breeches and stockings, buckled shoes, sword, sash, gloves, hat and powdered wig, Adams had ridden to court in Foreign Secretary Lord Carmarthen's coach. First ushered to an antechamber "very full of ministers of state, lords and bishops, and all sorts of courtiers," he was taken thence to the king's "closet" where George III waited. It was June 1, 1785, eleven years to the day since the king had closed the Port of Boston in Adams's home state in retaliation for the Boston Tea Party.

It had been a dramatic moment when Adams, envoy of the victor, bowed the requisite three times to the vanquished monarch—the New England farmer facing the ruler of the greatest empire on earth—two short, round, proud, and stubborn men whose very names in each other's lands had so long stood for conflict and destruction of the established order. Both men were nervous and uncomfortable, Adams reported to America's Foreign Secretary, John Jay, but the speech Adams had written and memorized was conciliatory, almost tender, praying for renewed esteem between the mother country and her now free and grown offspring.

"I felt more than I did or could express," Adams said later, and the king listened to his words "with a most apparent emotion . . . very much affected."

The monarch's voice trembled, Adams noticed, when George III answered, "Sir, the circumstances of this audience are so extraordinary, the language you have now held is so extremely proper and the feelings you have discovered so justly adapted to the occasion, that I must say that I not only receive with pleasure the assurance of the friendly dispositions of the United States, but that I am very glad the choice has fallen upon you to be their minister."

A pause ensued, Adams said, and the king seemed to be searching for words before continuing, "I will be very frank with you. I was the last to consent to the separation; but the separation having been made, and having become inevitable, I have always said, as I say now, that I would be the first to meet the friendship of the United States as an independent power."

A few weeks later, Adams attended a court party where the king held him in a long friendly conversation. Afterwards Adams wrote that he "is the greatest talker in Christendom . . . It is but justice to say that it was agreeable and instructive to hear . . . His Majesty said as many things which deserved to be remembered as any sage I ever heard."

Before six months had passed, Abigail had been able to write

Jefferson: "You will find by the public papers what favorites we are at court. The Prince of Wales supping with us, Mr. Adams holding frequent conferences with His Majesty and yesterday going to Windsor for the same purpose." But, she added shrewdly, "It is said by some that these are ministerial maneuvers to keep up the stocks . . . Others say it is to seek out the minds of the people with respect to a [commercial] treaty with America, of which . . . some symptoms have lately appeared tending to that point. But this is said in confidence, Sir, as I must not betray secrets."

Both Abigail and John liked England better than France. "The noise and bustle of this proud city almost turned my brain for the first two or three days," Abigail told Jefferson. "The figure which this city makes in respect to equipages [carriages] is vastly superior to Paris, and gives one the idea of superior wealth and grandeur. I have seen few carriages in Paris and no horses superior to what are used here for hackneys."

In their idle hours, John and Abigail saturated themselves in theater and concerts—John a passionate lover of Shakespeare's works, Abigail fond of most entertainment. As when her initial blushes at the sight of Parisian can-can dancers had yielded to admiration, Abigail became fascinated with the prowess of a beautiful girl in the Sadler's Wells tumbling act who danced on a tightrope, performed somersaults, and stood on her head. Abigail's embarrassment that "delicacy, modesty and diffidence [were] wholly laid aside" was somewhat eased by the fact that the girl was "well clad . . . with drawers."

A performance of Handel's *Messiah* was "sublime beyond description," Abigail sighed. "I should sometimes have imagined myself among a higher order of things, if it had not been for a troublesome female who was unfortunately seated behind me and whose volubility not all the powers of music could still."

They disliked many things about London and the British, too. John complained about "the smoke and damp of this city . . . such whiffs and puffs assault you every few steps as are enough to breed the Plague if they do not suffocate you on the spot." Abigail hated the British habit of staring, thought English manners in general bad, and was horrified at London's taste for violence. "Scarcely a day passes without a boxing match," she noted, even in the most elegant squares of the city. "My feelings have been repeatedly shocked to see lads not more than ten years old, stripped and fighting until the blood flowed from every part, enclosed by a circle who were clapping and applauding."

The other half of John's and Jefferson's portfolios, their roles as trade ministers, placed John in hostage negotiations with the Barbary states which his adroit pen could not resist painting in full for Jefferson.

Adams called upon the ambassador from Tripoli and was received in a room with "two great chairs before the fire, one of which was destined for me . . . Two secretaries of the legation . . . standing upright in the middle of the room without daring to sit during the whole time I was there, and whether they are not yet upright upon their legs, I know not."

The ambassador barely spoke English, but they understood each other well enough, John said, and the talk eventually turned to tobacco. " 'We make tobacco in Tripoli,' " John quoted the minister, " 'but it is too strong. Your American tobacco is better.' " Now, John said, one of the servants brought two pipes already lighted. It had been years since Adams had smoked, but from politeness, he "took the pipe with great complacency, placed the bowl upon the carpet, for the stem was fit for a walking cane, and I believe more than two yards in length, and smoked in awful pomp, reciprocating, whiff for whiff, with His Excellency, until coffee was brought in."

John took a cup, then the ambassador, who "alternately sipped at his coffee and whiffed at his tobacco, and I wished he would take a pinch in turn from his snuff box for variety. And I followed the example with such exactness and solemnity that the two secretaries appeared in raptures and [one] cried out in ecstasy, *'Monsieur, vouz etes un Turk!'* "

When they finally got to the "business," as Adams called it, the minister announced that America was at war with Tripoli. "I was 'sorry to hear that,' 'had not heard of any war with Tripoli,' " Adams told Jefferson, but the ambassador explained that it was so, because there was no treaty of peace. The Turks and Africans ruled the Mediterranean Sea and the navigation upon it, so America would be required to make treaties with Tripoli, Constantinople, Algiers, and Morocco.

The "treaties," of course, were extortion and ransom in the piracy and hostage-taking by which the Barbary states had for a century reaped profits and would go on doing for years more. America had to develop its policy, now that the shipping raids were her problem, not England's, and the task fell partly to Adams and Jefferson.* Adams and Jefferson debated their assignment earnestly in their letters, but both men realized it was all academic.

The truth was, America was at a standstill in her ability to operate in foreign affairs. A dozen weeks after Adams arrived in London, he had met with the prime minister, William Pitt, to discuss the full range of issues between the two countries. He had left feeling that the British might choose to do nothing to restore ties with America, and time had proven him right.

The king and his ministers wanted "the most cordial friendship with America" and to "dissipate every little animosity," Lord Carmarthen had told Adams a year and a half ago. But Great Britain had continued her commercial war with America—barring American vessels from carrying American goods to England and its colonies while Americans continued to buy British goods imported on British ships.

In fact, some ninety percent of imports to America were British in the late 1780s, despite Americans' declared outrage that their own vessels were coming and going half-empty. Adams knew the king and his ministers were convinced that

---

*Initially, Jefferson had thought that, as long as America intended to carry on her own commerce, Congress should fund a navy under John Paul Jones, who "with half a dozen frigates would totally destroy [the Barbary] commerce . . . by constantly cruising and cutting them to pieces by piecemeal."

The confederation being almost bankrupt, Congress settled for authorizing $80,000 as America's "peace" offering to the pirates—which would not rescue many Americans, with the Dey of Algiers demanding $6,000 for a shipmaster, $4,000 for a mate, and $1,500 for each sailor he was holding. Frustrated, Jefferson sounded out Lafayette and the French Foreign Minister about a joint operation against the pirates, run by a council of small-country ambassadors out of some foreign court, perhaps Versailles. The scheme, however, did not win French approval, which Jefferson attributed to suspicion that America would fail to carry her financial share.

Americans lacked the will to impose retaliatory restrictions and that no treaty of commerce was necessary. And, to his despair, he received advice from John Jay that in Congress the southern states were pouring "cold water" on proposals to regulate trade, preferring "to leave to foreign powers to manage the commerce of the United States."

Nor could Adams make progress on other problems. The British, contrary to the peace treaty, continued to hold the forts at Erie, Detroit, Niagara, and Michilimackinac, which it had agreed to surrender "with all convenient speed." Not only did this cut off American access to the northwest fur trade, it posed a security threat both direct and indirect—through the British provisioning the Indians with arms and ammunition, along with agents to direct them in skirmishes with American militia. Adams had protested this early to Carmarthen, and had continued to press it for months.

But this was America's fault, came the blunt answer finally. Surely Adams realized that the violations on his country's side were much more serious. The king's subjects had suffered "the utmost degree of difficulty and distress," because all the American states had passed laws erasing their citizens' valid debts to British creditors, permitting other obligations to be paid in paper money, and providing permanent confiscation of property and other abuses of Tory Americans who had remained loyal to the Crown. All of these acts were outright violations of specific articles prohibiting them in the peace treaty.

"I can assure you, sir, that whenever America shall manifest a real determination to fulfill her part of the treaty, Great Britain will not hesitate to prove her sincerity," Carmarthen told Adams. When that time came, America could depend upon Britain "for carrying every article . . . into real and complete effect."

At last, Adams had written Jay asking him to advise Congress that none of the concessions Britain had made on paper would be carried out until the individual states conformed with the treaty. However they might criticize him for saying so, Adams said, America looked shabby protesting violations "when the British court have it in their power to prove upon us breaches of the same treaty of greater importance . . . every law of every state which concerns either debts or loyalists, which can be impartially construed as contrary to the spirit of the treaty of peace (should) be immediately repealed and the debtors left to settle with their creditors" or submit their disputes to the courts.

Now, at the end of July, 1787, John and Abigail were merely marking time waiting for Congress to accept his resignation. The diplomatic mission had to end: Great Britain still refused to send an ambassador to America; the commercial war went on; the sore subjects in the peace treaty continued sore.

About the federal convention underway in Philadelphia, Adams had no qualms. Its members possessed "such ability, weight and experience that the result must be beneficial to the United States," he told Jay.

Adams had reason to feel he was in Philadelphia in spirit. In the early spring, with the Shays uprisings tarnishing the image of America's government experiments and lending credence to her public critics, he had locked himself in his room for weeks to write a tract, *In Defense of the American Constitutions.*

His purpose was to answer European advocates of single-house legislatures who accused the American states of having imitated the British system in setting up their governments. But Adams's reply exploded into a treatise on American republicanism that boldly defended both strong government and representation for "aristocrats."

The governments of the United States "have exhibited perhaps the first example of governments erected on the simple principles of nature," Adams wrote. They were "contrived merely by the use of reason and the senses."

In democratic governments, the wealthy and wellborn could accumulate overwhelming influence, Adams explained. They would then dominate a single-house legislature, and at last corrupt it. Those men should be formed into a single upper branch of the legislature, where the country would benefit from their talents and ambitions and where the "democratical branch" would keep them in check. At the same time, "the people's rights and liberties can never be preserved without a strong executive . . . If the executive power or any considerable part of it is left in the hands of either an aristocratical or a democratical assembly, it will corrupt the legislature as necessarily as rust corrupts iron or as arsenic poisons the human body. And when the legislature is corrupted, the people are undone."

Long and diligently, Adams wrote and buttressed his thesis, building the case of a strong executive and a "little council" of the most important men. Some men inevitably strive to rise above others in talents, fortune, ability. "These sources of inequality which are common to every people can never be altered by any, because they are founded in the constitution of nature. This natural aristocracy among mankind . . . is a fact essential to be considered in the institution of government. It forms a body of men which contains the greatest collection of virtues and abilities in a free government." And, if not "judiciously managed in the constitution . . . it is always the most dangerous."

Although he had also waxed euphoric about democracy and the people and written that a free government, even with the perils of the ancient Greek city-states, was better than the most benevolent monarchy, when he showed the completed book to Abigail, she was anxious about it. People would think, she warned him, that he wished for a king.

But Adams had not worried. *In Defense of the American Constitutions* had been published in London, and Jefferson was having it translated into French. Best of all, it had been printed in Philadelphia and gone on sale there at the end of May, right after the start of the convention.

3

Toward Philadelphia

THE FARTHEST THING from either Adams's mind or Jefferson's was that the convention in Philadelphia might propose to set up a sovereign national government over the states. The idea was a kind of non sequitur, illogical and unjustified.

True enough, by the close of the Revolution, they, like all Americans, called themselves a "nation" while basking in the glory of what they had done. The world rang with praises of the ideal society rising in the young, richly blessed New World. On both sides of the Atlantic, the hopes of political philosophers were pinned on "the American experiment" underway in the thirteen former colonies.

No one put their high sense of destiny better than George Washington when he said, in his circular letter to the governors, that the people of America were "from this period to be considered as the actors on a most conspicuous theatre, which seems to be peculiarly designated by Providence for the display of human greatness and felicity."

Two hundred years later, perhaps the most difficult thing to conceive about America is this: at the time Washington wrote those words, most of America's political leaders did not dream that her destiny would be pursued in the actual form of a sovereign nation. America was not internally a single country.

From Thomas Jefferson and John Adams on down to the lowest private in George Washington's army, the fact was that a man's state was his "country" and the United States was a federation—an alliance of sovereignties formed by mutual consent for defense and certain limited, mostly external advantages. And the Articles of "Perpetual Union" were not arbitrary; the thirteen small republics had yielded only such sovereignty as needed to obtain those ends. This system, it was believed, represented the only secure road to fulfilling the ideals of the Revolution.

A "republic"—every citizen having a voice through elected representation—was the pinnacle of political virtue, tying the people and their political leaders closely so that the government would rest on their consent. And it was an established principle that a republic could only extend over a limited geographical region containing culturally similar citizens. Expanding sovereignty over a larger, more diverse area would sacrifice liberty by demanding a monarch to keep order—a return, in fact, to the system that had just been overthrown. To say it the way it soon would be put: a national government would be "destructive of the political happiness of the citizens of the United States" and would "in its operation, produce a monarchy or a corrupt oppressive aristocracy."

Until late 1786, Americans had been happy with the principle of confederation. The only real irritant was the way trade and monetary conflicts kept erupting among the states—and that, it was felt, would settle down. Few state leaders were eager to surrender more sovereignty to the Union to harmonize their commerce; it smacked of failure. But some people were calling for just such a step, contending that the buffeting would only get worse. And a handful were even warning that the states' sovereignty was a centrifugal force that sooner or later would burst the confederation, leaving the infant republics naked to predators, both foreign and domestic. Listening uneasily, the state leaders could not dismiss the doomsayers as cranks: they were led by Washington, James Madison and Alexander Hamilton. And it was those three men who had finally brought about the Philadelphia convention.

THE AMAZING MISFIT

"The bastard brat of a Scotch pedlar," was the elderly John Adams's pronouncement on Alexander Hamilton some thirty years after the convention. "A colossus," a "host within himself," Jefferson would say in 1792—and beg Madison "for God's sake, take up your pen and cut him to pieces."

"Perhaps no man in the United States has sacrificed or done more for the present Constitution than myself," Hamilton would tell Gouverneur Morris in 1802. "And contrary to all my anticipations of its fate, as you know, from the very beginning, I am still laboring to prop the frail and worthless fabric."

It was the truth. From Hamilton in 1780 came the first forceful call for a constitutional convention; to him afterward fell the burden of building when it seemed impossible to be done. He wanted America to be a nation and when he was given a few sticks and nails, he built it. And yet, "No man's ideas were more remote from the plan than his were known to be," Hamilton would say at the end of the convention, "but is it possible to deliberate between anarchy and convulsion on one side, and the chance of good to be expected from the plan on the other?"

As John Adams inelegantly said, Hamilton was illegitimate, born in the West Indies of a love match without marriage between the runaway wife of a doctor and the gentle but useless scion of a titled Scottish family. His mother died when he was eleven, leaving him a practical orphan, for his father had long since wandered away. But a local clergyman and the merchant who employed Hamilton considered him a prodigy, and in 1772, shortly before he turned sixteen, they packed the boy off to America for an education.

Letters of introduction from Hamilton's sponsors carried him straight into a circle of friends who would be among New York's leaders in the Revolution—John Jay, Gouverneur Morris, Elias Boudinot, William Livingston and others—and the teenager seized upon it. By early 1776, he had abandoned his studies at Kings College (now Columbia) to establish an artillery unit, drilling daily to meet the British when they moved down from Boston toward New York.

Washington had heard about Hamilton before the year was out, and although his aides were supposed to come only from the "best families," he offered him a position as an aide de camp. Hardly another year had passed before Hamilton was chief of staff, and another founder, the dyspeptic Dr. Benjamin Rush, was complaining that "the Commander in Chief, at this time the idol of America, (is) governed by . . . Colonel Hamilton, one of his aides, a young man twenty-one years of age."

All the romantic notions of the glorious cavalier found an eager sponsor in young Hamilton. At age thirteen, he had written a friend that he hated "the groveling condition of a clerk to which my fate has condemned me," and, taken to the side of the man already being called the "father of his country" and the "idol of America," Hamilton grasped the godsend with ferocity.

Hamilton was the "Little Lion" in the gentle teasing of his compatriots in Washington's group of young aides; he was the self-assured Colonel Hamilton whom a French visitor to winter headquarters described at the commander in chief's table proposing toasts "as they occurred to him, without order or formality"; he was the Casanova who had his older comrade, Washington's secretary, Robert Harrison, clucking sympathetically for "poor Polly" whom Hamilton had overthrown. He was the writer who, composing Washington's correspondence, "held the pen of our Army," in the remembrance of another aide.

At the army's winter camp early in 1780, Hamilton fell in love with Elizabeth Schuyler, the daughter of General Phillip Schuyler, one of New York's wealthiest and most distinguished upstate landholders. He married Betsey the following winter and secured for himself not only a position near the very top of the New York power structure, but in perhaps the most devoted and forgiving family in the history of America.

Through battle, controversy, and partisan bloodletting, through estrangement from Washington and reconciliation, through the humiliation of Hamilton's publishing a detailed account of his own adultery and blackmail, through his overthrow as head of his party, through the death of Hamilton's son defending his father's honor in a duel, to Hamilton's own death dueling with Aaron Burr, the Schuylers stood as one behind their Hamilton. In the melodrama of Hamilton's life, he was the most fortunate of star-crossed heroes.

On the wings of his engagement to dark-eyed Betsey, Hamilton began his rise into the political stratosphere, launching his campaign for a constitutional convention on September 3, 1780. In a nine-thousand-word letter to a New York member of the Continental Congress, Washington's twenty-three-year-old chief of staff indicted the confederation system as "neither fit for war nor peace" and labelled its "fundamental defect . . . a want of power in Congress."

The blame, Hamilton said, lay in "an excess of the spirit of liberty which has made the particular states show a jealousy of all power not in their own hands" and a Congress "timid and indecisive in their resolutions, constantly making concessions to the states till they have scarcely left themselves the shadow of power . . .

". . . the particular states have no further attended to it than as suited their pretensions and convenience . . . The idea of an uncontrollable sovereignty in each state . . . will defeat the other powers given to Congress and make our union feeble and precarious." He thought the convention should be held two months later; it would not happen for almost seven years.

A few months later, Hamilton took to the pen again, building upon his letter to write "The Continentalist," a six-part newspaper series outlining the defects of the federation and urging a convention of the states to correct them.

After the battle of Yorktown (where he badgered Washington into letting him lead the final charge), Hamilton returned to New York, studied law for six months and was admitted to the bar. He schemed with his father-in-law, who was then a state senator, to make New York the first state to officially call for a constitutional convention—the measure Hamilton wrote passing in the spring of 1782. The Schuyler bloc then saw that

Hamilton was elected to Congress, where he took his seat in the fall of 1782.

There Hamilton called again for a constitutional convention, while working hand in hand with James Madison trying to strengthen the authority of the confederation. He wrote and circulated a resolution for the Congress to endorse the convention, but had to put it away for lack of support.

The impotence of Congress, New York's reluctance to pay its congressman's expenses, and the allure of his new home life and first child led Hamilton to serve only a single term in the Continental Congress. On becoming once again a private citizen, he virtually dropped out of political affairs. But while front-line political struggle had lost its appeal, the issues had not.

Tardily acknowledging a letter from Gouverneur Morris, Hamilton joked, "I would have sooner told you how much pleasure it gave me, if I had had time, but legislative folly has afforded so plentiful a harvest to us lawyers that we have scarcely a moment to spare from the substantial business of reaping."

The "legislative folly" was New York's program of reprisals against Loyalists and Tories—the same laws that were jeopardizing the peace treaty with England as they multiplied in the different states. Taking the unpopular side representing Tories, Hamilton was fashioning the cornerstone of his practice from lawsuits over confiscations, broken contracts, and rejected debts—and making the unprecedented argument that the statutes were invalid because they were in conflict with the national authority. Beginning with a test case watched by Washington and nationalists in every state, Hamilton's attacks on anti-Tory laws proved so damaging that, in 1784, a group of disgruntled plaintiffs hatched a scheme (soon squelched) to challenge him to consecutive duels until one of them managed to kill him.

WASHINGTON

The galleries were packed with ladies, the editor of the *Maryland Gazette* wrote the night of December 23, 1783, and "few tragedies ever drew so many tears from so many beautiful eyes as the moving manner in which His Excellency took his final leave of Congress." Early the next morning, Christmas Eve, Washington departed Annapolis, and reached Mount Vernon the same day.

"I am now a private citizen on the banks of the Potomac," Washington wrote to the governor of New York on New Year's Day, 1784. "I feel myself eased of a load of public care. I hope to spend the remainder of my days in cultivating the affections of good men and in the practice of the domestic virtues."

Life was good at Mount Vernon, even though the workings of the huge estate were in some confusion after so long an absence by its owner. With six weeks of unusually severe winter weather to keep him indoors, Washington was able to straighten out the plantation accounts, plan his spring crops, and answer the correspondence that got through to him. He also made up his mind that his two-story "cottage," with just four rooms to a floor, was too small and began laying plans to enlarge it and redo the landscaping, too.

And yet, he found it hard to adjust to private life: "I am just beginning to experience that ease and freedom from public cares," he told his old comrade in arms, General Henry Knox, late in February. "Strange as it may seem, it was not till lately I could get the better of my usual custom of ruminating as soon as I waked in the morning on the business of the day and of my surprise at finding, after revolving many things in my mind, that I was no longer a public man, nor had anything to do with public transactions."

As a matter of fact, Washington had not got the better of his interest in public cares—he had hardly even tried. His "retirement" was only five days old when he began once more to write about his fears for the union, and, in corresponding with every political friend from then on, he continually enlarged on his theme. And, before his first year of retirement was up, he set off in hungry pursuit of a private interest that would lead to the first small step toward creating a stronger union.

Washington's new campaign began in September with a glorious six-week-long, 680-mile ride through northwestern Virginia, to inspect the lands he had acquired after his service in the French and Indian War in the 1750s. For years, he had dreamed of a canal that would connect the Ohio Valley to the eastern seaboard by way of the Potomac River, and in 1774, just before the Revolution, he had tried to raise money to support its construction. The dream had not died, and now it was clear to him that, beyond its bold excitement, the project could help secure the loyalty of the numerous Americans who already had moved into that wilderness and promote western development as well.

The general who had beaten the British knew how to storm a redoubt, and that is about the way Washington renewed his drive for a Potomac canal. "The earnestness with which he espouses the undertaking is hardly to be described," James Madison wrote wonderingly to Thomas Jefferson a few months later, "and shows that a mind like his, capable of great views and which has long been occupied with them, cannot bear a vacancy."

Along with his canal, Washington continued to fret over the union. The winter thaw had brought floods of visitors to Mount Vernon and Washington pumped them all for news from the other states. Correspondence escalated too, from congratulations on his retirement to a steady stream of political reports from everywhere. That America's principal character could not withdraw to privacy was soon apparent to everyone. He demanded and dispatched so much information that, in Paris, one of his former aides concluded that Washington had become "the focus of political intelligence for the new world."

What Washington was learning could not have been more disheartening. The state parochialism that haunted the war effort was not being resisted, as he had urged in his letter to the governors. It was getting worse, and, writing to confidants such as Knox and John Jay, his reaction ran from panic to petulance.

"I have to thank you very sincerely for your interesting letter," he told John Jay in 1786. "Your sentiments, that our affairs are drawing rapidly to a crisis, accord with my own ... What astonishing changes a few years are capable of producing. I am told that even respectable characters speak of a monarchical form of Government without horror . . . what a triumph for our enemies to verify their predictions!

"Retired as I am from the world, I frankly acknowledge that I cannot feel myself an unconcerned spectator. Yet having happily assisted in bringing the Ship into Port . . . it is not my business to embark again on a sea of troubles. Nor could it be expected that my sentiments and opinions would have much weight on the minds of my countrymen; they have been neglected, though given as a last legacy in the most solemn manner. I had then, perhaps, some claims to public attention. I consider myself as having none at present."

Washington's gloom might not have been nearly so deep if he could have known that his canal had already put in motion the chain of events that would lead to a new constitution, by forcing Virginia and Maryland to face up to their disputes over interstate traffic.

MADISON

Since Washington's return to Virginia, a kind of friendship had developed between him and James Madison, who, at thirty-four, was twenty years younger and just coming into his own as a political star. Theirs was a bond of mutual regard, not kindred spirits. Except for their shared belief in a national destiny, two men more different from each other would be hard to imagine.

Madison, a dedicated intellectual, drew his philosophy from rigorous study and only adjusted it in consulting with others. Washington, a man of action, developed his ideas in conversation with more studious men and consulted scholarship himself only casually. Madison was inept with women and often left a bad impression; Washington enjoyed their attention, loved dancing and flirting, and sent many away smitten with him. Madison was an introvert who mixed best with a small crowd; Washington was a tireless extrovert who, but for his careful seriousness, could have been labelled a butterfly. At 5-foot-4-

inches and 100 pounds "Little Jemmy" was a foot shorter than Washington and half his weight; and Madison was as enthusiastic about his reading chair as Washington was for chasing foxes all day. Even their handwritings are dissimilar—Washington's big, loopy letters are like a schoolboy's; Madison's tight characters march across the page with microscopic precision, barely one-sixteenth of an inch high.

At twenty-one, Madison had been a singularly grim young man. To his best friend from college he once wrote praising him for having "seen through the romantic paintings with which the world is sometimes set off by the sprightly imaginations of the ingenious . . . I hope you are sufficiently guarded against the allurements and vanities that beset us on our first entrance on the theater of life . . . Pray do not suffer those impertinent fops that abound in every city to divert you from your business and philosophical amusements."

Growing a little older, he decided that "poetry, wit and criticism, romances, plays, etc. captivated me much," but "something more durable and more profitable befits a ripe age." This balance—favoring his scholarly side—prevailed through his life, leaving him a strong-minded loner and one not very well padded against the scrapes and bruises of politics and love.

Madison and Thomas Jefferson discovered each other in 1779, when Jefferson was serving his first term as Virginia's governor and Madison was elected to the governor's Privy Council. The eight years' difference in ages was irrelevant; they were kindred spirits. Both were soft-spoken, philosophical worshippers of the written word. Both were disestablishmentarians—committed to knocking down the Virginia laws that protected aristocratic estates and the Anglican Church. More important, their differences were complementary: Madison's intellectual rigor balanced Jefferson's tendency to flightiness; Jefferson's social skills balanced Madison's inwardness. Their teaming up to fight for freedom of religion in Virginia put their friendship on the map, and Jefferson's selection of Madison as a collaborator set the emerging young politician firmly on the road to his destiny.

The only time Jefferson led Madison astray was when he decided to fan the flame of a romance for Madison, who was definitely a late bloomer. No woman wrote a meaner description of Madison at that time than the social butterfly Martha Bland: "Mr. Madison," she said, "a gloomy, stiff creature, they say is clever in Congress, but out of it he has nothing engaging or even bearable in his manners—the most unsociable creature in existence."

Thus characterized, Madison had reached the age of thirty-one without leaving a trace of any earlier romance, but that had changed in the spring of 1783, the beginning of his fourth year in Philadelphia as a delegate to Congress. At the boardinghouse where he lived during the sessions, Madison fell in love with Kitty Floyd, the pretty, blond, fifteen-year-old daughter of a fellow boarder, New York Congressman William Floyd.

Staying there briefly while his diplomatic assignment was in limbo, Jefferson had noticed Madison's infatuation and wrote him gleefully to make his compliments "to Miss Kitty particularly." The teasing of the other boarders, he coaxed his friend, "strengthened by my own observation, gave me hopes there was some foundation for it. I wished it to be so, as it would give me a neighbor whose worth I rate high and as I know it will render you happier than you can possibly be in a single state. I often made it the subject of conversation, more exhortation, with her and was able to convince myself that she possessed every sentiment in your favor which you could wish." But matchmaking was not one of Thomas Jefferson's talents.

For a while he seemed to have succeeded: Madison wrote happily that a few days before Kitty and her parents left on a trip to New York, she had accepted his proposal of a November marriage. And Madison had already told his friends that he had "plans" that would keep him from finishing his term. But three puzzling months later, he received a letter from Kitty breaking their engagement. With childish cruelty, it is said, she sealed her message with a lump of rye dough.

Comforting Madison as best he could, Jefferson felt terrible. "No event has been more contrary to my expectations and these were founded on what I thought a good knowledge of the ground. But of all machines, ours is the most complicated and inexplicable."

Eleven years would pass before Madison would risk his heart again and propose to the widow who would become Dolley Madison.

Limited by law in the number of congressional terms he could serve, Madison was probably glad to decamp from Philadelphia and return to Virginia. There, he accepted election to the legislature starting in 1784 and began to get better acquainted with Washington.

Washington had good reason for a high opinion of Madison. During the period in which the army officers had crept so close to a coup, Madison and Hamilton had been joint captains of the effort in Congress to construct a financial plan that would mollify the angry soldiers. Although the plan never went into effect, it had been distributed to the states with an eloquent appeal for compliance written by Madison, which Washington had admired enough to praise in his own circular to the governors.

That Madison was a thoroughgoing nationalist must have come as a pleasant shock to Washington. His own nationalism rose from his visionary temperament, while that of the foreign-born Hamilton had not needed to overcome a state attachment. But Madison, a mental giant, seemed to confirm by the power of reasoning what the other two knew instinctively—that America was a national entity that would need to govern itself that way.

Washington did not hesitate to enlist Madison in the cause of the Ohio-Potomac canal, and Madison dutifully sponsored a canal incorporation bill in the Virginia legislature. But he was peevish about it at first, because he thought a more urgent problem faced the western settlers than tying them more securely to the eastern states.

A major storm had blown up over Foreign Secretary John Jay's negotiations with the Spanish ambassador over control of the Mississippi River. Jay had offered to surrender navigation rights on the waterway for twenty-five years in exchange for a favorable commercial treaty between the United States and

Spain. The southern states, whose claims extended to the Mississippi, were outraged, convinced that Jay had sold out the South in order to line the pockets of New England shippers and money men.

Perhaps Washington and Madison's own nationalism deceived them: both were aware of and badly underestimated the fury of their fellow Southerners. That smoldering resentment, hardening to distrust of the whole North, would follow them into the convention, jeopardize ratification of the Constitution, and dog the early years of the new government.

In any case, Washington, to Madison's dismay, supported Jay. The treaty with Spain would benefit the whole seaboard, Washington thought, while free navigation of the Mississippi would do nothing to promote unity between the West and the East. His own plan made better policy.

Madison was certain that after twenty-five years, the only way of retrieving use of the Mississippi would be by force, and, worried that the canal would clinch the argument in Jay's favor, he hesitated. But under Washington's pressure, and prodded by a letter from Jefferson praising the project, Madison guided it to approval in the Virginia Legislature in December, 1784.

Washington then rode off to Annapolis to lobby the Maryland legislature to approve incorporation of the canal company and soon wrote Madison "with an aching head" that the day had been won there, too.

By blessing the canal, Maryland and Virginia brought to center stage their old conflict over the Potomac River and Chesapeake Bay, the states' boundaries and shipping tolls Maryland was collecting. Now Madison was able to convince his own legislature to invite Maryland to seek a settlement, and a meeting was set for March, 1785, at Alexandria, Virginia. Maryland appointed four commissioners to attend, and so did Virginia, but Virginia's governor, Patrick Henry, forgot to notify his state's commissioners about the meeting.

The slip-up may have been innocent, as Henry said, or it may have been a slap at Madison and his supporters by the old firebrand: for Patrick Henry had gone sour on national ideas because of Jay and the Mississippi. When it came to continental measures, Madison and Henry's relations had been bumpy all along. Henry would cooperate with Madison on state actions propping up the Congress, only to turn around and maneuver to defeat or weaken them. As Henry aged, his Americanism seemed to bend before localism, and Jay's "sellout" had provided the last straw.

Also, Madison's formidable legislative skills had smashed many of Henry's projects. In fact, since Madison's return from Philadelphia, Henry had only one major victory to his credit, a tax to support religious education. That dust-up had been so long and arduous that Madison had had time to seek advice from Jefferson in Paris (Jefferson's disgusted reply was, "What we have to do, I think, is devotedly to pray for his death.") Madison opted for helping elect Henry governor to get him out of the legislature and repealing the tax once he was gone.

Whatever the reason for Henry's oversight, Washington saved the Maryland-Virginia conference from miscarrying when he learned about it from a Maryland commissioner who paid a courtesy visit to Mount Vernon en route to the meeting. Washington zoomed into action. "Major Jenifer came here to dinner," Washington advised his diary, "and my carriage went to Gunston Hall to take Col. Mason to a meeting of commissioners at Alexandria for settling the jurisdiction of the Chesapeake Bay and the rivers Potomack and Pocomoke between the States of Virginia and Maryland."

Major Jenifer stayed overnight and dined again with Washington before heading for Alexandria himself. Washington kept busy around the plantation the next morning, but then rode up to Alexandria for dinner and came back the same night. A day and a half later, he dispatched his carriage again to collect Mason from Alexandria and bring him back to Mount Vernon "according to appointment." The next day, "at about One Oclock," the three Maryland commissioners and the second Virginia commissioner, Alexander Henderson, came trooping in.

Washington, who had been conscientiously planting pine trees for several days, abandoned the trees to his "jobbers." Only when the conferees finally went away on the fourth day

after their arrival does Washington seem to have stepped outdoors again, and the only letter he appears to have written
during the week of the meeting was a reply to one involving
money owed him.

Alert to the impropriety of intruding on formal negotiations,
Washington was perfectly capable of the silence of the sphinx.
But some, if not all, of his guests knew that his style of hosting
was to give visitors the run of the house while he went on with
his daily work and hobbies. And in this case, Washington's
diary and correspondence for the week irresistably summon the
vision of a tall, anxious figure lingering outside his own dining
room door, never opening his lips except perhaps to bite his
nails.

The commissioners would have been made of stone not to
feel pressured to make the conference productive. And it was.
When the negotiators "went away before breakfast and Colo.
Mason [in my carriage] after it," they had settled numerous
issues.

Madison was galvanized when he read the report. It contained a golden opportunity: the commissioners had agreed to
make their meeting annual in order to adjust policy as circumstances changed. Madison instantly saw that, as commerce in the
Chesapeake did not just involve Maryland and Virginia, Delaware and Pennsylvania could be invited next time as well. If
everyone could agree to that, the case might be made that it was
time to settle commercial differences that were causing problems among all the states.

In concluding that the time had come to think continentally,
Madison was helped by a rising clamor among Virginia merchants for the state to do something about the British cutoff of
American trade with the West Indies. With another legislator,
he introduced a resolution calling for federal regulation of
commerce. However, Madison had misjudged the situation and
alert antifederal men in the legislature beat the bill soundly with
a series of crippling amendments over two days of debate.
Watching the measure go down, Madison was shocked to find
that Patrick Henry "shewed a more violent opposition than we
had expected."

A different tack was needed. Madison held back until the legislature battered itself almost insensible trying to solve the merchants' problem and then, on the last day of the session, introduced a resolution calling for a convention of all the states "to take into consideration the trade of the United States." The resolution carried easily, designating the meeting place as Annapolis, Maryland, and the date as the first Monday of September, 1786.

ANNAPOLIS FIZZLES

Just about the time Shays was gearing up for rebellion in Massachusetts, the convention delegates began to pack for the trip to Annapolis. The legislature of New York had appointed Hamilton and five other men to attend, while Virginia named Madison, the state attorney general, Edmund Randolph, and three others. Nine states in all named delegates to Annapolis, but only five were actually represented when the meeting began. The state in which they were meeting, Maryland, did not even bother to appoint anyone.

Under their instructions, the delegates were too few to officially even open the business, but simply packing up and going home would mark their cause as a loser. Madison summed up the dilemma this way: the weak attendance signaled "a belief that the time had not arrived for such a political reform" as he wanted, "but the convention, thin as it was, could not scruple to decline" its assignment.

Paper always being the best cover for embarrassment, the delegates appointed a committee to produce a report, and Hamilton seized the initiative of writing it. His quick eye had spotted something in the New Jersey delegates' instructions that the Annapolis convention could exploit: while all the delegates were authorized to talk about commerce, New Jersey's had been told to consider "other important matters as well" and to recommend measures to "provide for the exigencies of the Union."

Anything could happen with such flexible authority, Hamilton knew, so he brashly shifted the focus of the report from the failure in attendance to the inadequacy of the delegates' power. His draft resolution called for another convention—one that would propose "all such measures as may appear necessary to cement the Union of the States and promote the permanent tranquility, security and happiness."

Virginia's Edmund Randolph balked at the clarity of the draft, and Hamilton almost wrecked his own initiative by sticking stubbornly to it until Madison took him aside. "You had better yield to this man," he told Hamilton, "for otherwise all Virginia will be against you."

While Madison smoothed Randolph's ruffled feathers, Hamilton rewrote the report, softening the assertion that something *must* be done. Now the draft spoke only of a possibility that greater central powers might be needed and "may require correspondent adjustment of other parts of the federal system." This time, the group accepted it unanimously.

Annapolis had not failed after all. Discerning antifederal men would immediately see that they had been better off without any special assembly calling attention to the union's problems. But before a controversy could erupt over the convention's action, word spread of Shays and the rebels in Massachusetts and events began to push the politicians. Things looked as frightening here as they had to Abigail Adams in London.

"The malcontents are in close connection with Vermont, and that district, it is believed, is in negotiation with the government of Canada," Col. Henry ("Light Horse Harry") Lee wrote Washington. "In one word, my dear general, we are all in dire apprehension that a beginning of anarchy with all its calamities is made, and we have no means to stop the dreadful work."

Some people, Lee said, wanted Washington to help. "Knowing your unbounded influence, and believing that your appearance among the seditious might bring them back to peace and reconciliation, individuals suggest the propriety of an invitation to you . . . to pay us a visit."

Washington exploded. "I am mortified beyond expression when I view the clouds which have spread over the brightest morn that ever dawned upon any country . . . You talk, my good sir, of employing influence to appease the present tumults in Massachusetts. I know not where that influence is to be found; nor, if attainable, that it would be a proper remedy for these disorders."

Angrily Washington underscored his next words: *"Influence is not government.* Let us have a *government,* by which our lives, liberties, and properties will be secured; or let us know the worst at once."

4

"The eyes of the United States are turned upon this assembly"

PHILADELPHIA, THE LARGEST CITY IN AMER-
ica, was athrob with excitement over the gathering of the convention on the confederation in May, 1787. As far back as early
April, newspapers had been publishing tributes and advice for
the delegates to consider when they got down to work. A
hero-worshipper using the pen name "Alexis" inserted a poem
to George Washington in the *Independent Gazette*, "On the coming of the AMERICAN FABIUS to the Federal Convention in
May next":

> *The hero comes, each voice resound his praise*
> *No envious shaft can dare to chill his rays;*
> *All hail! great man! who for thy country's cause,*
> *Flew at her call to protect the laws . . .*

The *Pennsylvania Gazette* ran a commentary from Boston reminding the readers that "The states of America cannot be said
to be under a federal head . . . The breath of jealousy
has blown the cobweb of our confederacy asunder. Every link

in the chain of union is separated from its companion."

Quarrels in print between those who were eager for reform and those who thought the crisis exaggerated had been raising eyebrows. Finally, a correspondent, outraged over a writer's blaming financial speculators for Pennsylvania's economic troubles, damned the author as an evil stranger: "to madden thee at once, learn that Pennsylvanians are—honest. Retire then to thy native infamy; hide thyself in—Rhode Island."

Philadelphia's men of affairs, too, were keeping their pens busy, gossiping about the prospects and the delegates in their private correspondence. Dr. Benjamin Rush advised a friend in London that Benjamin Franklin, who was a delegate, had said "it is the most august and respectable assembly he ever was in in his life . . . and . . . Mr. Dickinson (who is one of them) informs me that they are all united in their objects . . . (and) . . . Mr. Adams's book has diffused such excellent principles among us that there is little doubt of our adopting a vigorous and compounded federal legislature."

And the city's more than one hundred taverns were scrambling to provide lodgings not only for convention delegates, but for two other large gatherings scheduled at the same time. Delegates to the Presbyterian Synod were here to write their constitution, and the triennial meeting of the revolutionary officers' Society of the Cincinnati was underway as well.

The *Pennsylvania Packet* could hardly contain itself: "Perhaps this city affords the most striking picture that has been exhibited for ages. Here, at the same moment the collective wisdom of the continent deliberates . . . a religious convention clears and distributes the stream of religion throughout the American world, and those veterans whose valour accomplished a mighty revolution are once more assembled . . ."

Such stirring goings-on were not all seriousness by far. The presence of so many important visitors was a challenge to Philadelphia's capable and dynamic society leaders. For the experienced hostesses of the city, the stimulation of the most exciting summer in years would be long remembered. But for one, Anne Willing Bingham, this summer would be the beginning of a stunning and famous social career.

On the morning of May 21, at the corner of Third and Spruce streets, the Binghams' Mansion House bustled with activity. In the banquet room, servants laid out the best blue, gilt-edged Sèvres china, the silver-pronged forks (the first seen in America), silver bowls, and ladles. Vases filled with spring flowers were set every few steps on both sides of great white marble staircase that rose from the center hall of the house. In the parlors, the drawing room, the library, and the study, all was carefully dusted and polished; outside, a pair of fawns played while the gardeners trimmed, pinched, and plucked the greenery and trees on the three-acre grounds.

Tall, and slim, Anne Bingham, the twenty-three-year-old mistress of this fabulous domain, moved lightly from room to room, inspecting her household staff's work. This afternoon's dinner would be the most important she had given since she and her husband returned from their long tour of Europe a year ago. General Washington was her honored guest, along with several of the delegates from various states already in for the convention. From the way Washington had been greeted, she knew her entertainment would be watched eagerly.

When the general had arrived just one week ago, the city company of light horse, commanded by Col. Samuel Miles, had gone out to welcome him at Gray's Ferry and escorted him to the outskirts of the city. There the artillery had been drawn up, its officers arranged in review, and all the city's bells were pealing. A huge crowd had gathered at the fine boardinghouse operated by Mrs. Mary House to catch a glimpse of the great man as he emerged from his carriage. Not to Anne's surprise, her father's former business partner, Robert Morris, had been waiting too and had spirited His Excellency away from poor Mrs. House, insisting upon his own hospitality.

Anne was aware that hers would be the first grand dinner Washington would attend. As was proper, first he had dined with the Morrises and their large family alone; then with his revolutionary officers in town for the meeting of the Cincinnati; then with the president of Pennsylvania, Dr. Franklin; with her own aunt and uncle, Samuel and Elizabeth Powel, who were among his oldest friends; with more old friends across the river.

Now at last, he would be here—the celebrated man her family had known since her childhood, whom she had last seen five years ago.

Wife of Philadelphia's leading banker, Anne Bingham was believed to be the richest and most beautiful woman in America. After she and her husband William visited London, where Abigail Adams had presented her at the court, Abigail had written her son, John Quincy Adams, that "I own I felt not a little proud of her. St. James did not, and could not, produce another so fine woman . . . 'She shone a goddess and she moved a queen' . . . The various whispers which I heard around me and the pressing of the ladies to get a sight of her was really curious . . . 'Is she an American, is she an American?' I heard frequently repeated."

Abigail's daughter, just two years younger, thought Anne was "possessed of more ease and politeness in her behavior than any person I have seen. She joins in every conversation in company [and] she will . . . convince you that she was all attention to everyone."

The Mansion House had not been completed until a few months earlier. William Bingham had been determined to build the finest home ever seen in America and had ordered one hundred thousand feet of cedar and pine boards for its construction, as well as door jambs, mantels, and floor slabs all of marble, brass hardware for the doors and windows, and stone ornaments of all kinds. He and Anne had shopped all over Europe, sending back paintings and busts from Italy, carpets and china from France, and furniture, china, and more than a hundred pounds of silver in the form of candlesticks, ladles, dinner utensils, vases, and bowls from England. Eighteen large mirrors, seventy-four chairs, a harpsichord, a pianoforte, seven knife cases, fourteen brass lamps, and a seven-foot square mahogany bedstead were part—but not all—of the shipment.

The Binghams' palatial residence, a bemused Quaker girl soon wrote in her diary, "causes much talk here." The grounds were three acres, the house three stories; a high wooden fence surrounded all. Set back from Third Street, the front was reached by a circular driveway. The floor of the entrance hall was marble in a mosaic pattern; the library, the study, several parlors, the ballroom, and the banquet room all were on the ground floor. The card room, drawing room, dining room and bedchambers were on the second; the Binghams' state bedroom and boudoir on the third. The gardens included orange, citron and lemon trees, a greenhouse, and the two little deer that always evoked smiles of delight.

In Paris, Anne had become a convert to the European salon and what she called the "happy variety of genius" that French women brought to their conversation. She had cultivated that happy genius and brought it home to Philadelphia, where, less than four years after the convention, she would become the unrivaled queen of the society surrounding the first administration of Washington.

For now, however, she would have been pleased to discover that her grand dinner drew a rare characterization in Washington's always terse diary notes: "Dined and drank tea at Mr. Bingham's, in great splendor," the general wrote.

Another star, too, was about to burst ablaze. Five blocks away, in Mrs. House's boardinghouse, James Madison was exceedingly busy. He had soared far beyond the vague ideas that he had tried out on Jefferson in March. "Temporizing applications will dishonor the councils which propose them," he had since decided. "Radical attempts, although unsuccessful, will at least justify the authors of them."

For months, he had been mulling over a dilemma: the states' individual independence was incompatible with federal sovereignty, but, on the other hand, consolidation of the states "into one simple republic" was impossible, too. Then, a month earlier, he had found "middle ground" adequate to produce "a due supremacy of the national authority and not exclude the local authorities wherever they can be subordinately useful."

The secret, the key, would be to change the way the states were represented in the federal legislature. Under the Articles of Confederation, each state currently had one vote—Delaware, one-sixteenth the size of Virginia, possessed exactly the same amount of power as Virginia in the Continental Congress.

He was sure that a ratio of representation should be substituted for this rule, so that a congressman from Virginia would be representing the same number of people as one from a smaller state. It would be fair, and he had found himself "ready to believe that such a change would not be attended with much difficulty."

Madison's optimism was odd: The one-state-one-vote rule had been drafted into the Articles of Confederation in 1777 only after a long and acrimonious battle between the large states and small who, as Jefferson said at the time, were "bitterly determined not to cede" to proportional representation. The lack of an uproar later—when Madison drafted a narrow version of the idea into the 1783 plan to pay the army—might have reassured him. Or perhaps he thought the crisis of the union, so apparent to all, had overborne such concerns.

In any case, convinced of his scheme now, he had written very long letters explaining it to Edmund Randolph, now Virginia's governor, and Washington—both of whom had been appointed delegates to the convention. Madison also had fleshed out his other concepts, of a national supremacy in commercial regulation, the veto over the states, a judiciary, an executive, and a power of taxation.

After spelling out his ideas for Washington and Randolph, Madison next had written for himself a paper he headed "Vices of the Confederation." In it, he drew upon his voracious scholarship on ancient and recent confederacies to damn the American federation—an indictment which he had brought with him to Philadelphia.

Arriving in Quaker City eleven days before the scheduled opening day, Madison had been full of anticipation, with good reason: as Shays and the Massachusetts insurgents had become more terrifying, things had started to drop into place for the convention. Several of the states named delegates without waiting for Congress to approve the call, and when it finally did, the rest of the states—except for Rhode Island—followed suit.

"Federal men"—as those known to support a stronger Congress were called—were amply represented in the lists of delegates that Madison had received. He could not guess what they would say to so radical a scheme as his, but he was sure they would listen carefully.

Not since the Continental Congress of 1776 had so highly regarded a group been summoned by the states. Among them were eight who had signed the Declaration of Independence, seven who either were now or had been the governors of their states, fifteen who had served in the Continental Army and felt the full force of the federation's defects, and thirty-nine who had grappled with its political impotence as members of the Continental Congress. Of enormous importance to public confidence was that both Washington and Benjamin Franklin would attend. The two most revered characters in the country had not only blessed the purpose but dramatized the urgency by setting aside their private pursuits to participate in the deliberations. Remarkably, too, Madison knew or had been in political service with more than thirty of the men appointed to the convention.

One of the best minds on the convention floor, he knew, would be James Wilson of Pennsylvania. Wilson's Scot's burr, pronounced even after more than twenty years in America, was a familiar sound to Madison: they served together in Congress in 1783 and again in 1786. His arguments were never grandiose, but they were clear, copious, and forceful, and though markedly aristocratic in demeanor, he had more confidence in "the people" than anyone of such intellect that Madison knew, except perhaps Jefferson. Wilson was also as meticulous a scholar as Madison himself and they were in close accord on their ideas for reform. Only one problem: though a good man, "James the Caledonian" somehow rubbed people the wrong way.

Madison would have to watch his own impatience with Gouverneur Morris, who was also on the Pennsylvania delegation. If Morris had disciplined himself in youth, he might have been a great scholar, but it was said that he wrote his final college oration on "Love" or "Beauty," which, although reportedly brilliantly conceived and delivered, was unorthodox, even glib. Another tale was that the carriage accident that had cost Morris his leg had occurred during a flight from an angry husband, but that was doubtful—Morris would have talked his way out of danger. In any case, he was a staunch nationalist, a bold and interesting speaker (for all his maddening inconsistencies), and would be a powerful advocate for the cause.

What the Connecticut delegation would say to his propositions Madison could not guess. The man to convince was probably Roger Sherman, the former shoemaker, whose gestures during a speech, someone had said, always looked as if he were sewing a shoe. He was an old Puritan, but an honest and practical one. Dr. William Samuel Johnson was a classicist, celebrated for his legal knowledge, intelligent in politics and very much the gentleman. At forty-two, Judge Oliver Ellsworth was the young man of that delegation (Sherman was sixty-six and Johnson fifty-nine). Madison had served with him in Congress in 1782–83, where Ellsworth displayed a talent for humorously demonstrating weaknesses in adversaries' arguments without being antagonistic. He used snuff, and when he was deep in concentration, he dipped often, letting it sprinkle down into little piles around his chair.

Madison liked Elbridge Gerry of Massachusetts, although some called him a "Grumbletonian." Forty-three and recently married to the seventeen-year-old daughter of a prosperous New York merchant, Gerry was small, thin, nervous, and had a stammer that frayed the tempers of those who disliked his complaining ways. Having observed Gerry in Congress, Madison knew he would be useful in debate, but whether he might emerge a "federal man" was anyone's guess.

Since Virginia was considered the instigator of the convention, Madison knew that his state would be allowed—probably expected—to take the lead on the floor. He had no intention of letting the opportunity slip away. In his letter to Randolph he had urged the governor to come early too, so that they could develop Virginia's presentation. He also had in mind working on Randolph himself, who could make or break Virginia's acceptance of whatever the convention accomplished.

And Randolph was not going to be an easy case. Even though he was national in spirit and had joined in the Annapolis report urging the convention, his opinion was that the Articles of Confederation needed only to be amended, not scrapped. He was by no means eager to construct a whole new government.

One modern historian has called Edmund Randolph "Aristotle's tragic hero"—a victim not of evil impulse but of his own bad judgment—and eight short years would bear that out. In 1795, Randolph would be forced to resign as Washington's second secretary of state when an intercepted dispatch from the French ambassador showed him confiding secret information—and implied that he had also solicited a bribe of "several thousands of dollars." Randolph was known to be in financial trouble and to be a French sympathizer, but the French envoy's insinuation was never proved true. Randolph returned to Virginia and built a prosperous law practice, but he had been labeled a traitor and his reputation was irreparably tarnished.

But as Madison joined the governor for a strategy session, it would have taken a seer to predict it. Not yet thirty-four, Randolph was a member of the tidewater dynasty that had ruled Virginia since before independence. His father had been the King's Attorney under Crown rule and Edmund himself had been the first attorney general under Virginia's new constitution. His uncle, Peyton Randolph, had been speaker of the colony's House of Burgesses and president of the First Continental Congress; his cousin, Beverley, was now lieutenant governor. And they all were distantly related to Thomas Jefferson, whose mother was a Randolph.

Besides wealth and power, the handsome young man had a good scholarly mind, the gift of eloquence, and, in the words of a convention delegate, "a most harmonious voice, a fine person and striking manners."

Randolph's drawback, as Madison was aware from serving with him as far back as Virginia's constitutional convention in 1776, was that he tended to vacillate under pressure. Balancing that was the fact that Randolph admired Madison unreservedly. If anyone could persuade Randolph of the need for radical action, Madison could. However, it was worrisome that Randolph had not come early as Madison had urged.

In fact, when Madison found himself one of only two out-of-state delegates in town for almost ten days, his initial optimism lost some of its bloom and gave him fair warning that his own eagerness for the meeting might not be matched by others—even the known "federal men," however earnest they seemed.

Come the convention's opening day, Madison was reinforced. Washington had arrived, as had the rest of the Virginia delegation, except for Randolph and Dr. James McClurg, who finally showed up two days late. The only other delegation with a quorum was Pennsylvania's, and only four other states had even one delegate on hand. Each day a few more men arrived, but not until May 25, eleven days late, was a quorum of seven states represented so that the convention could begin.

Though Madison chafed at the delay, he tried to put the best face on it in a letter to Jefferson, blaming bad weather and muddy roads. But Washington grumped, after six days of waiting, when just four states had a quorum, that "these delays greatly impede public measures and serve to sour the temper of the punctual members, who do not like to idle away their time."

Not that the idle time was unpleasant. Like Washington, most of the delegates went out paying visits, and on the afternoon of the sixteenth Benjamin Franklin entertained all of the delegates who had arrived—about twenty by then. He opened a cask of porter for a dinner in their honor and wrote to the man who had given it to him that "its contents met with the most cordial reception and universal approbation. In short, the company agreed unanimously that it was the best porter they had ever tasted." And maddening though it might have been to the impatient Washington and Madison, many of the delegates benefited from the time to visit and compare attitudes, and, in a few cases, to meet each other for the first time.

George Mason, author of the famous Virginia Declaration of Rights, wrote to his son that the Virginia deputies "meet and confer together two or three hours every day, in order to form a proper correspondence of sentiments; and to grow into some acquaintance with each other." These meetings, Mason said, along with conversations with a handful of delegates from the other states, "are the only opportunities I have hitherto had of forming any opinion upon the great subject of our mission."

Mason, whose more than twenty years of public service had

never been outside his state, was to be one of the most catalytic members of the convention. At age sixty-two, the wealthy plantation owner was still strong and vigorous, owing perhaps to his puritanical ways. A light drinker and a careful eater, he kept his head shaved and ducked it in cold water before donning his wig every day. He was impatient, curmudgeonly, and a reluctant politician, one who could turn churlish and sarcastic in debate. But he also was a stout champion of the rights of the people and, in the convention, would resist whatever he thought encroached on them. Right now, he was not sure how he felt about finding so many men of a continental bent. But, he told his son, he was surprised that "the most prevalent idea . . . seems to be a total alteration of the present federal system and substituting a great national council or parliament, consisting of two branches of the legislature . . . and an executive; and to make the several state legislatures subordinate to the national . . . It is easy to foresee that there will be much difficulty in organizing a government upon this great scale . . . I doubt not but it may be effected. There are," he added, "among a variety, some very eccentric opinions upon this great subject."

Mason did not explain what he meant by the interesting phrase, "very eccentric," but the swirl of discussion likely had carried to his ears the many shot-in-the-dark suggestions that had been circulated in recent months—running from dividing the union into three confederacies to inviting one or another European prince to serve as king of America.

That the convention was bursting with possibilities was not apparent just to those in Philadelphia. Everywhere, imaginations tingled—or trembled—at what might emerge.

The suspicious included Patrick Henry, named a delegate by the Virginia legislature, who declined, pleading financial problems. He had fooled no one; it was widely suspected that Henry had stayed away to leave himself free to oppose the result. He later would say that he had refused to attend the convention because he "smelt a rat."

Even more suspicious was New York's governor, George Clinton. And there the Hamilton-Schuyler magic had failed. Hamilton arrived on May 18 with news that he was saddled, in a manner of speaking, with bodyguards. In the New York maneuvering on convention appointments, Hamilton's name had survived, but the other two delegates were from Clinton's camp, hidebound antinational men—a state supreme court justice, Robert Yates, and John Lansing, the mayor of Albany. Hamilton would be in the awkward position of opposing his delegation in debate; and when he voted, he most probably would be outnumbered. The most he could do would be to exert all the influence he could—off the floor.

Dreams of great things produced a mini-scramble for the position of convention secretary. The clerk of the Virginia House of Delegates, John Beckley, had come with Randolph in hopes of getting the appointment, Benjamin Franklin's grandson, William Temple Franklin, hoped to be named, and several weeks earlier, Maj. William Jackson, former aide de camp to the revolutionary general Benjamin Lincoln, had begun rounding up sponsors, including Washington, for the job.

When Jackson's solicitation reached Mason via another Virginian, Mason wrote back, "I understand there are several candidates, which I am surprised at, as the office will be of so short duration, and merely honorary, or—" he added, *"possibly* introductory to something more substantial." A new national government certainly would offer "something more substantial" to ambitious young men.

The cumulative effect of the waiting and hobnobbing was to heighten the sense of anticipation and to let ideas be circulated—and then for anxiety to set in.

"I wish you were here," the Delaware deputy, George Read, wrote to a straggler in his delegation. "I am in possession of a copied draft of a Federal system intended to be proposed." This was a plan different from Madison's. It called for a house of delegates appointed by the state legislatures with the number of members to be proportioned to population. A senate would be picked by the house of delegates, which would divide the United States into four great senatorial districts for that purpose.

"By this plan," Read warned, "our state may have a representation in the House of Delegates of one member in eighty. I suspect it to be of importance to the small States that their deputies should keep a strict watch upon the movements and propositions from the larger States, who will probably combine to swallow up the smaller ones by addition, division or impoverishment; and, if you have any wish to assist in guarding against such attempts, you will be speedy in your attendance."

As new delegates arrived, they were drawn into the game, as were a number of political figures hovering anxiously on the sidelines. On May 24, the day before a quorum was reached, William Grayson, a Virginian in Congress at New York, hurried this note to Madison: "Entre nous. I believe the Eastern people have taken ground they will not depart from . . . *One legislature* composed of a lower house tri-ennially elected and an *Executive and Senate* for a good number of years. I shall see Gerry & Johnson, as they pass and may perhaps give you a hint."

Alert to the prospect of dangerous coalitions forming early, Rufus King of Massachusetts dispatched an urgent message to Connecticut. "I am mortified that I alone am from New England," he wrote. "The Backwardness may prove unfortunate—Pray hurry on your Delegates . . . —Believe me it may prove most unfortunate if they do not attend within a few days."

As delegates continued to come in, Madison began gaining confidence in a consensus, but he was not ready to bank on it. "In general," he notified former Virginia governor Edmund Pendleton, "the members seem to accord in viewing our situation as peculiarly critical and in being averse to temporising expedients. I wish they may as readily agree when particulars are brought forward."

But Congressman Grayson in New York was overcome by pessimism. "What will be the result of their meeting," he wrote to James Monroe in Virginia, "I cannot with any certainty determine, but I hardly think much good can come of it. The people of America don't appear to me to be ripe for any great innovations, and it seems they are ultimately to ratify or reject. The weight of General Washington, as you justly observe, is very great in America, but I hardly think it is sufficient to induce the people to pay money or part with power."

To back up his point, Grayson listed the mood of the states as he saw it: ". . . in Massachusetts, they think that government too strong and are about rebelling again, for the purpose of making it more democratical. In Connecticut, they have rejected [paying to support Congress] decidedly, and no man there would be elected to the office of constable if he was to declare that he meant to pay a copper towards the domestic debt. Rhode Island has refused to send members—the cry there is for a good government after they have paid their debts in depreciated paper—first demolish the Philistines, i.e. their creditors . . .

"New Hampshire has not paid a shilling since peace and does not ever mean to pay one to all eternity—if it was attempted to tax the people for the domestic debt, 500 Shays would arise in a fortnight. In New York they pay well because they can do it by plundering New Jersey and Connecticut. Jersey will go great lengths from motives of revenge and Interest. Pennsylvania will join provided you let the sessions of the Executive of America be fixed in Philadelphia and give her other advantages in trade to compensate for the loss of State power. I shall make no observations on the southern States, but I think they will be (perhaps from different motives) as little disposed to part with efficient power as any in the Union."

Washington was not prepared to construe anything from the early informal discussions. "The business of this convention," he wrote to Thomas Jefferson, "is as yet too much in embryo to form any opinion of the conclusion. Much is expected from it by some; not much by others; and nothing by a few."

But George Mason was shaken to his roots. It had occurred to him that the convention might well become a second revolution.

"The eyes of the United States are turned upon this assembly and their expectations raised to a very anxious degree. May God grant we may be able to gratify them by establishing a wise and just government. For my own part, I never before felt myself in such a situation, and declare I would not . . . serve in this convention for a thousand pounds per day.

"The revolt from Great Britain and the formations of our new governments at that time, were nothing compared to the great business now before us. There was then a certain degree of enthusiasm, which inspired and supported the mind. But to view, through the calm, sedate medium of reason, the influence which the establishment now proposed may have upon the happiness or misery of millions yet unborn, is a object of such magnitude as . . . in a manner, suspends the operations of human understanding."

5

"Resolved, that a national government ought to be established..."

LATE IN THE MORNING OF FRIDAY, May 25, the delegates made the now-familiar journey to the Pennsylvania State House through a light rain—some coming on foot over the slickened cobblestones the two blocks from Mrs. House's and the Indian Queen, others no doubt using carriages from the City Tavern and lodgings farther away. The start of the convention was now eleven days overdue.

Rollcall found Rufus King still the sole New Englander and the weather had kept Benjamin Franklin at home, but a quorum of Pennsylvania's deputies was in place. At last, New Jersey's David Brearly had been joined by his fellow delegates, William Churchill Houston and William Paterson. Twenty-seven men now were gathered, representing seven states—a quorum of the thirteen. The work of the convention could finally begin.

The high-ceilinged, chandeliered assembly chamber gave a sense of tranquility; it looked like a room meant for deliberation. The Declaration of Independence had been adopted and signed here, and it had been the home of the Continental Congress until 1783, save for the nine-month British occupa-

63

tion of Philadelphia. Most of the delegates knew it well.

Opening off the wide center hall of the state house, the chamber was spacious and wood-paneled, painted in a soft gray-blue. On the wall opposite the entry yawned two great fire-places; a door at one corner led to a committee room-library that was available for the convention to use. Centered a few feet forward of the fireplaces and framed by pilasters carved in Ionic style stood a low dais on which the presiding officer's table and chair were placed. Facing it in semicircles were tables and chairs for the delegates, each table covered in green baize and furnished with a brass candlestick, an inkwell, and quills. Running the length of the room on both sides were tall north- and south-facing windows that, with the dark green drapes drawn back and the venetian blinds raised, flooded the chamber with light even on gloomy days like this.

Always early and always purposeful, Madison arrived in plenty of time to get the place he wanted. "I chose a seat in front of the presiding member, with the other members on my right and left hand. In this favorable position for hearing all that passed, I noted in terms legible and in abbreviations and marks intelligible to myself what was read from the Chair or spoken by the members . . ." In this wonderfully laconic way Madison describes the beginning of an amazing achievement that he admitted to a friend later "almost killed" him: even though he was on his feet speaking more often than any other delegate but one, Madison's notes of the convention—including his own remarks—exceed 650 pages in modern print.

The basic elements of the Constitution are naturally the reason that Madison is called "the Father of the Constitution," but, as his self-assignment to be the comprehensive chronicler of its birth suggests, he deserves that title as much or more for the totality of his commitment to it.

For half a decade, Madison had steered his political career toward this moment. Over much of the last year, he had foresworn almost all else and buried himself in books, soaking up the origins, the philosophy, and the history of governance from antiquity to his times. He had reduced all his study to writing, and, for the last two weeks, he had been carefully working on his fellow delegates, listening and probing, learning who shared his boldness, who might see the merit in his scheme.

If any man now taking his seat in the assembly room did not at least respect James Madison's efforts, he never breathed a word of it at the time. Nothing exists to contradict William Pierce of Georgia, who, jotting "sketches" of the delegates, said of Madison: "what is very remarkable, every Person seems to acknowledge his greatness."

OFFICES

The first official action of the convention was to elect its presiding officer. When Robert Morris nominated Washington, Madison's pen made a quick parenthesis: "(The nomination came with particular grace from Penna, as Docr. Franklin alone could have been thought of. The Docr. was himself to have made the nomination . . .)" Of all the leaders in America, only Benjamin Franklin stood as high in the country's esteem and affection, but at age eighty-one and growing frail, Franklin was not to be risked in the role.

The vote unanimous, Washington was ceremoniously conducted to the chair, where "in a very emphatic manner," he thanked the convention for the honor. He was very embarrassed by his inexperience in such a situation, he said; he hoped the members would forgive any errors he might make. And those were the last opinions he offered in the assembly room, until the close of the convention.

This was classic Washington circumspection: not a formal hint of his fears and desires for the outcome, not a clue that his reputation was now hostage. Not the slightest acknowledgment that—as they all knew—he had been reluctant to attend because he feared the prospect was bleak. Not the least effort to plant a personal preference or to guide them in any way—though no one doubted he knew all the biases they had brought with them. He would just sit there, bigger than life, and hope he did not offend them with his mistakes. His modesty was not without purpose: whatever these men devised, they would have to support and live with, and like it or not, they would have to begin now.

For convention secretary, Franklin's grandson, William Temple Franklin, was nominated and Hamilton proposed Maj. William Jackson, who had been seeking the job. But John Beckley, clerk of the Virginia House of Delegates, who had come to Philadelphia with Randolph more than half-sure of winning the post, was not mentioned. The vote taken, Jackson defeated Franklin, five votes to two.

As the convention had not yet closed its doors, Beckley probably witnessed the public loss of his sponsors, and it is not farfetched to guess that his hatred for Hamilton dates from that moment. "A violent partisan and busybody," in the words of Hamilton's chief biographer, Beckley so fervently wanted to be a part of the convention that he remained in Philadelphia anyway. And so close did he stick to the official delegates that on that summer's subscription list for Carey's *American Museum,* he was described as a "delegate to said convention."

In two years, with Madison's help, Beckley would be elected the first clerk of the House of Representatives, and by 1792 would be the anti-federalist hatchet man against Treasury Secretary Hamilton. In 1796, he would plant a newspaper story that would corner Hamilton into revealing to the world his private scandal of adultery and blackmail. And, in one of those perversities of fate, Beckley would have to keep all of this from his wife's favorite uncle, Hercules Mulligan—Hamilton's first and oldest friend in America.

The convention moved on to the delegates' credentials, reading into the record the authority given by the states to their deputies. Most offered no sign of the political mindset back home, but straightforwardly instructed them to devise and propose alterations to the Articles of Confederation that would meet the needs of the Union.

But everyone was listening for clues, and when the Delaware credentials were read, a whisper must have run through the room. "Provided," the significant phrase began, "that such Alterations or further Provisions . . . do not extend to that part of the Fifth Article of the Confederation . . . which declares that 'in determining Questions in the United States in Congress Assembled each State shall have one Vote.' "

Madison wrote "It was noticed" and Hamilton's watchdog, Judge Yates, jotted "N.B." at the same moment. Delaware had tied her delegates' hands on the most controversial feature of the Articles of Confederation—the small states' voting equality with the large—and on the reform that Madison considered most crucial to the success of the convention.

Finally the convention appointed George Wythe of Virginia, Charles Pinckney of South Carolina, and Hamilton as a committee to draw up the rules, named a doorkeeper and messenger, and adjourned.

RULES

Form may not be substance, but it is a container that can preserve substance or let it spoil. As far as the rules of the convention were concerned, they proved to be a valuable enclosure for protecting the work that was to be done. In combination, they enforced discipline, attention, and discretion, producing, as a result, an atmosphere that was both prohibitive of empty bombast and conducive to real debate and persuasion.

First, the committee decided to protect the convention from paralysis by absences or coercion by possible walkouts—seven states would continue to be a quorum, and a majority of those present would decide any question. They also decided that this was not the time to face the touchy voting rule, and recommended that each state have one vote as usual.

Total decorum, complete order would rule: "Every member rising to speak shall address the President, and whilst he shall be speaking, none shall pass between them, or hold discourse with another, or read a book pamphlet or paper, printed or manuscript." And everyone would have his say, but he would have to get it said by the second time: "A member shall not speak oftner than twice, without special leave, upon the same question; and not the second time before every other who had been silent shall have been heard . . . upon the subject."

No one could change the subject once a debate began, although, if a question was complicated, it could be divided into separate parts and debated piece by piece. Decisions could be postponed upon any state's request.

"When the House shall adjourn, every member shall stand in his place until the President pass him."

The convention adopted the rules almost unchanged, except for one important rejection—that a record be kept of individual delegates' votes. Frequent changes of opinion over the course of the convention, Rufus King said, "would fill the minutes with contradictions." George Mason added that "a record of the opinions of members would be an obstacle to a change of them on conviction," and if published, "must furnish handles to the adversaries of the result of the meeting." By deciding to avoid such dangers, the members gave themselves maximum flexibility—and that turned out to be invaluable.

The rule of the convention most famous today came from the floor at this point. It is the one Jefferson called an "abominable precedent"—the rule of secrecy (which is actually three rules): "That no copy be taken of any entry on the journal during the sitting of the House without leave of the House; that members only be permitted to inspect the journal; that nothing spoken in the House be printed, or otherwise published or communicated without leave."

No modern politician would dare propose, nor would any self-respecting newspaper stand still for, such a gag order, but the convention approved it without discussion and apparently no newspaper objected. The delegates were faithful to the rule, too, almost completely, although a few minor leaks (a word used then as it is now) did occur.

From the members' standpoint, the blackout would spare them premature controversy. As George Mason explained to his son, it was "a necessary precaution to prevent misrepresentations or mistakes—there being a material difference between the appearance of a subject in its first crude and undigested shape, and after it shall have been properly matured and arranged."

Nor, despite his best friend's opinion, did James Madison

ever regret closing the convention's doors. Forty-three years later he defended it, saying, "Much was to be gained by a yielding and accommodating spirit. Had the members committed themselves publicly at first, they would have afterwards supposed consistency required them to maintain their ground. Whereas, by secret discussion, no man felt himself obliged to retain his opinions any longer than he was satisfied of their propriety and truth, and was open to the force of argument."

The modern mind all asquirm at the furtive framers can perhaps grant some truth in the remark of Philadelphia's publisher and humorist, Francis Hopkinson: "Their business is to revise the Confederation and propose amendments. It will be very difficult to frame such a system of union and government for America as shall suit all opinions and reconcile clashing interests. Their deliberations are kept inviolably secret, so that they sit without censure or remark. But no sooner will the chicken be hatch'd but every one will be plucking for a feather."

THE VIRGINIA PLAN

The rules adopted, Washington nodded to Edmund Randolph, who was standing to be recognized. Madison's pen began to move, and as Virginia's governor began speaking, a rueful smile must have tugged at the corners of Madison's mouth.

"Mr. Randolph expressed his regret that it should fall to him, rather than those who were of longer standing in life and political experience, to open the great subject of their mission. But, as the convention had originated from Virginia and his colleagues supposed that some proposition was expected from them, they had imposed this task on him."

Not everyone caught Randolph's disclaimer. Yates recorded only that "in a long and elaborate speech" Randolph assailed the present federal government as "totally inadequate to the peace, safety and security of the confederation." There was, Randolph said, "the absolute necessity of a more energetic government," and he now offered fifteen proposals for reform.

Madison had done a good job with Randolph. The governor's resolutions together amounted to the basic principles of a new constitution. They were a "revision" of the Articles of Confederation in name only; they were, in fact, the "radical attempts" that Madison wanted.

To be sure, they began with a bow to the Articles: Resolution Number One declared that "the Articles of Confederation ought to be so corrected and enlarged as to accomplish the objects proposed by their institution, namely 'common defence, security of liberty and general welfare.'"

But Resolution Number Two proposed to weight a state's vote in Congress according to either the taxes it paid or to its population. Number Three offered to chop the Congress into two branches. Numbers Four and Five described how the two branches would be set up; Six defined the congressional jurisdiction—including a power of veto over all state legislation.

Number Seven introduced the idea of a "National Executive." Number Eight was a formula for an executive veto and for a legislative override of the veto. Number Nine called for a "National Judiciary." Numbers Ten and Eleven suggested uniform procedures for admitting new states. Number Twelve asked for a smooth transition from the old to the new government; Number Thirteen sought a method of amending the constitution; Number Fourteen would have required state officials to take an oath supporting the federal government; Number Fifteen called for the new constitution to be ratified by the people of the states.

Madison says that Randolph "concluded with an exhortation" to seize the opportunity to make the United States secure and happy. But the vigilant Yates heard something more: "He candidly confessed that [the proposals] were not intended for a federal government. He meant a strong consolidated union, in which the idea of states should be nearly annihilated."

"CONSTITUTION CHARLEY"

Randolph sat down and Charles Pinckney of South Carolina rose. In his hands was a plan of government (the one that had alarmed George Read into writing his "hurry up" letter to his straggling fellow delegates) which he read to the convention.

With this speech and plan, Charles Pinckney became a permanent pause in all accounts of the convention for a moment of historical heavy breathing. Pinckney is a favorite of historians who do not like Madison and a villain to those who do. Madison's principal biographer calls Pinckney a "sponger and a plagiarist," and a contemporary mockery of him, "Constitution Charley," follows him to this day. He was, more or less, an eighteenth-century Narcissus drowned in the pool of history—after James Madison gave him a rueful push.

An eager young man, Pinckney was, at thirty, one of the youngest in the convention, and a "high-flyer" (the slang for bright and audacious) like Madison and Hamilton. As much the strikingly handsome, fair-haired scion of a dynasty in South Carolina as Randolph was in Virginia, he would become a four-term governor, U.S. Senator, state legislator, and a member of the U.S. House of Representatives (yes, in that order) for his state.

Less intelligent than Madison and possessing less star-quality than Hamilton, Pinckney still had made a mark for himself while serving just after them in the Continental Congress. He jumped into the nationalist camp early, writing in 1783 about the need to amend the Articles of Confederation. In 1786, he led a congressional delegation to New Jersey in a successful appeal for that state to pay its federal assessments, arguing, among other things, that if New Jersey felt abused, "She ought immediately to instruct her delegates in Congress to urge the calling of a general convention of the states for the purpose of revising and amending the federal system . . . I have long been of opinion that it was the only true and radical remedy."

"A Gentleman of the most promising talents," William Pierce called Pinckney in his sketches of the delegates, "intimately acquainted with every species of polite learning, and [who] has a spirit of application and industry beyond most Men."

The hour was late when Pinckney read his plan, so, like the Virginia plan, it was not discussed. Washington ordered both referred to the Committee of the Whole, as the convention was to be designated for the first phase of its debates. As things worked out, Pinckney's plan was never debated by itself.

As the years rolled by, Pinckney became something of a crank on the subject of his role in the convention, shaving five years from his age to make himself the youngest delegate and talking about it enough to earn the nickname "Constitution Charley." At the same time, he was turning into a political maverick. He stayed on the nationalist side for a few years, then decamped with Madison in the 1790s when Thomas Jefferson launched his powerful opposition to the new government's policies. After becoming an ardent Jeffersonian democrat, Pinckney served as his leader's ambassador to Spain and went on to be a loyal champion of President James Madison's policies which led to the War of 1812. All of which explains why Madison hesitated to brand him a fraud until 1831, seven years after Pinckney's death.

The stain on the South Carolinian's name began in 1818, when John Quincy Adams, then secretary of state, asked Pinckney for a copy of his plan to include in the government's record of the convention. With the event thirty years in the past, Pinckney responded in a long, somewhat muddled letter enclosing a draft of "the one I believe it was." In 1819, Adams published it as part of the formal record. The Pinckney document was almost exactly like the final constitution.

At first, Madison did nothing, but eleven years later, the most ambitious historian of the day and future President of Harvard University, Jared Sparks, started stirring him up, traveling back and forth between Adams and Madison trying to get one or the other to explain why the Pinckney document was so much like the Constitution.

Now eighty years old, retired, and spending enormous amounts of time answering requests to interpret the Constitution, ex-President Madison said he had meant to ask Pinckney about that, but Pinckney died. The likeliest explanation, he told Sparks, was that during debates, Pinckney marked up a copy of the emerging plan and, after thirty years, mistook it for his own.

Ah, Sparks soon reported to Madison, but Mr. Pinckney sent

it to Adams with "a long letter . . . in which Mr. Pinckney claims to himself great merit for the part he took."

Poor Madison—it was forty-three years since the convention. He had steadfastly refused to publish his own notes, saying he did not want to provide a feast for demagogues. Unfortunately, Yates's notes had been published a few years earlier, others were publishing scraps of this and that, and together they were being used to hammer Madison in something that had nothing to do with Pinckney: a doctrinal struggle between the Jefferson-Madison party and a faction trying to strengthen itself by questioning Madison's democratic ardor. Now, came the Pinckney questions and a threat to Madison's primacy on the Constitution itself. Thus goaded, Madison began working, privately and almost feverishly, to prove that the published "Pinckney Plan" was not what Pinckney read to the convention.

Madison was right enough, although Pinckney was not entirely wrong to claim a little credit. Pinckney's original plan has never been found, but excerpts turned up among the papers of the chairman of the committee that prepared the first draft of a constitution. Deducing from those, various researchers believe that from twenty-one to forty-three elements in the Constitution first came before the convention from Pinckney. Among those are the terms "president" for the chief executive and "Senate" for the upper house, the power of the House to impeach the president, the president's annual State of the Union address, and the idea of the president as commander in chief of the armed forces. His ideas were not original—as he himself pointed out when he presented his plan—but that is true, too, of much in the Virginia plan. The convention was not a contest for novelty, but to make, from experience and prudence, a good government.

If indeed the convention actually intended to seek a new government . . .

That was the question asked as soon as Pinckney had finished. "It was observed by Mr. Hamilton before adjourning," wrote James McHenry of Maryland, "that it struck him as a necessary and preliminary inquiry . . . whether the United States were susceptible of one government, or required a separate existence" connected only by treaties of security and commerce.

With Hamilton's pointed suggestion to digest with their dinners, the members resolved to form the Committee of the Whole on the morrow and adjourned.

THE "RUNAWAY" CONVENTION

At ten o'clock the next morning, Wednesday, May 30, the convention re-formed as the Committee of the Whole and elected Nathaniel Gorham of Massachusetts chairman. Washington turned over the gavel, stepped down from the dais, and took his place with the Virginia delegation.

In membership, the convention and the Committee of the Whole were the same. However, the purpose of the committee was to search for an informal consensus, to talk through and vote unofficially upon the general objects of the convention. Randolph's resolutions would be argued over and changes made, and the result would be a "report" to the convention. Only after the convention accepted the report would it begin making firm decisions, which, though they could be modified, would be essentially no longer subject to change.

Randolph led off, asking for the first of his resolutions to be considered, and Gouverneur Morris was glad to oblige. The first resolution, Morris said smoothly, was unnecessary: it talked about "correcting" and "enlarging" the Articles of Confederation, which, in truth, was not what the rest of the resolutions did.

Randolph offered a substitute—a three-parter declaring that a union "merely federal" was inadequate, a compact among sovereign states was insufficient, and "a national government ought to be established, consisting of a supreme judicial, legislative and executive."

Charles Pinckney objected: if the convention agreed to the first two parts, "it appeared to him that their business was at an end" because they were empowered only to improve the confederation, not to declare it worthless. When Butler of South Carolina suggested dropping parts one and two, Randolph again agreed. What now remained seemed to stun the convention:

"Resolved, that a national government ought to be established consisting of a supreme legislative, judiciary and executive."

No one said a word.

No matter that most were expecting it. No longer were they sitting at the Indian Queen over pipe and tankard, trading "very eccentric ideas on the subject." They were in the Pennsylvania State House, and the confederation existed, with wheels that turned now and then. The futures of thirteen states awaited their decision. Could it be a resolution like this?

Perhaps eyes shifted to Washington, sitting quietly with his delegation. All had seen his "legacy" letter four years ago; they knew where he stood—"there should be lodged some where a supreme power to regulate and govern the general concerns of the confederated republic . . ." But was not "confederated republic" a contradiction? Perhaps he would speak, exhort them a little. But he did not.

The suspense froze Madison; his pen had not moved from the moment Morris had spoken. He could look around the room and be sure that debate would sort out the political science of the resolution. No man here was new to government forms; all could conceive how "supremacy" might work, for good or ill. But the politics was a much harder matter, and potentially far more dangerous to the decision before them. He himself was troubled by word just arrived from Virginia—that "there is good reason to believe that Patrick Henry is hostile to the object of the Convention and that he wishes either a partition or total dissolution of the Confederacy." Who else would soon hear such threats from home?

Radical was what Madison had called it and this dead hush said it was true.

"Mr. Wythe presumes from the silence of the house, that the gentlemen are prepared to pass on the resolution and proposes its being put [to a vote]."

No! Pierce Butler of South Carolina was on his feet. He "does not think the house prepared . . . he is not." Charles Pinckney wanted to know whether Randolph meant to abolish the states in their entirety. His cousin, Gen. Charles Cotesworth Pinckney, doubted the convention's authority even to discuss it.

"It is questionable," Elbridge Gerry of Massachusetts stammered, "not only whether this convention can propose a government totally different or whether Congress itself would have a right to pass such a resolution . . . If we have a right to pass this resolution, we have a right to annihilate the confederation."

"It is only meant to give the national government a power to defend and protect itself," Randolph soothed, "to take from the states no more sovereignty than is competent to this end."

Gouverneur Morris rose to reassure them of their authority. "Men seem to have affixed different explanations to the terms before the house," he said. The existing government was called "federal" but it was not, because a federal government could "compel every part to do its duty," while the American federation had to rely entirely on the good faith of the states. Since the states and the Congress had appointed the convention to provide for the common defense, security of liberty, and general welfare, he went on, they were practically obliged to establish a "supreme" government capable of doing so.

The states therefore already expected to give up sovereignty, Morris suggested. He could not "conceive of a government in which there can exist two *supremes*. A federal agreement which each party may violate at pleasure cannot answer the purpose . . . We had better take a supreme government now, than a despot twenty years hence—for come he must."

It was true, George Mason agreed. The confederation was not only deficient in the ability to provide for coercion and punishment against delinquent states, but "in the nature of things" it could not act against the people of states that thwarted it. What was needed was a government that would operate directly on individuals, so that it "would punish only those whose guilt required it."

Roger Sherman, who had taken his seat only that day, admitted that Congress did not have sufficient power, but he was wary, not "disposed to make too great inroads on the existing system." For one thing, he observed, the whole reform effort could be defeated by inserting a provision unacceptable to the states.

Read of Delaware moved, with General Pinckney seconding, for a substitute resolution calling for a "more effective" instead of a supreme government. But they were too late; their motion lost on a tie vote, four to four.

By a vote of six states to one (New York was not counted because Hamilton and Yates canceled each other out), Randolph's first resolution passed; the convention agreed that a national government with a supreme judicial, legislative, and executive ought to be established. At this moment they became a runaway convention; they had voted to overturn the system.

6

Groping for a Principle

HIS FAVORITE MOTTO was "When you are in a minority, talk; when you are in a majority, vote." Thomas Jefferson once pointed him out to a friend saying, "That is Mr. Sherman of Connecticut, a man who never said a foolish thing in his life." Adams called Sherman "an old Puritan, as honest as an angel," while Silas Deane said he was as comfortable for a dinner party as "a chestnut burr for an eye-stone."

Roger Sherman, who had just taken his seat this day, was the most startling figure in the convention. Sixty-six years old, the son of a shoemaker, apprenticed in that trade, and without any formal education, he had been a member of the committee to draft the Declaration of Independence and had helped frame the Articles of Confederation. He now was an entrepreneur with shops in three towns and a self-taught lawyer past his thirtieth year as a judge of the superior court.

But Sherman looked as though hacked from Connecticut rock and behaved that way, too. He was all jagged edges, bumps, and creases. He had huge, deep, dark eyes, a beak for a nose, and a hard, long slash for a mouth. The form was clad in suits slightly rumpled, the whole topped off with crinkly dark hair, combed down and immobilized at the back of the neck. His movements were economical, bordering on paralysis, and he was famous for his utter lack of sociability.

Adams wrote: "Sherman's air is the reverse of grace. There cannot be a more striking contrast to beautiful action than the motion of his hands. Generally he stands upright with his hands before him, the fingers of his left hand clenched into a fist and the wrist of it grasped with his right . . . it is stiffness and awkwardness itself, rigid as starched linen or buckram."

"Mr. Sherman exhibits the oddest shaped character I ever remember to have met with," wrote William Pierce of Georgia. "He is un-meaning and unaccountably strange in his manner . . . the oddity of his address, the vulgarisms that accompany his public speaking, and that strange New England cant that runs through his public as well as his private speaking, make everything that is connected with him grotesque and laughable. And yet he deserves infinite praise—no man has a better heart or a clearer head."

The three greatest men in the Continental Congress, Patrick Henry said, were Washington, Richard Henry Lee and Sherman, and of all the statesmen he had known, the two greatest were Sherman and Mason. Alerting Rufus King that the Connecticut delegation was coming, Jeremiah Wadsworth, a Connecticut merchant, wrote, "I am satisfied with the appointment—except Sherman, who, I am told, is disposed to patch up the old scheme of Government. This was not my opinion of him when we chose him. He is as cunning as the Devil, and if you attack him, you ought to know him well. He is not easily managed, but if he suspects you are trying to take him in, you may as well catch an eel by the tail."

Though Madison could not know it, Sherman's arrival heralded the coming to life of opposing forces. From now on, the consensus Madison thought was there for "radical attempts" would slip—slowly, slightly, steadily—beyond his grasp.

In trying its collective mind on the Virginia plan, seeing the magnitude of the questions the scheme posed, the convention would find itself uncertain, groping for a principle, and the grounds of strife would be marked. The gifted three-man Connecticut delegation alone would move to a position early and stand—more landmark than leaders—unyielding until the battle reached them.

DELAWARE THREATENS TO WALK

The "Gordian knot," as Madison forever would call it, was Randolph's Resolution Number Two: "that the rights of suffrage in the National Legislature ought to be proportioned to the quotas of contribution,* or to the number of free inhabitants, as the one or the other rule may seem best in different cases."

Here was Madison's key. "Equality of suffrage"—the expression for one-state-one-vote—was the essence of confederation, insisted upon as far back as the first tentative talk of alliance in 1774 when the small colonies argued "that a little Colony had its All at Stake as well as a great one." And when the Articles of Confederation had been finalized in 1778, it had been enshrined as Article V.

Madison's motive for changing the rule of suffrage was simple: if the United States were to be a republic instead of a federation, the people—not the states—would have to be represented. Under proportional representation, the majority would prevail, and Madison hoped to convince the smaller state delegates that the change was superior both in logic and justice. The convention, however, was not disposed to let him try; it immediately demonstrated that the Gordian knot already had been tied.

Rising first, Madison asked for deletion of the reference to population so as not to "occasion debates† which would divert the committee from the general question." Objection, said Rufus King of Massachusetts. The deletion would leave only a

*the estimated share of the expenses of the government that each state would be asked to pay

†Madison was concerned about the southern states causing a quarrel by demanding slaves be included in representation.

state's wealth as the basis of representation; it would cause all kinds of mischief. Madison conceded the point and Hamilton moved to restore "the number of free inhabitants." Someone else suggested putting off both phrasings, and the convention agreed.

That left just the first half of the resolution. Randolph and Madison patiently moved "that the rights of suffrage in the national Legislature ought to be proportioned." No. Someone else wanted to be more aggressive and add "and not according to the present system," which, Madison wrote, "was agreed to," until yet another wording was suggested. Whereupon, a motion was made to postpone the whole question, and the convention agreed.

Madison was not to be deflected; the voting rule was the heart of reform and he was determined to have it debated. He "moved, in order to get over the difficulties . . . that an equitable ratio of representation ought to be substituted." This, Madison noted, was "generally relished [and] would have been agreed to, when:

"The deputies from Delaware," George Read reminded everyone, were "restrained by their commission from assenting to any change in the rule of suffrage." And "in case such a change should be fixed on," he warned, "it might become their duty to retire from the convention."

Gouverneur Morris rose to speak diplomatically. "The valuable assistance of those members could not be lost without real concern . . . so early a proof of discord in the convention as a secession of a state would add much to the regret." If Read looked relieved, he was premature, because Morris continued: "the change proposed was, however, so fundamental an article in a national government that it could not be dispensed with."

Nor was Madison going to let Delaware scare the convention. An equal vote of states might have been justified when "the union was a federal one among sovereign states," he declared, but "it must cease when a national government should be put in place." Perhaps it would save the Delaware deputies from "embarrassment" for everyone to agree to the proposition in the Committee of the Whole, but leave it unresolved in the formal report, whenever made.

"This, however, did not appear to satisfy Mr. Read." Read was not naive; to cave in so early would surrender all of the small state influence at once. If the idea of changing the rule of suffrage were voted now, it would go into the final report, no matter what Madison said. Read sat silent while the nationalists' criticism virtually made his point.

"By several it was observed that no just construction of the act of Delaware could require or justify a secession of her deputies," even if the convention chose to withhold the face-saving device Madison had offered. With Read refusing to budge, "It was finally agreed, however, that the clause should be postponed," as the Delawarian had urged.

DOUBTS ABOUT DEMOCRACY

Much easier was the question of whether to create a two-house legislature. In all but one state, two houses—the lower an "assembly" or a "house of delegates" and the upper usually a "senate"—was the legislative structure. As a token of respect to Benjamin Franklin, who had given Pennsylvania a "unicameral"— a single house—legislature, the same style was proposed by his delegation. (Franklin might have smiled; he would have known the Pennsylvania government was universally regarded as a horror.) The convention listened amiably, then voted for two houses without debate.

But democratically electing one of those houses was controversial. As George Mason had remarked before, a "supreme national government" would be able to exercise "coercive powers"—something between begging (as the federation did now) and using military action (which was unthinkable)—over the people themselves. Since government coercion would work only if the people were confident that they were represented, the nationalist approach to creating confidence was to allow the people to elect their representatives. Hence, the Virginia plan's

Resolution Number Four: "the members of the first branch of the National Legislature* ought to be elected by the people of the several states."

For many delegates, the idea was insupportable. Protectors of state sovereignty saw it (correctly) as a way to deprive the states of a hand in forming the first branch. For some of the political philosophers, it was a recipe for disaster, introducing the passions of the mob into the work of the national council. However much "democracy" resonated with virtue, it was an "enthusiasm" that, in action, produced anarchy.

Roger Sherman and Elbridge Gerry jumped up to head off democracy, startling Yates of New York so that he scribbled "strange to tell," as he described their arguments. One reason that Yates was surprised was that Connecticut and Massachusetts were two of the most liberal states in the union, but it was especially "strange to tell" that Sherman would seem to distrust the class from which he sprang. But though Sherman was a self-made man, that did not make him a populist.

"The people," Sherman declared, "immediately should have as little to do as may be about the government . . . They lack information and are constantly liable to be misled." The first branch should be chosen by the state legislatures, he said.

Gerry of Massachusetts, unwilling host to Shays's infamous rebellions, agreed: "The evils we experience flow from the excess of democracy," he said. The people do not lack virtue, "but are the dupes of pretended patriots. In Massachusetts, it has been fully confirmed by experience that they are daily misled into the most baneful measures and opinions by false reports circulated by designing men, and which no one on the spot can refute." Gerry said he "had been too republican here-

---

*The terms "first branch" and "second branch" as the delegates used them are confusing today, because we are accustomed to referring to *all* of Congress as a "branch," to the executive as a another branch, and to the Supreme Court as the third. But in 1787, the three-branch principle meant: a "first branch" that was a broadly based, democratic assembly or house; a much smaller "second branch" or senate that would be aristocratic or conservative; and thirdly, an "executive" branch. The judiciary was not yet fully incorporated in the idea of "checks and balances."

tofore. He was still, however, republican, but had been taught by experience the danger of the levelling spirit."

As surprising as the antidemocratic views of Sherman and Gerry was the quarter from which came the warmest argument in favor of the democratic principle. The wealthy Virginia patrician, George Mason, made the case both on the point of honor and by reminding the convention of a peculiarly American reality—equal opportunity for both upward and downward mobility.

The first branch "was to be the grand depository of the democratic principle of the government. It was, so to speak, to be our House of Commons. It ought to know and sympathise with every part of the community . . . We had been too democratic," Mason acknowledged, but now he was "afraid we would incautiously run into the opposite extreme. We ought to attend to the rights of every class of people."

Mason said he had "often wondered at the indifference of the superior classes of society to this dictate of humanity and policy—considering that however affluent their circumstances or elevated their situations might be, the course of a few years not only might, but certainly would, distribute their posterity throughout the lowest classes of society. Every selfish motive, therefore, every family attachment, ought to recommend such a system of policy as would provide no less carefully for the rights—and happiness of the lowest than of the highest orders of citizens."

In the twentieth century, the theory became popular that the framers were really an elite acting to secure their privileges against encroachment by the common folk. Mason's speech is one of the best of many in the convention that undermine the theory. Mason chose the argument that would hit home: class-conscious his listeners certainly were, but they also prided themselves on their honor and liberality, which was considerable for their day. In personalizing the principle by invoking their offspring, Mason reminded them that their status was maintained largely by hard work and ability—not bred in the bone as in the Old World—and that their wealth "not only might, but certainly would" vanish. With some of his most distinguished listeners staggering under a mountain of debt, this was something they all understood.

James Wilson of Pennsylvania (who would face the threat of a debtors' prison himself) rose to add another argument to Mason's. He "contended strenuously for drawing the most numerous branch of the legislature immediately from the people. He was for raising the federal pyramid to a considerable altitude and for that reason wished to give it as broad a basis as possible. No government could long subsist without the confidence of the people . . ."

Many states, Madison reminded them, had barriers to popular influence—usually by way of electors standing between voters and candidates. If the convention erected another such barrier in creating the first branch, "the people would be lost sight of altogether and the necessary sympathy between them and their rulers and officers too little felt." He approved of "successive filtrations" for popular enthusiasms, Madison said, but "thought it might be pushed too far."

The convention accepted election by the people, but barely. The ayes were six, nos two, and two states were divided.

THE "CHASM" APPEARS

John Adams would have been fascinated to see his ancient "Thoughts on Government" sprouting in the debate on the upper house—especially because it was an unconscious error, a flashback to 1776 in the minds of Sherman and Mason.

Resolution Number Five envisioned that the first branch would elect the members of the second—the Senate, as the delegates soon began calling it—from a pool of candidates nominated by the state legislatures.

Such an election procedure would further water down state influence, North and South Carolina protested. How far, Pierce Butler asked, did Mr. Randolph mean to go and how many members did Mr. Randolph mean to assign to the second branch? "Taking so many powers out of the hands of the states," Butler warned, would tend to "destroy all that balance and security of interests which it was necessary to preserve."

Randolph rose, testy. He had given his views on the nature of his propositions; the details had been properly left out. His general object for the Senate was to check in the national government a tendency that was pronounced in the state governments: "the turbulence and follies of democracy."

Well, then, said Butler, "until the number of the Senate could be known, it would be impossible for him to give a vote on it."

The second branch should be small—a select body, James Wilson and Rufus King volunteered. If every state legislature elected members according to population, King said, the second branch would balloon to at least eighty seats in order to assure Delaware of having just one. Wilson supposed excessive size could be prevented by joining several states, small and large, for the purpose of electing the second branch.

"The mode pointed out in the original propositions is best," Madison insisted. He had seen Wilson's idea in operation in Virginia, where senators were chosen by combined counties, he said. Big-county candidates always won, even if the little counties had better candidates.

Here Sherman and Mason mixed up Madison's proposal for election *by* the first house with Adams's 1776 recommendation that senates be elected *from* the legislatures' first houses: "If the Senate was to be appointed by the first branch and out of that body," Sherman protested, "it would make them too dependent" and destroy the value of the Senate as a check on the first branch. Absolutely, said George Mason. Plus "it would be highly improper to draw the Senate out of the first branch"; it would create vacancies in the larger house that "would cost much time, trouble and expense to have filled up."

Charles Pinckney bounced up. "Divide the continent into four divisions," he urged [did he wave his plan in the air?]. Nominate a certain number of persons from those divisions and appoint the Senate from that group. He called for a vote to delete "nomination by state legislatures" from resolution Number Five and got it: Rejected, nine to nothing.

Then Randolph's whole proposal for the second branch also

went down to defeat. As Madison put it, "So the clause was disagreed to and a chasm left in this part of the plan." When the chasm came to be closed, it would only set the stage for a much greater cleavage in the convention.

GETTING TOUGH ON THE STATES

The debate had been sloppy, and Madison was turning irritable. The proposed national government now had one house and a chasm. But the views of the delegates were showing divergence and there was little he could do about it: the question was looming—what would happen to the states in the national scheme? The question would drag at the feet of the convention until it brought the convention to a complete stop.

Without debate the delegates agreed unanimously that each branch of the national legislature should originate laws and that all the legislative powers of the existing Congress should be transferred to the new legislature.

Disagreement broke out again on providing the national body with "legislative power in all cases to which the state legislatures were individually incompetent." Regulating trade between the states was an obvious subject for the national legislature, but what else might this power take in? Charles Pinckney and his fellow South Carolinian, John Rutledge, objected to "the vagueness of the term 'incompetent.'" They could not decide how to vote without "an exact enumeration of the powers comprehended . . ."

Butler of South Carolina put the pressure on Randolph again. He feared "we were running into an extreme in taking away the powers of the states"—and called on Mr. Randolph for the extent of his meaning.

Defensive and angry, Randolph disclaimed "any intention to give indefinite powers to the national legislature!" He was "entirely opposed to such an inroad on the state jurisdictions, and . . . he did not think any considerations whatever could change his determination. His opinion was fixed on this point!"

Sturdy up to now, Randolph was buckling, Madison could

see, the old vacillation beginning to emerge. Forgetting how early, tentative, and fragile the consensus on a national government really was, he leaped up to deliver a sharp lecture.

It was necessary to adopt some general principles: "we were wandering from one thing to another." He himself "had brought with him into the convention a strong bias in favor of an enumeration and definition of the powers," Madison said, "but had also brought doubts concerning its practicability . . . his doubts had become stronger." He did not know what his final opinion would be, but he would "shrink from nothing which should be found essential" to make the government effective. And, he added imperiously, "all the necessary means for attaining it must, however reluctantly, be submitted to."

Madison may have been pleased that the delegates gave him what he wanted, passing the proposition nine to nothing, with Connecticut divided by Sherman's immovable no. But it appears that they had decided to get Madison off their backs: without debate or dissent, they next approved the proposed power to make laws in cases "in which the harmony of the U.S. may be interrupted by the exercise of individual [state] legislation" and then agreed that the national body should have the power to veto "all laws passed by the several states contravening in the opinion of the national legislature the articles of union."

No protest of such sweeping authority? Did Madison mean to flatten debate so thoroughly? His next remarks seem to be made in a vacuum, or to a roomful of men no longer listening. The papers of all the notetakers add to that impression: none but he wrote down a word he said after his tonguelashing.

The final clause of the resolution would allow the new government to use force against "any member of the union failing to fulfill its duty" under the new constitution—authority to wage civil war. Into the continuing silence, Madison observed that "the more he reflected on the use of force, the more he doubted . . ." He went on to discover problems in the idea and wound down with the suggestion that consideration be postponed. Agreed—without debate or discussion. Were the delegates supine or sulking?

DESIGNING THE EXECUTIVE

The next morning was fair, warm, and breezy, but the convention's spirit was sodden and still. The question now on the table was fundamental—Resolution Number Seven asked that "a national executive be instituted" chosen by the national legislature for an [blank] term of years and ineligible thereafter. But nobody had anything to say.

Charles Pinckney and James Wilson tried provocation—Pinckney warned of "a Monarchy of the worst kind, to wit an elective one," and Wilson moved for an executive consisting of a single person, with Pinckney somewhat fickly seconding him. Nobody followed up.

With "a considerable pause ensuing and the Chairman asking if he should put the question," Benjamin Franklin clucked at the tied tongues. This was "a point of great importance," Franklin observed. He "wished that the gentlemen would deliver their sentiments on it before the question was put."

John Rutledge tried to stir the stillness. He "animadverted on the shyness of gentlemen on this and other subjects . . . it looked as if they supposed themselves precluded—by having frankly disclosed their opinions—from afterwards changing them." He favored a single executive, but "not giving him the power of war and peace."

That roused Sherman. The executive was "nothing more than an institution for carrying the will of the legislature into effect." The legislature was "the depositary of the supreme will of the society" and "the best judges of the business which ought to be done by the executive." The legislature absolutely should appoint the executive—as the resolution proposed—and furthermore, the legislature should be "at liberty to appoint one or more as experience might dictate."

No, Wilson spoke up, not a plural executive. A single magistrate would give the most "energy, dispatch and responsibility to the office." People should stop worrying about the British monarch, he added. The plan did not model its executive on the king, who had, for instance, legislative powers.

A single executive would be "feasible," Gerry allowed. Why not try "annexing a council to the executive, in order to give weight and inspire confidence."

Randolph surged to his feet. He "strenuously opposed" a single executive—it was "the foetus of monarchy."

Madison moved quickly to cut off a clash between Wilson and Randolph. Perhaps, he suggested, before deciding between a single or a plural executive, they should define the powers of the executive. It "would assist the judgment in determining how far they might be safely entrusted to a single officer."

Randolph's responsibility for the Virginia plan had run its course. By introducing it, he had given it Virginia's blessing and made it respectable, but the easily bullied young governor was neither strong enough nor committed enough to succeed as its floor manager.

The time had come for Madison to step fully into the lead, although Randolph could not have chosen a more awkward moment to let the mantle of responsibility slip from his shoulders. Madison's overbearing lecture had brought debate to a standstill that had lingered overnight. He himself and those watching him must have wondered if it would happen again—and again. "Greatness" was what others saw in him, and no one is ever ready for "greatness." But, by God, Madison would try.

In line with his suggestion, he moved that the executive have general power to carry out national laws, to make appointments to offices, and to execute other powers (but not legislative or judicial) that the legislature might delegate. He gracefully accepted a redundant amendment, then waited patiently while the members discovered they did not like the extra words and voted to strike them. Finally his proposition came to a vote, and this time Madison had earned his victory—nine states agreed with him; Connecticut again was divided.

Madison's discipline appeared to work—the delegates seemed to square their shoulders and fix their lapels as they turned to the term of office for the executive.

Three years, said Wilson, but only if the executive could be reelected. Pinckney and Mason were for seven years. Assuming that the executive would be appointed by the legislature, Mason opposed reelection—the desire to be reappointed would invite the executive to make backroom deals with the legislature.

Seven years was far too long for Gunning Bedford of Delaware. "Consider what the situation of the country would be in case the first magistrate should be saddled on it for such period," he pleaded, "and it should be found on trial that he did not possess the qualifications ascribed to him, or should lose them after his appointment. An impeachment . . . would be no cure for this evil, as an impeachment would reach misfeasance only, not incapacity." The executive should serve for three years, and be ineligible for re-election after three terms, he urged.

The vote was tried on a seven-year term of office; it was the closest so far: five in favor, four opposed, one divided. Washington ruled that the divided state could not be counted; the five in favor formed an affirmative to pass it.

Agreement on who would choose the executive eluded them. An executive independent of the national legislature is "the very essence of tyranny if there was any such thing," Sherman's harsh voice pronounced. He should be appointed by the national legislature and be made "absolutely dependent on that body."

Election by the people was best, Wilson said. It was both "convenient and successful" in New York. (Hamilton must have winced—Governor George Clinton was as firmly enthroned in Albany as George III was in England.) Not only should both branches of the legislature derive from the people—without the intervention of the state legislatures—but the executive should also, Wilson added, "in order to make them as independent as possible of each other, as well as of the states."

Mr. Wilson should have time to "digest his idea into his own form," Mason urged. He liked it, but it seemed "impracticable." Agreeing, the delegates voted to give Wilson time, but a resolve to protect state powers seemed to harden overnight. Bad luck for Wilson, who came in the next morning with a novel scheme for picking the executive: have the people choose "electors" whose only task would be appointing the executive. If that sounds familiar, it is—Wilson is the father of the electoral college.

At that moment, however, Elbridge Gerry, while he "liked the principle," spoke against it: "it would alarm and give a handle to the state partisans, as tending to supersede altogether the state authorities," Gerry said. He thought "the community not yet ripe for stripping the states of their powers."

North Carolina's Hugh Williamson "could see no advantage"; it would mean "great trouble and expense."

Wilson's novelty took a drubbing: two ayes; eight nos. Instead, the convention agreed firmly (eight yes and two no) that the national legislature would elect the executive for a term of seven years.

The vote was no victory for state partisans. Rather it had the effect of spotlighting the still-undefined Senate as the remaining site for lodging direct state influence in the national government. Should all these informal decisions proceed on to final adoption, the Senate would clearly be the only place where state power might be made to count. And there was a strong likelihood that the democratically elected first branch would be a final decision.

MONEY AND POWER

In orchestral music, a cadenza is a solo, often improvised, in the middle of a concerto. In the hands of a master, it can be exquisite, even if greatly different from the composition it interrupts. In the convention, amid the debate on the executive, came a cadenza—an inspired solo on money and power from Benjamin Franklin. But he was not improvising; in a long, prepared speech, he moved that the executive be unpaid.

"As my opinion may appear new and chimerical," Franklin said, "it is only from a persuasion that it is right, and from a sense of duty, that I hazard it . . .

"Sir, there are two passions which have a powerful influence on the affairs of men. These are ambition and avarice; the love of power and the love of money. Separately, each of these has great force in prompting men to action; but when united in view of the same object, they have in many minds the most violent effects. Place before the eyes of such men a post of honor that shall at the same time be a place of profit, and they will move heaven and earth to obtain it . . .

"And of what kind are the men that will strive for this profitable pre-eminence, through all the bustle of cabal, the heat of contention, the infinite mutual abuse of parties, tearing to pieces the best of characters? It will not be the wise and moderate, the lovers of peace and good order, the men fittest for the trust. It will be the bold and the violent, the men of strong passions and indefatigable activity in their selfish pursuits. These will thrust themselves into your government and be your rulers. And these too will be mistaken in the expected happiness of their situation: for their vanquished competitors of the same spirit, and from the same motives, will perpetually be endeavoring to distress their administration, thwart their measures, and render them odious to the people . . ."

Let us not, Franklin said, "sow the seeds of contention, faction and tumult by making our posts of honor places of profit . . ."

He knew they would think it "an Utopian idea, and that we can never find men to serve us in the executive department without paying them well for their services. I conceive this to be a mistake . . . Have we not seen the great and most important of our officers, that of General of our armies, executed for eight years together without the smallest salary by a patriot whom I will not now offend by any other praise?"

Did they believe Washington a rarity? "Sir, I have a better opinion of our country. I think we shall never be without a sufficient number of wise and good men . . ." Honor, not thrift, was his object, Franklin concluded. If rejected, "I must be contented with the satisfaction of having delivered my opinion frankly and done my duty."

Franklin's speech does sound "utopian," as he realized, but perhaps a better term would be a wistful farewell to revolution.

For not only Washington, but they themselves in this convention and many of them for a year, two, or three, in the Continental Congress served without salaries. Sherman had done so for six years. This was part of the ideal then called "civic virtue," that the good, the able, the responsible—the elite—would enter high public office without monetary reward. But it belonged to the Revolution, when there was, as Mason had put it, "a certain degree of enthusiasm, which inspired and supported the mind." It could not last forever.

Madison noted that "no debate ensued, and the proposition was postponed . . . It was treated with great respect, but rather for the author of it, than from any apparent conviction of its expediency or practicability."

Impeachment and Removal

How to remove a bad executive was perplexing; here the short history of the states' independence had little to offer. John Dickinson of Delaware suggested providing for removal "by the national legislature on the request of a majority of the legislatures of individual states," because it "was necessary to place the power of removing somewhere." He did not favor a power of impeachment, he added.

Implacable as ever, Sherman argued that the executive should serve at the pleasure of the national legislature, which finally drew a protest from George Mason. "Making the executive the mere creature of the legislature," he complained, would be a "violation of the fundamental principle of good government."

Madison and Wilson shuddered at the idea of state involvement in a removal. "It would open a door for intrigues against him in states where his administration, though just, might be unpopular—and might tempt him to pay court to particular states whose leading partisans he might fear."

Dickinson, perhaps inspired by Franklin's speech, delivered a "discourse of some length" which not even Madison seemed able to sum up, except that he was defending removal at the request of state legislatures.

The vote in the end was for removal in case of "impeachment and conviction of malpractice or neglect of duty," but who would make these findings was left unsettled. Agreed to without debate for now was the proposal to bar the executive from a second term.

Charles Pinckney gave another tap to the nerve only a little less sensitive than state sovereignty when he moved formally that the executive should be one person.

Never! Randolph was on his feet. "With great earnestness," the young governor declared that he "should not do justice to the country which sent him if he were silently to suffer the establishment of a unity in the executive. He felt an opposition to it which he believed he should continue to feel as long as he lived."

Randolph feared that the people would reject a plan that included "a semblance of monarchy," and he was not alone. Others, though, did not add their voices, and the single executive passed, with three states voting in the negative.

JUDICIAL LAWMAKING REJECTED

Modern political argument, especially during the presidency of Ronald Reagan, has been hot and sometimes bitter on the subject of "judicial activism"—court rulings which amount to new legislation originating from the bench rather than the legislative branch. However, the impulse to involve the judiciary in lawmaking is not a modern development. Both Madison and Wilson proposed a formal role for the judiciary in creating law, not just interpreting it.

Madison conceived the Virginia plan's Resolution Number Eight, which called for a "council of revision" with authority to review all acts of both the National Legislature and the state legislatures and the power to veto them. The veto would not be absolute; the legislature would be allowed to override it.

Madison specified that a "convenient number" of judges would be included on the council of revision.

James Wilson supported Resolution Eight, but he wished for it to be carried even farther: the executive and judiciary, he thought, should jointly exercise an absolute veto over legislation. "They cannot otherwise preserve their importance against the legislature," he said.

But the convention rejected both ideas, accepting the arguments of Elbridge Gerry and Rufus King, who sound much like modern conservatives.

"Mr. Gerry doubts whether the judiciary ought to form a part of it, as they will have sufficient check against encroachments on their own department by their exposition of the laws, which involved a power of deciding on their constitutionality."

Judicial review for constitutionality was proper, Gerry said; the public approved. What bothered him about the proposed general veto power was that, he felt, it would improperly turn the courts into policymakers.

"In some states, the judges had actually set aside laws as being against the constitution. This was done too with general approbation," Gerry said. But he warned, "It was quite foreign from the nature of the [judicial] office to make them judges of the policy of public measures." Instead, he proposed, give the executive a veto, and allow the legislature to override it by a certain number of votes. Keep the policy-making in the hands of the elected officials—the executive and the legislature.

Rufus King agreed. "The judges," he said, "ought to be able to expound the law as it should come before them, free from the bias of having participated in its formation."

Neither Madison's council of revision nor Gerry's formula for an executive veto and legislative override went "far enough," Wilson insisted. The executive needed an "absolute negative" or the legislative branch would run wild and "sink [him] into nonexistence . . . Give the executive and judiciary jointly an absolute negative," he urged again.

An absolute veto would corrupt the executive, Franklin objected. When Pennsylvania was a colony, "The negative of the governor was constantly made use of to extort money. No good law whatever could be passed without a private bargain with him." The governor's greed grew, Franklin said, until it became the practice to present a Treasury check made out to him along with legislation to be signed. "When the Indians were scalping the western people," he added, the governor would not agree to raising arms and troops "till it was agreed that his estate should be exempted from taxation."

No one man, Sherman chipped in, should be able to "stop the will of the whole."

Making the veto difficult to override would "answer the same purpose as an absolute negative," Madison said. Not even King George III could flout the opinion of the whole Parliament, and giving the American executive "such a prerogative would certainly be obnoxious to the temper of this country—its present temper at least."

Wilson stuck to his guns: "The power would seldom be used," he argued. "The legislature would know that such a power existed and would refrain from such laws as it would be sure to defeat." Colonial governors may have abused the veto, but they had not been appointed by the people as this executive would be. It was more important that the executive be able to defend itself from legislative excesses.

But Wilson was all by himself on this one. Butler declared that "he certainly should have acted very differently" and voted against a single executive had he known an absolute veto would be considered; Gunning Bedford opposed any kind of veto or revisionary power.

George Mason and Benjamin Franklin both warned that the executive would be, in Franklin's words, "always increasing . . . till it ends in monarchy." Mason contended anxiously for a legislative power to override a veto. "We are, Mr. Chairman, going very far in this business," he warned. "We are not indeed constituting a British government, but a more dangerous monarchy, an elective one . . . Do gentlemen mean to pave the way to hereditary monarchy? Do they flatter themselves that the people will ever consent to such an innovation? If they do, I venture to tell them, they are mistaken. The people will never consent."

The absolute veto went crashing down—no ayes, ten nos. Adopted was the formula for a two-thirds vote of both houses of Congress to override an executive veto, the rule that governs today.

In a last ditch effort to join the judiciary and executive in the veto power, Madison suddenly placed before the convention his theory of clashing interests—the product of his extraordinary studies of the previous year and the theory for which he is most famous:

"The judicial ought to be introduced in the business of legislation," Madison began, in order to add sufficient weight to the check against the Legislative branches. It was "the only defense against the inconveniences of democracy consistent with the democratic form of government." All civilized societies, he said, leading his listeners carefully, divide into sects, factions and interests—rich, poor, debtors, creditors; the landed, the manufacturing, the commercial interests; inhabitants of different districts, followers of different political leaders, disciples of different religions.

"In all cases where a majority are united by a common interest or passion, the rights of the minority are in danger, and little or nothing restrains them," Madison said. Experience shows that "the maxim that honesty is the best policy is . . . as little regarded by bodies of men as by individuals. Respect for character is always diminished in proportion to the number among whom the blame or praise is to be divided."

These were the sources of persecution in all governments, ancient and modern. America feared Parliament because Great Britain had her own interests and would have pursued that interest at our expense. America, with slavery, commits the same injustice: "We have seen the mere distinction of color made, in the most enlightened period of time, a ground of the most oppressive dominion ever exercised by man over man . . .

"We must introduce the checks which will destroy the measures of an interested majority," he insisted. "A negative in the executive is not only necessary for its own safety, but for the safety of a minority in danger of oppression from an unjust and interested majority . . . Add the judiciary and you increase the respectability" of vetoing popular but unjust legislation.

"A very able and ingenious speech," Pierce wrote admiringly, that "proved . . . the propriety of incorporating the judicial with the executive in the revision of laws."*

But the convention did not think so, and voted eight to two to give "the executive alone, without the judiciary, the revisionary control on the laws."

FINISHING THE FRAME

The convention agreed easily on creating a national judiciary and dodged a potential dispute by deleting a clause in Resolution Number Nine providing for "one or more inferior tribunals." In laymen's language, that stood for lower courts and appeals courts, and the speedy deletion hints at suspicions that such courts were meant to replace the states' courts.

The method of appointing the judiciary was briefly troublesome. Appointment by the national lawmakers would be improper, Wilson said. "Intrigue, partiality and concealment were the necessary consequences." A principal reason for a single executive was so that such appointments could be made by one responsible person, he added.

Rutledge, however, "was by no means disposed to grant so great a power to any single person. The people will think we are leaning too much towards monarchy." He wanted, moreover, a supreme court only. "The state tribunals are the most proper to decide in all cases in the first instance."

Franklin was cool toward giving either branch the appoint-

*Madison, organizing his notes for publication, placed this famous speech within one he made two days later in support of his critical goal of establishing confidence in the idea of a large republic. However, Rufus King and William Pierce both heard Madison unveiling his theory here (a point where Max Farrand, the compiler of the standard reference work on the convention, found Madison's notes "quite defective"). I believe that Madison introduced his important new theory here, repeated it in fuller detail—and more usefully—on the day he shows himself giving it, and gave it still a third time. I suspect Madison found his tired listeners fairly uncomprehending this day. Pierce was dazzled, but did not follow it well; King did better. In future sessions, some delegates referred to the theory as if they were still digesting it.

ment power, and urged the delegates to try to think of something else, using the opportunity to tell another story "in a brief
and entertaining manner." The "good Docr.," as Madison
liked to call Franklin, "related a Scotch mode in which the
nomination proceeded from the lawyers who always selected
the ablest of the profession in order to get rid of him and share
his practice among themselves."

Madison admitted he was perplexed, too, and suggested leaving a blank that could be "hereafter filled on maturer reflection." That agreed to, the convention approved the creation of
a salaried judiciary that would hold office "during good behavi-
our" or, in effect, for life.

The convention hurried past Resolutions Ten through Fourteen, agreeing without debate that a procedure should be set
up to admit new states and that the Continental Congress
should keep operating until the first day of business of the new
government. They postponed debate on whether to guarantee
republican government in the states and territories, require
loyalty oaths from national officials, or allow the constitution to
be amended without the consent of the national legislature.

The fifteenth, and last, resolution, however, ignited a new
argument. This item called for popularly elected state conventions to ratify the constitution—another slap in the face for the
state legislatures.

The Articles of Confederation, Sherman growled, call for the
Congress and the state legislatures to amend the charter of the
union. Popular ratification is unnecessary.

And *that* is a defect in the Articles, Madison countered.
When state authorities oppose federal amendments, the state
almost certainly will prevail, because the power to ratify usually
rests in the legislature alone. The only safe way to ratify the new
Constitution was "by the supreme authority of the people themselves."

The people of Massachusetts, Elbridge Gerry protested,
"have at this time the wildest ideas of government in the
world." Gerry, Madison thought, "seemed afraid of referring
the new system to them."

The people tacitly agreed to a federal government, King

remarked. The legislatures, therefore, may hold the right to ratify—but he preferred a convention in each state.

The question wound down to a postponement—but not before Wilson raised the idea of letting "a partial union" begin operating after a fixed number of states had ratified and leaving the door open for holdouts to come in later. Madison suspected Wilson was trying to intimidate New Jersey and Delaware. "This hint was probably meant *in terrorem* to the smaller states . . . Nothing was said in reply to it," he jotted.

MAKING SURE

The first canvass of the Virginia plan had taken just one week, but the delegates now thought they knew the terrain they were on. They had a consensus on a two-branch legislature, but not on how it was to be constituted; they agreed on the need for an executive, but were split on how independent the executive should be; and they had not uncovered any deeply divisive conflict on a judiciary.

They had found some conflicts that boded to be serious. Completely murky was what to do about the states; some principle had to apply, but it eluded them. Next most troubling was a fear of planting the seed of monarchy on one hand and a distrust of democratic ideas on the other; and beneath it all was the nagging question of whether the country was really ready to overhaul the union.

The country's readiness was unknowable and unsolvable in convention, but a determined effort could perhaps bring solutions more clearly in view on the other questions. Their task was to work, not toward what would be acceptable, but toward what would be best—to "raise a standard to which the wise and honest can repair," as Washington had once put it. Accordingly, with scarcely a pause, the delegates took one last look to see if any views had changed.

They reconsidered popular election of the first branch, pushed by Charles Pinckney's motion for election by the state legislatures for the somewhat cynical reason that "The legislatures would be less likely to promote the adoption of the new government if they were to be excluded from all share in it."

Liberty itself hangs on the mode of election, said Gerry excitedly, renewing his warnings against democracy. In England, "the people will probably lose their liberty" because too few had the right to vote, but America was in the same danger "from the opposite extreme:

"In Massachusetts, the worst men get into the legislature. Several members of that body had lately been convicted of infamous crimes. Men of indigence, ignorance and baseness spare no pains, however dirty, to carry their point against men who are superior to the artifices practiced." Yes, the people should elect, he said, but with controls designed to "secure a just preference of merit." One method, he speculated, might be for the people to nominate candidates and the state legislatures to make the appointments.

This was too timid for James Wilson. He wanted vigor in the government—not of the monarchical sort, but "vigorous authority to flow immediately from the legitimate source of all authority. The government ought to possess not only, first, the *force,* but secondly, the *mind or sense* of the people at large. The legislature ought to be the most exact transcript of the whole society."

"If the state governments are to be continued," Sherman said, rising in his stiff way, the state legislatures must make the elections to the national government "in order to preserve harmony" between them. The "people's rights" in the national government would be secure because they elect the state legislatures.

Another reason not to involve the people, Sherman said, is that "the objects of the union are few. 1.defense against foreign danger. 2.against internal disputes and a resort to force. 3.treaties with foreign nations. 4.regulating foreign commerce and drawing revenue from it . . . All other matters, civil and criminal, would be much better in the hands of the states. The people are more happy in small than large states."

The objects listed by Sherman were "certainly important and necessary," Madison said. But he would add "the necessity of providing more effectually for the security of private rights and the steady dispensation of justice. Interferences with these were evils which had more—perhaps—than anything else produced this convention."

Half-agreeing with Sherman, Dickinson urged popular election in the first branch and election of the Senate by state legislatures. He was "for a strong national government, but for leaving the states a considerable agency in the system"; it was "as politic as it was unavoidable."

This troublesome matter of what to do about the states showed itself most remarkably in the paradox of George Read of Delaware: he was committed, consciously, to two opposite ideas. It was he who had drafted the Delaware instructions which forbade his delegation to agree to change the rule of suffrage, and he, too, who had warned that Delaware might walk out of the convention. As long as the system was federal, with the states sitting as sovereign governments, Read opposed anything that would reduce Delaware relative to the larger states. But he also wished to see Delaware erased—if all states could be erased.

The pity is that Read was not a better speaker. "His legal abilities are said to be very great," William Pierce noted, "but his powers of oratory are fatiguing and tiresome to the last degree. His voice is feeble and his articulation so bad that few can have patience to attend him." Read was a very good and amiable man, however, Pierce added.

"Too much attachment is betrayed to the state governments," Read said now. "We must look beyond their continuance. A national government must soon, of necessity, swallow all of them up." He was against "patching up the old federal system"; he hoped the idea would be dismissed. "It would be like putting new cloth on an old garment.

"The confederation was founded on temporary principles. It cannot last; it cannot be amended. If we do not establish a good government on new principles, we must either go to ruin or have the work to do over again."

Everyone had been trying to pretend this was not a concern, and Wilson rose anxiously to offset Read's remarks. He "saw no incompatibility between the national and state governments, provided the latter were restrained to certain local purposes— nor any probability of their being devoured."

The new vote was reassurance for Madison and the nationalists. Support for popular election of the first branch improved: the tally climbed from six to eight states in favor and three rejecting it.

Wilson and Madison, perhaps heartened by the win, asked for reconsideration of including the judiciary in revising legislation. They lost again, eight to three, picking up just one vote.

Fortitude finally was found to face the "chasm" left earlier on whether the first branch should choose the Senate. Three competing preferences were advocated from the floor: Dickinson called for the state legislatures to select the members; Wilson urged popular election; and Read suggested that the executive appoint the senate from candidates proposed by state legislatures.

This was the last debate on the Senate—for several weeks— that would be free of hostility, veiled or outright. The convention still searched for a consensus and was far from finding that it would be forced to settle for a compromise. They still felt there was principle to which they could all repair—one that might be superior to either the shaky alliance of small republics or Madison's giant sphere writhing with clashing interests—and since no obvious principle was lying around, perhaps one could be created on the spot.

John Dickinson mixed three metaphors—a collision, a solar system, and a river—trying to make one. The states were "indispensable" to the national government, he said. They would check its power by producing "that collision between the different authorities which should be wished for." The proposed national system could be "compared . . . to the Solar System, in which the States were the planets and ought to be left to move freely in their proper orbits." He accused Wilson of wanting to "extinguish these planets." If all power were drawn from the people at large, he argued, it "would only unite the 13 small streams into one great current pursuing the same course without any opposition whatever."

Wilson peered over his little round glasses. He was not for extinguishing the planets, he said. "Neither did he, on the other hand, believe that they would warm or enlighten the sun. Within their proper orbits, they must still be suffered to act for subordinate purposes" because of the size of the country.

"The great evils complained of," Madison observed patiently, were caused by the state legislatures. Involving them in the national legislature, instead of checking such a tendency, "may be expected to promote it." Nothing could be more contradictory, he said, than to say that, unchecked, the national legislature would behave like the states and "in the same breath that the state legislatures are the only proper check."

Dickinson's planets, however, were magic, exactly the right image to support what seemed to be the impossibility of excluding the states. Madison's minuscule allowance for state influence was not good enough; Wilson's proposed subordination of them was worse. George Mason now split with Madison and Wilson to support Dickinson. A total loss awaited both Madison and Wilson: appointment of the Senate by state legislatures passed ten to zero.

Overnight Madison mulled over the security of the planets in their orbits and found himself unhappy. The next morning, he swiftly seconded Charles Pinckney's motion to expand the national veto of state laws which had been silently approved after Madison's tonguelashing several days earlier. Pinckney's new motion proposed power for the national legislature to veto not only state laws in conflict with national laws and treaties, but *all* state legislation "which they should judge to be improper."

It is "absolutely necessary to a perfect system," Madison said. "This prerogative of the general government is the great pervading principle that must control the centrifugal tendency of the states which, without it, will continually fly out of their proper orbits and destroy the order and harmony of the political system."

"How can it be thought that the proposed negative can be exercised?" Bedford groaned. "Are the laws of the states to be suspended in the most urgent cases until they can be sent seven or eight hundred miles and undergo the deliberations of a body who may be incapable of judging them? Is the national legislature to sit continually in order to revise the laws of the states?"

The sweeping veto was defeated, three to seven, with one state divided. Massachusetts, Pennsylvania and Virginia agreed with it. Delaware was divided; with Read and Dickinson (who was perhaps delighted with Madison's seizing his metaphor) supporting it.

A HARBINGER OF THINGS TO COME

On Saturday, June 9, after two weeks of near total silence in debate, New Jersey suddenly spoke up to announce the presence of firm opposition. The Committee of the Whole, it was moved, should return to the question of proportioning the states' votes in the national legislature. (It had been carefully ignored since Read's threat to walk out at the beginning.)

New Jersey Supreme Court Chief Justice David Brearly seconded the motion, saying the rule of suffrage had been "rightly settled" when the confederation was established. Proportional voting was fair only in appearance, Brearly said. It would *operate* unfairly; the large states would "carry everything before them." The small states "will be obliged to throw themselves constantly into the scale of some large one, in order to have any weight at all." He would not claim that the equal vote was fair, only that it prevented the small states from being destroyed.

"Lay the map of the confederation on the table and extinguish the present boundary lines of the respective state jurisdictions and make a new division so that each state is equal," Brearly concluded scornfully, "then a government [as is proposed] will be just."

William Paterson, who had made the motion, now rose again, calling for another reading of the Massachusetts delegation's credentials. We see, he said when it was done, our authority is only to revise the Articles of Confederation, alter or amend the defects. "Can we on this ground form a national government? I fancy not . . . can we suppose that, when we exceed the bounds of our duty, the people will approve our proceedings?" No, the people of America were "sharpsighted and not to be deceived."

They were deputies of thirteen independent sovereign states here for federal purposes. "If we are to be considered as a nation, all state distinctions must be abolished. The whole must be thrown into hotchpot; and when an equal division is made, then there may be fairly an equality of representation."

If state distinctions are retained, what of the welfare of New Jersey with five votes in a national council to Virginia's sixteen? "The small states have everything to fear." It had been said that a national government would operate on individuals; a federal government could be made to do so too, Paterson declared.

Paterson now had a reply to the hint (*"in terrorem,"* as Madison had called it) "thrown out heretofore by Mr. Wilson, of the necessity to which the large states might be reduced—of confederating among themselves—by a refusal of the others to concur. Let them unite if they please, but let them remember that they have no authority to compel the others to unite.

"I therefore declare that I will never consent . . . and I shall make all the interest against it in the state which I represent that I can. Myself or my state will never submit to tyranny or despotism . . . Every state according to a confederation must have an equal vote or there is an end to liberty."

A furious Wilson came to his feet. Every citizen should possess the same representation as every other. "Shall New Jersey have the same right or influence in the councils of the nation with Pennsylvania? I say no. It is unjust—I will never confederate on his principles. The gentleman from New Jersey is candid in declaring his opinion—I commend him for it—I am equally so. I say again I will never confederate on his principles!"

Hugh Williamson of North Carolina sought to reassure Paterson by pointing out that counties of different sizes dwelt safely in states having proportional representation, but Paterson was not comforted. He won approval for a postponement of the vote on the equality rule, and the convention adjourned over Sunday.

However gratefully the delegates emerged from the state house into the warm Saturday afternoon, they were leaving the unhappy scene behind them only in body. Soon many of them were gathered, and undoubtedly discussing it, over dinner at the City Tavern.

Washington was clearly made anxious by the flareup between Patterson and Wilson, for he joined the City Tavern group—the second time in two days he had dined with his fellow delegates, which was unusual for him. From dinner, he went to the home of Samuel and Elizabeth Powel, who were among his oldest friends. There he would have been able to sort out his thoughts, for Eliza was a political confidante as well as his favorite of his female friends. He stayed until ten o'clock and was back the next morning for breakfast, before riding off with Eliza's husband to visit Philadelphia's botanical gardens.

The hostilities definitely troubled Benjamin Franklin, driving him back to his writing table where he prepared a long speech supporting proportional representation, but deploring the loss of "coolness and temper," and hoping that "it will not be repeated, for we are sent here to consult not to contend."

Roger Sherman, too, was searching for a way to head off a donnybrook.

Sherman was ready by Monday morning and as soon as the gavel fell was on his feet to propose a compromise that he thought would protect the small states against the large: establish proportionate representation in the lower house and give the states equality in the Senate. The seed landed on fallow ground; no one seconded him.

Since the Virginia plan could not be discharged from the Committee of the Whole without some action on each point, Wilson and King moved to secure at least the consensus that seemed apparent—that in the lower house voting would be proportional. After Wilson read Franklin's speech to support it, this passed with seven states voting "yes."

Now Sherman rose again and moved that each state have one vote in the Senate. "Everything," he warned, "depends on this. The smaller states would never agree to the plan on any other principle than equality of suffrage in this branch."

On a five-to-six vote, equal suffrage in the Senate was rejected, and Wilson and Hamilton moved quickly to clinch the victory. Their specific motion for proportional representation was agreed to, six to five.

The Committee of the Whole had finished its test of the mind of the convention. And the uncertainty that it had found was perfectly expressed as the last vote approached, when Rufus King rose to say plaintively: "It would be better first to establish a principle—that is to say, whether we will depart from federal grounds in forming a national government."

7

"You see the consequences of pushing things too far . . ."

THE DEBATES ON THE VIRGINIA plan had only churned up the philosophical ground under the notion of confederation—perhaps softened it some—but it had not yet been agreed that liberty would be secure under a supreme national government. And where the politics stood was another, much harder matter. Some delegates were starting to doubt the good faith of the critics of the plan, suspecting them of protecting local interest instead of principle.

On Wednesday, June 13, three held-over details were dealt with summarily, and the Virginia plan was ready to be reported. The resolutions Randolph had offered two weeks earlier—now including amendments—were ready to be approved as the basis for the convention's work and then taken up again line by line.

THE NEW JERSEY PLAN

Apart from the explosion between Paterson and Wilson, New Jersey had made no effort to fight the Virginia plan. But Paterson's speech had been the bellow of the bull about to break from the gate. On June 14, when the report from the Committee of the Whole was about to be considered, he rose to ask for a one-day postponement. The following day, he laid before the convention a plan that "several of the deputations wished to be substituted in place of that proposed by Mr. Randolph."

"You see the consequences of pushing things too far," John Dickinson told Madison privately. "Some members from the small states wish for two branches in the general legislature and are friends to a good national government. But we would sooner submit to a foreign power than submit to be deprived of equality of suffrage in both branches of the legislature and thereby be thrown under the domination of the large states."

Known instantly as the New Jersey Plan, Paterson's resolutions had been put together by delegates from Connecticut, New York, New Jersey, and Delaware, plus a new, soon to be cordially despised, delegate from Maryland, Luther Martin. It was a clear alternative—purely "federal," deriving all its power from the states and with no direct ability to govern the people except through the states. It tried to remedy the toothlessness, inefficiency, and bankruptcy of the old system without surrendering state sovereignty.

The New Jersey Plan called for creating an executive and a judiciary and strengthened the Continental Congress. Federalism would be preserved by lodging the key powers in Congress, which would remain under the dominance of the states.

Congress would be authorized to create sources of revenue and to regulate trade and commerce—brand-new powers. However, it would have to go to the state courts to deal with violators of regulations and treaties, and then state rulings could be appealed to the national judiciary that would be created.

The old "requisitions" system, which had been nothing more than Congress begging for donations from the states, would be made less arbitrary by basing assessments on population and more forceful by empowering Congress to order a state to pay up.

Congress would elect a paid executive body to serve a single fixed term and hold no other office during that time—a big change from the old system of appointing various congressmen to perform executive functions while representing their own states. The executive would be able to appoint other federal officers—instead of having to work with whomever Congress sent, as Washington had had to do during the Revolution.

The new national judiciary would consist of a supreme court that would be appointed by the executive. It would be the first resort only in impeachments of federal officers. In every other instance, including enforcing foreign policy and treaties, piracy, trade and commerce, and collection of federal revenue, it would be only the court of last resort. The federal body would have to resolve its legal problems through one state or another before it would get the last word.

Federal laws and treaties would be the "supreme law of the respective states" and the state courts would be bound by them, and—here was the shocker—"if any state or any body of men in any state shall oppose or prevent carrying into execution such acts or treaties, the federal executive shall be authorized to call forth the power of the confederated states . . . to enforce and compel an obedience . . ."

Jefferson had thought that the confederacy had such power implicitly, but New Jersey's plan spelled it out. Either way it was authority for civil war. That everyone generally believed its use unthinkable made it no less horrific in writing. If the use of armed force *was* thinkable, then it was also inevitable, because the plan did not interfere convincingly with the autonomy that gave rise to recalcitrant local behavior. Nothing made it formidable except the potential to initiate bloodshed.

A FUMBLED OPENING?

"The eagerness displayed by the members opposed to a national government . . . began now to produce serious anxiety for the result of the convention," Madison wrote later, with his usual understatement.

Actually, the small states' decision to bring in an alternative plan impassioned partisans on both sides. Rufus King, Hamilton, Paterson, and Wilson, departing from their jotting habits, were scribbling madly, covering page after page with notes and comments.

As the small state allies launched their offensive, it is hard not to think that they committed a strategic blunder: they asked for a clause-by-clause comparison of the New Jersey and Virginia plans, instead of the kind of unlimited hearing Randolph had received. Lansing of New York, who proposed the matchup, should have been tipped off when New York's nationalist bad boy, Hamilton, popped up to support it.

Hamilton amiably observed that neither plan appealed to him, but he supposed "both might again be considered as federal plans . . ." He would agree on taking them together to "be contrasted so as to make a comparative estimate of the two." Hamilton obviously foresaw—and the antinationalists did not—that by failing to force consideration of the New Jersey Plan on its own, they had guaranteed that the delegates would have great difficulty clearing their minds of national government notions to think about how they might perfect the federal system.

In consequence, the possibilities of the New Jersey plan were barely discussed. Rather, debate swiftly veered toward the Virginia plan and the small state objections to it.

Lansing began with what the coalition seems to have thought their best line of argument—that the convention did not have the power to propose a national government and that states would reject it. Paterson followed up to contend that his plan conformed to the convention's powers and would be acceptable to the people. His potentially fruitful point—that there was no reason to derive federal power from the people, because the people had placed that power in the states—sunk under his litany of fears of the Virginia plan. By the time he sat down, he had explained nothing that the New Jersey Plan would do except spare the convention from criticism for exceeding its authority.

Taking the floor next, Wilson did his duty to the format by mentioning each provision of the New Jersey Plan, then proceeded to devote himself to defending the apportionment principle. Charles Pinckney came next to accuse New Jersey of grabbing for power in the guise of defending federal principle. He "supposes that if New Jersey was indulged with one vote out of thirteen, she would have no objection to a national government."

Ellsworth of Connecticut could see where things were heading and asked for a discussion of Resolution Number Two in the New Jersey Plan, but Randolph was on his feet to keep attention fixed on the failure of the confederation and exhort all to courage and the Virginia plan.

Adjournment and the Sunday holiday sharpened the antinational coalition's thinking. Monday dawned warm, and when Dickinson spoke that morning he had a proposition capable of elevating the temperature in the chamber even more. He suggested rewording Paterson's first resolve to declare a federal responsibility for "the prosperity of the union."

It was a loaded idea. Ending the economic crisis had been the main reason for the convention in the first place, but the Virginia plan had not attempted to design the goal into the system itself. Declaring prosperity to be a purpose of a revamped federal form at least implied a solution to a crucial concern— which the timid could pretend to believe.

HAMILTON'S "MONARCHY" SPEECH

Before the substitute could be debated, Hamilton rose to do something that many historians ever since have called bizarre, inexplicable, or disappointing. Lavishing praise on the British system, he consumed the entire convention day, five or six hours, arguing for a national government so strong that his enemies would use his remarks to condemn him as a monarchist—and near-traitorous Anglophile—for the rest of his life.

Like everything else about Hamilton, opinion about his motive splits into two biased camps: those who dislike him hold that his vanity and arrogance overcame him and that the speech was his swan song before he quit the convention in pique. His modern admirers speculate that he deliberately hoisted a bogeyman alternative in order to make the Virginia plan look moderate.

The vanity argument is silly. Hamilton was intellectually daring and often a showoff, but he never took dangerous chances for shallow reasons. From his first documented risk to his future—quarrelling with Washington and resigning from the staff—to his 1783 attempt to hurry Congress into calling a constitutional convention, Hamilton paid attention to how far he could go to influence things he could not completely control.

In the case of his quarrel and resignation, Hamilton had realized that he would have to resign before Washington would give him the combat command that was essential to the resumé of a young man of his time and aspirations. He knew Washington would resent his departure no matter when he took it, so the best time to go was when Washington was in the wrong. He reciprocated Washington's painful attempt to patch things up by humbling himself to demonstrate a commitment to the cause that Washington could not help appreciating: he remained a revolutionary soldier, unemployed and estranged at headquarters for months, until Washington relented and gave him an assignment. Egotistical, yes; blind, no. And he did not now waste his growing luster as a political figure merely to strut his stuff before the constitutional convention.

Nor was Hamilton's speech a device. He was not capable of standing up and advocating something he did not believe in, especially for an entire day, merely to make another plan seem milder. In fact, he had given Gouverneur Morris the same general outline of his views in 1777—not once mentioning the British or monarchy, and coining the expression "representative democracy" to explain what he meant. He was *not* impressed with the Virginia plan, which at that early point already had—and was being encumbered with more—energy-sapping, federation-style flaws. He did admire the vigorous British system and he did wish that America could tailor it for herself.

Still, why did he do it? If anybody but Hamilton had made the speech, the question would not be asked, because the answer is obvious. As Madison said, the New Jersey Plan had created a near-crisis mood among the nationalists. When the convention agreed to a "supreme national government" on May 30, only eight states had quorums and just six had agreed to the proposition. By now, June 18, one of the six, Delaware, had gone over to the small state bloc that had been forming ever since. As state concerns were more often expressed, a timidity about a national government had set in.

For the previous thirty-six hours, delegates were out of session and talking to each other, dining together, evaluating the prospects of the New Jersey Plan. Its sponsors, too, were hard at work preparing for this morning. Given the communicative ways of these politicians and the fact that most of them were staying at the same boardinghouses and taverns, the nationalists had had plenty of time to discover both that they might be defeated if the New Jersey Plan were improved and that a new scheme was afoot to try to make it better.

At the very least, they had every reason to fear that what Hamilton said in his speech was true—movement toward the sort of government that would save the union was on the brink of being arrested. A good hard boot to the imagination of the convention was needed to try to loft its progress; it was vital.

The small states did not need to defeat the Virginia plan, but only to damage irreparably its support. A smart campaign for patching up the old system could so divide the convention that even if the Virginia plan emerged as the product, it would be eviscerated or hopelessly controversial. Either outcome could doom its ratification.

Whether the nationalists knew he was going to do it or not, no one was more perfect than Hamilton to deliver the kick. He had all the intellectual and oratorical skills to make an overleaping appeal for good government on the grounds of both philosophy and human nature.

Better still, he was the ideal choice to squelch the fears of monarchy that had been raised. The similarities between the Virginia plan and the British system were trivial, and Hamilton could argue from the heart that an even more similar system could be adopted without sacrificing principles of democracy and liberty. Unlike others who might have done this just as well—Gouverneur Morris, especially—Hamilton alone was invulnerable to the charge of nostalgia for the British system: he had never prospered under or participated in that system—nor did he come from a family that had.

How was his speech received? Gouverneur Morris, a good friend and kindred spirit, seemed to recognize that Hamilton had both jeopardized his political image and helped the nationalist cause. It was, he said, "a generous indiscretion." William Johnson of Connecticut reported that "every gentleman praises Mr. Hamilton, but no gentleman supports him." And finally, the next morning, Dickinson's proposal to include "prosperity" was defeated without debate at the opening of business, on a straight large states-small states vote.

Hamilton devoted about half his speech to exploding the idea that merely tinkering with a purely federal system could overcome its built-in tendency to disunion. But he also found fault with the Virginia plan: the moderate salaries for members of the first branch would "only be a bait to little demagogues." The Senate would be full of people looking for appointment to executive jobs. He was troubled by the difficulty of attracting good men from such a sprawling country to the "center of the community," because the plan left so much sovereignty with the states. "The real men of weight and influence" would remain at home to "add strength to the state governments." At bottom, he said, the Virginia plan was still federal—"pork still, with but a little change of sauce."

He conceded that it was "unwise" to talk of anything other than a republican government, but admitted that "in his private opinion . . . the British government was the best in the world and that he doubted much whether anything short of it would do in America. He hoped Gentlemen of different opinions would bear with him in this."

Repeatedly Hamilton reminded his listeners of the virtues of a model they knew best next to their own. The English House of Lords was a "noble institution" because its members held office for life and had nothing to gain from subverting public liberty. The king was good because he was a symbol to the whole nation and well enough paid to prevent his corruption by foreign intrigues. America could have her own version of those two institutions and still be republican—as long as they were elected by the people. He did not accept the idea that either the amount of power or the length of a term in office meant that its holder would be a tyrant.

Hamilton read his own plan of government, but did not formally offer it; he hoped it would suggest improvements in the Virginia plan. His scheme would have a supreme two-house legislature and an executive governor. The lower house members would serve for three years; the upper house and the executive would serve for life or good behavior. Lower house members would be directly elected by the people. The upper house and executive would be chosen by "electors" appointed directly by the people to perform that task—more democracy than the convention had already been willing to accept.

The executive would have: a veto (Hamilton did not say whether absolute or limited); treaty-making power—with the advice and consent of the senate; sole power to appoint executive department heads; power to appoint other executive officers with the advice and consent of the senate; and the power to issue pardons. The senate would have the sole power to declare war. The judiciary would be a supreme tribunal, with the question of setting up lower courts left to the national legislature to decide. The power of impeachment would involve the states.

State laws contravening the national constitution would be "utterly void," and to hold down the number of such state laws the chief executive of each state would be appointed by the national government and provided with veto power.

"Every gentleman" praised Hamilton because his plan had a stunning organic integrity; no gentleman supported him because it was politically unacceptable. But it did influence their thinking as he urged, and some parts of it—like Senate advice and consent on treaties and executive appointments—are improvements that became part of the final constitution.

DECISION

Madison squared off against the New Jersey Plan right after Dickinson's defeat the next morning, punching hard with specifics as he described how individual states had harmed the federation and still could do so under New Jersey's proposed amendments. Turning to sectional interests, he argued that the small states' devotion to sovereignty was the stuff of fantasy—they lacked the actual strength to defend their equality. Madison did not take seriously Paterson's alternative of redrawing the map to make thirteen physically equal states; agreement on what made any state equal to another would be impossible.

Madison relied so much on intellectual reasoning that sometimes he seemed inhuman. Yet he was not above playing to prejudices. One of the few examples of his doing so —reassuring to those who like humanity in the Founding Fathers—came in this speech. He not only played to prejudice, but conveniently forgot about having done it only a few weeks later.

Orating on the folly of equal influence among all the states, Madison reminded the small state men about "many new states to the westward" that were to be brought into the Union with the same rights as the states already there. If they had power according to their small populations, he said, "all would be right and safe." However, "let them have an equal vote and a more objectionable minority than ever might give law to the whole." When Gouverneur Morris in a few weeks would say this almost exactly, Madison would be utterly indignant.

As soon as Madison sat down, Rufus King moved to vote on the question of "whether Mr. Randolph's resolves should be adhered to as preferable to those of Mr. Paterson." Dickinson scrambled to save the format, urging that the convention "contrast the one with the other and consolidate such parts of them as the committee approve." But King's question was put, and the vote to consider only the Virginia plan was seven ayes to three nos, one divided.

In victory, nationalists Wilson and Hamilton immediately

attempted to be conciliatory. As the convention voted to start again with the first Randolph resolution—to establish a supreme national government—Wilson rose to comment that "I am for a national government, though the idea of federal is, in my view, the same . . . A general government over a great extent of territory must, in a few years, make subordinate jurisdictions."

Wilson erroneously labeled this a difference with Hamilton's views, and Hamilton was quick to respond. "I did not intend yesterday a total extinguishment of state governments, but my meaning was that a national government ought to be able to support itself without the aid or interference of the state governments and that therefore it was necessary to have full sovereignty." Hamilton qualified his olive branch by adding that "even with corporate rights some states will be dangerous to the national government and ought to be extinguished, new modified or reduced to a smaller scale . . ."

Did Rufus King use Washington's favorite exclamation of exasperation—"for God's sake!"—here? He "wished as everything depended on this proposition that no objections might be improperly indulged against the phraseology of it . . . the import of the terms 'states' 'sovereignty' 'National' 'federal' had been used in the discussion inaccurately and delusively."

The states were not " 'sovereigns' in the sense contended for by some. They did not possess the peculiar features of sovereignty. They could not make war, nor peace, nor allegiances nor treaties. Considering them as political beings, they were dumb, for they could not speak to any foreign sovereign whatever. They were deaf for they could not hear any propositions from such a sovereign. They had not even the organs or faculties of defense or offence, for they could not of themselves raise troops or equip vessels for war."

King was fighting a losing battle; political codewords, once adopted, have a way of sticking. Luther Martin of Maryland served notice that the claim for state sovereignty would continue. "The separation from Great Britain placed the thirteen states in a state of nature towards each other." He could "never accede to a plan that would introduce an inequality and lay the states at the mercy of Virginia, Massachusetts and Pennsylvania."

And the house adjourned its day of decision.

8

The Great Debate

"I DO NOT, gentlemen, trust you."

Tall, fat, and fiery, Gunning Bedford hurled the words at the delegates from Massachusetts, Pennsylvania, and Virginia. Only twice since his arrival five weeks ago had Delaware's attorney general entered the debate. A "bold and nervous speaker," according to Pierce's later description, Bedford now was making up for lost time.

Two full days had vanished in a wrangle over equal or proportionate voting in the Senate. The nationalists had hardened, begun questioning the motives of the small states, and bidding for the support of the ambivalent delegates on frankly political grounds. It all had become too much for Bedford.

"The little states will meet the large ones on no ground but that of the Confederation," Bedford stormed. No middle road lay between complete consolidation and a pure confederacy of the states. "We have been told with a dictatorial air that this is the last moment for a fair trial in favor of a good government. It will be the last indeed if the propositions reported from the committee go forth to the people . . .

"Will you crush the smaller states, or must they be left unmolested? Sooner than be ruined, there are *foreign powers who will take us by the hand.* I say this not to threaten or intimidate, but that we should reflect seriously before we act."

We will seek foreign intervention! Bedford's explosion—"this intemperance . . . a vehemence unprecedented in the House," as Rufus King soon said in rebuke—was one that the convention had been building to steadily. The date now was Saturday, June 30, eleven days since the convention had rejected the New Jersey Plan. The small states had not yielded an inch since their defeat.

"HE WILL GIVE IT EVERY OPPOSITION"

Confrontation had begun the day the convention became once again "the House"—June 20—when Washington reclaimed the presiding officer's chair from Nathaniel Gorham of Massachusetts, who had chaired the Committee of the Whole. On that day, the champions of the states, supported openly now by the distinguished Connecticut delegation, served notice that they would never submit to a purely national system.

Oliver Ellsworth of Connecticut, whose delegation had helped write—then voted to discard—the New Jersey Plan, raised the curtain for the reorganized attack on the Virginia plan.

"It would be highly dangerous not to consider the confederation as still subsisting," Ellsworth said. He moved to substitute the phrase "government of the United States" for the word "national" in the first line of the Virginia plan. He also "wished the plan of the convention to go forth as amendments to the Articles of Confederation" so that the state legislatures, not popular conventions, could ratify it.

No one doubted any longer that the word "national" was controversial; the convention agreed without hesitation—though Randolph advised "the gentleman who wished for it" that he rejected Ellsworth's reasons, "particularly that of getting rid of a reference to the people for ratification."

John Lansing of New York rose. "The true question here is whether the convention will adhere to or depart from the foundation of the present confederacy," he announced. The question, of course, had been answered by the convention's rejection of the New Jersey Plan, but Lansing ignored that. He moved to delete the two-branch national legislature and substitute "the powers of legislation ought to be vested in the United States in Congress"—giving, in other words, the old one-house Congress the power to make laws. It was the New Jersey Plan's second resolution, abbreviated, and was confederacy plain and simple, without even a pretense of introducing new principles.

The convention did not have the authority to propose a system like the Virginia plan, Lansing argued, and it would not be accepted. "Can we expect that thirteen states will surrender their governments up to a national plan?" Lansing asked. "If we devise a system of government which will not meet the approbation of our constitutents, we are dissolving the Union. But if we act within the limits of our power, it will be approved of."

Seeing that the New Jersey Plan sponsors were going to try to dismantle the Virginia plan piecemeal, George Mason rose, angry. He "did not expect this point would have been re-agitated." The convention was not precluded from proceeding on the Virginia plan. They had been called to *recommend;* the rest would be up to the people. Even so, "in certain seasons of public danger, it is commendable to exceed power."

Lansing had claimed that the people would never accept the Virginia plan, Mason said, but it was the New Jersey design that "could never be expected to succeed."

Not to offend any man sitting here who had served in Congress, Mason "meant not to throw any reflections" on it. However, he had the "privilege of age . . . to speak his sentiments without reserve on this subject." Americans never would permit the Congress to exercise the power of the sword, the purse, and the regulation of trade. They would never trust such important things to its "secret journal—to the intrigues—to the factions." If anyone thought the Congress was above such behavior, "let him consult their Journals for the years '78, '79 and '80."

The people are attached to the principle of two legislative

branches, Mason declared. They had set up every state legislature but Pennsylvania's that way. All, including Pennsylvania, were directly elected by the people. Only Congress was not. *That,* Mason said, was why Congress had been unable to increase its powers and why the New Jersey Plan would be doomed.

Lansing had claimed that the great powers contemplated for the national government would end in abolishing the states. Mason could not let that pass. He would repeat that, "notwithstanding his solicitude to establish a national government, he never would agree to abolish the state governments or render them absolutely insignificant. They were as necessary as the general government, and he would be equally careful to preserve them."

Washington next nodded to Luther Martin, attorney general of Maryland. "This gentleman," Pierce later wrote of Martin, "has a very bad delivery, and so extremely prolix that he never speaks without tiring the patience of all who hear him." Pierce was being kind.

Others leave a picture of an altogether unhinged temperament, a scant regard for truth, and near-perfect gall. A few months after the convention (from which Martin would depart in fury before the close), Ellsworth, using the pseudonym "The Landholder" in an open letter to Martin, savaged the Marylander for portraying himself as a friend and kindred spirit of Elbridge Gerry in the convention. Martin would remember, scoffed The Landholder, how his "genius provoked a sarcastic reply from the pleasant Mr. Gerry in which he admired the strength of your lungs and your profound knowledge in the first principles in government . . . This reply (from your intimate acquaintance) . . . had the happy effect to put the house in good humor and leave you a prey to the most humiliating reflections . . . You exhausted the politeness of the convention, which at length prepared to slumber when you rose to speak . . ."

Not everybody found Martin despicable. A century later, the historian Henry Adams cheerily called Martin "the rollicking, witty, audacious attorney general of Maryland, drunken, generous, slovenly, grand . . . the notorious reprobate genius." And in 1807, former Vice President Aaron Burr, who was also witty and audacious, who had killed Alexander Hamilton in a duel three years earlier, and who was about to be tried for treason for a freebooting scheme to conquer Mexico, asked Martin to serve on his defense team. Burr was acquitted. Six days after the July 4 deaths of Jefferson and Adams in 1826, Martin, about eighty years old, died bankrupt and mentally ravaged by alcohol, in Burr's home in New York.

At the time of the convention, Martin was about forty years old; he must have been a healthy bibulant, for Pierce thought him thirty-four. His portrait shows telltale puffs under the eyes and fleshiness of face, and his wrinkled clothes and soiled shirt ruffles already had been noticed,

Martin had not come to debate; he had come to fight. His position was that the confederation had been formed "on principles of perfect reciprocity"—the only just system—and "if any other principle is adopted by this convention, he will give it every opposition." He started now.

Martin saw no need for two branches. If that were important, the existing Congress could be divided in two. Congress already represented the people because the people elect the legislatures that appoint the Congress. The federal union was meant to protect the whole against threats from foreign powers and defend the small states against the large; the union was meant to support the sovereignty of the states, not swallow them up. A national judiciary extending into the states would appear so suspicious as to become useless. "This," Madison wrote, but then crossed the line out, "was the substance of a very long speech."

Roger Sherman rose. Of course the state legislatures had two branches, but two were unnecessary in "a confederacy of the states . . . Congress carried us through the war, and perhaps as well as any government could have done."* The states had much to apologize for in failing to support the confederation, but "they were afraid of bearing too hard on the people by

---

*One nearly contemporary account of the convention says that Washington let his reactions show in his expressions. If so, this is probably as close as Sherman ever came to being killed by a look.

accumulating taxes." The people did trust Congress, he was sure, and would be willing to enhance its powers.

The former shoemaker tried again to cobble together the compromise he had proposed in the Committee of the Whole: "If the difficulty on the subject of representation cannot be otherwise got over, he would agree to have two branches and a proportional representation in one of them, provided each state had an equal voice in the other." But he did not put his offer in the shape of a formal motion, and once more, the convention did not seize upon the solution.

Lansing's substitute was defeated, and the question of a two-house legislature was again before them. But Dr. William Johnson of Connecticut rose to divert the debate once more to the fate of the states and to talk of compromise as Sherman had done.

"The Jersey plan," Johnson said, was intended to preserve the state governments and even though the Virginia plan would not destroy them, it "was charged with such a tendency." He was sure that supporters of the substitute plan could accept the principles of the Virginia plan if they were guaranteed that state governments would not be in danger. In his opinion, giving the states an equal vote in the Senate would guarantee that they had the means to defend their sovereignty.

First Sherman, now Johnson. Two such towering figures could not go unanswered by the national men. The argument for a national government would have to be made again in order to, as James Wilson now put it, "solve the difficulty which had been started.

"If security is necessary to preserve the one," Wilson said, "it is equally so to preserve the other." Already the plan proposed that the state legislatures elect the Senate; should the national government then elect some branch of the state governments? He could not see why the state governments would feel endangered. Rather, "in spite of every precaution, the general government would be in perpetual danger of encroachments from the state governments."

Madison rose to agree. "All the examples of other confederacies prove the greater tendency in such systems to anarchy than to tyranny . . . and our own is proof of it."

Even if the nationalists proposed to abolish the states—which they did not—the greatest objection had been, Madison said, that the general government "could not extend its care to all the minute objects which fall under the cognizance of local jurisdictions." And that was an objection, not against the probable abuse of national power, "but against the imperfect use that could be made of it."

But suppose that the general government could do everything without the cooperation of the state governments: "The people would not be less free as members of one great republic than as members of thirteen small ones. A citizen of Delaware was not more free than a citizen of Virginia; nor would either be more free than a citizen of America."

When the vote was taken, Connecticut registered another straddle of the contending camps, having first voted for Lansing's substitute, but now joining the seven-to-three majority to approve a two-branch legislature.

The Shadow of Regional Conflict

The small states' line-by-line amendment strategy created an unremitting clash, but argument about the ends of the convention was at an impasse, and the small states were forced to proceed by trying to shape the means instead. Every item that could be remodeled in favor of the states' interest was challenged. And the nationalists in turn opposed each challenge on the grounds that the states would subvert the government.

Soon Ellsworth was driven to a complaint and a warning: "If we are jealous of the state governments, they will be so of us. If, on going home, I tell them we gave the general government such powers because 'we could not trust you'—will they adopt it? And without their approbation, your government is nothing more than a rope of sand."

The convention allowed itself to be pushed along this way because the delegates were loath to attack the real bone of contention as Sherman and Johnson had urged. But that reluctance harbored an insidious danger that Madison saw clearly: by moving sequentially through the Virginia plan, it was possible to disrupt its internal balance on a score of seemingly secondary provisions. This course could mongrelize the plan, and by the time they reached the provision for proportional representation, the provision might be either meaningless or truly unjust. Nor, by then, would the plan any longer be a schematic for a great republic or a confederation—or anything else anyone might recognize.

And that was not the only danger. As the convention was now debating means and not ends, interests less fundamental than state sovereignty tended to make themselves felt. The biggest of these was sectional rivalry, and the worst sectional rivalry was between South and North.

After the vote approving two branches, General Charles Cotesworth Pinckney of South Carolina, second cousin of young Charles Pinckney, rose with an amendment, and in doing so must have sent a wave of apprehension through Madison.

"The first branch, instead of being elected by the people, should be elected in such a manner as the Legislature of each State should direct," Pinckney intoned.

Until now, the South Carolina elders had seemed favorable to the Virginia plan, although very early this Pinckney had said he doubted their authority to exceed their instructions. He had also "wished to have a good national government and, at the same time, to leave a considerable share of power in the states." For him now to back up that wish with amendments was dismaying. Tellingly, Luther Martin seconded the motion.

Hamilton and George Mason rushed to the ramparts. The motion was "intended manifestly to transfer the election from the people to the state legislatures, which would essentially vitiate the plan," Hamilton charged. "It would increase that state influence which could not be too watchfully guarded against."

"Whatever inconveniency may attend the democratic principle, it must actuate one part of the government," Mason put in. "It is the only security for the rights of the people."

Backing his fellow South Carolinian, John Rutledge spooned a little flattery on the convention. Election by the people and election by the legislatures were the same thing, except that "An election by the legislature would be more refined than an election immediately by the people . . . If this convention had been chosen by the people . . . it is not to be supposed that such proper characters would have been preferred. The delegates to Congress," he added, were also "fitter men than would have been appointed by the people at large."

The difference between direct and indirect election, Wilson retorted, was "immense." The legislatures "have an official sentiment opposed to that of the general government and perhaps to that of the people themselves." True, said Rufus King. "The legislatures would constantly choose men subservient to their own views as contrasted with the general interest."

Without the slightest embarrassment, Pinckney acknowledged that. He was trying to carve a place for the state governments in the new system, because without an official role, "South Carolina and other states would have but a small share of the benefits of government . . . there is an *esprit de corps* which has made heretofore every *unfederal* member of congress, after his election, become strictly *federal.*"

Being circumspect, Pinckney did not elaborate. He did not have to; his listeners recognized the echo of "sellout"—the still-smoldering Southern resentment of John Jay's pro–New England Mississippi River deal with Spain. No belief was as firmly rooted as the southern conviction that northern commercial interests held sway over Congress. For many southern delegates, nothing was acceptable that might allow southern representatives to forget where they came from. With that hint, South Carolina decamped from the nationalists for the first time and voted with the small states.

"DIRTY POLITICKS"

Madison's argument, rather than any real conflict, enlivened debate over the clause establishing the term of office for members of the lower house. It reverberated with the footsteps of the younger political generation approaching. If elections were annual, he said, "none of those who wished to be re-elected would remain at the seat of government." This was because the voters would be "much more susceptible of impressions from the presence of a rival candidate . . . It must be supposed that the members from the most distant states would travel backwards and forwards at least as often as elections should be repeated."

Madison used this argument matter-of-factly, but only twenty years earlier he might have had to pretend that campaigns for office would *not* be a by-product of the system. However, treating public service as a sideline had become impossible once the former colonies had full burden of governing themselves, and a big change was under way in America: political office was to be made a respectable object, a prize to be won—not a call of duty to which a gentlemen's correct response was a protest and a promise not to become a politician.

The day was imminent when it would be rare to turn down public office, as James Duane had in 1767, saying "for this I must have been led into party and dirty politicks which I despise as beneath a man who would wish to be honest & wise." And even rarer would be the seven years it took to persuade Duane to change his mind, which he did in 1774, saying, "Unhappily for my repose, the alarming state of our publick affairs and the acts of my countrymen oblige me at once to plunge into the midst of a tempest . . ."

Old-timers like Sherman still suspected political eagerness. Opposing the motion for biennial election, Sherman argued: "I am for one year . . . Should the members have a longer duration of service and remain at the seat of government, they may forget their constituents . . . or there may be danger of catching the *esprit de corps.*" And Thomas Jefferson, upon returning to America four years hence, would be disgusted by the unhidden ambition pervasive in political life. Even organizing his own political party, he would have others act as his agents and spokesmen, while he conformed to the old tradition of pretending he wanted only to retreat to Monticello. Washington seemed to like the new style, but himself remained the grand master of longing for home.

GRABBING THE PURSE STRINGS

Oliver Ellsworth introduced the states' grab for the purse strings, calling for the salaries of members of the first branch to be paid by the state legislatures.

"The manners of the different states were very different in the style of living and in the profits accruing from the exercise of like talents," Ellsworth argued. Besides, he added, a salary that seemed reasonable in some states might be very unpopular in others and might "impede the system."

And consider the new states in the west, warned North Carolina's Hugh Williamson. They would be poor, would pay very little into the common treasury, and would have "a different interest from the old states." The old states should not "pay the expenses of men who would be employed in thwarting their measures and interests."

Both arguments were specious. And Williamson, declaredly a faithful nationalist, must have irritated Randolph, who snapped that putting the salaries in the hands of the states "would vitiate the whole system. The whole nation has an interest in the attendance and services of the members. The national treasury, therefore, is the proper fund for supporting them."

State legislatures "were always paring down salaries in such a manner as to keep out of offices men most capable" of filling them, Gorham contributed. And "those who pay are the masters of those who are paid," remarked Hamilton.

Trickier, however, was the nonpartisan question of fixing the amount—which was part of the pay clause. Except for Sherman's suggestion that it, too, be referred to the state legislatures, the nationalists debated it among themselves.

"We could not venture to make it as liberal as it ought to be without exciting an enmity against the whole plan," Gorham said. The constitution should be silent on it. "Let the national legislature provide for their own wages from time to time, as state legislatures do."

Wilson sided with Gorham, but King disagreed. Failing to set an amount, King said, "would excite greater opposition than any sum that would be actually necessary or proper."

"It would be indecent that the legislature should put their hands in the public purse to convey it into their own," Madison objected. They should not determine their own wages and the rate should be fixed in the constitution. The actual amount perplexed him, though. It might, he said, be attached to a "standard" that would adjust automatically to economic changes—something such as a commodity, perhaps the price of a bushel of wheat.

Two votes were taken—one approving payment by the national treasury and the other changing "fixed stipend" to "adequate compensation." But now South Carolina threw a procedural block, asking for a vote on the two ideas combined in a single clause. Someone objected that the motion was out of order, but when Washington asked the House to rule, the request was agreed to. Then South Carolina moved to postpone the vote. When it was taken the next day, the pay provision lost on a five-to-five vote.

PURIFYING PUBLIC OFFICE

"Ethical conduct" is a modern phrase, but the whole question of political morals was very high on the eighteenth-century list of concerns. Sides were taken in much the same way—those who believed in trying to legislate political ethics and those who doubted that it could be done.

Men were divided, too, on the principle that the government has a responsibility to promote a virtuous society. Some, like George Mason, saw a link between political corruption and degeneracy in society, and thought the government should try to stamp out both; others thought, as Hamilton said, that "the science of policy is the knowledge of human nature," and the government should try to channel men's venal tendencies toward useful ends.

An anticorruption provision in the Virginia plan brought on a great struggle. The clause barred legislators in the first branch from holding any other public office—state or national—during their term of service, and from accepting any national office for one additional year afterward. Its purpose was to prevent the creation of lucrative and unnecessary offices for personal gain or for the legislators to reward each other or be rewarded by their states for special favors. The practice was notorious from before the Revolution when the Crown's governors had offered high-paying public offices to win back dissident American leaders. And in some states, signs of lawmakers exploiting their power of appointment to public offices had surfaced anew.

The debate began tamely enough as a straightforward disagreement about attempting to legislate ethics, but the small states men soon identified their own interest in it.

Nathaniel Gorham, Rufus King, and James Wilson called for deleting the extra-year ineligibility. Gorham thought it "unnecessary and injurious," and argued that, even with abuses, the government might be better served by being able to fill public offices as it saw fit. "We refine too much by going to *utopian* lengths. It is a mere cobweb," agreed King.

"Strong reasons must induce me to disqualify a good man from office," Wilson said. "We ought to hold forth every honorable inducement for men of abilities to enter the service of the public . . . Shall talents which entitle a man to public reward operate as a punishment? While a member of the legislature, he ought to be excluded from any other office, but no longer. Suppose a war breaks out and a number of your best military characters are members. Must we lose the benefit of their services?"

In Great Britain, "this was the source of the corruption that ruined their government," argued Pierce Butler. "Men got into Parliament to obtain offices for themselves and their friends." It was a necessary precaution against intrigue.

"It is necessary to shut the door against corruption," George

Mason agreed. "Are we not struck at seeing the luxury and venality which has already crept in among us? If not checked, we shall have ambassadors to every petty state in Europe, the little republic of San Marino not excepted." The clause "will prevent the people from ruining themselves," was "the cornerstone on which our liberties depend."

Strike it, said Hamilton. "We must take man as we find him, and, if we expect him to serve the public, must interest his passions in doing so. A reliance on pure patriotism has been the source of many errors . . . we suppose mankind more honest than they are. Our prevailing passions are ambition and interest, and it will ever be the duty of a wise government to avail itself of those passions in order to make them subservient to the public good." The only rule should be that when a legislator takes his seat, he must vacate every other office, he said, echoing Wilson.

A perfect division appeared in the vote: four yes, four no, and three divided; the one-year prohibition stayed in the clause.

Now more and more clearly in harness with the small states, General Pinckney rose to ask for deletion of the reference to state offices.

If a man were forbidden to hold an important state office while serving in the national body, Pinckney said, "the first and best characters in a state" might be made ineligible or unwilling to serve in the national council.

Wilson spied something at work besides good intentions for the national system. "I perceive," he remarked, "that some gentlemen are of opinion to give a bias in favor of state governments. This question ought to stand on the same footing." Wilson had not forgotten that state offices had depopulated the Continental Congress during the war. They would be similarly employed by the states to control national legislators under the new system.

The convention, however, was inclined to go along with Pinckney—including Madison, who found himself unenthusiastic about fencing off the national legislature as a political steppingstone. He would be content to minimize the chance of corruption. He offered substitute wording to rule out only national offices created or made more remunerative while a legislator was serving, with the ineligibility existing just during the members' terms and one year afterward.

"The unnecessary creation of offices and increase of salaries were the evils most experienced. If the door was shut against them," Madison explained, "it might properly be left open for the appointment of members to other offices—as an encouragement to the legislative service."

A narrowly framed amendment, it kicked up a startling fuss, beginning with resistance from two South Carolina delegates who insisted it "did not go far enough" toward making the national council "as pure as possible."

Madison might have expected "purity" from state-minded men bent on disabling the national legislature, but his ally and colleague, George Mason, pounced on him from the other side of the political generation gap. Mason first scolded him, then embarrassed him.

Mason "appealed to Mr. Madison as a witness of the shameful partiality of the Legislature of Virginia to its own members" in creating offices and appointing one another to them. He could not believe that no citizen could be found to enter legislative service without the inducement of possible future office. "Genius and virtue, it may be said, ought to be encouraged," Mason said. "Genius, for aught he knew, might. But that virtue should be encouraged by such a species of venality was an idea that, at least, had the merit of being new," he scoffed.

They were "refining too much in this business," King again complained. The idea of preventing intrigue and solicitation of offices was "chimerical. You will say that no member shall himself be eligible to any office. Will this restrain him from availing himself of the same means which would gain appointments for himself to gain them for his son, his brother or any other object of his partiality?"

Wilson dropped the usual deference in a rejoinder to Mason. Madison's amendment was the proper remedy, Wilson said sharply. Mason's remarks were improper, "stigmatizing with the name of venality the laudable ambition of rising into the honorable offices of the government—an ambition most likely to be felt in the early and most incorrupt period of life and which all wise and free governments had deemed it sound policy to cherish, not to check."

Roger Sherman swung in beside Mason, predicting elaborate schemes to get around the limitation. "It might be evaded by the creation of a new office and the translation to it of a person from another office, and the appointment of a member of the legislature to the latter." One scenario, for example: "A new embassy might be established to a new court and an ambassador taken from another, in order to create a vacancy for a favorite member."

On the defensive, Madison tried to explain that he "had been led to this motion as a middle ground between an eligibility in all cases and an absolute disqualification." He appeased neither Mason nor the other opponents, who rose again to heap criticism on it.

Madison's proposal was buried eight to two, leaving a clause that barred national legislators from any other national office during their term of service and one year after.

If it had remained in the final Constitution, all the modern senators and congressmen who are recruited by presidents to serve as ambassadors and cabinet officers would not be able to accept the jobs. However, late in the convention, when the underlying conflict had ended, Madison brought his amendment back and it became the version (minus the extra one year) finally accepted.

The week that had opened with Hamilton's dramatic speech had finished with the plan for a great republic rattled but not ruined. The outlines of the first branch of the national legislature were complete. The protectors of the states had only managed to temporarily kill the pay clause, which would have to come back sometime, and to slam the door to political advancement through the national legislature.

The small states had decisively lost three crucial arguments: Lansing's motion for a single-house Congress; General Pinckney's for state legislatures to elect the members of the first branch; and Ellsworth's for the states to pay the legislators' salaries. The Senate, as had seemed likely, now remained the only chance for the states to enter into the national system.

This was Saturday; the delegates had the rest of the weekend to draw a deep breath and think about Monday, when they would begin framing the Senate. Washington let the delegates alone; he went to dinner at the home of Dr. Thomas Ruston before returning to Robert Morris's in time for tea and then "spent the evening in my chamber."

The delegates must have been fatigued, especially the New Englanders who were not accustomed to Philadelphia's summer weather. Temperatures all week had been in the low eighties, and, although the convention had not yet shut its windows against eavesdroppers as it would do later, the warmth would have made the Assembly Room where they sat disagreeably close. To make things worse, the street noise coming in the windows had become unbearable. Mercifully it would be taken care of: the city's street commissioners had voted Friday "upon complaint to this board of the very great difficulty arising from the carriages passing in front of the state house so that the Honorable Convention now sitting there are much interrupted by the noise of the same—*Resolved* that a quantity of gravel now hauling out of the sewer in Fourth Street be laid on Chestnut Street." Not elegant, but effective.

Before the end of July, the climate would drive away four of the six wives who had accompanied their husbands to Philadelphia, among them Betsey Hamilton, who was vivacious but not strong, and Mary Alsop (Mrs. Rufus) King, who had just become pregnant. (Her progress became perhaps the most anxiously watched pregnancy in America late the next January: she was expected to give birth during the closely divided Massachusetts ratification convention, causing numerous letters of inquiry to be written, on both sides, as to the dates King might be absent to be with her.)

The convention summer was the time in which King and Hamilton became close friends, and the two young couples must have been an attractive sight. Twenty-nine years old, Betsey Hamilton was petite and shapely, "a brunette," wrote a defeated suitor, "with the most good-natured lively dark eyes that I ever saw, which threw a beam of good temper and benevolence over her whole countenance . . . she was the finest tempered girl in the world." Quiet and cherubic, Mary King was also dark-haired, pretty, and, said Hamilton, "sweet." Their husbands—Rufus, thirty-two, and Alexander, thirty— had in common the impression they made on their colleagues: talent, eloquence, grace, and good looks. The two men would become such close friends that in 1804, Rufus would be one of only two others to know of Hamilton's impending fatal duel with Aaron Burr.

On a weekend like this one, the Kings and the Hamiltons might have sought relief from the heat by picnicking or visiting the popular Bartram Gardens. Ordinarily, a visit to Philadelphia's exciting public market would have been an adventure—strolling by four blocks of fresh produce, fruits, and meats as well as goods imported from everywhere, even China. But according to the *Evening Herald,* the city's efforts to make more space for the vendors and shoppers were not working. "We find the market people so attached to their old stations," the newspaper said, "that in Second and Market streets the foot pavements are impassable, and so much of the middle way is encroached upon that there is hardly sufficient room for the passage of a single horse. This inconveniency, and the mischievous practice of engrossing [keeping the best produce for favored customers], demand the immediate attention of the officers employed in this department of the public police."

A quieter way of whiling away the time would have been Hamilton's preference anyway. This summer King was in Philadelphia as a rather reluctant reformer, and Hamilton was working on him. The effort succeeded—Hamilton later said he "revolutionized his [King's] mind."

Lamps in Mrs. House's parlor, the Indian Queen, and the City Tavern may have burned late Sunday evening, June 24, with some delegates gathered to ready their next moves. One delegate, it is certain, made good use of his time: young Charles Pinckney worked on the argument he would use to present his own senatorial plan.

WHAT IS AN AMERICAN?

Whatever Charles Pinckney's vanities and peccadillos, the oration he polished in his room at Mrs. House's was one of the best speeches given by anyone during the convention—not so much for its purpose, but for its vision of America as she believed she was and would always want to be. Even hostile Irving Brant, Madison's biographer, grudgingly calls Pinckney's performance "remarkable," and Wilson, Gorham, and Madison all seemed to salute it by allusion. Pinckney delivered it immediately when business resumed Monday morning.

Anticipating the same analogies that had been raised in the first debate on the Senate, Pinckney warned that trying to create an American version of the British House of Lords was futile. The history of the two lands was too different; the system "must be suited to the habits and genius of the people it is to govern and must grow out of them.

"The people of the United States are perhaps the most singular of any we are acquainted with," Pinckney declared. "Among them are fewer distinctions of fortune and less of rank than among the inhabitants of any other nation. Every freeman has a right to the same protection and security, and a very moderate share of property entitles them to the possession of all the honors and privileges the public can bestow. Hence arises a greater equality than is to be found among the people of any other country, and an equality which is more likely to continue.

"I say this equality is likely to continue, because in a new country, possessing immense tracts of uncultivated lands, where every temptation is offered to emigration and where industry must be rewarded with competency, there will be few poor and few dependent—every member of the society almost will enjoy an equal power of arriving at the supreme offices and consequently of directing the strength and sentiments of the whole community.

"None will be excluded by birth and few by fortune, from voting for proper persons to fill the offices of government—the whole community will enjoy in the fullest sense that kind of political liberty which consists in the power the members of the state reserve to themselves, of arriving at the public offices, or at least, of having votes in the nomination of those who fill them . . ."

The British system was admirable, Pinckney said; he would "confess that I believe it to be the best constitution in existence." But America had no need to create an aristocratic body to act as a balance between a Crown and the people. Nor would she succeed if she tried.

"If equality is, as I contend, the leading feature of the United States, where, then, are the riches and wealth whose representation and protection is the peculiar province of this permanent body?" He doubted that a wealthy class in need of protection would ever arise.

"Where are the sources from whence it is to flow? From the landed interest? No. That is too unproductive and too much divided in most of the states. From the monied interest? If such exists at present, little is to be apprehended from that source. Is it to spring from commerce? I believe it would be the first instance in which a nobility sprang from merchants."

The British system reflected British society. The peers, the people, and the royalty each "must of necessity be represented by itself, or the sign of itself." But the United States contain "but one great and equal body of citizens . . . These are, I believe as active, intelligent and susceptible of good government as any people in the world . . . all that we have to do then is to distribute the powers of government in such a manner and for such limited periods as . . . will reserve to the people the right of election they will not or ought not frequently to part with."

Fitting the government to the people, Pinckney declared, meant that the states needed to be represented in the new American system. "They are the instruments upon which the union must frequently depend for the support and execution of their powers" because of the geographic immensity of the country. "State governments must remain, if you mean to prevent confusion." From this line of reasoning, Pinckney said, "I am

led to form the second branch differently . . . I propose this plan
. . . if no better plan is proposed, I will then move its adoption."

By a trick of fate (or as Pinckney's admirers contend, a trick
of Madison's pen), Pinckney's idea for the Senate is lost. He
obviously had proposed giving the states actual control of the
Senate, but his exact scheme is not recorded in Madison's notes
and Yates jotted only "(reads it)."

MADISON LOSES THE SENATE

Pinckney's speech was an eloquent beginning for a nasty confrontation. As if sizing up the situation, Madison said nothing
right away. Randolph moved to take up the Senate resolution
clause by clause, but Gorham of Massachusetts tried to push
past it.

"Sixteen members from one state will certainly have greater
weight than the same number of members from different
states," Gorham said. "We must therefore depart from this rule
of apportionment in some shape or other—perhaps on the plan
Mr. Pinckney has suggested."

But Wilson wanted to hold off that fight. The question on the
floor, he chided, was whether the Senate should be elected by
the state legislatures. "In every point of view, it is an important
question."

Sidestepping Pinckney's plan, Wilson both countered and
exploited the powerful chord the young South Carolinian had
struck. He mused that "when he considered the amazing extent
of country, the immense population which is to fill it, the influence which the government we are to form will have, not only
on the present generation of our people and their multiplied
posterity, but on the whole globe, he was lost in the magnitude
of the object . . ."

But his meditation led him to a conclusion wholly different
from Pinckney's: "I must therefore lay aside my state connections and act for the general good of the whole. We must forget
our local habits and attachments. The general government
should not depend on the state governments . . . we have

unanimously agreed to establish a general government—that the powers of peace, war, treaties, coinage and regulating of commerce ought to reside in that government. And if we reason in this manner, we shall soon see the impropriety of admitting the interference of state governments into the general government . . . I therefore move *that* [Yates's quill began underlining] *the second branch of the legislature of the national government be elected by the electors chosen by the people of the United States.*"

Ellsworth came in bone-dry, brushing off the lofty emotions preceding him to remind them that the convention had shown its will by its vote in the Committee of the Whole. He "saw no reason for departing from the mode contained in the report." The states were necessary. Without them, "it would be impossible to support a republican government over so great an extent of country . . . The largest states are the worst governed," he added. Virginia cannot control the district of Kentucky; Massachusetts cannot keep the peace one hundred miles from her capital; Pennsylvania would have the same problem, the only question was when. The only chance for a general government to succeed "lies in engrafting it on that of the individual states."

Suddenly Madison spoke up. "It would obviate the difficulty" if they postponed the senate discussion and went straight to the resolution on the voting rule.

This was a desperation strategy: on electing the senate, the small states had prevailed overwhelmingly in the Committee of the Whole. The large states had then won on apportionment, though just by a single vote. If the convention would just duplicate the apportionment vote, the small states might think twice about a method of election that would produce numerous senators acting as agents of the large states. It was at least a slim possibility.

The debaters, however, went on as if they had not heard Madison, until Butler, declaring that "we were put to difficulties at every step by the uncertainty" over equality or apportionment in the Senate, moved to skip on to that.

No. The delegates turned aside the proposition, eight to three, and then, without further discussion, voted nine to two for state legislatures to elect the members of the Senate. That decision stood until 1913, when the Constitution was amended to allow popular election.

It was a major loss for Madison. Sitting silent, he recorded the convention mutilating his great republic—deleting any reference to "insuring senators' independency," agreeing that senators should be at least thirty years old, and haggling over the term of office, which Madison thought should be nine years. When the delegates began to consider paring down the duration from seven, to six, then to five, and finally to four years— upon General Pinckney's warning that the senators might "lose sight of the states they represent," Madison's pen stopped moving and he was on his feet.

"We are proceeding," he accused them, "in the same manner that was done when the confederation was first formed: Its original draft was excellent, but in its progress and completion, it became so insufficient as to give rise to the present convention." Turning, possibly, to Pinckney he added, "By the vote already taken, will not the temper of the state legislatures transfuse itself into the senate? Do we create a free government?"

Madison's loss of the Senate election fight still bothered him fifty years later. When he was preparing his notes for publication, he marked the vote with an asterisk and a footnote saying, "It must be kept in view that the largest states, particularly Pennsylvania and Virginia, always considered the choice of the 2d Branch by the state legislatures as opposed to a proportional representation—to which they were attached as a fundamental principle of just government."

Why the two concepts were "opposed" is not clear on its face—the number of senators per state could still be determined by population, even if elected by state legislatures. But when Madison says "opposed" here, he does not mean "opposite"; he means "subversive."

Madison's anguish was natural. The original Virginia plan called for the people to elect the first branch with the number of members apportioned by population. The first branch would elect the Senate also proportionate to population, and the two branches together would elect the executive. Under this formula, all three branches depended on the people equally, and all were accountable for the national, not the local, interest. He had not the slightest doubt that the competing principle of states' interests would be as subversive of the new government as it had been of the confederation.

Worse, the state influence created by these votes did not affect just the Senate. As the plan now stood, the senators, agents of the state legislatures, would carry that influence into the selection of an executive, creating even more schizophrenia.

In short, the vote totally messed up the plan. The states had won the right to choose the Senate. Now proportional representation took on a bitter urgency: for the nationalists, apportioning would at least approximate the equality of all citizens, however palely; for the small states, now they really were fighting to prevent domination by the large states—albeit that situation had just been wrought by their own hand.

MADISON TRIES TO RESCUE THE SENATE

Madison rejoined the fray over senators' terms of office the next morning, trying mightily to make the convention understand his vision of the senate's purpose. It was a speech he perhaps should have made earlier (and without its pouting introduction as "reflections" that would be "becoming" to "a people deliberating in a temperate moment and with the experience of other nations before them . . .").

The senate should protect the people from their rulers and from themselves, Madison said. Protection from rulers' abuse of power was accomplished by dividing the public trust among different bodies to watch and check each other.

Protection from errors was just as important. The people themselves "were liable to temporary errors, through want of information as to their true interest"; the short-term politicians elected to the lower house would err for that same reason. One branch of the government should be constituted so that its members would serve long enough to acquire "a competent knowledge of the public interests." Errors also would spring from "fickleness and passion" and the Senate should be a body of "enlightened citizens whose limited number and firmness might seasonably interpose against impetuous counsels."

Again Madison brought forth his theory of clashing interests to show that the Senate would check a majority attempt "to commit injustice on the minority." Ringing and egalitarian as it sounds in modern times, Madison's point actually was that he viewed the Senate as the protector of property interests.

Acknowledging that he was contradicting Charles Pinckney, Madison said, "there will be particularly the distinction of rich and poor." In America, distinctions of rank were not hereditary nor were there extremes of wealth and poverty. "We cannot, however, be regarded even at this time as one homogeneous mass . . . In framing a system which we wish to last for ages, we should not lose sight of the changes which ages will produce.

"An increase of population will of necessity increase the proportion of those who will labour under all the hardships of life and secretly sigh for a more equal distribution of its blessings. These may, in time, outnumber those who are placed above the feelings of indigence. According to the equal laws of suffrage, the power will slide into the hands of the former. No agrarian attempts have yet been made in this country, but symptoms of a leveling spirit . . . have sufficiently appeared in certain quarters to give notice of the future danger."

Protection against the levelling spirit, Madison said, would have to come from "a body in the government sufficiently respectable for its wisdom and virtue, to aid on such emergencies, the preponderance of justice by throwing its weight into that scale."

However it looks today, Madison's view was not a baldly economic one. Nor was he a sycophant of wealth infatuated with the idea of an aristocracy. To Madison, a close scholar of Enlightenment philosophy, liberty was the central question before them; it was the most noble and ideal object of government.

In calling for the "enlarged sphere" of a great republican government, he had already explained how the liberty created by democracy would create many clashing interests as all men strove to improve their lot. Now he put another layer on it: a larger, more general division would occur between those who acquired property and those who did not. An additional clash would develop between the majority—the unpropertied—who would form "interested coalitions" against the propertied minority.

The Senate was the place to lodge the property interest, Madison felt, because with powers of their own they could check the majority against them. And why should property interests be defended? This Madison did not have to say in his time: men of property, that is to say, wealth, had a stake in society and would pursue stability. More important, their reputations, their "respectability," depended upon "wisdom and virtue" which all the "better characters" worked at with varying degrees of success. And finally with wealth came the obligation to undertake public service in the general interest for its own sake.

If they were not already equipped with inclinations to stability, wisdom, virtue, and public service, Madison wanted the Senate designed to give them a chance to become so. So he argued for a nine-year term of office; he was for making them ineligible for re-election so that they would not pander to public opinion; and he wanted an older age qualification so that inability to be re-elected would not be "inconvenient."

Reviews were mixed: Roger Sherman held up 132 years of stability in Connecticut to show that frequent elections were necessary. The oratorical equivalent of applause came from Hamilton, who profusely agreed with Madison and needled Sherman, saying that "of late" Connecticut government had practically closed down to prevent riots. Elbridge Gerry grew testy and twisted Madison's theory of property interests to warn that "not one one-thousandth part of our fellow citizens . . . were not against every approach to monarchy."

Still losing, but less dramatically, Madison saw his nine-year proposal rejected in favor of six, his hint about increasing the age qualification untaken, and his recommendation for non-re-electability ignored. He had the satisfaction of helping narrowly defeat (six to five) an attempt to give the senate purse-strings to the states. Finally from Mason came what seemed to be a pat on the back for Madison, a suggestion that it might be desirable to require that Senate candidates own property.

DEADLOCK

"It was now," the inexhaustible Luther Martin told the Maryland legislature four months later, "that they who disapproved the report [the Virginia plan] found it necessary to make a *warm* and *decided opposition,* which took place upon the discussion of the seventh resolution."

On June 27, the morning after Madison's defeat, the convention agreed to jump ahead to Resolutions Seven and Eight, which said: "7. *Resolved,* that the rights of suffrage in the first branch of the national legislature ought not to be according to the rule established in the articles of confederation, but according to some equitable ratio of representation, namely, in proportion to the whole number of white and other free citizens and inhabitants, of every age, sex and condition, including those bound to servitude for a term of years, and three fifths of all other persons, not comprehended in the foregoing description, except Indians not paying taxes in each state." Number 8 said that the voting rule in the second branch (the senate) should be the same as described in number 7.

The debate that opened this date continued until July 16, almost three weeks later, when a compromise was reached.

As soon as the convention agreed to take up the two resolutions, Luther Martin came to his feet, armed with books and papers, to lay out, as Madison wrote, "at great length and with great eagerness," the argument against proportional representation.

The pens of both Madison and Yates soon flagged. Martin spoke more than three hours; he read passages from Locke, Vattel, Lord Summers, and Priestly to prove that "individuals in a state of nature are equally free and independent." Then he read more from Locke and Vattel and threw in some Rutherford to prove that states were also equal. "His arguments," Yates's notes sigh, "were too diffuse, and in many instances desultory. It was not possible to trace him through the whole or to methodize his ideas into a systematic or argumentative arrangement."

Finally Martin announced that "he was much too exhausted," Madison says, "to finish his remarks, and reminded the House that he should tomorrow resume them."

"I cannot resist," Ellsworth as The Landholder seethed in his open letter to Martin, "drawing the veil of the convention a little farther aside . . . The day you took your seat must long be remembered by those who were present . . . You had scarcely time to read the propositions . . . when, without requesting information or to be let into the reasons of the adoption of what you might not approve, you opened against them in a speech which held during two days and which might have continued two months, but for those marks of fatigue and disgust you saw strongly expressed on whichever side of the house you turned your mortified eyes."

Actually Martin had taken his seat almost three weeks earlier, but The Landholder's point—that Martin's mind was utterly closed to the nationalists' arguments—was true. Nor was Martin ashamed of it.

State sovereignty was Martin's bottom line; when individuals elected a state government, they entrusted their *individual* liberty to that government. Therefore, in a state's relations with outside entities, it was to be treated as the embodiment of each individual within it. By this reasoning, irrelevant factors like size and wealth did not give one state the right to exercise more power than another. A large state's liberty was not more precious than that of a smaller or poorer state. For Martin, no distress that the union had felt, and no efficiency to be gained from the Virginia scheme, rendered this principle less true.

State sovereignty. Lansing of New York and Jonathon Dayton of New Jersey punctuated Martin's speech with a motion to strike the word "not" from Resolution Seven. And the convention began its slide into deadlock.

After voting in the Committee of the Whole for proportional

representation in the lower branch, the delegations from Georgia and the Carolinas had sympathetically cast most of their subsequent votes with the small states. But they wavered in the face of this new demand that they back up and support the whole state sovereignty argument.

If politics were mathematics, Williamson of North Carolina said, it might be demonstrated "that, if all states were equally sovereign now and parted with equal proportions of sovereignty, they then would remain equally sovereign. He could not comprehend how the smaller states would be injured in the case and wished some gentleman would vouchsafe a solution of it."

Madison rose. Everything he wanted to do, he had to do now; he must attack as hard as he could and leave no opposing argument unscathed. He struck at the unity of the small states coalition. Had not New Jersey's delegates themselves conceded that the equal vote was unjust? Had they not themselves proposed that it might be necessary to "throw the union into hotch-pot" and redraw the map? Had not even the New Jersey Plan proposed to give the general government some powers over individuals?

Wheeling on the small states' dread of combination by the large states, Madison attacked again. On what grounds could the large states—Virginia, Massachusetts, and Pennsylvania—conspire? Geographically "they could not have been more effectually separated from each other by the most jealous citizen of the most jealous state." In manners, religion, and other possible ties, they were "not more assimilated than the other states." Not even the means by which they sustained themselves were similar, Madison said. "The staple of Massachusetts was *fish,* of Pennsylvania *flour,* of Virginia *tobacco.*"

So the only common aspect left was that they were all big, and history proved that among big states "rivalships were much more frequent than coalitions." Consider the enmity between England and France: "To this principle we owe perhaps our liberty. A coalition between those powers would have been fatal to us."

If the small states thought that the large states individually would threaten their neighbors, they should welcome a government that would operate as implacably upon the large as upon themselves. "The more lax the band," Madison said, "the more liberty the larger will have to avail themselves of their superior force."

Rarely does it seem a babble breaks out on the convention floor, but June 28 was apparently one such instance. Of the four sets of notes still existing from that day, not one agrees with the other as to who spoke or when, once Martin had finished and the Dayton/Lansing motion had been made.

Amidst the excitement, Benjamin Franklin spoke once again—directly, without having James Wilson read his remarks for him. He thought the time had come to pray. "The small progress we have made after four or five weeks' close attendance and continual reasonings with each other, is methinks a melancholy proof of the imperfection of human understanding," Franklin said.

"We indeed seem to feel our own want of political wisdom, since we have been running about in search of it . . . In this situation of this Assembly, groping, as it were, in the dark to find political truth, and scarce able to distinguish it when presented to us—how has it happened, Sir, that we have not hitherto once thought of humbly applying to the Father of lights to illuminate our understandings?"

When America was preparing to declare independence, Franklin said, the Continental Congress had had daily prayers —in this very room. "Have we now forgotten that powerful Friend? or do we imagine that we no longer need His assistance? I have lived, Sir, a long time, and the longer I live, the more convincing proofs I see of this truth—that *God* governs in the affairs of men. And if a sparrow cannot fall to the ground without his notice, is it probable that an empire can rise without his aid?"

Franklin moved to bring in one or several of the Philadelphia clergy to lead the convention in a daily prayer. Although Sherman seconded the motion, other delegates anxiously rose to oppose it. If they had hired a clergyman at the beginning, they warned, it would have been considered routine. But to do so now would alert the whole watching world that the convention was in difficulty.

Williamson of North Carolina made the inarguable point that

"the true cause of the omission could not be mistaken. The Convention had no funds." Randolph suggested a subterfuge—that the convention request a Fourth of July sermon and then ask for prayers to continue daily thereafter. However, "after several attempts for silently postponing the matter by adjourning, the adjournment was at length carried, without any vote" on Franklin's motion.

"The controversy must be endless whilst gentlemen differ in the grounds of their arguments," Dr. Johnson of Connecticut complained the following morning. Since they could not agree whether to treat the states as political units or districts of people, "the two ideas embraced on different sides, instead of being opposed to each other, ought to be combined—in one branch the people ought to be represented, in the other, the states." It was the same compromise Sherman had twice urged, but the same deaf ear was turned to it again.

The argument swirled on, and now the nationalists began to raise the specter of dissolution—of the convention and of the union—if the convention failed to produce a reform. Aiming his remarks at Delaware, Gorham observed that "a rupture of the Union would be an event unhappy for all," but surely the large states would be able to take care of themselves.

"On the whole," he added, he "should consider it as his duty . . . to stay here as long as any other state would remain with them in order to agree on some plan that could, with propriety, be recommended to the people."

Massachusetts was merely upset by Shays and his rebels, George Read shot back. Delaware was tranquil, and probably always would be. But to get to the point, he "should have no objection to the system if it were truly national, but it has too much of a federal mixture in it."

As he had before, Read urged erasing the states. Suspicions that the large will combine against the small "are inseparable from the scheme of leaving the states in existence. They must be done away . . . He repeated his approbation of the plan of Mr. Hamilton and wished it to be substituted in place of that on the table."

Madison had been stymied by the fact that some opponents,

like Martin, were defending the states sovereignty, while others feared for the small states against the large. Now he aimed at the fearful, abandoning the abstract.

"Under the proposed government," Madison coaxed the small states listeners, "the powers of the states will be much farther reduced. According to the views of every member, the general government will have powers far beyond those exercised by the British Parliament when the states were part of the British empire. It will in particular have the power, without the consent of the state legislatures to levy money directly on the people themselves . . ."

Warning again of disunion, he "entreated the gentlemen representing the small states to renounce a principle which was confessedly unjust, which could never be admitted and if admitted, must infuse mortality into a constitution which we wished to last forever. He prayed them to ponder well the consequences of suffering the confederacy to go to pieces."

Hamilton played the bully to Madison's reasonable man. The sovereignty argument was contrived. "States are a collection of individual men," he declared. "Which ought we to respect most—the rights of the people composing them or of the artificial beings resulting from the composition? Nothing could be more preposterous or absurd" than to sacrifice the people for the states. "It has been said that if the smaller states renounce their equality, they renounce at the same time their liberty. The truth is, it is a contest for power, not for liberty."

"Though from a small state," Pierce of Georgia spoke up, he considered himself a citizen of the United States. The voting rule of the confederation had been the great source of public difficulties. "State distinctions must be sacrificed as far as the general good required," he said plaintively, but without destroying the states.

"We never were independent states," Elbridge Gerry burst out. We were "not such now and never could be—even on the principles of the confederation. The states and the advocates for them were intoxicated with the idea of their sovereignty." Now that the confederation was dissolving, "instead of coming here like a band of brothers belonging to the same family, we

seemed to have brought with us the spirit of political negotiators."

Perhaps goaded by Gerry's calling sovereignty advocates
"intoxicated," Luther Martin announced that he would read the
Articles of Confederation to the convention, since "the lan-
guagage of the states being sovereign and independent was
once familiar and understood, though it seemed now so strange
and obscure."

The vote on Resolution Seven, at last, was taken: First,
should Lansing's deletion of "not" be accepted, thus restoring
equal suffrage the first branch? *No,* six to four. Does the convention endorse a change in that rule? *Yes,* six to four. Proportional representation was secure in the first branch.

Ellsworth now moved for equal suffrage in the second
branch. He was "not sorry on the whole," he said, that proportional voting had passed for the first branch. He hoped it would
produce a compromise on the second branch. It would, he
admitted, make the new government "partly national, partly
federal," but he thought it "will secure tranquility and still
make it efficient."

Perhaps looking at Madison as he spoke, Ellsworth argued
that proportional representation in the first branch embodied
"the national principle"; the large states would be protected
against the small. The nationalists must reciprocate by granting
the states equal voices in the senate. That would honor the
federal principle and was necessary to "secure the small states
against the large." Declaring he was "not, in general a half-way
man," Ellsworth spoke long and fervently for the compromise.

The large states' influence would protect their superiority in
spite of the equal vote, and "the power of self-defence was
essential to the small states. Nature had given it to the smallest
insect of the creation." He could never admit that there was not
danger of combinations among the large states.

"Let a strong executive, a judiciary and legislative power be
created, but let not too much be attempted, by which all may
be lost." If it did not work out, Ellsworth added, it could be
amended later.

Speaking for the first time in almost three weeks of attendance, Abraham Baldwin of Georgia urged that the Senate represent wealth in some way, instead of either state governments or state populations. In Massachusetts, he said, forty senators were elected from thirteen districts in proportion to the state tax paid by each district.

The southerner's citation of a New England constitution seemed to bring back something Madison meant to say and he rose again. "The great danger to our general government is the great southern and northern interests of the continent being opposed to each other. Look to the votes in congress, and most of them stand divided by the geography of the country, not according to the size of the states."

The convention was divided and everyone inside knew it. New Jersey moved that Washington write to the governor of New Hampshire to urge the immediate attendance of that state's delegation. "The difficulties of the subject and the diversity of opinions called for all the assistance we could possibly obtain," he said. Madison put in parentheses that "it was well understood" that the small states expected New Hampshire to be on their side.

With Rutledge objecting that it would take too long, King assuring them that New Hampshire was expected soon, and Wilson warning of a breach of secrecy that would cause alarm, the convention rejected the motion.

Except for Hamilton's charge that the struggle was for power, not liberty, the nationalists had rarely attacked the small states' high moral tone. Even when warning that the opposition was risking the future of the union, the nationalists had been careful.

Wilson now cast off the restraint. Let a breakup come, Wilson said: "This neither staggers my sentiments nor my duty. If the minority of the people of America refuse to coalesce with the majority on just and proper principles, if a separation must take place, it could never happen on better grounds.

"The opposition to this plan is as twenty-two to ninety of the people of America . . . shall less than one-fourth of the United States withdraw themselves from the Union, or shall more than

three-fourths renounce the inherent, indisputable and unaliena-
ble rights of men in favor of the artificial systems of states?

"Can we forget for whom we are forming a government? Is
it for *men,* or for the imaginary beings called states? Will our
constituents be satisfied with metaphysical distinctions? . . . We
talk of states till we forget what they are composed of."

Ellsworth's compromise was not really a compromise, Wilson
said. The states acting through the Senate could undo anything
done by the lower house. "We shall leave the United States
fettered precisely as heretofore, with the additional mortification of seeing the good purposes of fair representation of the
people in the first branch defeated in the second."

The confederation still existed, Ellsworth answered. It had
been entered into solemnly. "We are running from one extreme to another. We are razing the foundations of the building, when we need only repair the roof."

"The party claiming from others an adherence to a common
engagement ought at least to be guiltless itself of a violation,"
Madison said roughly. Of all the states, Connecticut was perhaps least able to plead for faith in the confederacy. It was she
who, "by a pretty recent vote positively refused to pass a law
for complying with the requisitions of congress and had trans-
mitted a copy of the vote to congress."

Now Madison made an undisguised bid to end Georgia and
the Carolinas' flirtation with the state sovereignty bloc. The
"great division of interest" in the United States resulted "partly
from climate, but principally from the effects of their having or
not having slaves," Madison said. These two causes made the
"great division of interests in the United States." It did not lie
between the large and small states; it lay between the northern
and southern. "And if any defensive power were necessary, it
ought to be mutually given to these two interests."

He was "so strongly impressed with this important truth"
that he had been "casting about . . . for some expedient that
would answer the purpose." He had doubts, but here it was: in
one branch slaves should not be counted at all, while in the
other they should be counted as if free. "By this arrangement,
the southern scale would have the advantage in one house and
the northern in the other."

Chaos followed Madison's foray into expediency. As if discovered suddenly naked, the debaters stampeded, hurling themselves into the bushes of their old arguments. Ellsworth defended Connecticut's performance in confederation. Sherman growled that Madison had not proved the old system fatally deficient. Davie of North Carolina thought the Senate would be too large. Wilson and Franklin suggested minor compromises that would still allow proportional representation.

King was "prepared for every event, rather than sit down under a government founded in a vicious principle of representation." Dayton of New Jersey charged that "assertion is given for proof and terror substituted for argument." Martin roared that he would never confederate except on just principles. Madison retreated to arguing that the Senate would be dependent on the states.

It was now that Gunning Bedford blew up. Every state here acts "from interested and many from ambitious motives," he thundered. "Look at the votes which have been given on the floor of this house . . . Even the diminutive state of Georgia has an eye to her future wealth and greatness. South Carolina, puffed up with the possession of her wealth and negroes, and North Carolina are all, from different views, united with the great states."

The large states "we find closely united in one scheme of interest and ambition, notwithstanding they endeavor to amuse us with the purity of their principles and the rectitude of their intentions in asserting that the general government must be drawn from an equal representation of the people . . . they insist that, although the powers of the general government will be increased, yet it will be for the good of the whole . . . *I do not, gentlemen, trust you!*"

The small states would seek a foreign power to help them. "If we once leave this floor and solemnly renounce your new project, what will be the consequence? You will annihilate your federal government and ruin must stare you in the face. Let us then do what is in our power—*amend and enlarge the confederation, but not alter the federal system!*"

The moment of truth came at the opening of business Monday, when the vote was at last taken. The lineup of votes was almost the same, but with two crucial changes. Daniel St. Jenifer of Maryland, a nationalist, was absent, allowing Luther Martin to cast his state's vote with the small states, and William Few and William Pierce of Georgia were absent, leaving that state's vote divided and depriving the nationalists of a victory. The final tally was five states for, five states against, and one divided. The convention was deadlocked.

9

The Path of the Two-Headed Snake

' ' THE FEDERAL CONVENTION! May the result of their meeting be as glorious as its members are illustrious!" "The Grand Convention! May they form a Constitution for an eternal republic!" Lifting glasses to join their Philadelphia friends' Fourth of July toasts, the convention delegates laughed, huzzaed and swallowed a groan along with their wine, knowing the stalemate at which their labors stood.

The *Pennsylvania Herald*'s reporter started counting with 1776 to make July 4, 1787 "the Twelfth Anniversary of the Independence of the United States of America," which, the newspaper enthused, "was celebrated . . . with the heartfelt satisfaction the auspicious event first dictated and inspired."

The great celebration had begun early in the morning when "the light horse artillery, light infantry, together with Colonel Will's battalion of militia assembled on the Commons; and, after performing various evolutions, etc., fired a feu de joye. The train of artillery fired the salute of the Thirteen United States with three times thirteen rounds. The officers of the militia, with the corps in uniform, then the State Society of the

Cincinnati, who met at the statehouse, marched in procession, with accompaniments of music from martial instruments and ringing of bells, to the new German Lutheran Church, in Race St., where an ovation, well adapted to the occasion, was delivered to a very numerous and crowded auditory, by James Campbell, Esq."

This was a day for George Washington to put aside his anxieties and indulge himself in a justifiable pride. To his fellow Americans, it was a day on which he was as much honored as American liberty itself.

The very name of the Society of the Cincinnati which marched in the procession was inspired by his image as an American Cincinnatus, the classic Roman farmer-war hero. The martial tunes of the parade undoubtedly included a "Washington March" or two (three of such marches written in his honor already had become indispensable for patriotic celebrations). And no patriotic display ever failed to include his name, face, or figure rendered in portraiture, flowers, papier-mâché, or whatever the occasion offered.

So, while he committed to his diary only the usually cryptic entry, he must have allowed himself a moment of quiet satisfaction when he awakened to the booming guns and pealing bells and set out in the clear, warm morning to enjoy the festivities. He went to hear James Campbell's oration, and liked it enough to quote some lines in his diary:

"Why should we travel back to antiquity for examples of the dignity of conduct and sentiment inspired by a republican form of government—we have beheld the citizens of the United States raised by their personal interest in the government of their country to a pitch of glory which has excited the admiration of half the globe." And "may every proposition to add kingly power to our federal system be regarded as treason to the liberties of our country." Those were thoughts agreeable to Washington, who had often expressed them himself in his own way. Campbell's words against kingly power verified his to Madison a few months ago regarding the panicky outcry for a king. He was, Washington said, "fully convinced that those who lean to a monarchical government . . . have not consulted the public mind."

However, when Campbell announced, "Methinks I already see the stately fabric of a free and vigorous government rising out of the wisdom of the federal convention," Washington could be forgiven if his fingers crossed while his hands rested in his lap. Or perhaps he threw a glance at Dr. Johnson of the stubborn Connecticut delegation, who was listening to the same oration.

"Entertainments," the *Herald* went on to say, "were prepared at the City Tavern, at Epplee's, Gray's Ferry, Fish-House, Wigwam, Geisse's and Lilliput, on the Jersey shore, etc. where different parties from this city and Jersey met with mutual humour, which always mark and characterise the Sons of Freedom on this glorious festival."

And Philadelphia loved to celebrate. Four days earlier, the *Pennsylvania Packet* had announced an "apparatus" to be erected opposite the City Tavern, and "the most elegant *FIRE WORKS* that ever had been exhibited. Not labor or expense will be spared to gratify the curiosity of the spectators, and to prevent accidents, there will be no rockets." Tickets could be obtained at the City Tavern for seven shillings and sixpence each, "without which, no person will be admitted to the aforesaid City Tavern."

Summer was also the best time of year for celebratory eating in the biggest city in America. Fresh fruits of all kinds—"we have strawberries, pineapples, oranges," one delegate had written home—fresh produce, and every sort of meat, game, and seafood came through the busy harbor to be sold at Philadelphia's magnificent four-block-long open market.

City Tavern's festive dinners for Independence Day probably included great quantities of the usual chickens, ducks, ham, veal, beef, rockfish, sea turtles, soup, green peas, asparagus, spinach, pies, cherries, strawberries, apricots, and bananas, and were embellished with relishes, olives, a variety of nuts, plus the favorite fancy desserts, "floating islands," and cleverly sculpted "jellies."

The delegates, with few exceptions, drank pretty much on the scale of everyone else—that is, at least triple the amount a man could tolerate today. For a party a few weeks later, City Tavern would serve fifty-five men—Washington, several delegates, and the members of the Philadelphia cavalry—fifty-four bottles of madeira, sixty of claret, fifty of "old stock," porter, beer, and cider, and seven bowls of punch.

Outdoors, celebrants could see, besides parades and fireworks, puppet shows, dancing bears, horse shows, races and cock fights. Parties meant music performed, group singing, cards and dice, and always dancing, which often began at eight in the morning.

Some celebrants went to "subscription" balls, a favorite stylized amusement, at rented halls. A leading young man would be chosen "manager" to "preside" over the affair, presenting the dancers with "billets" folded up to conceal a number. "Thus fate decides the male or female partner," a French traveler explained. The "dances are previously arranged and the dancers are called in their turns." The dances "have some relation to politics: one is called 'the success of the campaign,' another 'the defeat of Burgoyne,' " and, inevitably, "Washington's March." And, the foreigner added happily, "strangers have generally the privilege of being complimented with the handsomest women."

Washington himself spent some time at the wax museum of Dr. Abraham Chovet, not far from the German Lutheran Church. Then he joined the Society of the Cincinnati for what must have been a nostalgia-filled dinner at Epplee's Tavern, before heading on to a party at the Powels'.

Some of the delegates celebrated independence elsewhere. William Livingston was in Trenton, where he delivered a patriotic speech to a Fourth of July celebration. Yielding to the appeals of Charles Thomson, secretary of the Continental Congress, three Williams [Blount of North Carolina, Pierce and Few of Georgia] had slipped away to New York to form a quorum for that body, and paid their tribute to independence there.

The whole fact of the celebration of independence was a

renewed reminder of the delegates' duty to justify the blood of eight years' war in the Revolution. As the *Herald* declared, "With zeal and confidence, we expect from the Federal Convention a system of government adequate to the security and preservation of those rights which were promulgated by the ever memorable Declaration of Independency."

To that end, some members of the convention probably were not celebrating at all—but busy putting into final form the report of the grand committee that had met yesterday.

THE COMPROMISE

The grand committee—consisting of one delegate from each state—had been appointed by the convention to seek a compromise after the deadlock had been reached. It had been General Pinckney's idea, and Madison and Wilson had fought it to no avail. Even Gouverneur Morris had supported it.

Formation of the grand committee marked the end of the convention's effort to come to a single view on the right manner of government. Something other than proportional representation would have to be done with the Senate; the friends of the principle could not carry the day. As Madison said afterward, the convention acted "with a view to some compromise, the indications being manifest that sundry members from the larger states were relaxing in their opposition and that some ground of compromise was contemplated such as finally took place."

How things had changed! From having come into the convention holding the initiative for a great republic, Madison now found himself and the nationalists in "opposition." The attachment to federation not only had held, it had struck back with unexpected force.

To make sure that compromise would result, the convention had elected to the grand committee just one large-state man unsympathetic to small state concerns, Elbridge Gerry. From the other two large states, Virginia and Pennsylvania, they chose men who were disposed to accommodation—not Madison and Wilson, but Mason and Franklin. The rest of the appointees were the most committed defenders of the states (Martin, Bedford, Paterson, and Ellsworth) and those nationalists who had either voted already for state equality in the Senate (Baldwin and Davie) or had supported other proposals to empower the states (Rutledge).

That is not to say the committee's job was easy. For one thing, the small states had shown no willingness to be satisfied with equality in the Senate alone. Whether in earnest or just posturing, they had persuaded everyone that they might withdraw from the convention if they could not have equality in both branches. As for the nationalists, even if they were more flexible than Madison and friends, they could be counted on to urge something other than equality in order to protect the new system from the evils that had wracked the old.

And so they did, for hours, until all the arguments in the convention had been rehashed. But "... when it was found that nothing could induce us to yield to the inequality in both branches," Martin said later of the negotiations, "they at length proposed, by way of compromise, if we would accede to their wishes as to the first branch, they would agree to the equal representation in the second branch."

In Martin's angry eyes, this was "only consenting, after they had struggled to put both their feet on our necks, to take one of them off—provided we would consent to let them keep the other on."

But for Martin's comrades it was enough, and the bargain was struck. After further dickering, the nationalists were able to walk out with something designed to at least make their loss on the Senate appear less than total.

Gerry, chairman of the committee, had the report ready for the opening of business on the morning of July 5. The compromise, he pointed out as he began, was recommended only on the strict condition that all its parts would be adopted.

For the basis of representation in the first branch—the first question submitted to the committee—a population ratio of forty thousand was proposed, though each state containing fewer inhabitants would still to be allowed one representative. On the second question, the voting rule in the Senate, the committee proposed an equal vote of the states.

Additionally, Gerry announced to the hushed room, the committee recommended that "all bills for raising or apportioning money, and for fixing salaries of the officers of government of the United States shall originate in the first branch . . . and shall not be altered or amended by the second branch and . . . no money shall be drawn from the public treasury but in pursuance of appropriations to be originated in the first branch."

The committee had by no means been asked to consider the jurisdiction of the legislative branches, but the purpose was clear: having given the states equality in the Senate, to try to curb their influence by putting the power to tax and spend entirely in the hands of the majority in the popular branch.

Nathaniel Gorham demanded explanations, while Gerry hastened to add that not even the committee members really supported the compromise, but "agreed to the Report merely in order that some ground of accommodation might be proposed."

To which Martin added unnecessarily, "the one representation is proposed as an expedient for the adoption of the other."

"The committee," Wilson objected angrily, "has exceeded their powers."

Clearly considering the opposition on the run, Martin called for a vote on the report, but Wilson jumped to his feet again: "I do not choose to take a leap in the dark. I have a right to call for a division of the question on each distinct proposition."

Finding his voice now, a grim Madison declared that "I restrain myself from animadverting on the report, from the respect I bear to the members of the committee. But I must confess I see nothing of a concession in it." State equality in the Senate was the same as shackling the lower house.

In every way, Madison said, the compromise caved in to the small states and would "perpetuate discord." At every turn, he predicted, the small states would try to thwart the majority of the people who populated the large states. The convention "was reduced to the alternative of either departing from justice in order to conciliate the smaller states and the minority of the people . . . or of displeasing these by justly gratifying the larger states and the majority of the people. He could not himself hesitate as to the option he ought to make."

An unwearied Gouverneur Morris, just back a few days since from a month's absence settling the affairs of his estate, rose on his wooden leg to throw fuel on the fire the holiday had banked.

The restriction on amending as well as the compromise itself was "objectionable," everything about it "wrong." He came here as a representative of America, he flattered himself he "came here in some degree as a representative of the whole human race, for the whole human race will be affected by the proceedings of this Convention."

Stop thinking of the present, your local politics, he implored. If he were to believe "some things" he had heard, he would think that "we were assembled to truck and bargain for our particular states." He could not "descend to think that any gentlemen are really actuated by these views." Let the convention do the right thing, and "all who have reasonable minds and sound intentions will embrace it."

America must be made one nation. "If persuasion does not unite it, the sword will . . . The scenes of horror attending civil commotion cannot be described." After triumphing in civil war, "the stronger party will then make traitors of the weaker, and the gallows and halter will finish the work of the sword."

Would foreign powers become involved? He did not know, but, perhaps gazing at Bedford of Delaware, he remarked, "Threats that they will be invited have, it seems, been thrown out . . ."

Bedford heaved to his feet. He had been misunderstood! "Foreign nations having demands on this country would find it in their interest to take the small states by the hand, in order to do themselves justice." That was all he had meant.

However! "No man can forsee what extremities the small states may be driven by oppression." Having repeated the threat, Bedford swiftly added "in apology that some allowance ought to be made for the habits of his profession in which warmth was natural and sometimes necessary."

As long as he had apologized, Bedford wanted to hear apologies by Morris for saying "that the sword is to unite, and by Mr.

Gorham that Delaware must be annexed to Pennsylvania and New Jersey divided between Pennsylvania and New York." (Bedford was decanting all his grievances at once: Gorham had warned early in the Senate debate that if the union dissolved, Delaware would be at the mercy of Pennsylvania, a fate worse than if the new plan really did combine the states, and that New Jersey would be taxed by New York and Pennsylvania until "she would beg of all things to be annihilated.")

Williamson took the floor to defend Morris, followed by Paterson of New Jersey standing up for Bedford. To the ensuing welter of charges and countercharges about swords and gallows, George Mason, his old ears heartily sick of the sound, decided to call a halt.

The compromise was "preferable to appeal to the world by the different sides." Settling the matter themselves was what they had come there to do. Nobody was suffering any more inconvenience from being stuck in Philadelphia than he, "but he would bury his bones in this City rather than expose his country to the consequences of a dissolution of the convention without anything being done."

Overheated, sullen, talked-out, unreconciled, the convention took a deep breath and essayed an orderly debate of the representation ratio—just long enough to achieve a dignified adjournment.

WORD FROM THE OUTSIDE

Hamilton, meanwhile, had taken advantage of his trip home to New York to make inquiries along the way about what fears and suspicions the public might be conjuring up in the vacuum of information from the secret proceedings. His optimistic findings reached Washington on July 10.

The people, Hamilton wrote, were far less afraid of what the convention might do than were the delegates themselves. "The prevailing apprehension among thinking men is that the Convention, from a fear of shocking the popular opinion, will not go far enough. They seem to be convinced that a strong, well-

167

mounted government will better suit the popular palate than one of a different complexion."

By the time this upbeat assessment reached Washington, nothing could lift the gloom that had settled over the convention president. He thanked Hamilton and then burst out that the deliberations "are now, if possible, in a worse train than ever . . . In a word, I almost despair of seeing a favourable issue to the proceedings of the Convention and do, therefore, repent of having had any agency in the business.

"The men who oppose a strong and energetic government are, in my opinion, narrowminded politicians, or are under the influence of local views," Washington fumed. "I am sorry you went away. I wish you were back. The crisis is equally important and alarming, and no opposition under such circumstances should discourage exertions until the signature is fixed."

The idol of America was depressed indeed—and no wonder: that same day, Hamilton's two fellow New Yorkers, Lansing and Yates, had packed up and left the convention, never to return. Even if Hamilton came back, he alone could not represent New York. The constitution, if they managed to produce one, would go to the people without that important state as a signatory.

A young French officer, De Maussion, who had served under Washington during the Revolution, was visiting Philadelphia during these weeks. He saw his former commander in chief leaving the State House one day and wrote home, "The look on his face reminded me of its expression during the terrible months we were in Valley Forge Camp."

To Washington, the convention must have seemed his dream turned nightmare; his beloved American empire was a fantasy. He had to say something to someone; not even the rule of secrecy could stop him. Despite the danger of putting his thoughts on paper, he wrote of his despair not only to Hamilton, but, the day before the deadlocked vote, to another friend:

The result of the convention "the book of fate must disclose. Persuaded I am that the primary cause of all our disorders lie in the different state governments and the tenacity of that power which pervades the whole of their systems. Whilst independent sovereignty is so ardently contended for, whilst the local views of each state, and separate interests by which they are too much governed, will not yield to a more enlarged scale of politics . . . [all] must render the situation of this great country weak, inefficient and disgraceful."

Even then he did not reveal the devastation of his faith, but walking with Abraham Baldwin one morning, he told the Georgia delegate that "he did not expect the constitution would exist more than twenty years."

SLAVERY

Acceding to Wilson's demand, the convention broke up the compromise to debate it and Morris quickly asked for another, smaller committee to revise the basis of representation, so that both property and new states could be taken into account.

"Life and liberty were generally said to be of more value than property," Morris admitted, but "an accurate view of the matter would nevertheless prove that property was the main object of Society. The savage state was more favorable to liberty than the civilized, and sufficiently so to life. It was preferred by all men who had not acquired a taste for property; it was only renounced for the sake of property, which could only be secured by the restraints of regular government." This was a staple of political theory: a principal purpose of government was the security of property rights.

Property had been on many minds, the delegates agreed, and turned the job over to Morris in committee with Gorham, Randolph, Rutledge, and King. When Morris brought in his committee's revision, the convention's first protracted debate on slavery was ignited. Modern readers will shudder, but, save for brief moments, this was an argument over sectional power. Those delegates who were abolitionists (including the unique Luther Martin, who was also a slaveowner) would pursue their object later in the convention. To bring it up at this fragile point would have been as dangerous as it was futile. The ghost of the future was in the chamber, and two of the delegates—Rufus King and Gouverneur Morris—felt it.

With the Morris committee's effort to include wealth in determining representation, the convention soon was in confusion over whether slaves were people or property, and their struggle with it would stretch over much of ten days' debate.

Paterson of New Jersey did not want slaves counted. If they were property they should not be included in population; nor was he willing to encourage the slave trade by providing representation on the basis that they were wealth.

"He could regard negro slaves in no light but as property. They are no free agents, have no personal liberty, no faculty of acquiring property, but on the contrary are themselves property . . . Has a man in Virginia a number of votes in proportion to the number of his slaves? And if Negroes are not represented in the states to which they belong, why should they be represented in the general government?"

Representation, Paterson argued, was a substitute for the people meeting and making decisions themselves. "If such a meeting of the people was actually to take place, would the slaves vote? They would not. Why then should they be represented?"

The institution was disgraceful to America. He was "against such an indirect encouragement of the slave trade." Congress, he reminded them, had been "ashamed to use the term 'slaves' and had substituted a description" in its resolutions on taxes.

Up jumped Madison to happily push Paterson into a hole he had just dug for himself by describing representation as a proxy for town meetings: Paterson's principle was "the genuine one," he said—which "must forever silence the pretensions of the small states to an equality of votes with the large ones." They ought to vote in the same proportion in which their citizens would do if the people of all the states were collectively met.

Count slaves, all of them, along with free inhabitants, Madison urged as before—but only for representation in the Senate, the guardian of property. Count free inhabitants alone to determine representation in the lower house.

Rufus King saw no need to beat around the bush: He "always expected that as the southern states are the richest, they would not league themselves with the northern unless some respect were paid to their superior wealth." The states had agreed with a congressional proposal to count slaves in apportioning taxation, so the South had a right to count slaves in representation because (said the delegate from the home of the Boston Tea Party) "taxation and representation ought to go together."

The convention wrestled tediously with possible allocations of representatives for each state in the new legislature. But now the southern states—like the small states before—saw danger from the other states leagued against them.

Cut New Hampshire's representation from three to two, Rutledge and the senior Pinckney demanded. "Her numbers do not entitle her to three, and it is a poor state." Cut somewhere, echoed Williamson of North Carolina. "The southern interest must be extremely endangered . . . The northern states are to have a majority and the means of perpetuating it."

King scoffed at their protests to one list. The four "eastern" states (New Hampshire, Massachusetts, Rhode Island, and Connecticut), with some eight hundred thousand people, would have only seventeen representatives—almost a third fewer than the twenty-three proposed for the four southern states with only seven hundred thousand, including every five blacks counted as three. He had been trying to give the southern states security, but "no principle would justify giving them a majority. They were brought as near an equality as was possible."

General Pinckney did not care about equality with the eastern states; the whole north was the problem. If southern states "are to form so considerable a minority and the regulation of trade is to be given to the general government, they will be nothing more than overseers for the northern states."

Denials rained on him, but, unmoved and fighting hard now, Pinckney "dwelt on the superior wealth of the southern states and insisted on its having its due weight in the government."

Morris was annoyed with the new quarrel. The Southern states would get "more than their share of representation. Property ought to have its weight; but not all the weight. If the southern states are to supply money, the northern states are to spill their blood. Besides," he added sourly, "the probable revenue to be expected from the southern states has been greatly overrated."

The convention was diverted to a debate on the West, but South Carolina jerked them back to the question of slaves. Insisting that slaves be fully represented, Butler and General Pinckney moved to delete the words "three-fifths."

"The labor of a slave in South Carolina was as productive and valuable as that of a freeman in Massachusetts," Butler argued. "An equal representation ought to be allowed for them in a government which was instituted principally for the protection of property and was itself to be supported by property."

When the Continental Congress chose three-fifths as the rule for taxation, Gorham retorted, the slave-state delegates argued "that blacks were still more inferior to freemen. At present when the ratio of representation is to be established, we are assured that they are equal to freemen."

But while the south had argued black inferiority, Williamson shot back, "the eastern states on the same occasion contended for their equality."

Mason temporized. Slaves were valuable, he said. They "raised the value of land, increased the exports and imports and, of course, the revenue, would supply the means of feeding and supporting an army and might, in cases of emergency, become themselves soldiers." Therefore, they should be included in the estimate of representation, but not in their entirety. Though he was arguing against his own state's interest, he "could not consider them free men and vote for them as such."

The Butler-Pinckney motion went down to defeat, but the subject nagged. King was soon on it again. He was "much opposed to fixing numbers" in the rule of representation, was particularly so on account of the blacks. Admitting them along with whites "would excite great discontents among the states having no slaves."

Wilson agreed. On what principle, he asked, could they explain admitting blacks in the three-fifths ratio? "Are they admitted as Citizens? Then why are they not admitted on an equality with white citizens? Are they admitted as property? Then why is not other property admitted into the computation?"

In a rare moment of unity with Paterson, Gouverneur Morris announced he was "compelled to declare himself reduced to the dilemma of doing injustice to the Southern States or to human nature, and he must therefore do it to the former. For he could never agree to give such encouragement to the slave trade" by allowing them to count their blacks.

Finally the convention voted for the three-fifths rule for numerical representation. But as soon as they turned to taxation, they had to face the question again. Morris triggered it with a motion to exclude estimates of imports and exports in figuring representation.

General Pinckney jumped up. He "had been alarmed at Morris's remarks about the slave trade and is now again alarmed at what had been thrown out concerning the taxing of exports. South Carolina has in one year exported to the amount of £600,000 sterling, all which was the fruit of the labor of her blacks. Will she be represented in proportion to this amount? She will not. Neither ought she then to be subject to a tax on it." The constitution should flatly guarantee *no* tax on exports.

Trying to set the problem aside, Morris amended his motion to say that "direct taxation ought to be proportioned to representation." This passed unanimously, but the southerners were boiling mad.

It was "high time now to speak out," Davie of North Carolina said. "Some gentlemen," he saw, meant "to deprive the southern states of any share of representation for their blacks." His state "would never confederate on any terms that did not rate them as three-fifths. If the Eastern States meant to exclude them altogether, the business was at an end."

Davie's passion was unexpected—he was one of the quieter delegates—but Paterson, Morris, King, and Wilson, northerners all, seemed a conspiracy. And off the floor, things were happening that were just as threatening.

In New York, the Society for the Manumission of Slaves—which boasted as founding members Alexander Hamilton and the former president of the Continental Congress, John Jay—was thinking of petitioning the convention to abolish the slave trade, and early in June, the Pennsylvania Society for Promoting the Abolition of Slavery had drawn up and signed a formal petition to the convention to consider stopping the trade. It had been scuttled, as Hamilton would see done in New York, but both abolition appeals were known to the delegates.

The southerners felt besieged. Besides the threat to strip them of their laborers, they were convinced that the north would write all the commercial laws, tax the South's agricultural exports, force their products into expensive New England ships, conclude treaties of trade with foreign nations injurious to southern interests, and abandon their western populations to the depredations of the Spanish and Indians. To do battle, the southern states would be heavily represented in the new government, or they would walk out.

Randolph "lamented" the existence of "such a species of property," but called for immediately adopting a formula to count slaves that would be immune to legislative connivance. As such property did exist, "the holders of it would require this security." They perceived that "the design was entertained by some of excluding slaves altogether."

In an unusually devious suggestion, blunt-spoken Wilson proposed hiding slaves by including them in the rule of direct taxation—making it unnecessary to mention them in the rule of representation. "As representation was to be according to taxation, the end would be equally attained." In other words, figure slaves in the tax bill and give the tax-paying state an equivalent proportion of representatives.

Any "rule of numbers" would be unjust, said King, still trying to be fair to the South. You could count population in the North and get a rough measure of wealth: it was shops and farms, ships and commercial business. But the free population in the agricultural South was entirely out of proportion to its wealth, which was land and the labor of slaves. Festering sectional resentment would be the price of ignoring the difference, King warned. Someday it would lead to civil war.

Justice must be the basis of the union, or "it could not be of long duration," King said. "He must be shortsighted indeed who does not foresee that, whenever the southern states shall be more numerous than the northern, they can and will hold a language that will awe them [the North] into justice. If they threaten to separate now, in case injury shall be done them, will their threats be less urgent or effectual when force shall back their demands? Even in the intervening period, there will be no point of time at which they will not be able to say, 'do us justice or we will separate.' "

In the end, the convention combined Wilson's subterfuge with Randolph's demand for a formula now—representation would be proportionate to direct taxation and taxation would be based on a census taken every ten years counting all whites and three-fifths of blacks.

Randolph now tried to delete the word "wealth" from the rule of representation approved days earlier. With representation for the South's slaves now secure in the rule of taxation, this would eliminate the north's conventional wealth from representation—and tip the balance of representation toward the South.

"Incoherence . . . inconsistency," Morris exploded. He had given "deep meditation" to the way this business was proceeding, and felt he should state his conclusions.

"A distinction had been set up and urged between the northern and southern states," which until now he had considered "heretical." He still thought it groundless, but "it is persisted in" and "the southern gentlemen will not be satisfied unless they see a way open to their gaining a majority in the public councils.

"Either this distinction is fictitious or real: if fictitious let it be dismissed and let us proceed with due confidence. If it be real, instead of attempting to blend incompatible things, let us at once take a friendly leave of each other. There can be no end of demands for security if every particular interest is to be entitled to it."

"The security the southern states want," flashed Butler, "is that their negroes may not be taken from them which some gentlemen—both within and without doors—have a very good mind to do!"

THE WEST

While the deadlocked convention heaved and writhed, the Continental Congress had come back to life and was putting the finishing touches on the Northwest Ordinance of 1787, one of the five greatest documents in American history. Nurtured into shape by stages since 1784, the ordinance set out the rules and civil guarantees that would govern the immense territory surrendered by Great Britain northwest of the original states. It also established the basis on which the territories carved out there would then join the Union as fully equal states.

These were wild unknown lands, the source of myth as well as furs and whisky. Crèvecoeur's *Letters of an American Farmer*, published in the United States in 1786, drew this picture of the western settlers:

"By living in or near the woods, their actions are regulated by the wildness of the neighborhood . . . The chase renders them ferocious, gloomy and unsociable; a hunter wants no neighbors; he hates them because he dreads their competition. In a little time their success in the woods makes them neglect the tillage . . . to make up for the deficiency, they go oftener to the woods . . . Their wives and children live in sloth and inactivity; and [all] grow up a mongrel breed, half-civilized, half-savage."

The number of western settlers in the 1780s could only be guessed at. Almost certainly, white inhabitants still were just in the few tens of thousands, as the British had proclaimed the West closed in 1763 to keep a buffer against the French and Spanish beyond. But American occupation was bound to increase rapidly. As Lord Dunmore, Virginia's governor in the 1770s, had noticed about Americans, "wandering about seems engrafted in their nature, and it is a weakness incident to it that they should ever imagine the lands farther off are still better than those upon which they are already settled."

Already, by the time of the convention, as Elbridge Gerry said on the floor, there was a "rage" for moving west. Yet at the same time, even though contemporary Americans knew Crèvecoeur's portrayal was poppycock, few admired the western settler for romance, virility, and virtue as we do today. Except for the perpetual dreamer, George Washington, who had launched his military career there, most assumed that their brethren heading west were a lowly mix of religious dissenters, debtors eluding their creditors, failed farmers, speculators, and the merely restless.

Though the Continental Congress ultimately decided to lay out the Northwest Territory into five potential new states, the current information to the convention delegates was that it would be ten. In the north, east, and south, moreover, three additional districts (Maine, Vermont, and Kentucky) were at various points of seeking their own statehood.

Not surprisingly, many of the delegates worried, as Williamson did, that "the new states to the westward . . . would be small states; they would be poor states; they would be unable to pay in proportion to their numbers; their distance from market rendering the produce of their labour less valuable, they would consequently be tempted to combine for the purpose of laying burdens on commerce and consumption which would fall with greatest weight on the old states."

What is surprising is that this was a minority view, though shared by such highly respected members as King, Rutledge, Read, Gouverneur Morris, Gorham, and Gerry. The majority, perhaps having long ago reached an opinion in congressional debate, seemed content with the idea that however the constitution affected their states, their situation would not be much altered by the new ones in the West. With one glaring exception.

Urbane, exciting Gouverneur Morris, with his abhorrence of slavery, his cynicism about the rich, his polished oratory, flashing brilliance, and broad classical education, had a blind spot for—or more correctly, a nearly irrational fear and dread of— the new states rising in the West.

The twenty-sixth president of the United States so admired Morris that he wrote a full-length biography of him. But Theodore Roosevelt (whose own love for the West may have overcome him) described Morris's view as "the narrowest, blindest, and least excusable sectional jealousy . . . the gravest discredit alike on his far-sightedness and on his reputation as a statesman."

The convention did not exactly debate the west during their days of crisis—Morris attacked it while Mason and Madison fought back. But how depressing to Washington—champion and believer in the West—to hear his engaging colleague, his friend, derogating America's future states as ferociously as any small-state or slave-state man.

"Fickle and inconstant," convention delegate Pierce had written of Morris, and Morris was never so much so as when he set out to prevent the new states from being admitted as equals of the old. The rule of representation, he urged, "ought to be fixed so as to secure to the Atlantic states a prevalance in the national councils." It would not be unfair, he added, as western settlers would know about it before becoming pioneers.

Here was the visionary Morris who had said perhaps an hour earlier that he "wished gentlemen to extend their views beyond the present" and asked "who can say whether he himself, much less whether his children, will the next year be an inhabitant of this or that state?" And here was the stern advocate of majority rule who two days later lectured, "particular states ought to be injured for the sake of a majority of the people."

Did it deter him when Mason said "decidedly" no: The compromise committee agreed that new states "ought to be subject to no unfavorable discrimination"? Not at all. Morris got his own committee to propose giving the government authority to "regulate" representation for new states. "The Atlantic states having the government in their own hands," committee member Gorham explained, "may take care of their own interest by dealing out the right of representation in safe proportions to the western states."

The west, Morris proclaimed, would not know the public interest, would have *different* interests, would not hesitate to involve the original states in costly wars. Fix an irrevocable number of votes for the seaboard states so they would never be outvoted.

Morris fought Randolph's call for a census in determining representation. "Advantage may be taken of it in time of war," was his dire prediction, "by new states to extort particular favors . . . He dwelt much on the danger of throwing such a preponderancy into the Western scale . . ."

"Ought we," George Mason finally demanded, "to sacrifice what we know to be right in itself lest it should prove favorable to states which are not yet in existence? If the western states are to be admitted into the union as they arise, they must," he would repeat, "be treated as equals . . . They will have the same pride and other passions which we have and will either not unite with or will speedily revolt from the union if they are not in all respects placed on an equal footing with their brethren."

No! Mr. Mason had not changed Morris's opinion on the Western country. "Among other objections, it must be apparent they would not be able to furnish men equally enlightened to share in the administration of our common interests. The busy haunts of men, not the remote wilderness, was the proper school of political talents. If the western people get the power into their hands, they will ruin the Atlantic interests. The back members are always most averse to the best measures." We should, he insisted, trust the duty and honor of the new legislature to do the right thing for the old states.

Madison, immediately on his feet, tore into Morris. He was "not a little surprised to hear this implicit confidence urged by a member who, on all occasions, had inculcated so strongly the political depravity of men and the necessity of checking one vice and interest by opposing to them another . . .

"His reasoning was not only inconsistent with his former reasoning, but with itself. At the same time he recommended this implicit confidence to the southern states in the northern majority, he was still more zealous in exhorting all to a jealousy of western majority. To reconcile the gentleman with himself, it must be imagined that he determined the human character by the points of the compass."

Few sights are so painful as the hero unhorsed. Perhaps that is why George Mason rose again after Madison to say gently, "he agreed with Mr. Gouverneur Morris that we ought to leave the interests of the people to the representatives of the people, but the objection was that the legislature would cease to be the representatives of the people . . . As soon as the southern and western population should predominate, which must happen in a few years, the power would be in the hands of the [northern] minority and would never be yielded to the majority unless provided for by the constitution."

Although in denouncing the North-South "distinction" Morris resurrected his dread of the rising west, he never again called for subordinating it—not even when Gerry later made a formal motion to curb its representation.

That is an example of what Madison meant fifty years later when he said about Morris, "It is but due [him] to remark that, to the brilliancy of his genius, he added what is too rare: a candid surrender of his opinions when the lights of discussion satisfied him that they had been too hastily formed, and a readiness to aid in making the best of measures in which he had been overruled."

But so ill-timed and unnecessary was Morris's campaign that the grace of his surrender undoubtedly eluded the despairing Washington. It all must have been enough to make the Father of His Country want nothing more than to weep.

"The Power of Giving Away the People's Money"

The compromise committee's decision to give the lower house what George Mason called "the power of giving away the people's money" came dressed as a concession. It was a proposition the convention had decisively, eight to three, rejected almost three weeks ago, and the nationalists flogged it again, now wearily, but this time to no avail.

Madison was quick to complain that he "could not regard the exclusive privilege of originating money bills as any concession on the side of the small states." The Senate would contrive to invade the power: "If seven states in the second branch should want such a bill, their interest in the first branch will prevail to bring it forward. It is nothing more than a nominal privilege."

The same was true for the power to amend. "Amendments could be handed privately by the Senate to members in the other house." The Senate could also refuse to approve bills until the lower house rewrote them "in the desired shape." Just as bad, if the Senate did not engage in back room maneuvering and simply approved what the lower house passed, the Senate's value as a checking body would be lost.

Wilson, too, "could see nothing like a concession here on the part of the smaller states. If both branches were to say yes or no, it was of little consequence which should say yes or no first." Several states' constitutions had borrowed this idea from the British system, Wilson said, and, if the result were examined, "it would be found to be a trifle light as air."

Whimsically, Gerry admitted it might not be a big concession, but it surely *was* a concession because "it would make it a constitutional principle that the second branch were not possessed of the confidence of the people in money matters—which would lessen their weight and influence."

"The consideration which weighed with the committee," Mason said in defense, "was that the the first branch would be the immediate representatives of the people. The second would not." If the Senate "have the power of giving away the people's money, they might soon forget the source from whence they received it. We might soon have an aristocracy."

That was all Morris needed to set off on his second-favorite theme: "his creed was that there never was, nor ever will be a civilized society without an aristocracy. His endeavor was to keep it as much as possible from doing mischief." Giving only the lower house the privilege to originate or amend money bills "will take away the responsibility of the second branch—the great security for good behavior." The senators would be more likely to approve "an obnoxious money bill." They could say they disliked it but constitutionally could neither amend it nor safely reject it. "On the whole," he said, "the restriction would be either useless or pernicious."

"It was always a matter of importance," Benjamin Franklin spoke up, "that the people should know who had disposed of their money and how it had been disposed of." That would be best achieved if money affairs were to be confined to the democratically elected branch. The mischief of Senate vetoes could be avoided by giving that branch no right to disapprove—or, he added (half-seriously?) "by declaring there shall be no such branch at all."

The origination clause passed on a plurality of just five votes because three states were divided on the question, but later in the convention, the clause was changed to permit the Senate to amend money bills. The Constitution still restricts the right of origination to the House of Representatives—and Madison's and Wilson's predictions about its operation have come true in recent years. The most prominent example occurred in the Ninety-ninth Congress (1985–86), when the Senate openly wrote its own tax overhaul bill, superimposed it on the House tax bill as an amendment, and thereby forced both plans into a closed conference committee where they were redesigned into a bill satisfactory to both branches. Some dismay was voiced about the Constitution's origination clause, but everyone seemed to find, with James Wilson, that it is "a trifle light as air."

THE TWO-HEADED SNAKE

Near dark on Friday evening, July 13, a teatable was spread under the mulberry tree in Benjamin Franklin's garden. A week-long heat wave had finally broken; the night promised to be soft and cool, an added treat for the good doctor's visitors— several gentlemen from the convention, some with their ladies, and the Rev. Manasseh Cutler, chatting pleasantly in the deepening dusk.

Franklin had been delighted to meet Cutler, but no more so than the Massachusetts minister, botanist, and land speculator himself, who had arrived at the Indian Queen the night before bearing his letters of introduction. Gratifying Cutler's eagerness to see Franklin, Gerry had brought him to call that afternoon.

They had found the philosopher hatless and in good spirits "upon a grass plat under a very large Mulberry" with company. The old doctor had taken Cutler's hand and "begged me to seat myself close to him . . . Here we entered into free conversation and spent our time most agreeably until it was dark."

While Franklin's daughter, Sarah Bache ("a very gross and rather homely lady," Cutler thought), poured tea, Franklin brought forth a strange object for his fellow scientist to see.

Cutler was fascinated. "The Doctor showed me a curiosity he had just received and with which he was very much pleased. It was a snake with two heads, preserved in a large vial."

The situation of this snake, Franklin told Cutler in his cheerful, low voice, is such that, "if it was traveling among bushes and one head should choose to go on one side of the stem of a bush and the other head should prefer the other side, that neither of the heads would consent to come back or give way to the other."

More amusing even, Franklin went on, was that, in the convention today, after he had compared the snake to America—"but the secrecy of convention matters was suggested to him, which stopped him and deprived me of the story he was going to tell."

Whatever transpired in the State House when Franklin had come up with his two-headed America had probably brought as much relief in laughter as the fresh, cool air coursing into the city that afternoon. The delegates had needed respite badly, and perhaps those two factors did the most to give them the courage to face the next day's debate—the debate they had avoided as long as they could.

Twice the convention had reached for the compromise clause on equality in the Senate, and twice drew back. On the third day after the report was presented, someone had suggested simply striking the line. The convention, though, voted six to three to let it stand, agreeing to it, in effect. It was only a dodge, to avoid another plunge into declamations and squabbles, and Madison wrote, "Note. Several votes were given here in the affirmative or were divided because another final question was to be taken on the full report."

The dodge did not work. When Gerry suggested debating the powers of Congress in general, Madison sulked that the powers of Congress could not be defined until it was known how the states were to be represented. Echoing his earlier outburst in defeat on the method of electing senators, he declared himself "apprehensive" that, as during the writing of the Articles of Confederation, "the new government would be rendered as impotent and as short lived as the old."

The remark outraged New Jersey's Paterson, to whom it was evident that Madison did not want to compromise at all. As proportional representation was decided in the first branch, Paterson flared, "There was no other ground of accommodation. His resolution was fixed. He would meet the large states on that ground and no other."

Gouverneur Morris "had no resolution unalterably fixed," except to do what he thought was right. It had been said that compromise would make the new government partly national, partly federal. The "national" protected individuals; "federal," the states. But how was it to protect "the aggregate interest of the whole?" Morris demanded. Among the many provisions which had been urged, he had "seen none for supporting the dignity and splendor of the American Empire."

No federation ever protected the whole; they were always unstable, sapped by local interests. "Good God, Sir!" he appealed to Washington, "is it possible they can so delude themselves? What if all the charters and constitutions of the states were thrown into the fire and all their demagogues into the ocean? What would it be to the happiness of America?"

No one answered him, and the subject had been dropped from that day, July 7, until this, Saturday, July 14.

For all of the debate and dozens of votes, the crucial decision had not been made. The basis of representation in the first branch had been hammered out and originating money bills agreed to —but the whole compromise had to be adopted or rejected. And on equality in the Senate, not a pebble had tumbled from the two granite blocks of obstinacy, the big states and the small.

Luther Martin precipitated the final imbroglio by seizing the floor at the opening of business that Saturday morning, calling for adoption of the compromise committee report. Gerry and King lobbed in countercalls to re-debate representation; it was important, they said, to talk about the West. Rutledge wished to reconsider money bills and debate the Senate clause, too.

Martin repeated his motion.

Wilson "traced the progress of the report through its several stages," concluding that the house remained divided. It still seemed to him that one-third would control two-thirds of the people, and the point was "of such critical importance that every opportunity ought to be allowed for discussing and collecting the mind of the convention on it."

"The states that please to call themselves large," Martin shouted, "are the weakest in the Union. Look at Massachusetts. Look at Virginia. Are they efficient states? He was for letting a separation take place if they desired it. He had rather there should be two confederacies, than one founded on any other principle than an equality of votes in the second branch at least."

Gerry and Wilson flew at him. Wilson was not surprised that someone more interested in the minority would also "say that the minority is stronger than the majority. He supposed that the next assertion will be that they are richer also—though he hardly expected it would be persisted in when the states shall be called on for taxes and troops—"

Gerry interrupted Wilson to fire at Martin—as Madison put it, he "also animadverted"—for citing Massachusetts and to support the requests to reconsider the Senate clause only.

Which was, Madison wrote, "tacitly" agreed to.

Probably Martin had heard that the friends of proportional representation intended to propose amendments to the Senate compromise and decided to pull the rug out from under them.

Indeed Gerry had had a clever idea: give each state the same number of senators and count each senator's vote separately, instead of one vote per state—which he said "would give a national aspect and spirit to the management of the business." And Charles Pinckney had cast aside his beloved four Senatorial Districts, to offer a thirty-six-member Senate apportioned state by state—which Wilson endorsed almost before the last number left Pinckney's lips.

Alas, all there was to say had been said before, and even Madison's notetaking seems weary. As usual the small states "would in no event yield" (Dayton); the compromisers pleaded for "the state governments which could not be preserved otherwise" (Sherman); those firm on majority rule remained firm; those fearing dissolution cried again for accommodation. King made a long speech and so did Madison. Here and there sputtered a new idea: make all state debts a national obligation so that all can begin with a clean slate; create a third branch of the government to represent the states; make the Senate proportionate, but let states vote as equals in special cases.

By and by, though, only the nationalists were talking, until the house adjourned for the weekend on an inconclusive note.

"Monday, July 16. In Convention" [Madison's notes begin]: "On the question for agreeing to the whole report as amended and including the equality of votes in the second branch. It passed in the affirmative . . . Ayes–5; noes–4; divided–1."

Stunned, Randolph slowly came to his feet. "The vote," he said, "has embarrassed the business extremely . . . When he came here this morning, his purpose was to have offered some propositions that might, if possible, have united a great majority of votes." From the division in the vote, it would be in vain. Now he "wished the convention might adjourn, that the large states might consider the steps proper to be taken in the present solemn crisis of the business, and that the small states might also deliberate on the means of conciliation."

If Randolph would just make that a formal motion, Paterson said, "He would second it with all his heart . . . it was high time for the convention to adjourn, that the rule of secrecy ought to be rescinded and that our constituents should be consulted."

No! General Pinckney "could not think of going to S. Carolina and returning again to this place . . ."

Adjournment "would be fatal," cried Broome of Delaware, only his third utterance since May. "Something must be done by the convention . . ."

My state will now concur in the adjournment, Gerry announced.

I see no need of an adjournment, Rutledge objected, because I can see no chance of a compromise. "The little states were fixed, they would yield or not."

After Randolph, embarrassed, explained that he meant only temporary adjournment, the convention voted to adjourn overnight.

The nationalists gathered well before the hour of the convention the next morning; a few of the small states men were with them, according to Madison's only account of a delegate caucus off the convention floor.

"The time was wasted in vague conversation, without any specific proposition or agreement." Among those who opposed equal voting in the senate, Madison says, no consensus could be reached and some feared the convention would dissolve. Some "supposed that no good government could or would be built on the compromise," but that it might be better received if "the principal states" were sponsors; others "seemed inclined to yield to the smaller states and to concur in such an act, however imperfect."

"It is probable," Madison concludes, his words hollow with the disappointment and depth of his loss, "that the result of this consultation satisfied the smaller states that they had nothing to apprehend from a union of the larger in any plan whatever."

The two-headed snake had gone past the bush.

10

"Unanimity Hall"

''SO GREAT IS THE UNANIMITY that prevails in the convention upon all great federal subjects," the Pennsylvania *Gazette* reported on July 18, the day after the caucus, "that it has been proposed to call the room in which they assemble 'Unanimity Hall.' "*

The *Gazette*'s cheery notice was an exaggeration, but the delegates were relieved. In fact, two days later, Sherman and Johnson actually left Philadelphia for Connecticut. "I believe the older men grow, the more uneasy they are [away] from their wives," their colleague Ellsworth wrote his own wife lightheartedly. "Mr. Sherman and Doctor Johnson are both run

*The *Gazette*'s anonymous item is one of the minor mysteries of the convention: it appeared less than twenty-four hours after the large states surrendered to the compromise and is suspected of being deliberately planted while the convention was in danger of breaking up, possibly to counter rumors about the dissension. As Franklin was the newspaper's founder, he is generally thought to have been the source, even though the rest of the item does not sound like him. The people of America, it continued, had cherished the federal government in the Revolution and had only begun suffering turmoil at home and disrespect abroad after "they set up the idol of *state sovereignty.*" The uncharitable writer hoped that enemies of the new government, "whether in Rhode Island or elsewhere," would "meet with the fate of the disaffected in the late war."

home for a short family visit. As I am a third younger than they are, I calculate to hold out a third longer, which will carry me to about the last of August."

Catching up on his correspondence, even Madison seemed to have patted down his thin hair, shot his cuffs, and settled with a sigh into the remaining business. He still could not reveal the proceedings, he wrote Jefferson, but "I . . . have little doubt that the people will be as ready to receive as we shall be able to propose a government that will secure their liberties and happiness."

If Madison was quickly reconciled to losing the battle over the compromise, it probably stemmed from signs, evident as soon as the convention began to move on, that equality in the Senate had wholly placated the small states. Guaranteed their share in the government, Madison's adversaries now seemed to think, as William Paterson of New Jersey wrote his wife, "we shall eventually agree upon and adopt a system that will give strength and harmony to the union and render us a great and happy people."

Should that satisfaction be real, Madison could at least hope that the systematic effort to debilitate his frame for a great republic had ended, leaving room to adjust for the awkwardness introduced by the federation-style Senate. Only pressing ahead would tell, and it soon did.

The arguments for state sovereignty and the small republic, used to good effect by the states' champions, vanished from the debates, lending credence to Hamilton, Wilson, and Madison's previous accusations that the struggle had been about power, not principle. Now that state interests would, as General Pinckney had said so early on, "share in the benefits" of the government, they became eager to heap powers upon it. At the same time, confirmation was shaping up on the sectional interests that Madison had drawn attention to. The common cause made between the Carolinas and Connecticut (which Madison had tried to sunder with his proposal to count slaves for representation in the Senate but not in the lower house) settled into a firm partnership culminating in a bargain on slavery. Thus, in a backhanded and coldly realistic way, Madison discovered that the republic would be proposed and that the work of the convention now was aimed at making it presentable to the constituencies back home.

That harmony reigned was a blessing, because so much—so very much—remained to be done. How powerful would the national legislature be? How should they set up the new executive? What about impeachment—was it a good idea? Should certain types of people be barred from holding office? Who should have the power of appointing judges and making treaties? Who should approve the new Constitution? And of course, the only other really hard, dangerous issue facing them: how would the commercial interests of the Union, including the slave trade, be governed?

The roles of Madison, the Connecticut delegation, Mason, and Wilson were to shrink; these questions—their moral dimensions notwithstanding—were less susceptible to "greatness" and leadership than to skillful political management. Those who had steered the convention this far were more often to share the reins with men like Gouverneur Morris, the senior Pinckney, John Rutledge, and Hugh Williamson of North Carolina—the harder, more political luminaries of the convention, whose constituents in the end must be secured in favor of the constitution.

THE SUPREMACY CLAUSE

After the caucus had broken up, the convention had gone into session and quickly faced a good test of its current disposition toward the states: the clause giving Congress authority to veto state laws in conflict with the Constitution. The earlier failure of young Charles Pinckney, Madison, and Wilson to expand this power over all state laws which the national body "should judge to be improper" proved now to have foreshadowed a retreat from the whole idea.

Even Gouverneur Morris, nationalistic to the core, thought a congressional veto excessive. It was "likely to be terrible to the states," he objected, "and not necessary if sufficient legislative authority should be given to the general government."

Roger Sherman and Luther Martin agreed. The state courts "would not consider as valid any law contravening the authority of the Union," Sherman said. "Shall all the laws of the states," Martin asked, "be sent up to the general legislature before they shall be permitted to operate?"

Madison fought for it again, but this time without help from either Pinckney or Wilson.

But Morris declared that he was "more and more opposed to the negative. The proposal of it would disgust all the states." A state law that deserved to be vetoed, he said, "will be set aside in the judiciary department" and, if not, could be repealed by a national law. In fact, Roger Sherman needled Madison, "such a power involves a wrong principle, to wit, that a law of a state contrary to the articles of the union would, if not negatived, be valid and operative."

By a seven-to-three vote, the convention rejected any congressional veto of state laws. Surprisingly however, it was Luther Martin who immediately offered a substitute to make concrete what had merely been Sherman and Morris's supposition that the courts would give precedence to national law over conflicting state laws. Martin moved that national laws and treaties "shall be the supreme law of the respective states . . . and that the judiciaries of the several states shall be bound thereby in their decisions, anything in the respective laws of the individual states to the contrary notwithstanding." The convention agreed unanimously with this approach.

Madison probably felt a trace of amusement in spite of losing the direct veto. Martin's new-found magnanimity toward the national government carefully skirted the potential that the *constitutions* of the states—not just their respective laws—might run contrary to national laws. But that kind of omission might be (and, in fact, was) rectified quietly in the actual drafting of a Constitution that was soon to come.

EXECUTIVE MERRY-GO-ROUND

Defining the national executive set spinning a merry-go-round of confusion and doubt. In fact, after four full days of debate,

Gerry urged his colleagues to let the drafting committee handle it because "We seem to be entirely at a loss." To their credit, the delegates declined to shirk the job, and stuck with it for another two days, making and unmaking decisions before ending up precisely where they had started—with a seven-year, unre-electable executive appointed by the national legislature and impeachable by a still undesignated authority.

In small ways, both North-South differences and large state-small state conflict impinged on the debate, but by far the biggest issues dogging it were the twin fears of laying the groundwork for a monarchy and of retreating from republicanism by curbing the people's representatives in the legislature. At the time of the Revolution, all the states, avoiding both offenses, had created notoriously weak executives that everyone knew were tyrannized by the legislatures. Yet the urge to risk the same outcome was almost as powerful as the delegates' appreciation of a balanced government. It was a bind that ultimately would take the convention some sixty votes to sort out. Nor was their timidity baseless. Just as they started debating the executive, rumors began circulating outside the convention that "it is intended to establish a monarchical government, to send for the Bishop of Osnaburg, etc." (the prince of Orange and nephew of George III) to launch an American monarchy. So persistent did the story become, that, late in August, the convention found it necessary to issue a denial saying, "though we cannot affirmatively tell you what we are doing, we can negatively tell you what we are not doing—we never once thought of a king."

The executive merry-go-round developed from the convention's discovery that Resolution Nine—defining the executive—could not be debated in fragments as the others had been, since each clause altered the executive relative to the national legislature. From one moment to the next, the executive was either dangerously subordinate to the legislature or dangerously beyond its reach, as round and round the argument went.

Gouverneur Morris, aristocrat, showed himself a champion of the people, opposing election of the executive by the national legislature. "He will be the mere creature of the Legislature," Morris warned. "He ought to be elected by the people at large . . . If the people should elect, they will never fail to prefer some man of distinguished character or services, some man . . . of continental reputation. If the legislature elect, it will be the work of intrigue, of cabal and of faction. It will be like the election of a pope by a conclave of cardinals."

A quick embrace between Connecticut and South Carolina was the reply. Sherman objected, with Charles Pinckney echoing him, that the people "will never give a majority of votes to any one man. They will generally vote for some man in their own state and the largest state will have the best chance for appointment."

While calling Morris inconsistent, George Mason seemed inconsistent. In spite of having earlier criticized Sherman for trying to subordinate the executive to the legislature, Mason now thought "it would be as unnatural to refer the choice of a proper character for chief magistrate to the people as it would to refer a trial of colors to a blind man. The extent of the country renders it impossible that the people can have the requisite capacity to judge" the candidates.

On a motion that the executive be eligible for re-election, Sherman seconded and Morris praised it. Restriction to a single term, Morris said, "tended to destroy the great motive to good behavior—the hope of being rewarded by a re-appointment. It was saying to him, 'make hay while the sun shines.' "

Re-eligibility approved, a little game started. Broome of Delaware swept off in the wrong direction by moving to shorten the seven-year term of office, but Dr. James McClurg of Virginia, who had been silent throughout the convention, came to his feet.

"Strike out seven years and insert 'during good behavior,' " McClurg said. Having the executive eligible for re-election "would keep him dependent forever on the legislature" when his independence was as essential as that of the judiciary.

Madison, who favored a nonrenewable seven-year term, speculated in a coy footnote that "the probable object of this motion was merely to enforce the argument against re-eligibility" by raising the specter of a monarch. In fact, Madison most likely schemed with McClurg to offer the alternative, which he himself had raised many weeks ago when the question was before the Committee of the Whole. In any case, McClurg was poking a hornet's nest that not even Gouverneur Morris had wanted to be first to stir up.

In ecstasy, Morris seconded McClurg. The motion gave him "great pleasure . . . This was the way to get a good government." His previous fear that "so valuable an ingredient would not be attained" had led him to suggest popular election, but he was "indifferent how the executive should be chosen, provided he held his place by this tenure."

Aha! Broome suddenly caught on and "highly approved the motion. It obviated all his difficulties."

You can almost see the glint in Sherman's eye while he watched those performances. Lifetime tenure, he said menacingly, was "by no means safe or admissible. As the Executive magistrate is now re-eligible, he will be on good behavior as far as will be necessary. If he behaves well, he will be continued; if otherwise, displaced, on a succeeding election."

Madison thought it best to extricate McClurg—or, as he put it, "to aid in parrying the animadversions likely to fall on the motion of Dr. McClurg, for whom J.M. had a particular regard. The doctor, though possessing talents of the highest order, was modest and unaccustomed to exert them in public debate."

Accordingly, Madison played his part with a little sermon suggesting that they could design impeachment to assure executive and judiciary independence, and urged that McClurg's motion receive "a fair hearing and discussion until a less objectionable expedient should be applied for guarding against a dangerous union of the legislative and executive departments."

George Mason took him seriously. Impeachment was no balance for a dangerous proposal, he said. "It would be impossible to define the misbehavior in such a manner as to subject it to a proper trial and perhaps still more impossible to compel so high an offender . . . to submit to a trial." An executive during good behavior was "a softer name only for an executive for life . . . an easy step to hereditary monarchy."

Madison retorted with marked impatience. The American experience so far revealed "a tendency in our governments to throw all power into the legislative vortex. The executives of the states are in general little more than ciphers, the legislatures omnipotent." If the convention did not devise an effective check, "a revolution of some kind or other would be inevitable."

Yes, Morris added, declaring himself "as little a friend to monarchy as any gentleman . . . the way to keep out monarchical government was to establish such a republican government as would make the people happy and prevent a desire of change."

McClurg, apparently enjoying his assignment, pitched in anew. He was "not so much afraid of the shadow of monarchy as to be unwilling to approach it, nor so wedded to republican government as not to be sensible of the tyrannies that had been and may be exercised under that form." It was crucial to make the executive independent and the only mode left for effecting it, after the vote permitting his re-election, was to appoint him during good behavior.

A one-day postponement to think things over gave Gouverneur Morris the chance to do what he did best, wooden leg and all: circulate. As he said later, "some gentlemen, I was told, passed their evenings in transcribing speeches from shorthand minutes of the day . . . My faculties were on the stretch to further our business, remove impediments, obviate objections and conciliate jarring opinions." His conversations told him that the crux of the problem was that his colleagues felt more fear than conviction on the subject of the executive. The little game they had played with McClurg's lifetime-tenure motion had been inadequate, if not stupid. The convention, he realized, was heading down the road to a dangerously weak executive when the whole future of the union might depend on a well-fortified one.

"It is necessary," Morris urged as soon as the debate resumed, "to take into one view all that relates to the establishment of the executive . . . It has been a maxim in political science that republican government is not adapted to a large extent of country, because the energy of the executive magistracy cannot reach the extreme parts of it. We must either then renounce the blessings of the Union, or provide an executive with sufficient vigor to pervade every part of it."

The subject was so important, he added, that he hoped they would indulge his taking "an extensive view of it"—which he did, in one of his most dextrous speeches of the convention.

"One great object of the Executive is to control the legislature," Morris said, which would "continually seek to aggrandize and perpetuate themselves and will seize those critical moments produced by war, invasion or convulsion for that purpose." That required the executive to be the "guardian of the people, even of the lower classes, against legislative tyranny" and against the wealthy who Morris expected would "in the course of things" take over the legislature.

"Wealth tends to corrupt the mind and to nourish its love of power and to stimulate it to oppression," Morris said. "History proves this to be the spirit of the opulent." The check provided by the Senate was not a check on "legislative usurpations of power, but on the abuse of lawful powers . . . It is no check on legislative tyranny." The second branch might "seduce" the first, leaving only the executive to serve as "the great protector of the mass of the people."

On Morris raced, through the argument for executive appointment of government officers down to the question of barring his re-election. Not only would it destroy the incentive for the executive to exert himself, but "it may give a dangerous turn to one of the strongest passions in the human breast—the love of fame is the great spring to noble and illustrious actions. Shut the civil road to glory and he may be compelled to seek it by the sword. It will tempt him to make the most of the short space of time allotted him to accumulate wealth and provide for his friends. It will produce violations of the very constitution it is meant to secure."*

*Since passage in 1951 of the Twenty-second Amendment limiting the president to two terms, four presidents—Truman, Eisenhower, Nixon, and Reagan—have served under an ineligibility for reelection. Two (Nixon and Reagan) saw their second terms ruined by scandals in which the need to make the most of the second term was a factor, making Morris perhaps half-right.

Impeachability was a counterproductive deterrent: the executive might be too deferential to the legislature or become the tool of "some leading demagogue in the legislature."

Those were the flaws of the executive as now proposed. "Can no better establishment be devised?" Morris urged. "If he is to be the guardian of the people, let him be appointed by the people. If he is to be a check on the legislature, let him not be impeachable. Let him be of short duration, that he may, with propriety, be re-eligible."

If the legislature could know who the best candidates were, Morris said, then they would have "such a notoriety and eminence of character that they cannot possibly be unknown to the people at large." Would an unimpeachable magistrate be dangerous? All his officers would be impeachable; "without these ministers, the executive can do nothing of consequence." Would the legislators try to influence or subvert re-election? "If the administration of the executive were good, it would be unpopular to oppose his reelection; if bad, it ought to be opposed and a reappointment prevented. And lastly . . . this indirect dependence on the favor of the legislature could not be so mischievous as a direct dependence for his appointment."

When several more delegates confessed second thoughts in favor of popular election, Wilson, the first to call for it, crowed a little that he "perceived with pleasure that the idea was gaining ground."

Even Madison admitted he might be changing his mind. He was leaning toward popular election, but, he observed shrewdly, "the right of suffrage was much more diffusive in the northern than the southern states and the latter could have no influence in the election on the score of the Negroes." Substituting electors, Madison thought, might redress the difference.

Consistent to the core, Gerry dragged out his "few designing men" who would mislead the uninformed people. Anything but popular election, Gerry groaned; it "would certainly be the worst of all. If he should be so elected and should do his duty, he will be turned out for it" like the governors of Massachusetts and New Hampshire had been after putting down rebellions.

THE MYSTERY OF THE IMPEACHMENT CLAUSE

"Corruption and some few other offences ought to be impeachable," admitted Gouverneur Morris, who had been opposing impeachment, "but . . . the cases ought to be enumerated and defined."

To this, congressional investigators of President Nixon and Watergate in the early 1970s probably shouted a loud "Amen" when they read it while rummaging the convention debates. But the Framers did not enumerate and define impeachable offences, and they left a real mystery as to their intentions when they decided to make the executive removable by impeachment.

Interestingly, however, those delegates who entered the debate seemed to expect the question to arise often and to be as applicable to political wrongdoing as to actual criminality. Madison gave it the broadest basis of all, saying it was "indispensable that some provision should be made for defending the community against the incapacity, negligence or perfidy of the chief magistrate. The limitation of the period of his service was not sufficient security. He might lose his capacity after his appointment. He might pervert his administration into a scheme of peculation or oppression. He might betray his trust to foreign powers." Had Madison's idea of reasons for removing a chief executive found their way explicitly into the Constitution, practically every president, from George Washington (who Jefferson hinted was "impaired by age" in his second term) to Ronald Reagan would have been subjected to an impeachment attempt from one quarter or another.

Charles Pinckney and Gouverneur Morris moved to strike out the reference to impeachment in the first place, Pinckney saying flatly "he ought not to be impeachable whilst in office."

If he is not, William Davie replied, "he will spare no effort or means whatever to get himself re-elected." Impeachment was "an essential security for the good behavior of the Executive."

"He can do no criminal act without coadjutors who may be

punished," Morris argued. "In case he should be re-elected, that will be sufficient proof of his innocence."

"No point is of more importance than that the right of impeachment should be continued," declared Mason. "Shall any man be above Justice?" When "great crimes" were committed, Mason said, "the principal as well as the coadjutors" should be punished. By then, the convention had opted for choosing the executive through "electors," who, Mason said, posed "the danger of their being corrupted by the candidates . . . a peculiar reason in favor of impeachments whilst in office. Shall the man who has practised corruption and, by that means, procured his appointment in the first instance be suffered to escape punishment?"

"What was the practice before this in cases where the chief magistrate rendered himself obnoxious?" Benjamin Franklin asked. "Why, recourse was had to assassination in which he was not only deprived of his life, but of the opportunity of vindicating his character. It would be the best way, therefore, to provide in the Constitution for the regular punishment of the executive where his misconduct should deserve it and for his honorable acquittal when he should be unjustly accused."

Morris wavered: corruption *was* a reason to impeach. But Pinckney was unmoved. Impeachments, he said with certainty, "ought not to issue from the legislature who would in that case hold them as a rod over the executive and . . . effectually destroy his independence.

"A good magistrate will not fear them; a bad one ought to be kept in fear of them," Gerry said, endorsing impeachments, adding that he hoped "the maxim would never be adopted here that the chief magistrate could do no wrong."

King "wished the House to recur to the primitive axiom that the three great departments of governments should be separate and independent." Judges' tenure was for life, so impeachments were needed, but the executive "would periodically be tried for his behavior by his electors, who would continue or discontinue him in trust according to the manner in which he had discharged it . . . therefore, he ought to be subject to no intermediate trial by impeachment."

"The propriety of impeachments," Randolph said almost insouciantly, was "a favorite principle" with him. "Guilt, wherever found, ought to be punished. The executive will have great opportunities of abusing his power, particularly in time of war when the military force and, in some respects the public money, will be in his hands. Should no regular punishment be provided, it will be *irregularly* inflicted—by tumults and insurrections."

The arguments had changed his mind, Gouverneur Morris announced. The executive ought "to be impeachable for treachery. Corrupting his electors and incapacity," he added, were "other causes," but for them, "he should be punished not as a man, but as an officer, and punished only by degradation from his office. This magistrate is not the King, but the prime minister. The people are the King. When we make him amenable to justice, however, we should take care to provide some mode that will not make him dependent on the legislature."

The convention voted to retain the line providing virtual *carte blanche* on attempts to remove the executive by "impeachment and conviction of malpractice or neglect of duty" and did not debate the subject again until the words had been greatly changed. In fact, the important decision to strip the wording of its political temptations was reached mostly behind closed doors.

First, the Committee on Detail's draft constitution emerged providing for impeachment and conviction "of treason, bribery or corruption." (In one of two existing committee documents that contain this line, the change is in Rutledge's handwriting, but the idea could have been somebody else's.) There was no floor debate on the clause, until after a subsequent committee, the "Committee on Remaining Matters," deleted "corruption."

On the convention floor, then, George Mason complained vociferously that treason and bribery alone were too narrow. He moved to add "or maladministration," but changed it to "other high crimes and misdemeanors against the State" after Madison and Morris objected on political grounds. The convention approved the second wording and also unanimously refined it by changing "the State" to the "United States." The

"Committee on Style and Arrangement" deleted the words "against the United States," but left no clue as to whether it was thought redundant to "high crimes and misdemeanors" or intended to enlarge the possible reasons for impeachment.

THE MERRY-GO-ROUND STOPS

The four days given to debating the executive brought the convention to the point where the executive would serve for six years instead of seven and be eligible for re-election. He would be chosen by twenty-five electors, allocated according to state size and named by the state legislatures. He would be removable by impeachment, but who could impeach him was still undecided.

Everything, it seemed on Monday, July 23, was settled about the executive, and the convention moved along to the remaining resolutions on ratifying and amending the constitution. But, just before the close of business, came another call for a review of the mode of electing the executive because of "the extreme inconveniency and the considerable expense" of bringing the twenty-five electors together for a single purpose. And the merry-go-round started up again, with all the executive clauses re-debated as if for the first time.

The electoral approach they had created was too "complicated" and might put the choice into the hands of second-rate men. Hugh Williamson of North Carolina had especially severe problems with the whole composition of the executive: The best electors, he thought, would have gone into the Senate or lower house; a three-man executive would be better able to deal with regional differences; and "a single magistrate . . . will be an elective King and will feel the spirit of one. He will spare no pains to keep himself in for life and will then lay a train for the succession of his children." Williamson was "pretty certain" that eventually we would have a king, but he wished to delay it as long as possible.

Gerry thought the executive could also be made more independent by lengthening his term of office. A good idea, several delegates agreed—but for how long? Eleven years, said one; fifteen, said another; eight, said a third. "Twenty," Rufus King mocked them. "That is the medium life of princes."

The longest term, Wilson griped, would not equal a proper form of election. They were assuming that, at a certain time of life, the executive and the public would no longer want the executive to continue in office. But experience showed otherwise: the doge of Venice was elected after he was eighty years old, and Catholic popes "have generally been elected at very advanced periods, and yet, in no case, had a more steady or a better concerted policy been pursued than in the Court of Rome." What if the executive takes office at age thirty-five to serve a fixed fifteen-year term? "At the age of fifty, in the very prime of life and with all the aid of experience, he must be cast aside like a useless hulk."

They even debated seriously a motion from Wilson that a group of not more than fifteen national legislators be chosen by lottery and locked up together until they named an executive. At least the executive's dependence "would be diminished."

"We ought to be governed by reason, not by chance," King objected. Wilson gave a verbal shrug. He had not said lottery was the best way; he himself was still "unshaken that we ought to resort to the people for the election."

Madison's change of heart was now complete: "With all its imperfections," he liked election by the people at large. The convention, however, shied away from joining him and toyed with a half-dozen other ideas.

Charles Pinckney offered up a kind of rotation—that the executive be eligible for no more than six years in any twelve— but Morris said rotation "formed a political school in which we were always governed by the scholars, and not by the masters." Rotation would not make the executive independent either; he still would look forward to reappointment, even if he was un- likely to live that long. "Such is the nature of man . . . that although he knows his existence to be limited to a span, he takes his measures as if he were to live forever," Morris argued.

Williamson thought the lurking problem with popular elec- tion was "the disadvantage under which it would put the smaller states." He proposed that each voter choose three candidates, two of whom would have to be from states other than the voter's own. Good, said Morris, but make that just two candidates—with one from another state.

"Radically vicious," cried Gerry, who finally gave a name to the designing men he feared: the Order of the Cincinnati. "They will, in fact, elect the chief Magistrate in every instance, if the election be referred to the people." Belatedly, he absolved the president of the Cincinnati, George Washington: Gerry's respect for the characters composing this society could not "blind" him to the "danger and impropriety of throwing such a power into their hands."

George Mason and Benjamin Franklin thought re-election was wrong in the first place. The "polestar" of political conduct, the preservation of the rights of people, Mason declared passionately, made it essential "as the very palladium of civil liberty, that the great officers of state, and particularly the executive, should, at fixed periods, return to that mass from which they were at first taken, in order that they may feel and respect those rights and interests."

Surrendering office to become a private citizen again, Franklin said, "seems to have been imagined by some . . . degrading to the magistrate." This was "contrary to republican principles. In free governments, the rulers are the servants, and the people their superiors and sovereigns." For rulers to return among the people, therefore, "was not to *degrade* but to *promote*" them. In fact, Franklin said, re-election "would be imposing an unreasonable burden . . . to keep them always in a state of servitude and not allow them to become again one of the masters."

Gouverneur Morris could be acid when he thought he was hearing rubbish, and he was now: "On the same principle, the judiciary ought to be periodically degraded," and so should lawmakers, "yet no one had proposed or conceived" that they be barred from re-election. Addressing Franklin by name, Morris had "no doubt that our Executive, like most others, would have too much patriotism to shrink from the burden of his office and too much modesty not to be willing to decline the promotion."

At long last, the merry-go-round ground to a halt where it had begun—at a seven-year executive appointed by the national legislature and ineligible for reappointment.

ZIPPING ALONG

During the one-day interruption in the executive debate, the delegates had polished off seven resolutions: the two-thirds override of the executive veto was reaffirmed, as were the clauses creating a supreme court, life tenure for the justices, and establishing that they would be paid salaries that could be increased but not reduced during their service. The supreme judiciary's jurisdiction was approved along with granting Congress the power to create lower courts if needed. They rejected executive appointment of the justices, but postponed a decision on any other method of appointing them.

Resolution Fifteen, which would have kept the Continental Congress alive until a specific date and guaranteed fulfillment of its obligations, was rejected in order to remove any barrier to starting up the new government as soon as enough states had approved—although Wilson worried that failing to mention the existing obligations would raise fears that lawful contracts with the confederation might be dissolved.

Resolution Sixteen, "That a republican constitution and its existing laws ought to be guaranteed to each state by the United States," drew complaints, beginning with Morris who called it "very objectionable" and declared himself "very unwilling that such laws as exist in Rhode Island should be guaranteed."

Wilson, Mason, and Randolph chided him. The resolution was intended to protect the states against insurrections and rebellions, Wilson said. Rebellions against the national government, Mason added, would start in and against individual states. The general government "will be in a bad situation indeed . . . [if] it must remain a passive spectator of its own subversion."

Maybe, Madison suggested, the wording should be "that the constitutional authority of the states shall be guaranteed to them respectively against domestic as well as foreign violence."

No. The constitution of Georgia was "a very bad one," said William Houstoun of that state; he was against anything that could prevent its being revised. No, said Luther Martin, the states should be left to suppress rebellions themselves. No, said Rutledge, Congress could cooperate with any state in subduing a rebellion.

"As a better expression of the idea," Wilson suggested new wording: "that a republican form of government shall be guaranteed to each state and that each state shall be protected against foreign and domestic violence," which passed unanimously.

WHO SHALL RATIFY?

Haunted by the rising question of the states, the Committee of the Whole had approved popular ratification of the Constitution with only brief debate. The time had now come for confirming that decision—and, as it turned out, a chance to see how far they really had travelled from their first nervous vote to overturn the old Confederation.

No one had forgotten that Paterson had introduced the New Jersey plan and Ellsworth had led the effort to install it piecemeal after its rejection. Accordingly, the nationalists were heads-up when the formidable duo joined again to lead the charge on behalf of the states—Ellsworth moving, and Paterson seconding, that the Constitution be referred to the state legislatures for ratification.

Taking a highly legalistic tack, Mason replied first. As far as he knew, none of the state constitutions provided this power to their legislatures, so the national Constitution must be approved by the people "with whom all power remains that has not been given up." Further, the act of one legislature could be repealed by a later legislature, so "the national government would stand in each state on the weak and tottering foundation of an Act of Assembly." Finally, some state governments' very legitimacy was in doubt, and, therefore, their approval of the Constitution would be disputed.

Randolph, who had been almost silent since early in the

convention deadlock, spoke up strongly for ratifying conventions. "Local demagogues who will be degraded by it . . . will
spare no efforts" to defeat it in the legislatures, he predicted.
Moreover, Randolph pointed out, in some states common law
had been ruled to take precedence over the Confederation,
which rested merely on the approval of legislatures.

"The arguments of Colonel Mason and Mr. Randolph prove
too much," Gerry said smartly. "They prove an unconstitution-
ality in the present federal system . . . Both the state governments and the federal government have been too long acquiesced in to be now shaken." They were obliged to follow
the amendment form spelled out in the Articles of Confederation—and seek ratification from the state legislatures. Anyway,
Gerry was sure (naturally) that "great confusion . . . would
result from a recurrence to the people. They would never agree
on anything."

Did Gorham throw his fellow Massachusettsan a glance of
exasperation as he rose? "Men chosen by the people for the
particular purpose," Gorham declared, "will discuss the subject
more candidly than members of the legislature who are to lose
the power which is to be given up to the general government."
He had four other arguments: Some legislatures had "several"
branches which would make it harder to get the plan through
them than through a convention. Some states excluded from
their legislatures able men, including "many of the clergy who
are generally friends to good government," who could be
elected to a convention, and the legislatures would be interrupted by other business, especially diversions dreamed up by
opponents of the constitution. Finally, if the Articles of Confederation were followed, all thirteen states would have to approve. "But will anyone say that all the states are to suffer
themselves to be ruined if Rhode Island should persist in her
opposition to general measures?" He expected New York to
oppose the constitution too: "The present advantage which
New York seems to be so much attached to —of taxing her
neighbors by the regulation of her trade—makes it very probable that she will be of the number" refusing to ratify.

Conventions, Ellsworth said stubbornly, were "a new set of

ideas [that] seemed to have crept in . . . The legislatures were considered as competent. Their ratification [of changes in the Articles of Confederation] has been acquiesced in without complaint . . . The fact is that we exist at present, and we need not enquire how, as a federal society." If the "urgency and necessity of our situation" was so great, he added, the Articles' requirement for unanimity could be safely overlooked.

"A non sequitur," Morris pounced. "If the confederation is to be pursued, no alteration can be made without the unanimous consent of the legislatures. Legislative alterations not conformable to the federal compact would clearly not be valid; the judges would consider them as null and void." But all that was irrelevant: "The amendment moved by Mr. Ellsworth erroneously supposes that we are proceeding on the basis of the Confederation. This convention is unknown to the confederation."

Mildly, Rufus King agreed with Ellsworth. "The legislatures had a competent authority—the acquiescence of the people of America in the confederation being equivalent to a formal ratification by the people." Still, he preferred popularly elected ratifying conventions "as the most certain means of obviating all disputes and doubts concerning the legitimacy of the new Constitution, as well as the most likely means of drawing forth the best men in the states to decide on it."

As he had learned to do when a flammable debate occurred, Madison had kept silent until he had a good idea of its range. Now he rose. He also doubted the legal authority of the legislatures, he said. But more important: "the difference between a system founded on the legislatures only and one founded on the people [was] the true difference between a *league* or *treaty,* and a *Constitution.*

"The former," he said, "in point of *moral obligation* might be as inviolable as the latter; in point of *political operation,* there were two important distinctions in favor of the latter." First, judges might uphold future state laws violating the "treaty," but "a law violating a constitution established by the people themselves would be considered by the judges as null and void." Second, under the Law of Nations, breach of a treaty by one party frees all the other parties from their obligations under it. "In the case of a union of people under one Constitution, the nature of the pact has always been understood to exclude such an interpretation."

The Ellsworth-Paterson motion was defeated; approved by a nine-to-one vote was "to refer the Constitution, after the appro-bation of Congress, to assemblies chosen by the people." No one seemed to notice, just then, that they had failed to debate the phrase, "after the approbation of Congress."

Screen Out Undesirables?

Apropos of no resolution, Mason urged that the Committee of Detail, soon to begin patching all the decisions into a prelimi-nary constitution, be given a clause "requiring certain qualifica-tions of landed property and citizenship of the United States in members of the Legislature, and disqualifying persons having unsettled accounts with, or being indebted to the U.S., from being members of the national legislature."

"If qualifications are proper," Morris protested, they should be "in the electors rather than the elected." Not many men owed the union money, but quite a few were owed something. "Such a discrimination would be both odious and useless, and, in many instances, unjust and cruel . . . What will be done with those patriotic citizens who have lent money or services or property to their country, without having been yet able to obtain a liquidation of their claims? Are they to be excluded?"

Madison commented that he had seen men with business connections to the state governments "get into the legislatures for sinister purposes." But he thought "it might be well to limit the exclusion to persons who had received money from the public and not accounted for it."

"A precept of great antiquity as well as high authority," Morris insisted, was "that we should not be righteous over-much . . . we ought to be equally on our guard against being wise overmuch." Washington himself could have been victi-mized by such a provision. The commander in chief's bill for secret services "was so moderate that everyone was astonished at it, and so simple that no doubt could arise on it. Yet had the auditor been disposed to delay the settlement, how easily might he have effected it, and how cruel would it be in such a case to keep a distinguished and meritorious citizen under a temporary disability and disfranchisement."

It was a telling example, however embarrassing it might have been to Washington listening from the chair, and it put their feet back on the ground: Gerry, King and Dickinson all weighed in with Morris.

After a series of votes picked apart Mason's motion, Wilson rose. "We should consider that we are providing a constitution for future generations, and not merely for the peculiar circumstances of the moment. The time has been, and will again be, when the public safety may depend on the voluntary aids of individuals." Those people would then do business with the government and it would "be a characteristic of patriotism."

Gerry saw the convention drifting toward ruling out any exclusions and tried to stop it: "We might have a legislature composed of public debtors, pensioners, placemen* and contractors . . . the proposed qualifications would be pleasing to the people. They will be considered as a security against unnecessary or undue burdens being imposed on them." In fact, Gerry formally moved to disqualify pensioners from holding office, but the convention voted his motion down.

Morris had another example close at hand: excluding public debtors "will exclude every importing merchant" because importers henceforth would be liable for the import duties on foreign merchandise. He did not have to add that such people as John Hancock and Robert Morris would be sacrificed, as well as up to ten members of this convention.

Ellsworth delivered the crowning blow to Mason's attempt to impose financial qualifications for holding office: Leave "the wisdom of the legislature and the virtue of the citizens the task of providing against such evils," Ellsworth said. "Is the smallest as well as the largest debtor to be excluded? Then every arrear

---

*A contemporary pejorative, similar to "bureaucrat" today.

of taxes will disqualify. Besides, how is it to be known to the people when they elect who are or are not public debtors?"

Time has tested this debate, including Wilson's remarks on a future crisis when it would be hard to distinguish between the profiteer and the patriot doing business with the government. That was a factor in the Civil War and both world wars, though by the Second World War, the American government was vigorous enough to scruple over shady deals without endangering its ability to make war at all. By leaving refinements to successive generations of lawmakers, instead of imbedding them in the Constitution, the convention allowed ethics to evolve along with the government. And officeholders today are as rigidly controlled as Mason could have wished—by conflict-of-interest and disclosure laws, rather than by the Constitution itself.

Now the proceedings, Madison says, "were referred unanimously to the Committee of Detail and the Convention then unanimously adjourned till Monday, August 6, that the Committee of Detail might have time to prepare and report the Constitution."

A MUCH-NEEDED BREAK

The three dozen men strolling out of the State House on the cool, damp Thursday afternoon of July 26 knew that at least another month of close, demanding work lay ahead. The hardest part, though, was done. It had taken exactly two months, but the main supports for the framework were in place. For the next ten days, all—except the five delegates comprising the Committee of Detail—could scatter.

Some went home if they lived near; others headed for New York to rejoin Congress or wives who had fled before Philadelphia's mid-July heat wave had broken. With South Carolina's interests well-tended by the presence of John Rutledge on the Committee of Detail, General Pinckney promptly obtained a list of the best inns on the road to the famous Moravian community of Bethlehem, Pennsylvania, and set out with his wife to visit there. But some delegates, like Georgia's Abraham

Baldwin, stayed close for fear of leaving their states unrepresented while the committee was working, and a few merely lingered to enjoy the unexpectedly pleasant weather and the city's cosmopolitan pleasures.

For Washington the cosmopolitan pleasures were just about exhausted. He had been to the theater three times in the last two weeks and to several "concerts" before then, attended the Catholic, Episcopal, and Calvinist churches, sat three times for two portrait painters, reviewed the city's light horse and militia, and visited the local botanical gardens and museums. He had dined or drunk tea with Elizabeth Powel at least eight times since the convention began, supped with a half-dozen formal societies and informal dinner clubs at different taverns in Philadelphia, and visited for dinner, tea or "entertainments" no fewer than twenty-four other private homes, many of them twice. In fact, four out of every five days in Philadelphia he had spent all his free time socializing and enjoying what the city had to offer. He was ready for some rural excursions and did not hide his good spirits in the note he dashed off to Eliza.

"General Washington presents his respectful compliments to Mrs. Powel and would, with great pleasure, have made one of a party for the *School For Scandal* this evening, had not everything been arranged and Mr. Gouverneur Morris and himself on the point of stepping into the carriage for a fishing expedition . . . The General," he twitted her cheerily, "can but regret that matters have turned out so unluckily, after waiting so long to receive a lesson in the School for Scandal."

Washington and Eliza Powel shared an easy affection that has always charmed and enticed the first president's biographers. Mrs. Powel flirted with Washington unceasingly and he with her, and despite every effort curious historians have made to learn otherwise, their banter was innocent. An undercurrent of knowingness in their exchanges leaves an impression, almost piquant, of dignified lust—by agreement, never to be satisfied. But the friendship they shared looks to the prying eye more rare and valuable than any seeming sensuality—for Mrs. Powel was, above all, Washington's closest political confidant.

On the day of Washington's final speech to Congress in 1796,

Eliza would send a servant to the President's house, with a stomach remedy concocted of rum. "I think it would not be amiss if my good friend the President will take a glass on his return from the Congress," her note to Martha said. "I know his sensibility, diffidence and delicacy too well not to believe that his spirits will be not a little agitated on the solemn—and, I fear, last—occasion that he will take of addressing his fellow citizens."

The wife of Philadelphia's mayor, Samuel Powel, who had first welcomed Washington to their home in 1778, Eliza did know Washington's feelings, perhaps even as well as Martha did. When Washington decided to end his presidency at the close of his first term in 1792, Eliza would write him in words his other confidants would not have dreamed of using. Boldly pointing to his popularity (which it was his duty to ignore), she predicted that if he quit, his reputation would be "torn from you by the envious and malignant" who would whisper that "ambition has been the moving spring of all your acts." Washington's biographers firmly believe that her letter alone changed his mind.

The Powels occupied one of three mansions in the Willing family compound between Third and Fourth streets, four blocks from the State House where the convention sat. The rooms were done in mahogany woodwork, decorated with Irish cut glass chandeliers and Chinese wallpaper with painted scenes, an elegant and comfortable setting to which Eliza drew Washington during the desperate days of the constitutional convention.

That summer of 1787, Eliza Willing Powel was forty-five years old, and still called "beautiful." She was neurotic—gay and melancholy by turns—and the one person, male or female, who took verbal liberties with Washington. She goaded him about his chastity; she sassed him in her notes of invitations; she was excitable and melodramatic, but he relished her company. And he liked her this way despite evidence that she was a bit overwhelming to his contemporaries.

The French memoirist, the Marquis de Chastellux, visited her in 1782 and later wrote, "she talks a great deal; she honored

me with her friendship and found me very meritorious because
I meritoriously listened to her."

And in 1799, a dashing (and hardhearted) young Federalist,
Harrison Gray Otis, dined at her home a few days after Eliza
had received word of Washington's death. "The Dowager," he
wrote to his wife about his hostess, "is really afflicted at the
death of her old friend the General, but she thinks it necessary
to appear more so than she is in fact, and that she is called upon
in decency to shed tears whenever his name is mentioned. She
made out very well at first, but Mr. Hare with a maladroit
perseverance would talk of nothing else, so that before the cloth
was removed, the old Lady's stock of briny element being fairly
exhausted, she could only look piteous and at length begged a
truce of all conversation on the subject, which being granted,
she munched her pies with an air of consolation that was truly
edifying."

Undoubtedly some members of the convention attended the
play that Elizabeth was forming a party to see on the day that
Washington left to go fishing.

Because of the Quaker City's sumptuary law, R.B. Sheridan's
School for Scandal (performed for the first time in America only
three years before) was disguised in newspaper advertisements
as "A Comic Lecture in Five Parts on the Pernicious Vice of
Scandal." James Townley's *High Life Below the Stairs,* which
Washington had seen July 10, had been billed as a "concert"
entitled "The Servants Hall in an Uproar." *Hamlet* was "a
Moral and Instructive Tale as Exemplified in the History of the
Prince of Denmark." And the theater where the American
Company, the season's hottest troupe, was putting on the performances was euphemistically called the "opera house." De-
spite the fact that they were seldom respected, sumptuary laws
rested on the premise that individual conduct directly affected
the public welfare. And when the convention resumed, George
Mason would move, without success, to put such laws in the
Constitution, too.

Cerebral leisure was available to the delegates willing to
climb the two flights of stairs at Carpenters Hall to visit the

Library Company, a private subscription library founded more than fifty years earlier by Benjamin Franklin. Its directors had voted earlier in the month to offer the delegates free use of its books. Probably numerous delegates took advantage of the invitation, but a record of only two is left—because both men lost the books they borrowed, blamed the loss on their servants, and paid for replacements.

Rufus King checked out a sort of social history of France, *Letters to a Young Gentleman on his Setting out For France,* by John Andrews, and a travel book, John Henry Groce's *Voyage to the East Indies.* Luther Martin borrowed Sir William Jones's *Poems, consisting chiefly of translations from Asiatick Languages,* mostly sentimental poems such as "A Turkish Ode of Meshihi":

> *The smiling season decks each flowery glade*
> *Be gay: too soon the flowers of spring will fade*

In their fascinating "Daybook" of 1787, horrified scholars of the U.S. Park Service in Philadelphia, discovering what King and Martin had borrowed, wrote with a cry of pain "they are worse than irrelevant; they are, two of them at least, junk!"

Another popular spot was Charles Willson Peale's museum, "a Repository of Natural Curiosities" with a one-shilling admission fee. On display were the teeth of a mammoth discovered in Kentucky, stuffed exotic birds, animals and reptiles in habitat groups, a rattlesnake's fangs mounted under a magnifying glass, lifelike wax figures, Indian scalps, and a pair of shoes, four inches long, made in China for bound feet. Peale's collection was almost too popular: he had just had to order glass cases with sloping shelves because "I found that all small articles, especially those that are delicate, must be kept under glass to prevent the abuse of fingering."

For other delegates staying on, the recess was a shopping opportunity. Philadelphia's stores featured goods from all over the world; one merchant, Joseph Stansbury, possibly thinking of convention members, had advertised that "country orders" (out-of-town shipments) would be "carefully packed and executed at the shortest notice." Stansbury had just imported, among other things, "complete tea table sets of enameled china richly ornamented, Egyptian or black china teapots, sugar dishers and cream ewers; cut glass candelsticks, salts, mustard-pots, cruets, decanters and wine glasses, and cut tumblers of several sizes."

Shopping, however, was a good option only for those who had hard money. Paper money had "ceased to circulate very suddenly" in mid-July, Madison reported to Jefferson, because of a conspiracy of merchants not to accept it from "country people" on market days. Civic leaders had prevented a riot and got the conspirators to advertise that they would accept it. The depreciated paper had started circulating again, but sluggishly.

Remaining in Philadelphia himself, Madison was mulling a dilemma: the Virginia delegation was pretty clearly split. He, Washington, and McClurg were voting solidly nationalist, but more and more, Randolph, Mason, and Blair had been going their own separate ways. The trouble was that McClurg, who could be counted upon, had fled back to Richmond shortly after playing his intrepid part ten days earlier.

Madison decided to write McClurg to come back, but while feeling "anxiety about the result," McClurg refused: "If I thought that my return could contribute in the smallest degree . . . nothing should keep me away." The other delegates were good men and "my vote could only operate to produce a division and so destroy the vote of the state. I think that my attendance now would certainly be useless, perhaps injurious." As Madison said, McClurg was a novice; Madison knew that some votes were better divided than counted against the nationalist side.

With changeable Edmund Randolph on the Committee of Detail, Madison most likely did not wander far from the scene. The son of a planter, he did make time to round up for his father a report on Pennsylvania's crops, which had been "remarkably fine" although "the weather has been dry in spots in this quarter." He also passed along to Madison Senior a copy of the Northwest Ordinance and other news from Congress about western lands and Indian affairs. A tooth-gnashing letter from his cousin came along to give him a smile: "We are here, and

I believe everywhere, all impatience to know something of your conventional deliberations. If you cannot tell us what you are doing, you might at least give us some information of what you are not doing."

Neither a diary-keeper nor inclined to talk about himself in letters, Madison left a scant record of his free time, but he probably was on the preferred list of delegates to be invited to private gatherings. Certainly he was on the preferred list of targets for two of the most energetic visionaries of the time.

One was the visitor to whom Franklin had shown his pickled snake, the ebullient clergyman-scientist, Manasseh Cutler, who had just sealed a deal with the Continental Congress to buy himself five million acres of western land (today the southeastern quarter of Ohio) for "two-thirds of a dollar per acre." Although Cutler was supposedly in Philadelphia to see investors in the project, he spent most of his time socializing with convention delegates, most certainly to make sure that the convention would not subvert his deal. He had been careful to cultivate Madison during his visit, including Madison in the lavish private dinner he held for the delegates and in a breakfast picnic he had hosted on the banks of the Schuykill River.

The other man of vast ideas who sought out Madison during the recess probably always aroused mixed feelings in the solemn Virginian. He was the brash, ambitious, ardent nationalist, twenty-nine-year-old Noah Webster, who already had published America's first widely used speller but was still forty years away from publishing his first dictionary. Madison knew Webster from three years earlier when separately both had been trying to get the states to pass copyright laws. Madison admired and agreed with Webster's 1785 tract, *Plan of Policy for Improving the Advantages and Perpetuating the Union of the American States,* in which Webster had urged that Congress have the same legislative and compulsory power over states as states had over towns and counties. And Madison would not have argued with Webster's passionate promotion of an *American* language (his speller excised the British *u* from such words as "colour" and "labour"). But Madison, considering the practical use he had made of ancient history, might well have found it excessive that

Webster advocated dropping Latin and Greek from the curricula of all students not intending to become purely scholars. Their conversation must have been interesting; Webster probably called on Madison for help in signing up subscribers to his *American Magazine,* which he founded a few months later in New York and which failed soon after.

Like Cutler, Webster also paid a visit to Franklin. That man, whose old-age disabilities, though severe, have been overdramatized, was having only a partial holiday. As president of Pennsylvania, he had been presiding at the state's Supreme Executive Council meetings every day before the convention sessions. He was continuing his attendance there, though its agenda was routine, with things no more portentous than, for instance, a request from Philadelphia officials (on July 30) for some state land for a cemetery.

In town at last were New Hampshire's delegates—John Langdon, speaker of his state legislature and former governor, and Nicholas Gilman, who was in the Continental Congress and almost universally regarded as a mediocrity. They had taken their seats only three days before the recess adjournment. That they had arrived at all was Langdon's doing: the legislature, though unopposed to the convention, could not bring itself to pay for their attendance, and Langdon had finally decided to pay for both of them out of his own pocket. For them, the recess meant a chance to get familiar with what they had missed.

William Paterson went home to New Brunswick, New Jersey, but before departing Philadelphia, he dropped a note to John Lansing of New York, his erstwhile collaborator in the small states' strategy. Although Lansing and his colleague, Judge Yates, had walked out of the convention on July 10, either Paterson did not realize how hostile New York's ruling party was toward the proceedings, or he thought it politic to overlook the animosity. The convention had recessed, he told Lansing, to meet again on August 6. "It is of moment that the representation should be complete and I hope that you and Mr. Yates will not fail to attend on the very day . . . I hope to see you and Mr. Yates at New Brunswick on your way to Philadelphia."

Considering the turn New York politics had taken, Yates and Lansing's disregard of Paterson's call is no surprise. The battle over ratification of the coming Constitution was already starting. Having returned home with Betsey at the beginning of the month, Alexander Hamilton, just days earlier, had published in the *New York Daily Advertiser* a long article ending in an attack on Governor Clinton for having "in public company, without reserve, reprobated the appointment of the convention and predicted a mischievous issue of that measure . . .

"It is *unwarrantable* and *culpable in any man*" so nationally important as Clinton to try to "prepossess the public mind" against the still secret decisions "of a body to whose councils America has, in a great measure, entrusted its future fate," Hamilton wrote. "Such conduct in a man high in office argues greater attachment to his *own power* than to the *public good* . . . If there be any man among us who acts so unworthy a part, it becomes a free and enlightened people to observe him with a jealous eye, and when he sounds the alarm of danger from another quarter to examine whether they have not more to apprehend from *himself.*"

Mild compared to what would come later, Hamilton's was the first public shot fired in what would be one of the two hottest and bitterest struggles over adoption of the new system.

Another convention delegate sojourning in New York was also in the early throes of making history—of an entirely different kind. William Blount of North Carolina was laying the groundwork upon which he would become the first U.S. senator expelled from the new government.

Having come up from the convention a few weeks earlier at the request of the secretary of Congress to help make a quorum, Blount was in Congress when it concluded its deal with Manasseh Cutler. Already a speculator in North Carolina's western lands (around what is today Knoxville, Tennessee), Blount now wrote a nephew in London who had wanted to buy land in the Northwest, telling him that "the door is now open to such a speculation."

For himself, Blount wished his nephew to publish in English newspapers proof of the "very great" number of settlers heading west—as provided to Congress by army officials at the Ohio River: from Fort Harmer at the mouth of the Muskingum (today Marietta, Ohio, on the Ohio-West Virginia border) from October 10, 1786 to May 12, 1787, "177 boats containing 2,689 souls, 1333 horses, 766 cattle, 102 wagons and one phaeton beside a number which passes in the night unobserved." Most, Blount said, were settling in western North Carolina around the Tennessee and Cumberland rivers (the vicinities of Nashville and Knoxville where Blount owned land). Advertising in England "will be beneficial to himself and associates holding lands," Blount said, but the information should appear as a news item. Label it an "Extract of a Letter from a Gentleman in New York to his Friend in London," he said, "concealing the name of the writer and that of the person to whom it is addressed."

Blount was to move to his western land, build a mansion in Knoxville, help separate Tennessee from North Carolina and bring it into the Union in 1796, and become one of Tennessee's first two U.S. senators. But he already was far overextended in his land deals, one of which became the Yazoo Fraud, a gigantic 1795 Georgia scandal in which Blount had been a secret investor and which ended in title disputes affecting all the land involved. In 1797, in financial desperation, he hatched a scheme to raise the value of his good holdings by driving the Spanish out of Louisiana and Florida with a force of frontiersmen and Indians, and he went to the British for naval support. But a letter Blount had written about this plan fell into the hands of the new president, John Adams, who forwarded it to the Senate. When his letter was read aloud in front of the Senate, Blount chartered a boat and vanished, after which the Senate expelled him. The House, which thought that under the Constitution it had to impeach, did—but the Senate dismissed the articles for lack of jurisdiction. Blount, meanwhile, was welcomed back in Tennessee as a hero and elected to the state senate.

Those stubborn stalwarts of Connecticut, Sherman and Johnson, met with a pinch of poetic justice for having slipped away early for their vacations. Sherman—maybe because a rock is not supposed to float—was seasick, though the ship's captain logged smooth water and fair sailing, and Johnson had a hard time getting back, stalled twice by adverse sailing weather and a third time when his ship ran aground on an island north of Philadelphia.

11

The Draft Constitution

''RETURNED TO PHILADELPHIA,'' Maryland delegate James McHenry wrote on Saturday, August 4. "The committee of convention ready to report. Their report in the hands
of Dunlap, the printer, to strike off copies for the members."

The convention was not over, and secrecy had not been
lifted. Printing was the only way to provide all the convention
members with identical copies of the five-thousand-word Committee of Detail report; had it been necessary for the delegates
to individually copy it from the original, as they had been doing
with the various resolutions, it would have taken weeks.

"Dunlap the printer" was the establishment, located on Market Street, of John Dunlap and David C. Claypoole. The Continental Congress had been using the firm since 1775 for the
official printing of such documents as the Declaration of Independence and the Articles of Confederation. The Constitutional Convention's strictly guarded secrecy was as safe with
Dunlap & Claypoole as the draft Articles of Confederation had
been a decade earlier when the printers had put their signatures
to a paper stating that "We and each of us do swear . . . that

we will not disclose, directly or indirectly, the contents of the said confederation.''

At this time, Dunlap most likely was away in New York coordinating congressional printing, so that his partner probably set the type and struck off the first proofs and the final corrected copies of the Committee of Detail's draft constitution. The printer was able to deliver about sixty copies of the document in the space of a weekend.

When the gavel fell in the Assembly Room on Monday, August 6, and John Rutledge, chairman of the Committee of Detail, rose to read the committee report, each delegate received his own copy, consisting of seven large folio sheets, the right-hand two-thirds of each sheet bearing the text while the left-hand third was blank for the delegates to use for notes and revisions.

The report began with a preamble: "We the People of the States of New Hampshire, Massachusetts . . . [all thirteen states were listed] . . . do ordain, declare and establish the following Constitution for the Government of Ourselves and our Posterity." Twenty-three articles followed—no longer resolutions that the government "ought" to consist of this and its powers "ought" to be that, but that it "shall" comprise three branches, and so on. The convention's work at last looked like a constitution.

The committee—Rutledge, Edmund Randolph, James Wilson, Nathaniel Gorham, and Oliver Ellsworth—had filled up many blanks: the first branch of the national legislature now had a name, the "House of Representatives," and so did the executive—"his style shall be 'The President of the United States of America' and his title shall be 'His Excellency' " (which was both the usual form for governors and how almost everyone referred to George Washington). But there was much more.

Things were added that had not been debated at all: that the governors of the states would call elections to fill unscheduled vacancies in their states' representation; that the House would choose a Speaker and have the sole power of impeachment; that punishment in impeachment would extend no farther than removal from office; that the state legislatures would schedule and make the rules for elections, but that Congress could alter such regulations; that each house of Congress could judge its members' qualifications and could penalize members' absences or misbehavior; that each house would keep a record of its proceedings and publish it from time to time.

The draft also ignored the convention's express vote against enumerating the powers of Congress and contained a list of eighteen powers, the last and most important of which was the power to "make all laws that shall be necessary and proper for carrying into execution the foregoing powers . . ." Nine of the listed powers had not been discussed either, but were obvious or essential for a sovereign government—the power to coin money, fix standard weights and measures, establish post offices, create a uniform rule of naturalization, punish felonies committed on the high seas, borrow money on the credit of the United States, regulate commerce with foreign nations and among the states, make war, raise armies, and build a navy.

In its essentials, the draft remained the revised Virginia plan, but the committee had freely added snippets from the New Jersey plan, touches of young Charles Pinckney's plan, phrases from writings the committee members considered important, fragments of their own ideas and those of other delegates. Provisions that had served well were taken from the Articles of Confederation and the states' constitutions, prominently (and ironically, considering the state's walkout) from New York's.

One long memorandum found among George Mason's papers late in the nineteenth century may be the first draft on which the committee worked. It is in Randolph's handwriting and contains an extensive sketch of a constitution with insertions by Rutledge as well as checkmarks suggesting items that were carried over to later drafts.

Whatever Randolph lacked in courage and decision, this memorandum shows the Virginia governor's able and thoughtful mind to good advantage. "In the draft of a fundamental constitution," he began, "two things deserve attention:

"1. To insert essential principles only, lest the operations of government should be clogged by rendering those provisions permanent and unalterable which ought to be accommodated to times and events, and

"2. To use simple and precise language and general propositions . . . for the construction of a constitution, of necessity, differs from that of law."

A preamble would be "proper," he went on, for a brief declaration of the reason for establishing a supreme government.

The burden of the convention's business now was to make sure that the details fit the principles the members had established—and, of course, as they moved through the document clause by clause, to refine and adjust many of their ideas.

QUICK DECISIONS

A blessing of the last phase was that some issues were easy to handle. They were solved by experience or tradition in law and government. Some were choices without any cataclysmic implications at all—like whether to fix a time for Congress to meet.

Those who thought Congress had been given too many powers said no. "The public business might not require it," said Morris. "A great vice in our system," added King, is "that of legislating too much. The most numerous objects of legislation belong to the states."

The executive should not be left running everything, others said. "There should be one meeting at least every year as a check," Gorham recommended. Mason was sanguine in agreement: "The extent of the country will supply business."

After debating each season of the year, the convention agreed with Wilson and Ellsworth that winter was "the best time for business" and approved the first Monday in December, as the Committee of Detail had proposed.

A provision that now costs American taxpayers $18 million a year—publication of congressional proceedings—was briefly imperiled by objections to letting one-fifth of the members demand a roll call of each member's vote. "The people have a right to know what their agents are doing," Wilson insisted. Not providing it, Mason added, "would give a just alarm to the people."

An important decision—whether the new government should be able to issue paper money—was briefly controversial, but less so within the convention than the delegates knew the subject would be among the public. The Committee of Detail had explicitly provided for the power "to emit bills," but Gouverneur Morris urged deletion. It would still leave room for a "responsible" executive to act in an emergency, he said.

While Mason felt "a mortal hatred to paper money," he called for retaining the words. He could not foresee all emergencies and was "unwilling to tie the hands of the legislature," he said. Ellsworth thought the time had come to "shut and bar the door forever." The convention voted to delete after Read predicted that the words "would be as alarming as the mark of the Beast in Revelations."*

Another creation of the Constitution far less portentous in the delegates' minds than it seems today was the Supreme Court. Madison warned of "going too far" in giving the court the power to interpret the Constitution, and Dickinson and some others even opposed a judicial power to set aside a law as unconstitutional, but the majority of delegates' comments leave it clear that they expected the court to exercise that power. The convention, however, never did say one way or the other, and the court did not decide the constitutionality of any law until 1796, when Alexander Hamilton defended a federal carriage tax before the court. The Justices, who happened to include former convention delegates James Wilson and William Paterson, ruled the law constitutional.†

Jurisdiction of the federal court was settled with relative ease, but the old argument about pay in public service bubbled up again when Madison and Mason moved to exclude sitting judges from participating in salary increases for the federal judiciary. As appointments were for life, someone objected, not

---

*In a footnote fifty years later, Madison said he was satisfied that they had "cut off the pretext for a paper currency and particularly for making the bills a tender either for public or private debts." The first paper money was issued under Lincoln, during the Civil War.

†The more famous case, *Marbury* v. *Madison,* did not come until 1803, when the Court, under Chief Justice John Marshall, ruled a portion of a federal law *un*constitutional. *Marbury* was the first time the Court asserted its power to void a federal law.

only would a judge's salary become worth less over time, but new judges would be seated at higher pay than the more senior jurists were receiving. "Men of large talents" would be needed for the federal bench, General Pinckney added, so the judges should get large salaries as well. The convention made no attempt to work in Pinckney's idea, but it did reject Madison and Mason's effort.

Another problem was the committee's definition of treason: "levying war against . . . and adhering to the enemies" of the United States. Although some members questioned whether they were narrowing or widening the idea of "adhering" to enemies, the convention accepted George Mason's proposal to add "giving them aid and comfort" which Mason insisted was "restrictive" of the phrase. Finally, testimony of two witnesses was required for a treason conviction, but Franklin urged that it read "two witnesses *to the same overt act.*" Prosecutions for treason were "generally virulent," Franklin said, "and perjury too easily made use of against innocence." Though Wilson noted that such acts were hard to prove "as in a traitorous correspondence with an enemy," the convention voted Franklin's preference.

Déjà Vu

Two provisions of the draft constitution were actually contrary to the convention's hard-made decisions on them, and seemed—on the face of things—certain to spark renewed tumult. One reversed the vote that Congress would be paid out of the national treasury and gave the authority to the states. The other changed the vote that, in the Senate, each *state* would have one vote: "each *member* shall have one vote." Neither caused trouble.

The committee, it turned out, had been stymied in its effort to find a "value," such as Madison's bushel of wheat, to which salaries could be linked in lieu of letting the legislators set their own pay. They had even considered a special body of wise men to ascertain the market price of wheat from time to time, but then had merely thrown the problem back to the convention to resolve once more. After running over the old arguments, the members at last voted to let the Congress set by law its wages, to be paid out of the national treasury.

More interesting was the utter lack of chagrin which greeted the idea of one vote per senator, instead of a single vote per state. It had been mentioned at the height of the deadlock by Gerry as an alternative compromise to "give a national aspect and spirit to the management of business" in the Senate. Luther Martin complained of "departing from the idea of the *states* being represented," but from the Connecticut table came Ellsworth's observation that he had "always approved of voting in that mode." That barely discussed change was one of the most important made in the convention. On national matters with no special state interest, where senators of a state held opposite views, both would be counted rather than neither—and, of course, this rule facilitated the making of coalitions.

The section barring legislators from taking other offices under the government was a different matter. A renewed motion to change it was debated as furiously as before, with Mason inveighing about "the present state of American morals and manners," and "encouraging that exotic corruption which might not otherwise thrive so well in American soil." They fussed their way to a three-week postponement and then went over the whole ground again before finally adopting the limited restriction that Madison had offered back in June.

Madison, Pinckney, and Morris tried quick sorties for their lost causes. Madison's national veto of state laws, resurrected by young Pinckney, was rejected again (which did not stop Madison from advocating it as late as September 12). Madison also revamped his idea for including the judiciary in the veto of new laws by proposing that the court conduct a separate review— also rejected on Dickinson's warning that the court could become "by degrees the lawgiver." Morris was luckier on his old phobia about the western states: almost casually he moved to delete the phrase "on the same terms with the original states" in the clause for admission of new states, so as not to "bind down the legislature." The convention agreed.

CALL OUT THE NATIONAL GUARD

Washington had, in 1783, called for establishing "the palladium of our security"—the states' militias—on "a peacetime footing absolutely uniform," and, on August 18, the convention came to the question of military security.

The draft constitution proposed to give Congress three powers: "to raise armies; to build and equip fleets; [and] to call forth the aid of the militia, in order to execute the laws of the Union, enforce treaties, suppress insurrections and repel invasions."

George Mason fathered the provision under which the states' militia were to evolve as the National Guard with his proposal that the national government regulate the state militias. It would be better than permitting a standing army in time of peace "unless it might be for a few garrisons," he said. However, no one immediately seconded him.

Instead, Gorham of Massachusetts moved to add to the first clause, "to raise armies," the words "and support," which was approved without debate or dissent, possibly drawing a concurring nod from Washington. However, Gerry was swiftly on his feet.

He "took notice that there was no check here against standing armies in time of peace." The people, he said, were "jealous on this head and great opposition to the plan would spring from such an omission." Gerry personally thought that an army would be "dangerous in time of peace" and he "could never consent to a power to keep up an indefinite number." He proposed a limit—two or three thousand—on the number of troops maintained in peace.

Like Mason's, his suggestion did not receive any reply at first. The convention went on to the power to build and equip fleets, making that clause read "to provide and maintain a navy."

Luther Martin stepped in to help Gerry, formally moving the troop limit Gerry had suggested, but General Pinckney objected, asking "whether no troops were ever to be raised until an attack should be made on us?"

"If there be no restriction," Gerry replied, "a few states may establish a military government," reflecting the widespread public view that a standing army, as the former Congress president, Richard Henry Lee, once said, "constantly" ends "in the destruction of liberty."

Williamson of North Carolina reminded Gerry that Mason wanted a restriction on the length of time for which funds might be appropriated. That might be "the best guard in this case."

The delegates seemed to be tired of Gerry. Langdon of New Hampshire "saw no room for Mr. Gerry distrust of the representatives of the people."

"Preparations for war are generally made in peace," Dayton added—with unassailable logic. "And a standing force of some sort may, for ought we know, become unavoidable."

Gerry was unanimously defeated, but Mason's time limit for appropriations was incorporated in a further report from the Committee on Detail over the weekend. As reported from committee, the limit was one year; the delegates later approved a two year limit.

Mason's proposal that the government regulate the militia also was adopted, giving the Congress the power to "provide for organizing, arming, and disciplining the militia." The appointment of officers and authority of training the militia was left with the states. New York was the first state, in 1823, to name its militia the National Guard. Other states followed slowly; the term was first applied universally in a congressional act in 1903.

12

The Fateful Slavery Compromise

THE SECOND AND LAST GREAT issue to bring the convention to near-fatal division was reached in this period of making the Constitution final. That issue was slavery.

When the question had been political representation, all five southern states had wanted to count slaves and, therefore, had brought about the "three-fifths" formula. That debate masked differences among the southern states themselves: they were not of one mind about what constituted *security* for their region.

The delegates from all five southern states shared a general distrust of the North. It was an axiom with them that the North would run the new country on the revenues from southern exports and regulate commerce entirely to its own advantage. If those fears had been the only focus of bargaining, the debate that now unfolded would not have been as divisive nor the outcome as fateful. However, two of the five southern states, South Carolina and Georgia, had a much more specific "security" in mind: protecting their ability to import slaves and a guarantee of noninterference with slavery itself.

As George Mason was to write later, they *"knew* [emphasis

added] that Congress would immediately suppress the importation of slaves." And they knew that slavery was widely abhorred, even in the South, and that sentiment to abolish it was strong.

The leading delegates to the constitutional convention were opposed to slavery, many actively. Benjamin Franklin was president of a Pennsylvania manumission society. Washington, Madison, and Mason had supported legislation in Virginia designed to encourage owners to free their slaves. Morris and Hamilton were longtime backers of manumission in New York. To them, the slave trade was a British legacy. In fact, Jefferson had included a powerful diatribe blaming George III for it in the Declaration of Independence, but the Continental Congress deleted it because it appeared hypocritical, since no move was being made to emancipate slaves. But the fact remained that the men at Philadelphia and many public leaders outside the convention despised the mortifying contrast slavery presented to their avowed principles.

In the Northwest Ordinance, enacted while the convention was sitting, the Continental Congress forbade slavery in the new states that would be formed. Already eight states had banned the importation of slaves and two had imposed heavy monetary penalties on it. The courts in two states—New Hampshire and Massachusetts—had held that their states' constitutions had set all slaves free; the would-be state of Vermont had written full emancipation into its constitution, and Pennsylvania had passed a law instituting gradual abolition of slavery.

No one expected to abolish slavery in the new constitution— the delegates would be unable to form a government if they tried. Rather, they would have preferred slavery not to be mentioned at all. They had good reason to believe that, if the government's hands were not tied constitutionally, the new Congress could, and *would,* bring an end to slavery by legislation. And that was what South Carolina and Georgia were out to prevent.

Two days before the Committee of Detail went to work, the senior Pinckney had announced that he would be "bound by duty" to his state to vote against the constitution "if the committee should fail to insert some security to the southern states against an emancipation of slaves and taxes on exports."

Now, in two sections of the draft constitution, the committee's proposed response to that demand lay before the convention: constitutional guarantees for the South's economic security—including the slave trade.

Article VII, Section 4, forbade any tax or duty on exports from any state or on the "migration or importation of such persons as the several states shall think proper to admit." Nor, Section 4 continued, "shall such migration or importation be prohibited." In other words, no export taxes and no tax on, or suppression of, the slave trade.

Section 6 of the same article specified that: "No navigation act shall be passed without the assent of two thirds of the members present in each house." Navigation acts were all those regulations by which nations nurtured domestic monopolies on shipping. They were the form of commercial regulation the South dreaded most. Yankee shippers wanted such a monopoly, but the South, using British ships at good rates, did not want to be forced into shipping in northern vessels. The two-thirds vote requirement was meant to enable the South to block passage of any navigation acts.

The proposed guarantees came as a shock to many of the delegates. Everyone knew that South Carolina and Georgia had supported the small states in the battle over representation in exchange for security for southern interests. Indeed, Madison's last-minute offer—to count slaves for the Senate representation—had been an effort to sever the alliance. But some appeared shocked that the trade-off had gone beyond counting three-fifths of the slaves in the rule of representation. Rufus King, for one, declared that he had yielded to that "most grating circumstance" because he did not expect the new government to be forever barred from interfering with the slave trade.

The deep South's grab for absolute security for slavery angered not only King but Gouverneur Morris as well. Like King, Morris had swallowed the three-fifths formula and found it barely digestible. Now he was ready to open fire on all fronts, including the compromise on representation.

Morris struck at the first opportunity during debate on the population ratio for representation in the lower house—of one member for every forty thousand inhabitants—by moving to insert the word "free" in front of "inhabitants."

Domestic slavery was "a nefarious institution," Morris declared, "the curse of heaven" wherever it was found.

"Travel through the whole continent and you behold the prospect continually varying with the appearance and disappearance of slavery . . . Proceed southwardly, and every step you take through the great region of slaves presents a desert increasing with the increasing proportion of these wretched beings."

Why were slaves included in representation? Morris demanded. "Are they men? Then make them citizens and let them vote. Are they property? Why then is no other property included? The houses in this city are worth more than all the wretched slaves which cover the rice swamps of South Carolina."

Granting representation for slaves, Morris went on, amounted to this: "the inhabitant of Georgia and South Carolina who goes to the coast of Africa and, in defiance of the most sacred laws of humanity, tears away his fellow creatures from their dearest connections and damns them to the most cruel bondages—shall have more votes in a government instituted for protection of the rights of mankind than the citizen of Pennsylvania or New Jersey who views with a laudable horror so nefarious a practice."

And what had the South proposed in order to compensate the northern states "for a sacrifice of every principle of right, of every impulse of humanity? They are to bind themselves to march their militia for the defence of the southern states . . . against those very slaves."

Excises and duties were to be limited to imports which would fall heavier on the north, Morris said. "The bohea tea used by a northern free man will pay more tax than the whole consumption of the miserable slave, which consists of nothing more than his physical subsistence and the rag that covers his nakedness."

Yet the South was to be encouraged to import "fresh supplies of wretched Africans" by being assured of an increase in voting power in the national government. He would sooner submit to a "tax for paying for all the negroes in the United States than saddle posterity with such a Constitution!"

Roger Sherman had brushed off Rufus King's opening of the subject, saying that representation had been "settled after much difficulty and deliberation [and] he did not think himself bound to make opposition." But Morris's powerful denunciation moved him to rise again.

"The admission of the negroes into the ratio," Sherman said, did not warrant "such insuperable objections." Slaves were merely included in the tax estimates; "It was the freemen of the southern states who were, in fact, to be represented according to the taxes paid by them."

Not even Wilson was prepared to encourage Morris's attack on the representation formula; it was too intrinsic to the compromise that had saved the convention. The amendment was "premature," Wilson hinted now; leaving the clause alone "would be no bar" to Morris's object. No question the members agreed: they rejected Morris's motion ten to one (New Jersey alone supported him).

When the convention reached the clause forbidding either taxation or suppression of the slave trade two weeks later, battle broke out in earnest, consuming most of two days.

South Carolina and Georgia made themselves perfectly plain—they would have guarantees or they would not join the union. North Carolina issued no threats, but the delegates knew she shared that attitude. To the extent objections must be acknowledged, the two southernmost states optimistically predicted that the institution would certainly die out on its own. But, said Rutledge belligerently, "If the convention thinks that North Carolina, South Carolina and Georgia will ever agree to the plan unless their right to import slaves be untouched, the expectation is vain. The people of those states will never be such fools as to give up so important an interest."

Throughout the fight, Georgia and South Carolina were supported by their Connecticut allies, Sherman and Ellsworth, who were now repaying the support they had received in the struggle between the big states and small. Sherman "disapproved" of the trade, but, as the states now had the right to import slaves and "the public good did not require it to be taken from them," it was "expedient to have as few objections as possible to the proposed scheme of government." "What enriches a part enriches the whole," said Ellsworth. "The states are the best judges of their particular interest . . . Let us not intermeddle . . . Slavery in time will be not a speck in our country."

But the attacks were heavy, and this time the attackers made no bones about their opposition to the institution of slavery itself. And the new assault was led not by the nonslave states, but by Maryland and Virginia, both of which had prohibited importation.

Luther Martin opened the fight by urging that either "a prohibition or tax on the importation of slaves" be allowed. The three-fifths representation formula already encouraged the traffic, even though "slaves weakened one part of the Union which the other parts were bound to protect." The right to import them was "therefore unreasonable," and "inconsistent with the principles of the revolution and dishonorable to the American character to have such a feature in the Constitution."

"Religion and humanity have nothing to do with this question," Rutledge shot back. "Interest alone is the governing principle with nations. The true question at present is whether the southern states shall or shall not be parties to the Union. If the northern states consult their interest, they will not oppose the increase of slaves, which will increase the commodities of which they will become the carriers."

"Let every state import what it pleases," agreed Ellsworth. "The morality or wisdom of slavery are considerations belonging to the states themselves."

"South Carolina can never receive the plan if it prohibits the slave trade," young Charles Pinckney warned, but "if the states be all left at liberty on this subject, South Carolina may perhaps by degrees do of herself what is wished, as Virginia and Maryland have already done."

George Mason rose. It was not a local matter and it would not just go away. "This infernal traffic," he snapped, "concerns not the importing states alone, but the whole union." The steps Maryland, Virginia, and North Carolina had taken against importation "would be in vain if South Carolina and Georgia be at liberty to import. The western people are already calling out for slaves for their new lands and will fill that country with slaves if they can be got through South Carolina and Georgia."

It is "essential in every point of view that the general government should have the power to prevent the increase of slavery," Mason avowed. "Slavery discourages arts and manufactures; the poor despise labor when performed by slaves . . . They produce the most pernicious effect on manners; every master of slaves is born a petty tyrant. They bring the judgment of heaven on a country . . . By an inevitable chain of causes and effects, Providence punishes national sins by national calamities."

Glancing perhaps at the importing states' bedfellows in the Connecticut delegation, Mason "lamented that some of our eastern brethren had, from a lust of gain, embarked in this nefarious traffic."

Ellsworth was on his feet immediately, full of sarcasm for the eloquent slaveowner from a state with a surplus of slaves. As he himself had never owned a slave, he "could not judge of the effects of slavery on character . . . however, if it was to be considered in a moral light, we ought to go farther and free those already in the country." A tax or prohibition on the trade would be patently unjust to South Carolina and Georgia: "Slaves," he said, "multiply so fast in Virginia and Maryland that it is cheaper to raise than import them, whilst in the sickly rice swamps foreign supplies are necessary."

Exactly, said General Pinckney, capitalizing on Ellsworth's lead, "South Carolina and Georgia cannot do without slaves. As to Virginia, she will gain by stopping the importations. Her slaves will rise in value and she has more than she wants." In any case, it was useless to try to persuade him and his colleagues; their constituents would not consent. He admitted that it was "reasonable" to tax slaves like other imports, but deleting the protection would amount to "an exclusion of South Carolina from the union."

Leave Georgia to herself, said Baldwin, and "she may probably put a stop to the evil." Meanwhile, he said, she would see any "attempt to abridge one of her favorite prerogatives" as proof that a national government was "the pursuit of the central states who wished to have a vortex for everything."

If South Carolina and Georgia were disposed to get rid of slavery, Wilson replied, "they would never refuse to unite because the importation might be prohibited."

Gerry doubted the authority of the general government to interfere with the states on slavery but, he added, "we ought to be careful not to give any sanction to it."

But Dickinson had no doubts. It was "inadmissible on every principle of honor and safety that the importation of slaves should be authorized to the states by the Constitution. The true question is whether the national happiness would be promoted or impeded by the importation and this question ought to be left to the national government, not to the states particularly interested."

Williamson put his state in the deep South's corner by pointing out that North Carolina had not abolished the trade, but was only taxing it. The southern states could not join the union without protection, he said; it was "wrong to try to force anything down not absolutely necessary . . . which any state must disagree to."

Rufus King was tired of the threats. If the two most southerly states would not agree to the constitution without the clause, other states would have "great and equal opposition" because of it.

Unexpectedly, General Pinckney turned conciliatory. He felt "bound to declare candidly that he did not think South Carolina would stop her importations of slaves in any short time." He urged the appointment of a committee to revise the clause "that slaves might be made liable to an equal tax with other imports." This, he thought, would be both "right and would remove one difficulty that had been started."

Gouverneur Morris supported the idea and urged inclusion of the clauses on export taxes and navigation acts, which also were of such great concern to the South. "These things may form a bargain among the northern and southern states," he observed.

Sherman and Butler raised their voices against including anything else, but Randolph argued for taking the chance that "some middle ground might, if possible, be found." The convention was in a dilemma, he said: protecting the slave trade "would revolt the Quakers, the Methodists and many others in the states having no slaves. On the other hand, two states might be lost to the union."

Ellsworth, with a vehemence unusual for him, opposed both the committee and the inclusion of the section on navigation acts. "This widening of opinions has a threatening aspect," he said. The plan was "middle and moderate ground." Otherwise two states would be lost, others might "stand aloof . . . fly into a variety of shapes and directions and most probably into several confederations and not without bloodshed." Ellsworth's panicky plea is a clue to the heat and resentment that must have attended the question of southern "security" during the drafting in the Committee of Detail.

The convention had already agreed to prohibit all export taxes, so it sent only the question of navigation acts into the committee along with the slave-trade issue. The compromise emerged two days later.

The committee recommended deleting the section on navigation acts entirely; restraining the new government for twelve years from interfering with the importation of slaves; and taxing slaves imported, but the tax should not to exceed the percentage levied on other imported goods.

George Mason was furious. Gone was the chance for the greater South to block navigation acts. The slave-importing states had sold out the rest of the South for a chance to protect the slave trade. He spelled it out later for Jefferson: so great was South Carolina and Georgia's fear of a cutoff, Mason said, that the two states had "struck up a bargain with the three New England states: if they would join to admit slaves for some years, the two southernmost states would join in changing the clause which required two-thirds of the legislature . . ."

The new coalition announced itself as soon as the compromise was taken up on the floor. General Pinckney moved to extend the time during which slaves could be imported from twelve years to twenty. Gorham of Massachusetts, one of three states where slavery had been abolished, seconded the motion.

Madison objected lifelessly that "twenty years will produce all the mischief that can be apprehended from the liberty to import slaves. [It] will be more dishonorable to the national character than to say nothing about it in the Constitution." But no one else bothered, and the change passed seven to four (Virginia, New Jersey, Pennsylvania, and Delaware against).

Morris stood upon his wooden leg, a hard glint in his eye, to request a change of wording to refer to "importation of slaves into North Carolina, South Carolina and Georgia." He wanted it to "be known that this part of the Constitution was in a compliance with those states."

No, Mason said sadly, it would "give offense to the people of those states."

But Dickinson realized that precisely something along that line was needed to avoid the appearance of overriding the states that already had banned importation. He proposed confining importation to "such of the states as shall permit the same." That passed without dissent.

The word "slaves" and the effort to set the tax on them caused the bargainers to writhe. Sherman found himself against "acknowledging men to be property," to which King and Langdon brutally replied that this was "the price of the first part" and General Pinckney "admitted that it was so." "Mr. Sherman," soothed Gorham, should see the tax "not as implying that slaves are property, but as a discouragement to the importation of them."

A last-ditch attempt to restore a special vote requirement for navigation acts gave General Pinckney an opportunity to publicly thank his New England allies. He positively oozed. Any regulation of shipping was against the interest of the South, he said. However, in view of New England's "liberal conduct towards the views of South Carolina and the interest the weak southern states had in being united with the strong Eastern states . . . no fetters should be imposed on the power of making commercial regulations." His constituents, "though prejudiced against the eastern states, would be reconciled to this liberality." Why, even he himself "had prejudices against the eastern states before he came here, but . . . he had found them as liberal and candid as any men whatever."

The interests of the southern and eastern states were "as different as the interests of Russia and Turkey," piped up Pinckney's colleague, Butler. He was "notwithstanding, desirous of conciliating the affections of the eastern states."

It has become commonplace to say that a moral flaw stains the convention of 1787—that the framers were tolerant of slavery and admitted it into the Constitution more or less in the routine course of things. However, the framers not only did not admit it without a fight, but they forced its proponents to accept only temporary protection. Although they dreaded what twenty years could bring, they felt they had managed to leave the new government technically in a position to do away with it. Abraham Lincoln gave them even more credit: he contended that the framers had tried to put slavery on the path of ultimate extinction.

Elbridge Gerry may have been oppressed by the unhappy portent of this deal, although he was not referring to it when he wrote his wife, Ann, the morning after the slavery compromise was unveiled: "I am exceedingly distraught at the proceedings of the convention. I am almost sure they will, if not altered materially, lay the foundation of a civil war."

13

"... It is a rising and not a setting sun"

GERRY'S DRAMATIC COMMENT to his wife was a feeling he had not kept hidden. A few days earlier, when the convention had debated standing armies, he had used similar words on the floor. He was afraid that the convention was packing the constitution with features that would infuriate zealous Democrats and fanatic Tories alike, to the point of bloody opposition. And while Gerry was the most agitated, others delegates beheld the emerging system with sensations running from edgy optimism to dismay.

For Madison, the success of the hardbitten team of Sherman, Ellsworth, Rutledge, and Pinckney, which became more apparent as the slavery debate unfolded through August, took its toll. Though he never missed a day of the convention, fatigue and the summer heat bowed him physically. His floor leadership dropped to a negligible level; his notetaking turned desultory. But Madison was not wholly in a slump. In this final month, he stepped over yet another threshold of political growth, redeploying his physical and philosophical reserves with a steely practicality that would become one of his most striking qualities. As a member of the committee that produced the slavery compromise, he would damp down his private opposition on the convention floor and make the "northern" case for navigation laws on continental grounds. At the same time, as the work marched toward conclusion, he would help nail together one last tradeoff to "elevate" the tone of the new government in a way that his most sophisticated intellectual pleas had been unable to do.

The full sails of Gouverneur Morris, on the other hand, seemed incapable of going flat. As men of more gravity and emotion flagged and anguished, he continued, tirelessly bold, energetic, and provocative. He really was a living argument for every old saw about never taking yourself too seriously. Only once, in reply to an outbreak of acrimony, would he snap out his own dissatisfaction with the system the delegates were producing.

In alarming contrast were Mason and Randolph. As August passed and became September, Mason grew ever more sour, critical and isolated, while Randolph drifted into a lagoon of disappointment, and dropped anchor.

Meanwhile, the convention hurried toward its finish. And even if the delegates' vision had become a little blurred, they were still awake to the call of principle and alive enough to produce a four-day battle over one last compromise.

Who Shall Govern America?

On "24th Ellul 5547 or Sept 7th 1787," George Washington, on behalf of the convention, received a letter from Jonas Phillips, "being one of the people called Jews of the City of Philadelphia, a people scattered and dispersed among all nations."

The constitution of Pennsylvania, Phillips told them, prescribed an oath for officeholders affirming belief in God and in divine inspiration of the Scriptures, both Old and New Testament. Despite a guarantee of freedom of religion in the state's bill of rights, "By the above law, a Jew is deprived of holding any public office," Phillips said, because "to swear and believe that the new testament was given by divine inspiration is absolutely against the religious principle of a Jew . . .

"It is well known among all the citizens of the thirteen united states that the Jews have been true and faithful whigs," Phillips said, "and during the late contest with England, they have been foremost in aiding and assisting the states with their lives and fortunes. They have supported the cause, have bravely fought and bled for liberty which they cannot enjoy."

If convention would alter or omit such an oath, Phillips urged, "then the Israelites will think themselves happy to live under a government where all religious societies are on an equal footing. I solicit this favor for myself, my children and posterity and for the benefit of all the Israelites through the thirteen united states of America."

Phillips's was a letter to give the convention quiet satisfaction. A week before they had unanimously approved Charles Pinckney's addition to the oath-of-office clause: "but no religious test shall ever be required as a qualification to any office or public trust under the authority of the United States."

But hardly anything else about restrictions on the right to vote and hold office had gone so smoothly.

To elect the members of the House of Representatives, the draft constitution said, voters must meet the same qualifications as required to vote for members of "the most numerous branch of their own legislatures."

Morris moved to limit voting rights to freeholders (owners of landed estates). John Dickinson agreed: freeholders were "the best guardians of liberty" and restricting the vote to them would provide "a necessary defense against the dangerous influence of those multitudes without property and without principle with which our country, like all others, will in time abound."

It was conventional political theory, but America was already on more radical ground. In states where the vote was more widely held, Wilson pointed out swiftly, it would be "very hard and disagreeable" for a man to be able to vote for state legislators but not for national lawmakers. There is "no right of which the people are more jealous," Butler warned, and shrinking it might lead to the rise of an aristocracy. Mason pointed out that eight or nine states did not require a freehold. "What will the people there say if they should be disfranchised?" he asked.

Morris insisted: he had long ago learned "not to be the dupe of words. The sound of 'aristocracy'" did not alarm him, he said. "If the suffrage was to be open to all *freemen,* the government would indubitably be an aristocracy. Give the votes to people who have no property and they will sell them to the rich . . . The time is not distant when this country will abound with mechanics and manufacturers who will receive their bread from their employers . . . the man who does not give his vote freely is not represented . . . The ignorant and the dependent can be as little trusted with the public interest."

"Ought not every man who pays a tax to vote for the representative who is to levy and dispose of his money?" Ellsworth countered. "Shall the wealthy merchants and manufacturers who will bear a full share of the public burdens be not allowed a voice?"

Morris was unsympathetic. "If they have wealth and value the right, they can acquire it. If not, they don't deserve it!"

"We all feel too strongly the remains of ancient prejudices and view things too much through a British medium," Mason chided. Because a freehold was required in England, "it is imagined" to be the only proper qualification. In his opinion, he said, "Every man having evidence of attachment to and permanent common interest with society ought to share in all its rights and privileges."

"In its merits alone," Madison remarked, freeholders would be "the safest depositories of republican liberty," but, he admitted, public reaction did worry him.

Benjamin Franklin was provoked; he did not wait to prepare remarks for Wilson to read on his behalf. "It is of great consequence that we should not depress the virtue and public spirit of our common people," he warned. American seamen, when captured during the Revolution, had chosen imprisonment rather than serve on British ships, while British prisoners "readily" served on American ships "on being promised a share of the prizes that might be made out of their own country." He also did not think the elected had any right to narrow the privileges of the electors.

Only Dickinson's state, Delaware, voted for Morris's motion, and the provision remained as the committee had written it.

As many of the delegates were foreign-born, citizenship requirements for officeholders scraped even more tender feelings. The Committee of Detail had set three years' citizenship for members of the House of Representatives and four years for the Senate. However, Mason, who "did not choose to let foreigners and adventurers make laws for us and govern us," successfully moved to extend the House requirement to seven years.

When Morris urged increasing the Senate requirement to fourteen years, however, the convention began to worry about the message within the idea.

If the Constitution gave stability and reputation to America, Madison said, "great numbers of respectable Europeans, men who love liberty and wish to partake of its blessings, will be ready to transfer their fortunes hither. All such would feel the mortification of being marked with suspicious incapacitations."

Too rigid a requirement, Ellsworth agreed, would discourage "meritorious aliens" from emigrating to this country. Franklin was not against "a reasonable time," but he "should be very sorry to see anything like illiberality inserted in the Constitution." Randolph recalled an obligation of "good faith" to foreigners invited to resettle during the Revolution, and took his stand on seven years.

Wilson's Scottish burr underscored his words as he pointed out that he rose "with feelings which were perhaps peculiar . . . not being a native" to describe the "discouragement and mortification meritorious foreigners would have from the degrading discrimination." When he had earlier moved to Maryland, he said, he found himself "under certain legal incapacities which never ceased to produce chagrin."

"We should not be polite at the expense of prudence!" said Morris, exasperated. Some Indian tribes "carried their hospitality so far as to offer to strangers their wives and daughters. Is this a proper model for us?" He would "admit them to his house . . . invite them to his table . . . provide them with comfortable lodgings, but would not carry the complaisance so far as to bed them with his wife. He would let them worship at the same altar, but did not choose to make priests of them." Immigrants, Morris said, could enjoy the privileges of America without being eligible to the great offices of government.

"Every society from a great nation down to a club has the right of declaring the conditions on which new members should be admitted," he lectured. "As to those philosophical gentlemen, those citizens of the world as they call themselves, I own I do not wish to see any of them in our public councils." He would not trust them. "The men who can shake off their attachments to their own country can never love any other."

The convention split the difference, voting to require nine years' citizenship for Senators. It stood firm on seven for the House after a reconsideration.

Having taken almost three days on those subjects, the convention was easily persuaded to delete entirely a provision that Congress establish property requirements for its members.

"By so general a 'no' that the states were not called," they rejected Charles Pinckney's motion that the president, judges, and members of the legislature be required to possess clear, unencumbered estates worth certain amounts (Pinckney thought $100,000 for the president and $50,000 for the others was right). Madison argued without success that "qualifications for electors and elected were fundamental articles in a republican government and ought to be fixed by the Constitution." The convention heeded Franklin's final impatient admonition that he "disliked everything that tended to debase the spirit of the common people." Some of the greatest rogues he had ever met, Franklin said, "were the richest rogues."

THE LAST TRADEOFF

The creature the Convention had formed for the executive nagged at Madison, Morris, Wilson, and the other nationalists.

"The President," as Hamilton would say, was "a Monster elected for seven years and ineligible afterwards, having great powers in appointments to office and continually tempted by this constitutional disqualification to abuse them in order to subvert the government."

The draft constitution was the first attempt to spell out the president's powers, and they were substantial. He would appoint all officers of the United States except the treasurer, justices of the Supreme Court, and ambassadors; he would execute all the laws; he would be commander in chief of the military forces. He would have a veto with some weight. And every one of those powers would be in danger of abuse, because the president would not be his own man.

Yet the manner of electing the executive and his term of service had been debated over and over and the resistance to anything that could be branded "monarchical" had been insuperable.

On August 8, however, two days after the Committee of Detail laid the draft constitution in front of the convention, a sudden deletion was made that burned and smoldered in the minds of George Mason and a few others until it finally became the basis for the bargain that would reshape the president's role. The clause deleted was none other than that "trifle, light as air"—the sole power of the House of Representatives to originate money bills. And the first man to see that it mattered enough to produce a compromise was George Washington.

Charles Pinckney set events in motion when he moved to delete the origination power as "giving no peculiar advantage to the House of Representatives and as clogging the government."

Mason flew to his feet. This would "unhinge" the compromise that had broken the representation deadlock. The Senate would be a small number of men serving long terms of office. Origination power should not be added to the "other great powers vested in that body." They were an "aristocracy . . . the government of a few over the many . . .

"An aristocratic body, like the screw in mechanics working its way by slow degrees and holding fast whatever it gains, should ever be suspected of an encroaching tendency," Mason cried. "The purse strings should never be put into its hands."

Back and forth it went for a while, and then Pinckney's motion passed by a vote of seven to four. Randolph rose to announce that he would move to reconsider, and five days later it was taken up again.

"When this plan goes forth," Dickinson warned, "it will be attacked by the popular leaders. Aristocracy will be the watchword; the shibboleth among its adversaries."

"When the people behold in the Senate the countenance of an aristocracy and, in the president, the form at least of a little monarch," Randolph said, "will not their alarms be sufficiently raised" without taking the purse strings out of the hands of their immediate representatives?

Tut, tut, said Rutledge. The people will say that "this restriction is but a mere tub to the whale . . . and will be more likely to be displeased with it as an attempt to bubble them than to impute it to a watchfulness over their rights."

The deletion was confirmed, seven to four again. This time, however, Washington voted with the origination advocates. He "gave up his judgment," he told Madison, because the issue was "not of very material weight" with him "and was made an essential point with others, who, if disappointed, might be less cordial in other points of real weight."

That quote is a fascinating bit of intelligence. Washington's extreme discretion as president of the convention would never have let him sit down and plot, but if his very specific observation was not a hint, it surely prompted Madison to wonder about the price Mason might pay for the origination clause. But were the clause's advocates fervent enough to bring it up again?

They were: two days later, they offered a substitute to exclude the Senate from originating. Seconding the motion, Mason declared himself "extremely earnest to take this power from the Senate who could already sell the whole country by means of treaties." Now although Mason fought for an immediate vote, it was postponed until the powers of the Senate were reviewed.

Annotating his notes years later, Madison explained what was going on, with the wonderfully dignified honesty that often enlivens his record: "Col. Mason, Mr. Gerry and other members from large states set great value on this privilege of originating money bills," he wrote. "Of this the members from the small states, with some from the large states who wished a high-mounted government, endeavored to avail themselves—by making that privilege the price of arrangements in the Constitution favorable to the small states and to the elevation of the government."

When the Senate's powers came up a week later, Madison and Morris raised a series of issues that tipped the clause into a committee for a possible overhaul. Now both the Senate and origination were in limbo—two pieces of a bargain set aside until they could be brought into play.

The next morning brought Article X of the draft constitution—the section on the president. His election by the legislature was endorsed again, but when the convention delegates found themselves getting nowhere on his term of office or re-electability, they postponed the section and moved on to complete the draft constitution without a backward look.

The rules of the convention frowned on this conduct. Postponed matters were supposed to be handled the day after postponement. Both the Senate and the origination clause, however, had been left hanging and so now was the president, joining about a dozen other clauses and proposals that were not so divisive as frustratingly resistant to decision.

The convention had a procedure for tidying up. On August 31, one more committee was appointed—the Committee on Postponed Matters—with a member from every state, including Roger Sherman, James Madison, and Gouverneur Morris. On September 4 and 5, this committee brought in its report.

The president, the committee proposed, should hold his office for four years, be elected more or less by the people through "electors" chosen for that purpose, and be eligible for re-election. He, and not the Senate, should have the power to make treaties and appoint ambassadors and justices of the Supreme Court—but with the advice and consent of the Senate, and a two-thirds vote of approval in the case of treaties. A postponed clause that would have designated the head of the Senate to succeed the president in event of death or disability was scrapped for one which invented a new officer, a "vice president." He would serve as president of the Senate without a vote, except in case of a tie.

The benefit to the large states was in the electoral device: each state would appoint electors, who would be equal in number to the state's total membership in the House and Senate. The electors would meet and vote for two persons, one of whom must reside in a different state. The electors would list all the names voted for, along with the tally of votes received by each candidate, and forward the list to the Senate, where the votes from all the states would be counted. The person who received a majority would be president; the second highest would become the vice-president. In case of a tie, the Senate would choose between them by ballot.

The final provision was the bait to draw the small states into the compromise: if no one candidate had received a majority of the electors' votes, the Senate would choose the president from among the five highest vote-getters.

Sherman, godfather of the small states, was betting that no one man would ever be well enough known continentally to receive a majority. The practical result would be that the Senate would elect the president, and since the Senate could choose among the *five* highest vote-getters, it would not even be obliged to pick the man who had amassed the most votes. The small states would have a solid chance to influence the outcome.

And the Senate would be excluded from the power to originate money bills, but it would be permitted to amend them.

The plan of committee, said Mason cautiously, had "removed some capital objections, particularly the danger of cabal and corruption" in choosing the president.

However, the "high-mounted government" was far from home free. Morris, for one, knew or sensed how unhappy Mason and Gerry really were, and when the origination clause came up before the president was fully debated, Morris moved for postponement. Origination had been agreed to as a compromise in committee, he said, but he wanted to be free to vote against it, "if on the whole he should not be satisfied with certain other parts to be settled."

Sherman reproached him, contending for "giving immediate ease to those who looked on this clause as of great moment and for trusting to their concurrence in other proper measures."

The convention was for keeping Mason and Gerry's feet to the fire, and approved the postponement nine to two, with only the two men's own states voting to trust them.

Nevertheless, this compromise wobbled and jolted like a carriage with ill-fitting wheels. It unsettled most of the men whose concerns it was supposed to meet. Origination proponents, small-state men, and large-state nationalists all resisted it. The new team of Sherman, Morris, and Madison had so much difficulty keeping it on course that for a few alarming days the plan seemed about to produce a new stalemate.

Randolph and Pinckney demanded explanations. Why was the final stage referred to the Senate and not to the whole Congress? "It might be better," Wilson said thoughtfully, "to refer the eventual appointment to the legislature than to the Senate and confine it to a smaller number than five of the candidates." Wilson's lukewarm reaction was telling—he had, after all, first suggested "electors" way back in June.

Even John Rutledge declared himself "much opposed," and moved to restore the original plan for the legislature to elect the president.

As long as he was not trusted to stick to the bargain, Mason felt free to voice his objections. Not only would the Senate usually choose the president, but an incumbent president would certainly be among the names from which the Senate would choose four years later, he said. Thus the president would not be independent during his term of office; he would work to ingratiate himself. Mason urged depriving the Senate of the eventual election—and moved for the highest vote-getter to be made president, whether he had received a majority or not.

But when Sherman "reminded" everyone that the idea was to tilt the electoral voting toward the large states and the Senate voting toward the small states, the specter of old divisions was enough. The convention turned Mason down flat.

Wilson, however, had settled on his opinion. He moved to strike out "Senate" and replace it with "Legislature."

Madison tried to hang on to his nationalists, only to be followed by Randolph's complaint that the plan already contained "a bold stroke for monarchy. We are now doing the same for an aristocracy."

Give it to the legislature, not the Senate, declared Dickinson, defecting like Rutledge from Sherman's old coalition. It is "too much influence to be superadded" to the Senate.

Still the compromise held: The convention rejected Wilson's motion, too.

Things became even more complicated. Madison and Williamson proposed that only one third of the total electoral votes, rather than a majority, be sufficient to determine the president, but the convention turned that down as well. Gerry suggested that the eventual election be made by six senators and seven representatives chosen by joint ballot, and Mason moved that only the three, instead of five, highest candidates be referred to the Senate. Sherman snarled that he "would sooner give up the plan." And the convention turned them all down again.

As the method of electing the president now stood, Mason announced, "it is utterly inadmissible." He would "prefer the government of Prussia to one which will put all power into the hands of seven or eight men and fix an aristocracy worse than absolute monarchy." The compromise was falling apart.

Sherman moved to hold it together the next morning. He would not mind if the choice fell to the whole Congress, he said, if it voted by states instead of proportionately in that case. No one answered him.

Wilson rose to condemn the committee's whole scheme and concluded that, while the election arrangement was an improvement that could be perfected by amendments, he "could never agree to purchase it" at the price of the rest of the report.

Morris was flabbergasted and said so, launching into a long speech to convince Wilson of his error. That did not help. Two more delegates rose up promptly to call the plan "aristocratic." And now even Alexander Hamilton went over the side—urging that the Senate be kept out of it and the highest number of ballots, a majority or not, be sufficient to appoint the president.

Madison saw what was coming when two members from North Carolina moved to replace the proposed four year term with seven. The next thing would be to make the president ineligible for re-election, he noted grimly. And the committee's plan would have unraveled.

But it held. The move was turned down; the convention crept, five words at a time, through the compromise, approving it bit by bit, until they reached to clause referring the five highest candidates to the Senate. Williamson rose for the fourth time to change it to the Legislature, adding now "voting *by states,*" but Sherman got up immediately with a surprise. The House of Representatives voting by states would be better than the whole legislature, he said, and he so moved. With what had to be a gasp of relief, the convention approved, ten to one.

As John Adams, Thomas Jefferson, and their successors were to discover, the office of vice-president was framed with a splendid indifference to self-esteem of the occupant.

Gerry was "against having any vice president," and especially to sit at the head of the Senate. "We might as well put the President himself at the head . . . The close intimacy that must subsist between the President and Vice President makes it absolutely improper."

Intimacy? Morris laughed it off: "The vice president then will be the first heir apparent that ever loved his father." If there were no vice president, he added, the president of the Senate would be the temporary successor, "which would amount to the same thing."

Sherman saw no danger. "If the vice president were not to be president of the Senate, he would be without employment," and one senator would lose his vote by having to occupy that place.

Randolph, Mason, and Williamson all weighed in against a vice president, but the convention approved the measure, eight to two, and went on to adopt the rest of the compromise, essentially as the committee had reported it.

The electoral system in the Constitution today is almost the same. The Twelfth Amendment, ratified in 1804, changed the voting procedure to require electors to specify the candidate voted for as president and the one voted for as vice president, and it reduced the number of top vote-getters referred to the House from five to three. Those changes resulted from the debacle of the election of 1800, when Thomas Jefferson and Aaron Burr received a tie vote, throwing the choice into the House. Balloting continued for six days before Jefferson finally prevailed.

Today, most states bind their electors to the popular vote, making their task purely ceremonial, and every presidential election year brings editorials and articles calling for the system's abolition. The argument for abolishing it rests on the fact that the winner's margin in the electoral count is usually wider than the margin in the popular vote—with the corresponding possibility that someday the electoral winner will actually be the popular loser. But America today, like the convention two hundred years ago, is not ready to dispense with the states. And those who consider the states crucial feel that the electoral system obliges national candidates and parties to pay attention to local differences. It is the only provision in the Constitution that requires the executive to remember that there are states, and for that reason, unless a loser in the popular vote ends up in the Oval Office, it is likely to remain.

"The *finish* given to the style and arrangement of the Constitution fairly belongs to the pen of Mr. Morris," James Madison wrote many years after the convention. "The task having probably been handed over to him by the chairman of the Committee, himself a highly respectable member, and with the ready concurrence of the others."

The Committee of Detail's forty-three articles had been modified, voted upon, modified again, and reworked in still further committees, such as the Committee on Postponed Matters. All that was left to do was to write the Constitution, and to Gouverneur Morris was entrusted the job.

How highly regarded his mind and writing skills actually were is brought home by the names of the other four men elected to the Committee on Style and Arrangement. Its chairman was William Samuel Johnson, soon to be president of Columbia College. Other members were James Wilson and James Madison, both lucid and experienced with the pen. The last was Alexander Hamilton, one of the finest writers of his time.

"A better choice could not have been made," Madison continued about the man he could not like. Certainly the draft helped organize the materials, and the succeeding resolutions were accurately written out for Morris's use, "but there was sufficient room for the talents and taste stamped by the author on the face of it. The alternations made by the Committee are not recollected. They were not such as to impair the merit of the composition."

Somehow it seems appropriate that Gouverneur Morris had once described himself as "constitutionally the happiest of men."

". . . MAKE MANIFEST OUR UNANIMITY . . ."

The morning of Monday, September 17 was clear and chill; autumn's approach was unmistakably in the air. In the Assembly Room of the State House, forty-one delegates gathered this day, the last meeting of the Constitutional Convention. They planned to dine together this afternoon at City Tavern, and, in twenty-four hours, they would be on horseback, in carriages and stages, and on board ship, taking printed copies of the proposed Constitution back to the states that had sent them.

Jacob Shallus, assistant clerk of the Pennsylvania General Assembly, joined convention secretary William Jackson before the session came to order, to hand Jackson four sheets of parchment on which Shallus had inscribed the completed Constitution. As requested, he settled himself outside the Assembly Room door to wait for the summons to engross the closing block that would read "Done, in Convention . . ."

From his usual seat at the front of the room, Madison could see a few empty chairs. Rhode Island, of course, had never arrived and the two New Yorkers, Lansing and Yates, had not come back. His friend McClurg had not returned—a disappointment. And there would be no piles of snuff around Ellsworth's chair; he had been called away by urgent business in Connecticut. Caleb Strong was gone for the same reason, but he was all for the plan and would be as quietly dependable for Massachusetts's ratification as he had been here. Not so the carping young Marylander, John Mercer, who had appeared for two weeks, thought the plan too weak, supposedly had made up a list of delegates who were "for monarchy," of all things, and gone back to Maryland. Unhappily, Madison saw, John Dickinson's seat was empty again, as it had been last Friday and Saturday. He would be deprived of the day by illness—though George Read had promised to sign the Constitution for him.

And rowdy Luther Martin was gone, off in a huff two weeks since. That was something to smile about. James McHenry said that when Martin had fumed to one of their colleagues about the new plan, "I'll be hanged if ever the people of Maryland agree to it," the other Marylander had advised him that he had best stay in Philadelphia, then.

Proud Alexander Hamilton had deposited himself at the New York table. He intended to give his signature, whether it was deemed official or not. James Wilson and Gouverneur Morris—the third and first most frequent debaters, respectively, these four months—had their heads together with Benjamin Franklin. Madison knew something was afoot there; it would be in Franklin's last speech, which Wilson would read for him.

The remaining two-thirds of Connecticut, Sherman and Johnson, occupied their chairs as usual. A lifetime ago, it seemed, William Paterson had presented the New Jersey plan and Gunning Bedford of Delaware had hurled "I do not, Gentlemen, trust you!" at the large states men. But both were here today, smiling and talking with the others.

Madison's eyes roamed the room to find the Massachusetts and Virginia delegates. Washington was pensive—something was on his mind. And Rufus King and Nathaniel Gorham at the Massachusetts table did not look too happy either. In fact, here were the most serious clouds over this long-wished-for morning: Gerry of Massachusetts had announced just before Saturday's vote on the whole Constitution that he would refuse to sign. And Mason and Randolph had been threatening to withhold their names, too.

Gaunt, stammering little Gerry—suspicious of everyone and everything—was a puzzle. Perhaps because many men in the convention knew his complaining ways, few had realized that he had actually turned against the plan. Certainly his chairmanship of the great compromise committee and his help in solving smaller stalemates had been misleading.

Ellsworth was furious with him. "No man was more plausible and conciliating upon every subject . . . mutual concession and unanimity were the whole burden of his song," Ellsworth, as "Landholder," would write in a dozen weeks, "till, toward the close of the business, he introduced a motion . . . founded in such barefaced selfishness and injustice that it at once accounted for all his former plausibility and concession." The convention's rejection of Gerry's proposal (for paying off the old Continental certificates, large numbers of which Gerry was rumored to hold) "inspired its author with the utmost rage and intemperate opposition to the whole system," Ellsworth charged.*

Liking Gerry, Madison was more tolerant—had "a very high esteem and a very warm regard" for him. He would take him at his word that he had developed a fatal accumulation of doubts. On Saturday, Gerry had condemned eleven provisions in the Constitution, including three that he thought threatened liberty, and all of which he said had convinced him to withhold his signature.

Gerry certainly could be faulted for one thing: most of his objections were entirely unexpected, such as to the length of senators' terms and their re-electability, which he had not opposed when decided upon, and the representation of slaves, in which his only comment had been to concur. It could not even

*Ellsworth was partly wrong: The convention agreed to Gerry's request to submit the problem of public securities to a committee. The committee did propose obligating the new government to pay the debt, but the convention softened this by simply giving Congress the power to do so. Gerry was not on the committee, but he might have been the informal author of its proposal.

be explained by his remark that he could "get over all these if the rights of the citizens were not rendered insecure" by three major flaws. There, too, Gerry had spoken out vigorously against only one, the lack of a prohibition on a standing army. He had moved to remedy another, the omission of trial by jury in civil cases, but had not put up a fight.

The third provision he found unacceptable, the power of Congress to make what laws "they may please to call 'necessary and proper,' " he had said nothing about. No one had; it had passed unanimously, without any discussion at all.

Mason, for his part, would be leaving Philadelphia "in an exceeding ill humor indeed," Madison knew. Mason considered the lack of a Bill of Rights, turned down flat by the Convention, a "fatal objection." In a way, Mason was as much to blame as anyone; he had never said a word about a Bill of Rights until five days earlier. But he deserved better than the members' near-total refusal to debate it, and Madison could see how the haste and fatigue plaguing the Convention had served "to whet his acrimony." Still, Mason had not announced, like Gerry, that he had decided not to sign the Constitution, and there might yet be a chance, Madison could hope, that Gouverneur Morris's stroke of genius for this morning's proceedings would win Mason back.

Randolph, naturally, was a much better candidate for being pulled back from the brink of refusal. His habit of vacillating might prove valuable now, and, despite his incantations of disappointment in recent days, the anger of a Gerry or Mason was missing from his attitude. In fact, a few delegates suspected that Randolph was only hesitating because of some "rival" in Virginia. On the other hand, he had linked a dangerously appealing proposal to his threats not to sign, and he might be perversely pleased enough at the impact he had had to carry through.

The state ratifying conventions, he had said, "should be at liberty to offer amendments to the plan and these should be submitted to a second convention, with full power to settle the Constitution finally." If that provision were not approved, he "should be obliged to dissent from the whole of it." Horrifyingly, Franklin himself had seconded Randolph's motion. The convention had gone so far as to refer it to the Committee on Style, which, of course, had not incorporated it, but Mason had seized on the idea, too, as had Gerry.

Agreeing, George Mason had professed that he "would sooner chop off his right hand than put it to the Constitution as it now stands," which had caused Morris to explode that he "had long wished for another convention that will have the firmness to provide a vigorous government, which we are afraid to do!"

Charles Pinckney had delivered one of his better orations on "these declarations from members so respectable at the close of this important scene [which] give a peculiar solemnity to the present moment." He urged them to think of the consequences of having the different states all devising amendments to the general government. "Nothing but confusion and contrariety could spring from the experiment. The states will never agree in their plans, and the deputies to a second convention, coming together under the discordant impressions of their constituents, will never agree." He recited his own objections, "but apprehending the danger of a general confusion and an ultimate decision by the sword," he intended to support the plan as it was.

Randolph's inconceivable suggestion had been the crowning tribulation in a subject that had continued troublesome to debate. Mercifully, no one had heeded Martin's renewed call for state legislatures to be responsible for ratification, but to Madison's consternation, Morris had some support for a motion to leave the method of ratification up to the states. So that had had to be considered before it was rejected.

The discussion then had snagged on whether to submit the Constitution to Congress *for approval* or just send it with the convention's "opinion" that Congress should transmit it to the states. To Gerry, failure to request congressional approval was tantamount to "an annulment of the confederation with . . . little scruple or formality," and even Hamilton agreed it would be "indecorum." But King had pointed out that if Congress must first approve, the Constitution might well never reach the states "and all our labor . . . lost." And the decision had been to say nothing about Congress's approval.

Hardest had been settling the number of states needed to put the new Constitution in effect, which had consumed nearly a day. Did they want to salvage the tattered fiction that they were here revising the Articles of Confederation? Then they would need approval from all thirteen states. Gazes swept to the Rhode Island table at that and Butler "revolted at the idea that one or two states should restrain the rest from consulting their safety." Yet several members, including Rufus King, had been strong for thirteen. Wilson had made a case for seven; Madison said he could agree to anything from eight to ten. They had voted on thirteen, ten, and nine, and nine had been the decision.

Washington brought down the gavel and nodded to Secretary Jackson while silence stole over the room. The young man rose and, from the four sheets of parchment, read out the completed Constitution.

Dr. Franklin stood up as soon as Jackson was done, his speech in his hand to be read, as often before, by James Wilson. Warm, personal, candid, Franklin's last plea for conciliation was also a veiled reproach to the men who planned to dissent.

"Mr. President . . .

"I confess that there are several parts of this Constitution which I do not at present approve, but I am not sure I shall never approve them. For, having lived long, I have experienced many instances of being obliged by better information or fuller consideration to change opinions, even on important subjects . . . It is therefore that, the older I grow, the more apt I am to doubt my own judgment and to pay more respect to the judgment of others. Most men, indeed, as well as most sects in religion, think themselves in possession of all truth . . ."

Never one to forego whimsy, Franklin quoted the British writer, Steele, on the infallibility of the churches of Rome and England—and recalled "a certain French lady who, in a dispute with her sister, said, 'I don't know how it happens, Sister, but I meet with nobody but myself that's always in the right.'

"Sir, I agree to this Constitution with all its faults, if they are such," Franklin said, "because I think a general government necessary for us . . . I doubt, too, whether any other convention we can obtain may be able to make a better constitution. For, when you assemble a number of men to have the advantage of their joint wisdom, you inevitably assemble with those men all their prejudices, their passions, their errors of opinion, their local interests and their selfish views. From such an assembly, can a perfect production be expected?

"It therefore astonishes me, Sir, to find this system approaching so near to perfection as it does, and I think it will astonish our enemies, who are waiting with confidence to hear that our councils are confounded like those of the Builders of Babel and that our states are on the point of separation, only to meet hereafter for the purpose of cutting one another's throats. Thus I consent, Sir, to this Constitution because I expect no better and because I am not sure that it is not the best."

Franklin would sacrifice his opinions to the public good—"within these walls they were born and here they shall die." If all of them reported their objections and sought support for them, he warned, they might damage the new government and injure the country in foreign opinion.

"On the whole, Sir, I cannot help expressing a wish that every member of the convention who may still have objections to it would, with me on this occasion, doubt a little of his own infallibility and, to make manifest our unanimity, put his name to this instrument."

Now came the motion that Morris had conceived to win back the dissidents, and, Madison knew, "put into the hands of Doctor Franklin that it might have the better chance of success"—a procedure for signing that would be ambiguous as to the opinions of the signers:

"Done in Convention by the unanimous consent of *the States* present the 17th of September &c—In Witness whereof we have hereunto subscribed our names."

"Consent of the States . . . In Witness whereof"—Would it work? The delegates had a few minutes to think. Then came another surprise.

"For the purpose of lessening objections," Nathaniel Gorham moved to reduce the ratio for members of the House of Representatives, from one for every forty thousand inhabitants to one per *thirty* thousand, and George Washington spoke for the first time in the convention.

He could not "forbear expressing his wish that the alteration proposed might take place . . . The smallness of the proportion of representatives had been considered by many members of the Convention as insufficient security for the rights and interests of the people . . . it had always appeared to himself among the exceptionable parts of the plan and, late as the present moment was for admitting amendments, he thought this of so much consequence that it would give much satisfaction to see it adopted."

"No opposition," Madison noted, "agreed to unanimously."

Now, "On the question to agree to the Constitution enrolled, in order to be signed. It was agreed to, all the states answering ay." This was the moment of decision.

Randolph came to his feet, prefacing his remarks with a reference to Franklin's speech. He "apologized for his refusing to sign the Constitution notwithstanding the vast majority and venerable names that would give sanction to its wisdom and worth." He did not mean by refusing that he would oppose its adoption; he "meant only to keep himself free." He could not pledge himself and thus be restrained "from taking such steps as might appear to him most consistent with the public good."

Urgently, other members argued that the form attested to the recommendation of the states, not the feelings of the members, and that the refusals would produce great mischief in the hands of opponents.

Hamilton rose—his "monarchy" speech, his long absences, his eagerness for a strong government well etched in the convention's mind—to plead his anxiety that every member should sign. A few men of consequence, by opposing "or even refusing to sign the Constitution might do infinite mischief by kindling the latent sparks" that were hidden by an enthusiasm for the convention which would wear off. "No man's ideas were more remote from the plan," than his were known to be, he argued, "but is it possible to deliberate between anarchy and convulsion on one side and the chance of good to be expected from the plan on the other?"

Dismayed, Franklin was back on his feet to express his "fears" that Randolph seemed to have felt himself the target of Franklin's speech. He had not known who might refuse to sign and he felt "a high sense of obligation to Mr. Randolph for having brought forward the plan in the first instance—and hoped that he would yet lay aside his objections."

Randolph did not acknowledge Franklin's olive branch. He "could not but regard the signing in the proposed form as the same with signing the Constitution." In refusing to sign, he would repeat, he took a step that "might be the most awful of his life, but it was dictated by his conscience."

Nervously and with a touch of anger, Gerry took the floor, describing "the painful feelings of his situation and the embarrassment under which he rose to offer any further observations." In his state were two parties, "one devoted to democracy, the worst . . . of all political evils; the other as violent in the opposite extreme. From the collision of these in opposing and resisting the Constitution, confusion was greatly to be feared . . . the plan should have been proposed in a more mediating shape in order to abate the heat and opposition of parties." As it was passed, "it would have a contrary effect." As for the proposed form of signing, it "made no difference."

As Randolph had done, Gerry referred to Franklin's remarks—and rejected Franklin's disclaimer by adding that he "could not . . . but view them as leveled at himself and the other gentlemen who meant not to sign."

"We are not likely to gain many converts by the ambiguity of the proposed form of signing," General Pinckney observed drily. He thought it "best to be candid and let the form speak the substance," not leave the meaning of the signers in doubt. He would sign the Constitution with the intention "to support it with all his influence and wished to pledge himself accordingly."

Perhaps now Washington looked toward Mason, sitting in stony silence with Randolph. But the convention president's oldest friend in this room, neighbor and mentor since Washington's youth, did not rise. He had carefully written down his reasons for dissenting, but the words on the paper were left unspoken.

Washington came to his feet to call for the question on Franklin's proposed form of signing. It was agreed to by ten votes.

Madison watched as the delegates approached Washington's desk, grouped in their states' geographical order, north to south, to fix their signatures. New Hampshire, Massachusetts, Connecticut . . . there was Hamilton, boldly stepping into the line for New York . . . Pennsylvania, Delaware . . .

As the line grew shorter and the last members were signing, Madison noticed Franklin looking at Washington's chair, its high back adorned with a painted sun on a horizon.

"Painters," Franklin said in his low voice, always "found it difficult to distinguish in their art a rising from a setting sun. I have often and often in the course of the session—and the vicissitudes of my hopes and fears as to its issue, looked at that behind the president, without being able to tell whether it was rising or setting. But now at length, I have the happiness to know that it is a rising and not a setting sun."

"The Constitution being signed," Madison now wrote, "the convention dissolved itself by an adjournment *sine die—*"

14

The People Speak

"DAMN HIM—DAMN HIM—everything looked well and had the most favorable appearance in this state previous to this, and now I have doubts," one Massachusetts supporter wrote another in November, two months after the convention. Once the New England newspapers began publishing a letter from Gerry to his state legislature defending his refusal to sign, friends of the Constitution had been unable to win a December date for the ratifying convention. Instead, it would be held in January, giving opponents more time to organize.

The new Constitution had appeared in Philadelphia's five daily newspapers on September 19 and in the near and distant states as fast as copies reached them. For a few weeks, the plan had enjoyed an enthusiastic, mostly unchallenged reception, but then the opposition began to find its voice and strategy.

By late November the battle was on, with antagonists of the document quickly drawing screams of agony from its supporters.

"Away ye spirits of discord! Ye narrow views! Ye local politics! Ye selfish patriots would damn your country for a six penny duty!" wrote one defender of the Constitution. "A swarm of paltry scribblers possessing posts of high emolument . . . the confirmed tools and pensioners of foreign courts" cried another, are "at this moment fabricating the most traitorous productions" in order to prevent adoption of the new government.

The first staging area for the opposition forces had been the Continental Congress in New York where Major Jackson had turned over the official engrossed* Constitution on the morning of September 20. There, incensed by the great powers proposed for the national government, its most formidable critic emerged as Richard Henry Lee of Virginia, an early Revolutionary leader and now a recent president of the Congress. He was joined by another well-regarded Virginia congressman, William Grayson, for the obverse reason that he thought it too weak.

"I look upon the new system as a most ridiculous piece of business," Grayson wrote a friend, "like the legs of Nebuchadnezzar's image: it seems to have been formed by jumbling or compressing a number of ideas together, something like the manner in which poems were made in Swift's flying island. However, bad as it is, I believe it will be crammed down our throats . . ."

R.H. Lee would have preferred that Congress simply roll up the parchment sheets and put them away, on the grounds that the convention had exceeded its authority, and Grayson was "for giving it only a silent passage to the states." But Madison and nine other congressmen, returning from the convention hot on the heels of their handiwork, had no intention of letting either be done. In two days of debate, they defeated Lee's final fallback—a set of amendments to go with the Constitution for the state conventions' action—and maneuvered the same "unanimous" vote of the states on the congressional resolution transmitting the document.

"The people do not scrutinize terms," a Virginia delegate cautioned, and congressional approval would be inferred. Washington thought so, too, and was delighted when he was informed. "This apparent unanimity will have its effect," he

---

*The original parchment prepared by the calligrapher and signed by the delegates.

wrote Madison. "Not everyone has opportunities to peep behind the curtain."

Transmittal of the Constitution to the states September 28 officially began the ratification process. Ten months would be needed to win approval in nine states, the number required to bring the new government into operation. It is in some ways a twice-told tale, because in the most closely divided state conventions, delegates debated the Constitution clause-by-clause, traveling the same ground that the federal convention had covered. Yet, in one respect, ratification was vastly more important than even the writing of the Constitution itself: it was the act (or series of acts) that breathed life into the new republic, the moment when the people themselves consented to become one nation.

For that reason, too, the contest over approval was happily a different one. The secrecy was gone; the decision to adopt was the business of everyone. The state conventions were preceded by public elections of delegates to attend them and the result was tumultuous debate. That in itself produced a further, unintended consequence: two national factions competing continentally for the first time—"Federalists" and "anti-Federalists," foreshadowing America's traditional two-party system.

From North to South, Federalists corresponded feverishly with each other passing on advice and intelligence from their states, while the Antis did the same, narrowing down their attacks to a few that seemed useful everywhere. Newspapers boosted both sides. They reprinted Gerry's letter from Massachusetts, a pamphlet by Mason in Virginia, the diatribes of "Cato" in New York, countless other essays and arguments published originally in states other than the reprinters' own. When the contest began to narrow, partisan leaders on both sides began to travel into the contested states, bringing printed essays and pamphlets to distribute, personal messages from friends for waverers, and guidance on how the other side had been handled in their own states. To be sure, it was all freewheeling and undirected, but it was the essence of a national campaign.

The names of the opposing sides caused some head-scratch-ing. For years, political leaders who exhorted their states to support the confederation had been informally known as "federal men," and though the new government would be national, or at least only "partly federal," these men—Hamilton, Madison, Morris, Wilson, and all their allies supporting the Constitution—almost immediately were known everywhere as "Federalists." Equally quickly, opponents were dubbed "anti-Federalists,"* a name they resented because they felt *they* were the real "Federalists" while their opponents aimed at monarchy or aristocracy. Doggedly, they described themselves as "Federal Republicans," but the term did not catch on.

One anti-Federalist writer struggled valiantly to make his point about the Federalists' secret monarchical aims by tracing the Latin root word *foedus,* meaning a league. As a label for those now calling themselves "Federalists," he avowed, it meant "in plain terms a conspiracy, and this is the fifth signification of the word *foedus* given by Ainsworth in his excellent Latin dictionary." Happily killing two birds with one stone, a pro-Constitution editorialist offered a distinction between the two sides that was also a reminder to his readers of the most important figure among supporters of the Constitution: "The *Federalists* should be distinguished hereafter by the name of WASHINGTONIANS and the *Anti-federalists* by the name of SHAYSITES in every part of the United States."

Public discusion sank noticeably from the high tones of the convention. One reason was that supporters wanted nothing more urgently than speed in ratification before the inevitable doubts about so radical a transformation could set in. Principles such as separated powers and proportional representation could not be lingered over; they would have to come second to argu-

---

*It would take Thomas Jefferson to rename the "Antis," as they came to be called, when he welded them into a cohesive political party early in the 1790s. The Federalists he labelled "monocrats," and to identify his faction by its principles, he called them Democratic-Republicans—"Republican" to soften the radical connotation of "Democratic." The present day Democratic party descended from them. The modern Republican party descends from the nineteenth-century Whigs and a conservative faction that split off from Jefferson's party. The Federalists, unable to keep pace with the political evolution stimulated by the Constitution they fought to establish, had vanished by 1820.

ments for public order and stabilization of the economy. For adversaries, delay was just as crucial, and getting it depended upon quickly finding and harping on fatal flaws in the Constitution. Political topics always produced vivid language and personal attacks anyway, and for an issue of such importance, the ablest pens were unsheathed on both sides to pour forth colorful and vicious rhetoric.

Gerry's opposition to the Constitution brought this from a Federalist penman: "Detractor! we can trace thee like a snail upon the rock, by the slime of defamation, which thou leavest behind thee."

To the Antis, the Federalists were a society of "Totos" recognizable by their insignia: "a man gaping very wide and straining hard to *swallow fish, tail foremost.*"

The Constitution was "gilded chains." It would substitute "an iron handed despotism" and back it with a standing army. In the end, "the poor man must . . . submit to the wealthy."

Dr. Benjamin Rush was moved to employ his pen in succor of the poor Constitution: "the hand of God was employed in this work, as that God had divided the Red Sea . . . or had fulminated the ten commandments from Mount Sinai!" Tut, tut, replied an Anti, do not blame "so imperfect a work" on God.

Of course, exceptionally fine campaign arguments would be published, too—by "Brutus" (possibly Robert Yates, one of the two New York delegates who had walked out of the federal convention) and "The Federal Farmer," both on the anti-Federal side; and "A Citizen of America" (Noah Webster) for the Federalists. But one project would be immortal: a series of eighty-five essays would begin appearing in a New York newspaper toward the end of 1787 under the signature "Publius." Initiated by Hamilton, who wrote more than fifty, and contributed to by Madison (with at least twenty-five) and John Jay (lost to the effort from illness after just five), *The Federalist* quickly was recognized as, and is still considered, the finest treatise ever written on the political principles of the American Constitution.

AND THEN THERE WAS ONE

The first state to ratify was Delaware, where public reaction was almost universally laudatory, a convention swiftly scheduled, and approval voted on December 6. Not so smooth were the proceedings in the state depicted in a widely reprinted cartoon as the "keystone"* of the federal arch, Pennsylvania.

Opposition in the Pennsylvania Assembly was western-led, full of "the cold and sour temper of the back counties," according to Gouverneur Morris. Failing to slow the ratifying rush, sixteen of those members balked it by vanishing and robbing the Assembly of a quorum just before its vote to schedule the state convention. When word spread that polite visits from the sergeant-at-arms asking the boycotters to return had met with refusal, a mob formed up eager to assist. They discovered two of the missing members at a tavern, dragged them through the streets of Philadelphia back to the State House, and dumped them—"clothes torn and white with rage"—into the Assembly Room, and blocked the door until the vote had been taken.

Unhappily, that was not the greatest indignity suffered by the anti-Federalists. The Federalists' two-to-one victory in electing delegates to the convention was marred on election night, November 6, when a drunk and triumphant Federalist mob descended on the Philadelphia home of an anti-Federalist leader, breaking windows and pounding on the door.

The short campaign in Pennsylvania was marked, too, by the earliest attacks on Washington and Franklin. Aspersions on Washington's intellect and Franklin's advanced age finally came into the open when the anti-Federalist penman, "Centinel," wrote that "the unsuspecting goodness and zeal of the one has been imposed upon, in a subject of which he must be necessarily inexperienced" and that "the weakness and indecision attendant on old age has been practiced on in the other."

The great Federalist villain was deemed to be James Wilson, whose brilliance and seemingly aristocratic demeanor combined to infuriate anti-Federalists. And when Wilson emerged

---

*giving birth to the state's permanent nickname, "The Keystone State"

270

as the leader in the Pennsylvania convention, the Antis would not forget it. After Pennsylvania on December 12 ratified by two to one, an anti-Federalist mob seized Wilson during a celebration, knocked him down, and would have beaten him to death if others had not intervened.

New Jersey accepted the Constitution on December 19, and Georgia followed on January 2, 1788—both unanimously. On January 9, Connecticut ratified with a vote of more than three-to-one, persuaded by, among other things, Ellsworth's reminder that the state needed protection from "the rapacity and ambition of New York."

In Massachusetts, the anti-Federalists' success in delaying the convention until January had begun to slow the Federalist sweep. By the end of December, as Madison would later report to Washington, the outlook was "very ominous."

According to his latest intelligence, Madison said, "there was very great reason to fear that the voice of that state would be in the negative." If so, he feared it would ricochet in New York, where opponents would succeed in blocking any call for a convention, and in Pennsylvania where "the minority . . . is very restless under their defeat . . . they will endeavor to undermine what has been done there. If backed by Massachusetts, they will probably be emboldened to make some more rash experiment."

Gerry's letter, a dissent from within the very convention, had "done infinite mischief," as Nathaniel Gorham put it, even though leadership of the anti-Federalist movement in Massachusetts was almost nonexistent. Samuel Adams was a declared but almost passive opponent of the Constitution, and Governor John Hancock was supposed to be against it but had been unwilling to show his hand. The Antis had the active labor of James Warren, the speaker of the state House of Representatives who was respected if not considered brilliant, but in terms of important names, that was all they could boast.

Massachusetts had its battle in print, of course, although the Federalists' most colorful scribe, "Landholder," hurled his bolts at Gerry from Connecticut. The anti-Federalists had a powerful home-grown warrior—the satirical revolutionary playwright, poet and historian, Mercy Otis Warren. Wife of James Warren and daughter of the deceased early revolutionary James Otis, Mercy Warren was the only woman to take a leading public role in the battle over the Constitution.

A handsome, elegant and spirited woman, Mercy Warren was sixty years old at the time of the ratification. She had been instrumental in helping start the Revolution, and although she would enjoy less success fighting the Constitution, she would see the anti-Federalists transformed into the "Republican" party and into control of the national government before her death in 1814 at age eighty-six.

"One half *The Group* is printed here, from a copy printed in Jamaica," John Adams had written James Warren from Philadelphia in 1775. "Pray send me a printed copy of the whole and it will be greedily reprinted here. My friendship to the Author of it."

The whole title of Mercy Warren's play was *The Group, a Farce as Lately Acted, and to be Re-acted to the Wonder of All Superior Intelligence, Nigh Headquarters at Amboyna.*" It was a stinging satire on British military officers that revolutionary patriots staged often and with zest.

She was among the closest of the friends of Abigail and John Adams, but in 1804 managed to offend the touchy then-expresident in her three-volume *History of the Rise, Progress and Termination of the American Revolution.* Her account of events, John wrote to her, contained some errors "in those passages which relate personally to me." Especially galling to him, after an unhappy, tumultuous presidency and defeat for reelection, was not her taking him to task for his "aristocratic" views, but her contention that "his prejudices and his passions were sometimes too strong for his sagacity and judgment." Four decades of friendship was not overturned by her criticism, but it did cool his affection for her.

When Adams wrote her ten long letters criticizing her history, she replied to each defending her work. It was a brave stand for a presidential friend to take in any era, but especially for a woman in her time—and especially because her analysis of him was true. The same insistence on saying what she considered true was what made her pamphleteering effective: she heaped damnation on her target using a particularity that made her attacks formidable to rebut.

Her quill tipped in as much venom as Ellsworth's "Landholder," Mercy Warren (writing as "a Columbian Patriot") branded the Federalists as "partisans of monarchy" and the constitutional convention as "the fraudulent usurpation at Philadelphia." She demanded a second convention "who may vest adequate powers in Congress for all national purposes, without annihilating the individual governments and drawing blood from every pore by taxes, impositions and illegal restrictions."

A huge gathering, the Massachusetts convention opened on January 8 with 330 delegates. Another twenty-five would take their seats before it closed, and the number would have been even larger if forty-six towns had not refused to be represented. By now, Rufus King wrote Washington, three clear factions could be discerned. Federalist in inclination were the commercial and landed men, the clergy, lawyers, and officers of the Revolution, and that coalition was the largest, he thought. Second in size was the Maine faction, leaning against the Constitution, and smallest, but rabid in opposition, was the populace of the western part of the state where Shays's marauding had occurred. The two smaller groups, the Federalists feared, boded to be a majority in the convention.

Three of the four Massachusetts members of the federal convention, Nathaniel Gorham, Caleb Strong, and Rufus King, had been elected to the state convention, but "Cambridge, the residence of Mr. Gerry, has left him out of the choice," Madison reported to Washington. Instead, Gerry's constituents had elected Judge Francis Dana, one of the negotiators of the peace treaty with England, and "another gentleman, both of them firmly opposed to Mr. Gerry's politics." Gerry was politically dead in the district where he long had been a leader.

The body, however, was exhumed promptly. "The opponents of the Constitution moved that Mr. Gerry should be requested to take a seat . . . to answer such inquiries as the convention should make concerning facts which happened in the passing of the Constitution," King notified Madison a week after the convention opened. This was considered "a very irregular proposal," King said, but, considering the temper of the proposers and "doubt of the issue had it been made a trial of strength, several friends of the Constitution united with the opponents . . . and Mr. Gerry has taken his seat."

King's next report to Madison was bleak. "The opponents affirm to each other that they have an unalterable majority on their side. The friends doubt the strength of their adversaries, but are not entirely confident of their own.

"An event has taken place relative to Mr. Gerry, which, without great caution, may throw us into confusion." Though Gerry ostensibly had been seated to answer questions only, "Yesterday, in the course of debate on the construction of the Senate, Mr. G. *unasked* informed the convention that he had some information to give . . . Mr. Dana and a number of the most respectable members remarked upon the impropriety of Mr. G's conduct. Mr. G. rose with a view to justify himself. He was immediately prevented by a number of objectors."

The quarrel over whether to hear him went on until it was time to adjourn, but the incident was not over. "Mr. Gerry immediately charged Mr. Dana with a design of injuring his reputation . . . and preventing his having an opportunity to communicate important truths to the convention. This charge drew a warm reply from Mr. Dana. The members collected about them, took sides as they were for or against the Constitution and we were in danger of the utmost confusion. However, the gentlemen separated, and I suppose tomorrow morning will renew the discussion."

Three days later, King had better news. "Our prospects are gloomy, but hope is not entirely extinguished. Gerry has not returned to the convention, and I think will not again be invited."

If getting Gerry out of the way did not raise King's spirits, it was undoubtedly because he was hearing so many angry speeches from the apparent majority. One typical orator was Amos Singletary, who prided himself on being a simple patriot in contrast to "these lawyers and men of learning and moneyed men, that talk so finely and gloss over matters so smoothly to make us poor illiterate people swallow down the pill." These fellows "expect to get into Congress themselves . . . and get all the power and all the money into their own hands, and then they will swallow up all us little folks, like the great *Leviathan,* Mr. President, yes, just as the whale swallowed up *Jonah.* "

Even if some back-country men felt as did Singletary, not all of them did. In immediate reply rose Jonathon Smith of Lansboro, in the Berkshires of western Massachusetts, the region of Shays's Rebellion. "Mr. President, I am a plain man and get my living by the plough," Smith began. "I am not used to speak in public, but I beg your leave to say a few words to my brother ploughjoggers in this house.

"I have lived in a part of the country," Smith said, "where I have known the worth of good government by the want of it. There was a black cloud that rose in the east last winter and spread over the west . . . burst upon us and produced a dreadful effect." Delegates from Shays's stronghold, Worcester County, tried to stop Smith, but he talked right over them.

"People, I say, took up arms, and . . . if you went to speak to them, you had the musket of death presented to your breast. They would rob you of your property, threaten to burn your houses, oblige you to be on your guard night and day. Alarms spread from town to town; families were broken up. The tender mother would cry, 'Oh, my son is among them! What shall I do for my child!' . . . Our distress was so great that we should have been glad to snatch at anything that looked like a government," even a monarchy.

"Now, Mr. President, when I saw this Constitution, I found it was a cure for these disorders . . . I got a copy of it and read it over and over . . . I did not go to any lawyer to ask his opinion . . . I formed my own opinion and was pleased with this Constitution.

"My honorable old daddy there," Smith said, pointing to Singletary, "won't think that I expect to be a Congressman and swallow up the liberties of the people. I never had any post, nor do I want one. But I don't think the worse of the Constitution because lawyers and men of learning and moneyed men are fond of it. I don't suspect that they want to get into Congress and abuse their power. I am not of such a jealous make.

"I say," Smith finished, "there is a time to sow and a time to reap. We sowed our seed when we sent men to the federal convention. Now is the harvest, now is the time to reap the fruit of our labor. And, if we won't do it now, I am afraid we never shall have another opportunity."

Happily as Smith's testimonial fell on Federalist ears, King and his allies knew that the strongest persuasion would be the acquiescence of those two icons, the most influential men in the convention—Samuel Adams and John Hancock.

A fortnight into the convention, the silent Adams, suffering the twin anguish of his son's mortal illness and his most respected friends' terror of the Constitution, seemed to remain implacably opposed. And Hancock, though the Federalists had helped elect him president of the convention from where he could maintain a plausible neutrality, had a ploy he liked better—he was staying home with the gout.

Desperate, the Federalists set out to win Hancock first, then encourage Adams. Certain that the Governor needed only a proposal that would let him recommend ratification without rebuffing his western constituents, the Federalists drew up a list of desirable checks on the new government and a speech for Hancock to give. They took it to him with a flattering appeal to save the convention and possibly the country—and an even more flattering hint: *"and we told him,"* Rufus King wrote a few days later, underlining it as if amazed at their own gall, *"that, if Virginia does not unite, which is problematical, he is considered as the only fair candidate for President."* Hancock also would have the "universal support of Bowdoin's friends [the influential former governor, James Bowdoin]," they told him. All he had to do was urge acceptance of the Constitution as written, to be sent to Congress along with the list of suggested amendments. If he would consent, they added, several strong young men would carry him to his carriage and into the convention hall. Hancock said yes.

The first break with Adams came suddenly: after a brilliant speech by Fisher Ames, a rising young Federalist who would one day be one of James Madison's most troublesome adversaries, Adams yielded on a provision in the Constitution hotly opposed by the Antis. If Adams was flexible after all, the Federalists decided, perhaps the followers who mattered most to him—the artisans and mechanics of Boston—could bring him around.

Grabbing their quills, the Federalists drew up a bare-knuckle set of resolutions attacking the anti-Federalists and called a meeting of Adams's supporters at the old Green Dragon Inn, the tradesmen's favorite gathering-place in the early days of the Revolution. The tradesmen voted their approval of the resolves, and appointed a delegation to carry it to Adams, headed by that message-bearer *par excellence,* the silversmith, Paul Revere. Adams quizzed the emissaries about the size of the meeting and, reassured that it had been very large and unanimous, agreed to consider their view.

The double strategy almost backfired. Good as his word, Hancock recovered from his gout, reclaimed the convention gavel, and at the appropriate moment of crisis delivered the speech the Federalists had written for him. Forgotten in all the maneuvering, however, was that Adams and Hancock had for years been political archrivals. Instead of jumping on the bandwagon, Adams struck back with his own list of amendments. After panic broke out in both camps, a Federalist observer later reported, Adams "perceived the mischief he had made," withdrew his motion, and gave his support to the Federal side. A roll call vote on the Constitution was immediately taken.

The decision of the Massachusetts convention on February 6, 1788, the sixth to ratify, was close: 187 Yes to 168 No.

Springtime in the seventh state, Maryland, found Luther Martin matching the savage "Landholder" open letter for open letter in that state's gazettes, a clash that began when Martin published a defense of Gerry in the *Maryland Journal* in January. True to his commitment, Martin was leading the anti-Federalist charge, and even had gone so far as to publish a thirty-thousand-word pamphlet, *The Genuine Information Delivered to the Legislature of the State of Maryland* in which he reported exhaustively on the proceedings of the convention at

Philadelphia. His penmanship, alas, served him no better than his lungs had before. On April 28, the Maryland state convention ratified the Constitution, 63 to 11.

In South Carolina, John Rutledge reported "tedious but trifling opposition," almost wholly from the inland counties, but led by the revolutionary general Thomas Sumter, former Governor Rawlins Lowndes, and Judge Aedanus Burke, all of Charleston. A certain inevitability pervaded a convention dominated by Rutledge, his brother Edward, and the Pinckneys, but the Federalists were careful. The upcountry men arrived in town to be welcomed by Charleston merchants holding open house for their pleasure, and the convention itself was distinctive for having an official bartender. The Federalist hospitality was not without value: the ratifying vote when it came was 149 to 73.

Now the approval of only one more state would bring the new government into existence—but the terrible truth was that the Constitution was in trouble in all five remaining states.

Two of them were effectively out of the running as the possible ninth. Rhode Island, continuing to defy the march of events, had refused to call a convention and instead sent the Constitution out to be rejected in individual town meetings. In North Carolina, a powerful anti-Federal movement had exploded and the spring elections for delegates to the state's convention had brought a two-to-one landslide for opponents of the Constitution. Federalists could only be grateful that North Carolina would meet in July, leaving the fate of the Constitution to be sealed in June—by Virginia, New York, and New Hampshire.

In New Hampshire, complacent Federalists had received a shock: a majority of delegates to that state's ratifying convention in February had arrived with instructions from their towns to reject. Friends of the Constitution had averted disaster only by winning a recess until June 18—mere moments before the convention would have voted defeat. The Federalists felt their chances had improved since then, but no one was celebrating yet.

The New York elections for the convention had been a

Federalist rout. Under the leadership of Governor Clinton, anti-Federalists had rolled up a more than two-to-one margin; forty-six opponents of the Constitution would go to Poughkeepsie on June 17 against nineteen Federalists. Barring a miraculous conversion, perhaps the only hope would be adoption in Virginia and New Hampshire—forcing New York to consider isolation.

Very cautious optimism was the outlook in Virginia, but the state was so huge and communication so slow that no serious prediction could be made. To all appearances, friends and foes had close to the same number of delegates. Virginia's convention was to open June 2; she could well become the ninth state.

However, neither Federalists nor anti-Federalists were under any illusion that making the Constitution official would magically produce a viable union. By staying out, New York and Virginia could reduce the Constitution to mere parchment; because of their wealth, geography, and political significance, their loss would fatally dismember the new republic. Rejection by New York alone would cut off the four New England states, by Virginia alone the three states south of her. *Both* had to come in.

Everywhere, leaders on both sides were acutely aware that the decision of any one of the three states meeting in June could be decisive in the other two. Because Virginia's convention opened first, out-of-state visitors descended on Richmond. Two, especially, drew mention—Gouverneur Morris, stumping on his wooden leg in and out of the convention hall with the Federalists and sending word back to Hamilton in New York, and the anti-Federalist publisher of the Philadelphia *Independent Gazetteer,* Eleazer Oswald, who wore a black patch over one eye and had come to make special arrangements for the Antis' correspondence because he believed the Federalists were stealing their mail.

In Massachusetts, Rufus King made arrangements for an express rider to bring news from the New Hampshire convention to Boston, from where a courier relay would take it on to Hamilton in convention at Poughkeepsie. Likewise, Hamilton asked Madison to set up an express from Richmond "authoriz-

ing changes of horses, etc., with an assurance to the person sent
that he will be liberally paid for his diligence."

"An Awful Squinting . . . Toward Monarchy"

Over the dirt roads from every part of Virginia came 170
delegates to the convention at Richmond. Riding hundreds of
miles through wilderness, the men of Kentucky arrived in their
buckskin leggings and hunting shirts, fully armed, "pistol and
hanger at belt." From the Tidewater came the lords of the great
plantations in their carriages, an attendant or slave or two following along. Farmers rode in from the middle counties and
south of the James River, college students from Williamsburg,
lawyers and merchants from Alexandria, and preachers from
almost everywhere.

The little capital was overflowing. Crowds already were on
hand for the year's great social event, the Jockey Club's annual
races, and the new arrivals packed the elegant Swan Tavern and
the local boardinghouses. The streets were thronged, and the
air of the town crackled with anticipation.

So full were the galleries at the Capitol on opening day, June
4, that the convention adjourned to the larger, recently built
New Academy on Schockoe Hill. No leaderless Antis or complacent Federalists were on hand this time, and the sides were
evenly matched. With nearly all the largest, even mythical,
figures of Virginia's revolutionary affairs involved, few hearts
that beat to the rhythm of politics could stay away.

Washington, though, did remain at Mount Vernon. His
name on the Constitution carried more than enough influence,
and he had decided the wise course would be to remain aloof
as the clash went on. He would be more the conciliator by
staying out of the fray—that would be needed when, as everyone was saying, he was elected the first President under the
system.

Foes of the Constitution in this state were not called anti-
Federalists. They were "Henryites," and they included the
frontiersmen of Kentucky and the farmers of southern Vir-

ginia—almost to a man. Twice-former governor, now back in the state legislature, Patrick Henry strode at the head of a faction that had come together in 1786 in rage over John Jay's proposed treaty surrendering navigation rights on the Mississippi River to Spain. The treaty was abandoned, but from that day to this sunny June morning two years later, Henry's followers viewed every measure favoring the central government as a plot to satisfy the avarice of the eastern states at the expense of Virginia. So bitter was the residue, in fact, that notwithstanding his anti-Federalism and his stature, R.H. Lee had been defeated for election to the ratifying convention for having supported the treaty.

Dark of complexion, grave in countenance, Henry was an irresistably dramatic figure. For his admirers he did not just arrive in Richmond, he "was seen advancing from the south side of the James, driving a plain and topless stick gig. He was tall, and seemed capable of enduring fatigue, but was bending forward as if worn with travel. His dress was the product of his own loom, and was covered with dust." Here was the "fine blue eye" flashing under long dark eyelashes and full brows, the appealing contrast of his "earnest manner" and his imperious high forehead and Roman nose, the electrifying voice that had demanded "Give me liberty or give me death,"

Henry would weave his spell, a contemporary says, with "a happy articulation and a clear, distinct, strong voice . . . every syllable was uttered. He was very unassuming as to himself, amounting almost to humility, and very respectful towards his competitor . . . He was great at a reply and greater in proportion to the pressure which was bearing upon him." At such moments, Henry's oratory would soar so swiftly and passionately that the convention stenographer later would confess he had been unable to capture it all.

The crowds expected the great confrontation to be between Henry and his rival of twenty-five years, Pendleton. But Henry himself probably had an inkling that his most dangerous adversary would be the small man with the faint voice and diffident manner whose efforts in framing the Constitution yet remained known just to an important few—James Madison, whom Henry despised.

In a short, almost pschoanalytical, memoir of Henry, his son-in-law, Judge Spencer Roane, tried to explain why Henry felt as he did about Madison. Henry, Roane wrote, "generally thought like the most of people, because he was a plain, practical man, because he was emphatically one of the people, and because he detested, as a statesman, the projects of theorists and bookworms. His prejudices against statesmen of this character were very strong."

As for Madison in particular, Roane thought Henry's youthful disadvantages played a role: "He was without a regular academical education. He was poor, married young and had a numerous family. For a great part of his life (though he died rich) he was struggling in debt and difficulties . . . Contrast him in these respects with Madison . . . Madison was born to affluence. His father early gave him a competent fortune . . . and Madison lived with his father, I believe, till past the age of forty, unencumbered with the cares of a family or with keeping a house. He had, besides, received a finished education at Princeton. He had every opportunity for improvement and his life was that of a recluse and student. Had Mr. Henry had these advantages and been as studious as Madison, he would have excelled him . . ."

During Madison's time as a Virginia legislator in the early 1780s, the judge added, Henry considered him "a man of great acquirements, but too theoretical as a politician and . . . not well versed in the affairs of men. This opinion increased in the convention of '88. He was astonished that Madison would take the Constitution, admitting its defects and in a season of perfect peace—and believed him too friendly to a strong government and too hostile to the governments of the states . . . Henry's prejudice against Madison always remained in some degree . . ."

The vast difference between the two men was never so clear as in the way each pursued the challenge that faced him in the ratifying convention. They plunged their listeners into a wrenching struggle between the head and the heart—Madison encircling Henry with cold precision and reason, and Henry's passion bursting through Madison's logic "with as much ease as Sampson did the cords that bound him before he was shorn."

The only other opponent of the Constitution anywhere near as formidable as Henry was George Mason, severely suited up in black silk as he stepped from his coach on his arrival in Richmond. In the eight months since Philadelphia, the author of the Virginia Declaration of Rights had grown, Madison said, "every day more bitter and outrageous in his efforts to carry his point" and would be, Madison correctly predicted, "thrown by the violence of his passions into the politics of Mr. Henry."

Henry had a problem that for a lesser politician might have been insuperable: the second declaration for which he was most famous was "I am not a Virginian but an American." But Henry made it impossible to hurl the phrase back at him by the ground he staked out for this fight. He was defending the *spirit* of American liberty—and Virginia would remain its true protector only by rejecting the Constitution. As Henry put it, "I mean not to breathe the spirit nor utter the language of secession; the dissolution of the Union is most abhorrent to my mind." However, "the first thing I have at heart is American liberty; the second thing is American union."

Madison and others who had served in Philadelphia had heard the opposition's specific points of attack before—notably from Luther Martin—but never with the same oratorical skill. Whether the topic was state sovereignty, the ratio of representation, trial by jury in civil cases, the "federal district ten miles square," the militia, or a standing army, Henry gave passionate proof that the plan was a threat to liberty.

"The question turns, sir," Henry said, "on that poor little thing—the expression, *We, the people,* instead of the states of America . . . Is this a monarchy, like England—a compact between Prince and people? . . . Is this a confederacy . . . ? It is not a democracy, wherein the people retain all their rights securely . . . Here is a revolution as radical as that which separated us from Great Britain."

Virginia would stand on the high ground if she refused the Constitution. "It is said eight states have adopted this plan. I declare that if twelve states and a half had adopted it, I would with manly firmness and in spite of an erring world, reject it. You are not to inquire how your trade may be increased, nor how you are to become a great and powerful people, but how your liberties can be secured, for liberty ought to be the direct end of your government . . . Guard with jealous attention the public liberty. Suspect everyone who approaches that jewel."

On providing for internal security, said Henry, the Constitution was clear, but on the rights of individuals it showed "an ambiguity, Sir, a fatal ambiguity." A standing army would spring up "to execute the execrable commands of tyranny" and the state's militia "is given up to Congress also." Hooping various clauses together, Henry warned that popular resistance would be suicidal, in face of the all-powerful government: "In what situation are we to be? The clause . . . gives a power of direct taxation, unbounded and unlimited, exclusive power of legislation in all cases whatsoever for ten miles square and over all places purchased for the erection of forts, magazines, arsenals, dockyards, et cetera. What resistance could be made? The attempt would be madness. You will find all the strength of this country in the hands of your enemies . . .

"Now, Sir, the American spirit, assisted by the ropes and chains of consolidation, is about to convert this country to a powerful and mighty empire . . . Such a government is incompatible with the genius of republicanism. There will be no checks, no real balances in this government. What can avail your specious imaginary balances, your rope-dancing, chain-rattling, ridiculous ideal checks and contrivances?"

The Constitution was said to have "beautiful features, but when I come to examine these features, Sir, they appear to me horridly frightful. Among other deformities, it has an awful squinting; it squints towards monarchy . . . Your president may easily become king . . . The army will salute him Monarch; your militia will . . . fight against you . . . What will then become of you and your rights?"

Henry's declamations on the president soared to such peaks that even the stenographer's quill was halted and he was only able to report that "here Mr. Henry strongly and pathetically expiated on the probability of the President's enslaving America and the horrible consequences that must result."

Testimonials to Henry's oratory are numerous in the papers

of his contemporaries. Some make him look ridiculous, as one tale that, in agitation, he would repeatedly push his brown wig out of place until by the end it had spun several times on his head. But others tell of listeners discreetly rubbing their wrists as if they could already feel the chains upon them, and of when, as Henry closed another hypnotic speech, a thunderstorm broke directly over the New Academy, momentarily convincing the terrified audience that, as one witness said, he had managed "to seize upon the artillery of Heaven and direct its fierce thunders against the heads of his adversaries."

Because of his oratorical gifts, Henry's image in history has tilted more and more toward his emotional effect, but that is not the whole light in which he was seen by his contemporaries. He was known, in the words of John Marshall, as "a learned lawyer, a most accurate thinker, and a profound reasoner. If I were called upon to say who, of all the men I have known, had the greatest power to convince, I should perhaps say Mr. Madison, while Mr. Henry had, without doubt, the greatest power to persuade."

The convincing Mr. Madison presented a touching contrast to Henry: he was so short that the spectators had to bob and crane to get a look at him and his voice was so soft that even the strategically placed stenographer had difficulty hearing him. And though he had performed with virtuosity before the few dozen friends and colleagues behind closed doors in Philadelphia, Madison also seems to have suffered stage fright here in front of hundreds of avid listeners. To fight it, he made numerous notes on the subject he knew so well, and the way he contrived to refer to them made him appear even more modest. According to one account, he "rose to speak as if with a view of expressing some thought that had casually occurred to him, with his hat in his hand and with his notes in his hat, and the warmest excitement of debate was visible in him only by the more or less rapid and forward seesaw motion of his body." Thus propped and disciplined, Madison managed to withstand Henry's gales and drive the debate again and again back to the logic of the Constitution.

It is always said that a close vote is won on the margins,

decided by just a few votes switched, so while Henry and Madison fought for every last one, certain other factors weighed in importance. The image of Washington was one. And Edmund Randolph's re-defection to the support of the Constitution was another.

Randolph had stunned the opposition, but his value to the Federalists depended mightily on how he dealt with the damaging charge of inconsistency. Wisely, he took the initiative in his first speech, explaining that he had wanted amendments before the new government went into operation, but with Virginia's convention occurring at such a late date, any further delay would be unwise. It would bring "ruin to the Union, and the Union is the anchor of our political salvation."

Henry, though, was giving no quarter. He managed to draw attention to a nasty rumor, spread outside the convention, that Randolph switched because Washington had offered him a job in the new administration. "I find myself attacked in the most illiberal manner by the honorable gentleman," Randolph exploded. "I disdain his aspersions and insinuations. His asperity is warranted by no principle of parliamentary decency nor compatible with the least shadow of friendship. And if our friendship must fall, let it fall like Lucifer, never to rise again!"

If tales were to be told, Randolph rushed on, he could disclose certain facts that would make "some men's hair stand on end." Henry did not retreat, but demanded that Randolph make his disclosure immediately. Randolph refused, and after adjournment, Henry and a "second" marched over to the governor's residence to challenge Randolph to a duel. Friends talked the two men into cooling off, however, and the incident ended.

Madison was to receive his own blow a few days later, when Henry rose brandishing a letter from Thomas Jefferson to a Richmond tobacco trader named Alexander Donald. "I say," Henry announced, "that his opinion is that you reject this government . . . This illustrious citizen advises you to reject this government till it be amended. His sentiments coincide entirely with ours . . . At a great distance from us, he remembers and studies our happiness. Living in splendor and dissipation, he yet thinks of bills of rights."

In almost a decade of friendship, Madison undoubtedly had observed Jefferson's devious streak, but this was the first time it had been turned against him. He knew well enough where he and his mentor held different views—in fact, he had sent Jefferson a copy of the Constitution with a seven-thousand-word cover letter designed to justify it. Jefferson's reply had been both positive and negative, but had Madison known of his friend's furious reaction to the first copy he received, from Elbridge Gerry, he might have guessed that there was more to come.

"There are things in it which stagger all my dispositions to subscribe to what such an assembly has proposed," Jefferson had written John Adams. "The house of federal representatives will not be adequate to the management of affairs either foreign or federal. Their president seems a bad edition of a Polish king.

"Indeed," he had added in an observation that would have floored Madison, "I think all the good of this new constitution might have been couched in three or four new articles to be added to the good old and venerable fabric, which should have been preserved even as a religious relic."

To another correspondent, Jefferson voiced even more anger. "Wonderful is the effect of impudent and persevering lying. The British ministry have so long hired their gazetteers to repeat and model into every form lies about our being in anarchy that . . . we have believed them ourselves. Yet where does this anarchy exist? Where did it ever exist, except in the single instance of Massachusetts? . . .

"God forbid that we should ever be twenty years without such a rebellion . . . what country can preserve its liberties if their rulers are not warned from time to time that their people preserve the spirit of resistance? . . . What signify a few lives lost in a century or two? The tree of liberty must be refreshed from time to time with the blood of patriots and tyrants. It is its natural manure. Our convention has been too much impressed by the insurrection of Massachusetts and, in the spur of the moment, they are setting up a kite to keep the henyard in order."

By the time Jefferson wrote Madison, he had given the Constitution more thought and it had begun to look better. He liked the organization of the government into three branches, and the congressional power to levy taxes, he told Madison. He felt a house chosen by the people directly would be "very illy qualified to legislate for the union, for foreign nations, etc.," but he approved of it "solely" because it preserved the principle that the people must be represented if they are to be taxed.

Jefferson was "captivated" by the compromise on equal representation in the Senate and with the way the presidential veto had been formulated, although—and this surely delighted Madison—"I should have liked it better had the judiciary been associated for that purpose or invested with a similar and separate power."

Henry was correct, Madison knew, in saying Jefferson decried the omission of a Bill of Rights—"what the people are entitled to against every government on earth," he had written Madison. But Madison must have wondered if, without warning him, Jefferson had settled his lingering doubt as to whether the Constitution should be ratified or, "after it has been duly weighed and canvassed by the people . . . to say to them 'we see now what you wish. Send together your deputies again, let them frame a constitution for you omitting what you have condemned and establishing the powers you approve.' " In other words, a second convention.

Jefferson had almost apologized at the end. "I own I am not a friend to very energetic government. It is always oppressive." But if the majority approved, "I shall concur in it cheerfully in hopes that they will amend it whenever they shall find the work wrong." By that, had not Jefferson declined to take sides?

Not exactly. Seven weeks later, Jefferson had thought up a bit of extortion and suggested it, not to Madison, but to the Richmond tobacco trader, Donald, in the letter that Henry was now using. "I wish with all my soul," Jefferson wrote, "that the nine first conventions may accept the new constitution because this will secure to us the good it contains . . . But I equally wish that the four latest conventions, whichever they be, may refuse to accede to it till a declaration of rights be annexed." Forcing the new government to limp into existence as a partial union, Jefferson predicted, would "probably command the offer of such a declaration."

Madison had written Jefferson that the opposition held "latent views of disunion" and were operating "under the mask of contending for alterations," and he was horrified to see Jefferson playing into their hands. Not surprisingly, he sounded a little stiff when he mentioned it afterward in a letter describing the convention to Jefferson.

"Among a variety of expedients employed by the opponents opinions expressed in a letter from you to a correspondent (Mr. Donald or Skipwith, I believe) and endeavored to turn the influence of your name even against parts of which I knew you approved." He assumed it would be "agreeable to yourself" that he had taken the liberty of replying with some of Jefferson's favorable comments. "I am informed that copies or extracts of a letter from you were handed about at the Maryland convention with a like view of impeding the ratification."

Jefferson's opinion about a bill of rights, coupled with the clamor for it by Henry and Mason, undoubtedly helped make the Federalists willing to introduce one early in the operation of the new government. They had not been convinced of its value at the close of the Philadelphia convention; both Madison and Washington had stood behind James Wilson's legal analysis that it was not necessary. But Massachusetts had demonstrated that the public was uncomfortable with the powerful government proposed, and Mason and Henry's much abler use of the issue in Virginia brought into view a real concern: that the people might never be happy under the government without such protection. And the need for it would be beyond doubt once the Federalists compared notes on New York and New Hampshire, where it would be a problem too.

The comings and goings of out-of-state opponents and their vigorous correspondence must have given frequent butterflies to Edmund Randolph, for he was hiding one more secret as carefully as he had hidden his change of heart: he had subverted the anti-Federalists' most promising tactic for aborting the convention. He was suppressing a letter from New York's anti-Federalist governor, George Clinton, inviting the Virginia convention to confer with New York's on the need for a second federal convention. It was an official communication in reply to an official Virginia communication, but Randolph locked it up until the last day of the convention, then delivered it to the Virginia House of Delegates just as the legislators rushed off to hear Henry's last speech before the vote on ratification.

"On the final question, the ratification passed—89 ayes, 79 noes . . ." Madison wrote Washington "in haste" on June 25.

"Mr. Henry declared," he added a couple of days later, "that although he should submit as a quiet citizen, he should seize the first moment that offered for shaking off the yoke in a *constitutional way.*" He believed Henry would try to unite two-thirds of the states on a petition for amendments "or to get a Congress appointed . . . that will commit suicide on their own authority."

Still weak from a fever that had knocked him out for several days early in the convention, Madison was exhausted. He had carried the main burden in the fight against Henry; seventeen of Henry's speeches had replied to Madison compared to fifteen answering all the other Federalists combined. But Madison was not able to vacation, not yet. He rushed Hamilton's messenger off to Poughkeepsie and then headed for New York, where he laid Virginia's ratification before the Congress two weeks later.

NEW YORK

"It is with unfeigned concern I perceive that a political dispute has arisen between Governor Clinton and yourself," George Washington had written Hamilton back in October. "But, as you say, it is insinuated by some of your political adversaries . . . 'that you *palmed* yourself upon me and was *dismissed* from my family . . . I do therefore explicitly declare that both charges are entirely unfounded . . . I have no cause to believe that you took a single step to accomplish, or had the most distant idea of receiving, an appointment in my family till you were invited thereto. And . . . your quitting it was altogether the effect of your own choice."

Hamilton had been forced into a humiliating request to Washington to vouch for him after someone using the pen name "Inspector" attacked him in the *The New-York Journal* as "an upstart attorney" who, during the Revolution, had imposed on Washington but "was at length found to be a superficial, self-conceited coxcomb and was, of course, turned off and disregarded by his patron." Published a few days after the close of the federal convention, the article was the fourth salvo in a public fight Hamilton had picked with the governor in July when he had returned to New York to discover that Clinton was predicting "a mischievous issue" from the work being done in Philadelphia.

After the Constitution was unveiled, the governor had refused to call elections for a ratifying convention and the fight intensified. Contributors defending both men ratcheted the newspaper rhetoric down a few notches—with a Hamilton partisan calling Clinton a "designing croaker," and the other side replying in verse, "To Hamilton's the ready lies repair/Ne'er was lie made which was not welcome there."

Washington exonerated Hamilton on "Inspector's" charge, but he added pointedly that, "when the situation of this country calls loudly for unanimity and vigor, it is to be lamented that gentlemen of talents and character should disagree in their sentiments for promoting the public weal." That was all the reprimand Hamilton needed. Within days, he had decided to switch his tactics.

First, he drafted his dark-eyed Betsey, now three months pregnant with their fourth child, to serve as general in charge of the home battlefield on a scale unparalleled in their married life. Two, three, four evenings a week she presided over her dinner table at their Wall Street home, while her husband talked, persuaded, and cajoled the men who had come to dine and learn the virtues of the new Constitution. Betsey oversaw everything—menu, seating, instructions to the servants on wine, when to withdraw the cloth, what the after-dinner service would be (walnuts, for some reason, were conducive to deep thought; the men would crack them and talk, crack them and sip their brandy, crack them and alternate with their pipes). At the right moment, she would rise and lead the ladies away for a card game and wine, leaving her husband to apply the last pressure to the men. When he was writing arguments for publication, the evenings would grow very long; she would wait up to see if he wanted her to read parts of his work—as he sometimes did.

Soon after receiving Washington's letter, Hamilton decided to elevate the public debate with a series of addresses to the people of New York. Sailing down the Hudson River from his in-laws' estate in Albany, Hamilton wrote the first "Publius" essay, which he would publish in the New York *Independent Journal* on October 27. Once home, he solicited help from Madison, Jay, Gouverneur Morris, and a bright, sophisticated ally named William Duer (who would bring Hamilton untold grief in a few more years). Morris was not interested, but Duer wrote two numbers, signed "Philo-Publius," which were not included when "Publius" was first collected in book form, under the title *The Federalist.*

"Publius" worked feverishly. In the early stages the writers showed each other their work, but then stopped doing so, Madison said, "there being seldom time for even a perusal of the pieces by any but the writer before they were wanted at the press, and sometimes hardly by the writer himself." The project was not intended to become as long as it did, but the work continued through the end of May, 1788, spreading out to be published by two or three of the New York papers, sometimes with more than one number appearing on the same day.

It is safe to say that many passages of the *Federalist* were written with a sigh and a grimace. After all, Hamilton felt "no man's ideas were more remote" from the Constitution than his, and Madison had been beaten on some of his favorite proposals. But the very test given their ideas in Philadelphia had instructed them on the premises of the document as it finally emerged. It provided them with an ability—totally beyond the power of any opponent—to cover all the ground, pro and con, that an openminded reader could want. Though too scholarly to be popular, Publius was influential because he left no stone unturned to let the public probe the Constitution. That was different from upbraiding the other side, and it put the Constitution on ground to which honest men could repair, if they had to. The only question was: what would force honest men to repair to it?

One thing certainly was the faint rumble of civil war. New York City was so Federalist that Antis mockingly called it "Hamiltonapolis," but the solidarity there underscored what John Jay was to write Washington shortly before the convention. "An idea has taken root," he said, "that the southern part of the state will, at all events, adhere to the union and, if necessary to that end, seek a separation from the northern."

Another was the fact that Governor Clinton was no Patrick Henry clinging passionately to a lofty ideal, however misperceived. The big, growly, popular New York leader was an out and out political boss bent on saving his regime.

Clinton was fifty-one years old and at the peak of his political power at the time of the ratification. His power base was upstate New York, where the attitudes resembled those of Patrick Henry's back-country men. He had been a general in the Revolution, albeit not a very successful one, but his constituents did not care. In 1777, they elected him both governor and lieutenant governor. Clinton graciously declined the lieutenant governorship in favor of being governor, withdrew from an active military role, and took control of the office he had held ever since. He was the champion of the people restraining the baronial Schuylers and Livingstons.

The upstart Hamilton, nationalist, son-in-law of General Phillip Schuyler (repairer of Clinton's military botches), and pro-Tory litigator, had stepped on Clinton's toes in 1782. Appointed receiver of Continental taxes, Hamilton had had the effrontery to call upon Clinton and inform the governor that he, Hamilton, would collect those taxes directly, himself. Their battle had been going on ever since.

Clinton had never tried to subvert the Continental Congress from his and his supporters' point of view. He had merely refused to let it interfere with his state, which seemed to them perfectly legitimate. They could also point to New York's record in paying confederation assessments, which was as good as or better than most of the other states.

The Achilles' heel of fighting for the status quo was that the status quo was going to change, and New York would be facing a whole new relationship with the members of the former confederation, with unknown consequences. As Henry Knox, the secretary of war, said, "it is a stubborn fact . . . the confederation has run down . . . the springs have utterly lost their tone and the machine cannot be wound up again." But New York's voters had not been quick to see the weakness.

Clinton had left it up to the legislature to call elections, which it had taken until February to do, and when the April vote tally for delegates was in, the shocking 46-to-19 margin for the Antis had made Hamilton grateful that the convention was still more than a month away. "Notwithstanding the unfavorable complexion of things," he had written Gouverneur Morris, friends of the Constitution had two reasons for hope—the possibility that nine states would have ratified before New York decided and his own intuition of "the probability of a change of sentiment in the people."

The state capital, Poughkeepsie, had a permanent population of only about three thousand. But as a busy port town on the Hudson River, it was accustomed to visitors and welcomed the illustrious sixty-five delegates to the convention by trimming its principal avenues with bright flags, colorful flowers, and greenery. For proponents of the Constitution, the time was come for a stiff upper lip. The *Poughkeepsie Country Journal,* playing both sides in a town divided about two-to-one for the Federalists, reminded them of the temper of the opposition in repulsive metaphor by printing a letter from "Turtle Dove" to "Mr. Soaring Lark":

"The hawks, owls, ravens, vultures, kites, etc. are gathering all the sour, nauseous, obscene and offensive matters . . . to burn our Phoenix. And out of her ashes is to arise an enormous big Eagle that is to prey upon us as long as there is feather, skin, flesh, muscle, fiber, entrail, etc. left; and then they are to take our bones to make nests of, to lay in, and to hatch more of those greedy birds of prey. But let us destroy their eggs, sir."

The little band of nineteen had two leaders—its titular head, the chancellor of New York, Robert R. Livingston, and its driving force, Hamilton. Fruitful and cordial, this alliance would be their last; failing to mind his political p's and q's later this year, Hamilton would alienate Livingston with a chain of damaging consequences that would leave his friends and party reeling. Third most important politically, and greater than Livingston intellectually, was John Jay, who would speak more often than any other proponent except Hamilton. The mayor of New York, James Duane, was the next-best-known and the fourth most frequent speaker on the team.

The Antis' whip was held, of course, by the governor, Clinton, but their side also boasted one of the state's finest thinkers, Melancton Smith. Smith would lead the Clintonians' fight, rising forty-five times either to propose amendments or to offer "acute and logical discussion," in the words of a Federalist spectator, in a "dry, plain and syllogistic" style. It behooved an adversary to think clearly in debate with Smith, "or he would find it . . . embarrassing to extricate himself from a subtle web." Next most heard-from would be John Lansing, Jr., who had led the fight in Philadelphia for the small states' bloc and then departed mid-convention with Robert Yates. Yates, too, had been elected to Poughkeepsie, so it was inevitable that Hamilton's "monarchy" speech would rise up to smite its author—though it was strange that Hamilton would be surprised.

Delay had been the enemy of ratification last fall, but now the Federalists' best hope was playing for time—to let the New Hampshire and Virginia results come in. Hamilton and Livingston quickly put their heads together and drafted an opening resolution calling for the convention to debate the Constitution clause-by-clause. Knowing that Clinton had in mind a quick vote and adjournment, they were skeptical—and surprised when the motion passed.

"We yielded," an uneasy Yates wrote to a friend, "to prevent the opposition from charging us with precipitation." Clinton was upset at the sacrifice of strategic advantage to such scruples and blamed Melancton Smith for wanting to show off his debating skill—saying later that "his vanity lost the state."

For a week, the convention waded through the clauses, sticking for several days on the ratio of representation, while the Federalists patiently chipped away at the prejudice that held the Antis together. Hamilton spoke, a listener said, with "energy and considerable gestures. His language was clear, nervous . . . His candor was magnanimous . . . His temper was spirited

but courteous . . . and he frequently made pathetic and powerful appeals to the moral sense and patriotism, the fears and
hopes of the assembly."

It was hard to come up to the Henrys, Hamiltons and Smiths
of the world, but Gilbert Livingston, Clintonian and a cousin
of the chancellor, was at least willing to try. Late in the first
week, he burst forth against the Senate in a speech that was
finally interrupted as he pleaded, "What, what will be their
situation in a Federal town? Hallowed ground! Nothing so
unclean as state laws to enter there, surrounded as they will be
by an impenetrable wall of adamant and gold, the wealth of the
whole country flowing into it!"

"What?" cried a Federalist. "What WALL?"

"A wall of gold, of adamant, which will flow in from all parts
of the continent," Gilbert blurted, his metaphor in hopeless
collapse. "At which," the stenographer wrote, "a great laugh
in the house."

The good news from New Hampshire arrived at the beginning of the second week, on June 25. By tirelessly campaigning
in the back country during the four-month adjournment, the
Federalists had brought in that state, fifty-seven to forty-six, in
a speedy three-day convention. The confederation was dissolved, announced Robert Livingston in Poughkeepsie. New
Hampshire was the ninth state. The Antis pronounced themselves unmoved—"It is still our duty to maintain our rights,"
said Lansing—but, Smith, while saying that he had long expected New Hampshire to ratify, acknowledged that he was
partly convinced though he would not budge in the absence of
amendments.

"Our only chance of success depends on you," Hamilton
wrote Madison two days later, not knowing that Virginia had
just ratified. "There are some slight symptoms of relaxation in
some of the leaders—which authorizes a gleam of hope if you
do well—but certainly I think not otherwise." Only a "gleam"
of hope was Hamilton's pessimistic assessment; he had heard
that Clinton several times had "declared the UNION [Hamil-
ton's emphasis] unnecessary" and, at least in his own anxious
mind, it was possible that a majority of the convention might
agree.

New York's potential isolation had been a main theme in the Federalist argument from the opening, and the ninth state's ratification, if not decisive, was pertinent enough. Both sides began to hit harder.

Hamilton struck the first blow directly against Clinton when the debate moved on to the power of direct taxation. An intrusion on state prerogatives, the Antis had contended; the old requisition system was best. But in a private conversation with James Duane, Clinton himself unthinkingly recalled its defects. Dashing to the archives, the Federalists unearthed a dozen of Clinton's old speeches and official letters and Hamilton introduced them the next day—"to prove," he said, "that this state, in the course of the late revolution, suffered the extremes of distress on account of this delusive system."

Furious, Clinton denounced Duane as "uncandid," but he was obliged to insist that he favored a strong, efficient government. The damage was done. Hamilton could pointedly ask why Clinton now defended a tax system that he formerly had damned, and go on with authority in a long speech defending the Constitution's unlimited power of taxation.

Before he finished, however, he sought to smooth any ruffled feelings in words oddly revealing of both his nature and his lifelong naiveté. "I am apprehensive, Sir, that in the warmth of my feelings, I may have uttered expressions which were too vehement. If such has been my language, it was from the habit of using strong phrases to express my ideas, and, above all, from the interesting nature of the subject. I have ever condemned those cold, unfeeling hearts which no object can animate. I condemn those indifferent mortals who either never form opinions or never make them known . . . If anything has escaped me which may be construed into a personal reflection, I beg the gentlemen once for all, to be assured that I have no design to wound the feelings of anyone who is opposed to me."

His lowly origins seem to be in his mind in his reply to the repeated claim that the Constitution would enslave and ruin the governed by giving all power to a few ambitious men. "If the gentlemen reckon me among the obnoxious few, if they imagine that I contemplate with an ambitious eye the immediate honors of the government—yet let them consider that I have my friends, my family, my children to whom the ties of nature and of habit have attached me. If today, I am among the favored few, my children tomorrow may be among the oppressed many . . . The changes in the human conditions are uncertain and frequent. Many on whom fortune has bestowed her favors may trace their family to a more unprosperous station, and many who are now in obscurity may look back upon the affluence and exalted rank of their ancestors."

John Lansing's eye did not moisten; he remembered Hamilton's monarchy speech and could prove that Hamilton advocated enslaving the states. He came to his feet charging "an inconsistency in Col. Hamilton's conduct." In the Philadelphia Convention, said Lansing, the gentleman "argued with much decision and . . . plausibility that the state governments ought to be subverted" and none of their laws should take effect "without an officer of the United States present."

Hamilton "interrupted Mr. Lansing and contradicted in the most positive terms" the charge of inconsistency, adding, "I think it highly improper and uncandid for a gentleman to mention in this committee arguments by me used in that convention."

With the chair calling for order, Lansing shouted back, "I am charged with being uncandid and improper . . . the matters of that convention were no longer secret when their proceedings were published."

Another call to order went unheard as Hamilton replied furiously, "A disingenuity is imputed to me—that honorable member ought to retract it—it is improper to be here introduced—because if my sentiments were improper—the convention thought differently—to bring forth individual sentiments to operate against the acts of convention—"

"A warm personal altercation," the *New York Daily Advertiser* said delicately, "engrossed the remainder of the day." However, as the incident "may wear a complexion not perfectly satisfactory to the parties, the Editor presumes that the public will excuse an entire omission of the subject." But the biographer of John Lamb, another New York anti-Federalist, wrote many years later that Colonel Oswald, the Philadelphia pub-

lisher who had been in Richmond making the Antis' mail secure, was now on the scene in Poughkeepsie and challenged
Hamilton to a duel with pistols—a challenge withdrawn after
a formal exchange of messages.

"Our arguments confound but do not convince," Hamilton
wrote Madison despairingly. "Some of the leaders . . . appear
to me to be convinced *by circumstances* and to be desirous of a
retreat. This does not apply to the Chief, who wishes to establish *Clintonism* on the basis of *Antifederalism.*"

About a half-hour after noon on July 2, New York's circumstances changed still more. While Governor Clinton was speaking, a messenger suddenly appeared at the door for Hamilton,
provoking "such a buzz through the House, that little of his
Excellency's speech was heard." The sight of the rider's foam-
ing bay horse drew a crowd of Federalists and, when they
learned that he carried news of Virginia's ratification, they
struck up a jubilant impromptu march—with fife and drum—
round and round the courthouse.

Ten states had joined the union; New York, Rhode Island,
and North Carolina alone remained outside. The prospect of
isolation was now coldly real. A spectator believed "a visible
change took place in the disposition of the House," and he may
have been right. But the anti-Federalists would not surrender
for more than three additional weeks.

On July 4, the convention delegates laid aside their contest
to exchange toasts to the twelfth anniversary of Independence
and to mingle cordially over dinner. But elsewhere party passions ran high and dangerous. In Brooklyn, thirteen Federalists
gathered at Dawson's Tavern to celebrate with "curses called
down" on the Antis. At Albany, a Federalist parade crossed
paths with an anti-Federalist procession and, in the resulting riot
of swinging bayonets, clubs and swords and hurled stones, one
person was killed and eighteen injured.

The wily Clinton realigned his troops; their declared position
became that they would accept the Constitution with the
amendments which they proposed to introduce. Hamilton and
the Federalists sat silent and listened to the amendments and the
bill of rights that Lansing had brought in. Hamilton became

desperate, like a man wielding a pickaxe who finally breaks through hard rock to spy still more below.

The Antis were playing an amendments game: ratification, but only to be effective after amendments; amendments with a deadline after which the ratification would be withdrawn; ratification with declarations as to which parts of the Constitution New York considered too ambiguous to adhere to; and, now, finally, talk was heard of merely recommending amendments.

On July 11, Jay offered the first resolution calling for ratification and Hamilton made a long and impassioned speech in support, finishing with an entreaty to the convention "to make a solemn pause and weigh well what they were about to do."

He "received from every unprejudiced spectator the murmur of admiration and applause," the *Daily Advertiser* reported. "Very different was the effect upon his opposers . . . Even the man who of all others should set the first example [Clinton] . . . Even he was incensed . . . This man, immediately after the adjournment, made a public declaration to this effect: 'I see the advocates of the Constitution are determined to force us to a rejection. We have gone great lengths and have conceded enough . . . if convulsions and a civil war are the consequence, I will go with my party.' "

Smith countered Jay's resolution with one of conditional ratification until a second convention could be held, during which time New York would not adhere to certain parts of the Constitution. This resolution was approved.

Hamilton dispatched "Philo-Publius," William Duer, on a fast horse to Madison, who had a few days earlier arrived in New York. Hamilton's dauntlessness had been daunted; he feared that Smith's version was the last stop. "Let me know your idea of the possibility," he begged Madison, "of our being *received* on that plan."

At once, Madison replied: The proposition "is a *conditional* ratification . . . it does not make New York a member of the new union, and consequently . . . she could not be received on that plan . . . The Constitution requires an adoption *in toto* and *forever*. It has been so adopted by the other states . . . any *condition* whatever must vitiate the ratification."

When Hamilton read the letter, no one asked "who elected Madison?" They knew he was speaking the truth; New York could not get away with it. But they kept on debating amendments anyway, Hamilton advised Madison, "without having decided what is to be done with them."

On July 23, a delegate named Samuel Jones, a Long Island lawyer and staunch Clintonian state assemblyman, rose with a three-word amendment to Smith's resolution. He called for "upon condition" to be deleted, and "in full confidence" put in its place. His amendment passed, thirty-one to twenty-nine.

But what to do about all of New York's objections remained. Lansing again moved that New York reserve the right to withdraw, but Hamilton argued that "it implied a distrust of the other states—that it would awaken their pride and other passions unfriendly to the object of amendments." In any case, he added, "it . . . was *no* ratification." The solution came in the form of a circular letter from the convention to the other states. Written by Jay and edited by Hamilton, the letter announced that "a majority of us" found several articles so objectionable that only their full confidence that the articles would be revised and "an invincible reluctance to separating from our sister states" had induced them to approve the Constitution.

The vote of the state of New York to accept the Constitution passed by a margin of just three—thirty to twenty-seven.

North Carolina did not enter the union until November 21, 1789—after Congress had passed and sent out to the states a bill of rights. Rhode Island ratified by only two votes on May 29, 1790.

15

Interregnum

EARLY IN THE MORNING OF APRIL 7, 1789, Charles Thomson, former secretary of the Continental Congress, boarded a southbound stage in New York, headed for Alexandria, Virginia. The dispatch he carried was short, but the new Congress had meant to pay him special tribute by appointing him to deliver it, a high honor for which he was grateful.

The message was signed by John Langdon of New Hampshire, president *pro tempore* of the United States Senate. "Sir," it said, "I have the honor to transmit to your Excellency the information of your unanimous election to the office of President of the United States of America. Suffer me, Sir, to indulge the hope that so auspicious a mark of public confidence will meet your approbation and be considered as a pledge of the affection and support you are to expect from a free and enlightened people."

Thomson could look forward to seven days of travel—barring bad weather—in which to consider his remarks for the moment of presenting the announcement to George Washington. He also would have plenty of time to reflect on the services he had rendered, as well as the retirement he craved. He could not be other than content as he settled in for the trip which would culminate in his escorting the first president back to New York.

Now sixty years old, Thomson had served as the secretary of Congress since 1774. He had, as far as is known, never missed a day of work in fifteen years. From the first exciting days when words of revolution rang the rafters in the Philadelphia State House, through eviction by British invasion, mortification by home-grown rebels, and the dwindling attendance in the later years, until the dreary and unnoticed death of the Congress just one month ago, Thomson had never accorded his duties anything less than his most perfect respect.

When important business had gone begging because too few members appeared, Thomson wrote beseeching their attendance. A scholar of Latin and Greek as well as a wealthy merchant, he was easily the peer of any delegate and much superior to some, but his letters unfailingly blended impeccable courtesy with his earnest insistence. "I think it of great importance to the honor and safety of the Confederacy that Congress should be in session and the form at least of government kept up in the present situation of affairs," was a typical plea.

Sometimes he used a light touch, as he did calling one young bachelor back to Philadelphia: "I acknowledge, my dear sir, the beauties and agreeable situation of Annapolis and will admit that the graces and charms of its nymphs are not excelled by those of the inhabitants of Calypso's isle . . . But these are not the objects of the patriot's pursuit . . . I confess, therefore, I should not be sorry if some kind mentor, I care not whether in the form of a mosquito or a fever and ague, were to drive you from that enchanting place . . . and force you to turn your attention to the concerns of this young and rising empire which demands your care."

In the summer of 1787, Thomson had even raided the federal convention at Philadelphia for a quorum to complete work on the Northwest Ordinance, over which the Congress had labored almost four years. His sense of history probably told him the bill would be the Continental Congress's greatest legislative achievement. And his realism probably warned that it might never be done over, no matter how good the new government might be.*

The last eight months of life of the old body had been, by turns, familiar and eerie—unlike anything Thomson had known. As soon as nine states had ratified the Constitution, the Congress, in a great burst of enthusiasm, had brought itself together—all thirteen states present for only the second time since 1776—to make the necessary arrangements for its own death and burial.

It had quickly set dates for the states to choose electors of the president, for the electors to meet and cast their ballots, and for the new Congress to assemble, count the votes, and commence the new government. But several weeks had been consumed in wrangling over *where* it should begin. Philadelphia lost when Delaware voted nay in an attempt to have Wilmington chosen; Lancaster, Pennsylvania was rejected in another vote and then—"to the surprise of everybody," as Madison had said— Baltimore was selected. However, the New England members complained bitterly, South Carolina's delegation changed its mind, and the vote was rescinded. When the contest was left between New York and Philadelphia, the delegates from Rhode Island—who were the necessary seventh vote for New York—quit the Congress, wounded by criticism of their making decisions for a government they had rejected. Things had stuck there for weeks.

Toward the end of July had come a day when nothing could be done: Even though New York's convention was still fighting over ratification, the city's Federalists had decided to mount a huge celebration of the Constitution. Uncharitable men held that the timing was meant to terrify upstate holdouts at Poughkeepsie, but Congress had been invited to participate and all but the North Carolina delegation did.

The centerpiece had been an enormous parade. Besides flag-

---

*The absence of two of Abraham Baldwin's colleagues in response to Thomson's quorum call made it possible for that Georgia delegate to cast his vote with the small states' bloc. Baldwin's vote divided the Georgia tally and produced the deadlock that almost ended the convention.

bearers, bands, and militia troops, the thousands of marchers and specially made floats included the city's bakers displaying an enormous "federal loaf"; the coopers' float depicted a barrel of thirteen staves which was being given new hoops; the furriers had a real Indian miming a delivery of pelts; the brewers produced a dray carrying a three-hundred-gallon cask of ale, with "a *living Bacchus,* a very handsome boy" perched atop. The tailors, the hatters, the wig-makers, the pewterers, the upholsterers, the blacksmiths, sailmakers, the block-and-pump makers, and even the farmers had displays. But the grandest entry was a thirty-two-gun frigate, more than thirty feet long and ten feet wide, drawn by ten white horses and manned by more than thirty seamen and marines in different uniforms. The ship, which fired a thirteen-gun salute as it moved down Broadway, was called *The Hamilton;* its figurehead was a sculpture of the thirty-one-year-old Federalist leader. The procession wound through the city, ending at "the Fields" on the edge of town where the members of Congress and six thousand guests feasted on bullocks and mutton roasted whole in open pits.

At mid-August, when North Carolina rejected the Constitution, that state's congressmen decided to abstain on any votes implementing it. That let Pennsylvania, Delaware, and three southern states hold out for Philadelphia, effectively blocking a decision until mid-September when they finally yielded to New York, for fear of "strangling the government in its birth."

Within days of the decision, Thomson was back on familiar ground: the quorum had vanished. It reappeared for two days, but at the end of September, the city of New York, in effect, evicted the Congress from City Hall by launching a noisy remodeling to ready the building for the new government. The remaining members regrouped in John Jay's office, where attendance dribbled away until only three states were represented. On October 10, however, a quorum was made to perform what turned out to be its last official act—rejecting a motion on an administrative problem.

The dying of the confederacy had been a slow one. Thomson recorded a handful of members late in October, four states fully represented and three partly in January, 1789, and even a day toward the end of that month when the old body came within one member of being able to do business. In February, the names became fewer until day after day had passed with no one present but Charles Thomson and his journal book. Thomson's last entry on the *Journal of the Continental Congress* was a note of attendance on March 2, 1789: "Mr. Phillip Pell from New York."

His own last official act had been a letter to the governors of the thirteen states: "I have now the honor to transmit to your Excellency, herewith enclosed, two copies of the Thirteenth Volume, which closes the Journal of the United States in Congress Assembled . . ."

Serving unofficially in the same post while the new Congress gathered, Thomson saw again an old, awful symptom. Opening day was March 4, 1789, but neither house had a quorum. Travelers reported bad roads and bad weather; word came that some elections had been delayed. Everyone had agreed it was true—and whispered uneasily of apathy. The new Congress had finally begun its business on April 6.

THE PRESIDENT-ELECT

At Alexandria on the morning of April 14, Dr. James Craik, who was an old family friend of Washington, met Thomson and took him on to Mount Vernon, where they arrived shortly after noon. Washington, delighted that Thomson had been sent, greeted them at the door and invited the emissary to rest and refresh himself before they proceeded with their business.

At one o'clock, the two men faced one another in Washington's formal dining room, where Thomson presented the dispatch from Langdon and made the plain, brief remarks he had prepared to announce Washington's election. Washington replied formally that "I cannot, I believe, give a greater evidence of my sensibility to the honor which they have done me than by accepting the appointment. I am so much affected by this fresh proof of my country's esteem and confidence, that silence can best explain my gratitude."

Even so, the president-elect could not hide his dismay at the late gathering of the first Congress. He explained that he was prepared to leave within two days, "considering how long time some of the gentlemen of both houses of Congress have been at New York, how anxiously desirous they must be to proceed to business, and how deeply the public mind appears to be impressed with the necessity of doing it speedily."

Washington's coach drew away from Mount Vernon at ten o'clock in the morning, April 16. Martha was not with him. She was still learning to accept the new disruption of their life. He had been called by the public, she knew, and he was responding "according to his ideals," but she had never thought "any circumstances could possibly have happened" to require his going "into public life again. I had anticipated," she wrote Marcy Warren with a touch of bitterness, that after sacrificing eight years in the prime of his life to the war "we should have been left to grow old in solitude and tranquility together."

Her husband had not hurried her. He knew how much the change involved—not only seeing to the safekeeping of the household they would leave behind, but making a new one in an unfamiliar city where she would also be a principal figure in society. He had written to Madison in New York to help find him either "rooms in the most decent tavern" or a house he could rent that would be "tolerably convenient." With the pressures bearing on both his purse and his wife, he was "not desirous of being placed *early* in a situation for entertaining."

Traveling with Washington were his former military aide, Col. David Humphreys, and Thomson. Washington was pensive. He wrote in his diary that he "bade adieu to Mount Vernon, to private life and to domestic felicity . . . with a mind oppressed with more anxious and painful sensations than I have words to express." To his old friend, the secretary of war, Henry Knox, he had been more explicit. "My movements to the chair of government will be accompanied by feelings not unlike those of a culprit who is going to the place of his execution." Every nerve warned him that perils awaited in leading his country onto unknown and uncharted ground.

The journey to New York sharpened the sensation with

307

almost unbearable poignancy. One tumultuous scene followed another as Washington made his way north. Alexandria had echoed with memory—its citizens were his neighbors and friends. They celebrated him with a farewell dinner, speeches, and toasts to which he replied "from an aching heart." At Baltimore, another dinner and hours of speeches and toasts were followed by a predawn rising and departure to the roar of a cannon salute and accompanied by a local delegation on horseback.

Two hours west of Philadelphia, Washington exchanged his carriage seat for a white horse which he rode toward the city, followed by a train of riders which grew longer as they were met at each crossroad. At Gray's Ferry, he found the bridge trimmed in fresh greenery, with triumphal arches erected at either end, and, as he rode across, "certain machinery" plopped a wreath of laurel on his head. Dreamed up by the painter, Charles Willson Peale, the maneuver had been executed by Peale's own charmingly garlanded fifteen-year-old daughter, Angelica, who had been hiding in the foliage on the bridge. However, the startled hero snatched off the coronet, to the regret of Philadelphia leaders who had hoped to preempt his refusal of it. The *Pennsylvania Packet* estimated that twenty thousand people lined Washington's route into the city, where he was welcomed by cannonades and troops of militia, while the parade behind him grew until "the column swelled beyond credibility itself." A grand civic banquet in his honor was followed by an evening of fireworks. He departed the next morning, taking advantage of a rainstorm to decline an escort of city light horse.

The greeting at Trenton tore at Washington's heart. Here he had crossed the icy, storm-whipped Delaware in darkness fourteen years earlier to mount the bloody surprise attack on the British, his only victory in the year-old war. Now a warm spring sun shone, and on the shore where his wet and freezing men had landed stood "a numerous train of white-robed ladies leading their daughters." Above them rose an arch of flowers upon which the blossoms had been arranged to say, *December 16, 1776—January 2, 1777. / The Defender of the Mothers Will Be the*

Protector of the Daughters. When the white-robed girls stepped forward singing and casting flowers before his horse's feet, tears filled Washington's eyes and he was hardly able to reply.

Each town having a church bell, a cannon, and a militia troop seemed to have a welcoming party until finally Washington reached Elizabethtown, New Jersey. There a great barge waited to carry him across the bay to Manhattan, its crimson-canopied deck crowded with city and state officials and members of the new House and Senate. The vessel received a thirteen-gun salute as it passed the battery at Staten Island and a Spanish warship, with a roar of its guns, unfurled the flags of more than two dozen nations to welcome the world's youngest nation. Private and public boats followed in procession, while barges carrying musicians and choirs drew alongside. One participant even saw a school of porpoises that "came playing amongst us." A carpeted staircase draped in red bunting awaited the barge at Murray's Wharf, and the view on approaching was one of "heads standing thick as ears of corn before the harvest."

Atop the platform, flanked by New York officialdom, waited Governor George Clinton, who obviously had ignored Washington's polite letter refusing a welcoming ceremony. Still friends despite Clinton's continuing exertions against the Constitution, the two men made the gestures of a formal greeting while the cheers of the crowd obliterated their words. Declining the carriage arranged for him, Washington walked the half-mile to his rented house on Cherry Street, a stroll that took half an hour because of the mob pressing around him. Inside the residence, he received the local leaders, influential citizens, and, of course, old friends and officers from the Revolution. With their departure, it was on to the governor's banquet and from thence a rainy ride through the streets to view the candle displays, called illuminations, placed in the windows of houses throughout the city.

Whole books can be written about the meaning of a triumphal arrival such as Washington's, but it is hard to imagine him needing them. He heard much more than the love and admiration he had earned by leading America's military struggle for freedom; he heard the frenzied anticipation that he would also lead her to happiness in peace. That night, exhausted, he made his regular entry in his diary. Describing briefly his welcome, he added that it "filled my mind with sensations as painful (considering the reverse of this scene, which may be the case after all my labors to do good) as they were pleasing."

THE VICE-PRESIDENT

Washington's inauguration was set for April 30, one week from the date of his arrival, and the president-elect gave over the interval to resting from his trip and receiving and paying visits.

Meanwhile, the three-week-old Senate was already hard at work in the "Federal Hall"—the old city hall at Wall Street and Nassau, now elegantly refurbished under the supervision of Major Pierre Charles L'Enfant.* Presiding over the debates from a desk set upon an elevated dais was Vice-President John Adams, who had been back in America about a year. Among the twenty-six senators arrayed before Adams were seven of the framers of the Constitution, including Oliver Ellsworth and William Johnson of Connecticut, William Paterson of New Jersey, and Pierce Butler of South Carolina. An eighth, Rufus King, would soon join them, taking his seat in July.

Details about the Senate's work in the first two years of the government very nearly eluded history, because while the Senate recorded its motions and votes as the Constitution required, it continued the tradition of the Continental Congress, meeting behind closed doors and making no transcript of debates. Fate intervened, however, in the form of Senator William Maclay, a farmer from near Harrisburg in western Pennsylvania, who kept a personal diary of the daily proceedings. Not only was he a faithful scribe in the privacy of his boardinghouse room, but, never intending to publish the journal, he created a record of the years 1789 to 1791 that is colloquial, opinionated, vividly colored, thoroughly malicious, and often hilarious.

*The same L'Enfant who would lay out the design for the City of Washington in the 1790s

Trained in law and the classics, Maclay was fifty-two years old, six feet, three inches tall, thin, with a great dome of a forehead, a long nose, and an air of severity. He believed that the ideal society was agrarian, and he loathed anything that smacked of pomp, ambition or high-toned government—in other words, the distinguishing marks of the Federalists who were running everything. Not surprisingly, he was neither happy nor comfortable with the company in which he found himself, but he went along with what he thought necessary, so that his journal provides a nearly panoramic view of life in the new government.

All ceremony was suspect to Maclay, even going with a group of senators to pay respects to the president-elect. "What a perfidious custom it is!" he wrote afterward. He had gone, "mind this, not to resent it, but to keep myself more out of his power." And that thought was very typical of William Maclay.

Maclay doubted everyone—he was completely nonpartisan in that way—but his most savage lampooning was reserved for John Adams, whose unfortunate self-consciousness all too often bespoke pomposity and left him naked to the scratchings of Maclay's quill. As the democratic-minded senator studied the characters around him for telltale signs of aristocratic tendencies, he repeatedly turned a cruel eye on Adams.

Adams gave him such an opportunity on Saturday, April 25. Maclay was out of sorts to begin with—he "did not embark warmly" that morning—and the subject at issue was the style the Senate should follow when the president entered the chamber to be sworn in next week.

"Ceremonies, endless ceremonies, the whole business of the day," Maclay complained. "The Vice-President, as usual, made us two or three speeches from the Chair. I will endeavor to recollect one of them." And he did, preserving for all time poor Adams's discovery of the dilemma of the office of vice-president.

" 'Gentlemen,' " Maclay quotes Adams, " 'I do not know whether the framers of the Constitution had in view the two kings of Sparta or the two consuls of Rome when they formed it; one to have all the power while he held it and the other to

311

be nothing . . . Gentlemen, I feel great difficulty how to act. I am possessed of two separate powers . . . I am Vice-President. In this I am nothing, but I may be everything. But I am president also of the Senate. When the President comes into the Senate, what shall I be? I cannot be president then. No, gentlemen, I cannot, I cannot. I wish gentlemen to think what I shall be.'

"Here," Maclay wrote, "as if oppressed with a sense of his distressed situation, he threw himself back in his chair. A solemn silence ensued. God forgive me, for it was involuntary, but the profane muscles of my face were in tune for laughter in spite of my indisposition.

"Ellsworth thumbed over the sheet Constitution and turned it for some time. At length, he rose and addressed the Chair with the utmost gravity:

" 'Mr. President, I have looked over the Constitution (pause), and I find, sir, it is evident and clear, sir, that wherever the Senate are to be, there, sir, you must be at the head of them. But further, sir (here he looked aghast, as if some tremendous gulf had yawned before him), I shall not pretend to say.' "

Adams was equally solicitous that the president be accorded at least as much respect as a European monarch. When Maclay contended that the Senate reply to the president's inaugural address should not refer to *His most gracious speech,* Adams, Maclay said, "rose in his chair and expressed the greatest surprise that anything should be objected to on account of its being taken from the practice of that government under which we had lived so long and happily formerly . . . he was for a dignified and respectable government and, as far as he knew the sentiments of people, they thought as he did."

Maclay was not so radically "democratical" that he was not embarrassed to find himself arguing with the vice-president, but he stuck to his position that the phrase would offend the people and that "if such a thing as this appeared on our minutes, they would not fail to represent it as the first step of the ladder in the ascent to royalty."

But the phrase had been his, Adams said. He "could not possibly conceive that any person could take offense at it." He was not opposing Adams personally, Maclay replied, "although it was a painful task, it was solely a sense of duty that raised me." While Maclay answered, "The Vice President stood during this time—said he had been long abroad and did not know how the temper of people might be now."

Adams took Maclay aside after adjournment and argued earnestly with him. Maclay remained unyielding in his "sense of duty" but "begged him to believe that I did myself great violence when I opposed him in the chair." Adams then, says Maclay, "got on the subject of checks to government and the balances of power. His tale was long. He seemed to expect some answer. I caught at the last word and said undoubtedly without a balance there could be no equilibrium, and so left him hanging in geometry."

Maclay blamed Adams and the unpredictable anti-Federalist, Richard Henry Lee, for a new controversy that broke out when it came time to decide how the Senate reply should be addressed. Some preferred "His Excellency," others "His Elective Excellency," while the Judicial Committee, led by Ellsworth, recommended "His Highness the President of the United States of America and Protector of the Rights of the Same." Maclay and others opposed to titles tried to get an adjournment, managing only to upset Adams—"for forty minutes did he harangue us from the chair."

The vice-president's speech concluded, Maclay says, with a plea that the president be entitled "something greater still" than the titles that abounded in foreign courts. "What will the common people of foreign countries, what will the sailors and the soldiers say, 'George Washington, President of the United States'? They will despise him *to all eternity.* This is all nonsense to the philosopher, but so is all government whatever."

Many senators resented Adams's persistent thumping for high-toned forms and they mockingly gave him the title "His Rotundity." But Adams was not unconscious that he was swimming upstream; he was speaking his convictions, even while wondering more than once if he had been too long gone from his country. Yet neither he nor it had actually changed: he always had been among a limited number of leaders who believed the trappings of power served beneficial purposes, and his countrymen had always associated those same devices with oppressive government. What Adams seemed not to have realized—perhaps because men like Roger Sherman, Richard Henry Lee, and Oliver Ellsworth still agreed with him—was how extremely unpopular this minority point of view had become in his ten years' absence.

He discovered it after the Senate rejected a report by a joint committee of both Houses that had concluded that the chief executive should be addressed by no other title than as provided in the Constitution, "President of the United States."

"The House was soon in a ferment," a Massachusetts member, Fisher Ames wrote later. Titles were "repugnant to republican principles, dangerous, vain, ridiculous, arrogant and damnable. Not a soul said a word *for* titles, but the zeal of these folks could not have risen higher in case of contradiction." Since House debates were open to the public, Ames was not sure whether all the excitement was meant to impress the galleries or to begin establishing an adversarial relationship between the two Houses. In any case, Ames accurately predicted that "the business will end here. Prudence will restrain the Senate from doing anything at present, and they will call him President . . . simply."

THE INAUGURATION

The taverns, boardinghouses and private homes of New York were groaning with the influx of thousands of visitors. "We shall remain here, even if we have to sleep in tents, as so many will have to do," wrote one Miss Bertha Ingersoll to a Miss McKean. "Mr. Williamson had promised to engage us rooms at Frauncis's, but that was jammed long ago as was every other decent public house; and now, while we are waiting at Mrs. Vandervoort's in Maiden Lane, till after dinner, two of our beaus are running about town, determined to obtain the best places for us to stay which can be opened for love, money or the most persuasive speeches."

The city announced the great day with a sunrise cannonade of thirteen rounds and residents and visitors were out early to get places with a good view of the balcony of Federal Hall where Washington would take the oath. By the time of the early afternoon ceremony, the crowd would be so dense that in the eyes of one young girl, Eliza Morton, it would look as if "one might walk on the heads of the people."

The skies were fair, though at about eight o'clock some clouds gathered on the horizon. They were gone by nine when the bells of all eight churches in the city pealed for half an hour and their congregations met to pray for "the blessings of Heaven upon the new Government, its favor and protection to the President and success and acceptance to his administration."

Services over, the people came out from the churches and military units began to march from their quarters "with flaunting banners and the liveliest music."

As noontime approached, Washington dressed in a suit which he had ordered with the idea of using this occasion to encourage American manufacturing. Tailored from brown Connecticut broadcloth, it had silver buttons decorated with spread eagles. To this he added white silk stockings, shoes with silver buckles, and his dress sword. Then he sat down to wait for the Congressional delegation that would escort him.

At twelve came the sound of the marching troops, and "soon after," Washington's secretary, Tobias Lear, recorded in his diary, "the committees of Congress and heads of departments* came in their carriages to wait upon the President to the Federal Hall. At half-past twelve, the procession moved forward, the troops marching in front with all the ensigns of military parade. Next came the committees and heads of departments in their carriages. Next the President in the state coach and Colonel Humphreys and myself in the President's own carriage. The foreign ministers and a long train of citizens brought up the rear. About two hundred yards before we reached the hall, we descended from our carriages and passed through the troops,

---

*New departments remained to be established by law, but the confederation departments of War and Foreign Affairs were continuing as formerly until then, under General Henry Knox and John Jay.

who were drawn up on each side, and into the Hall . . ."

The members of both Houses waited inside, among them, of course, Senator Maclay. "This is a great, important day," the Pennsylvanian wrote that evening. "Goddess of etiquette, assist me while I describe it."

The Senate had set eleven-thirty as their time to convene, but Maclay had been dressed and out of his lodgings shortly after ten.

"Turned into the Hall. The crowd already great. The Senate met." Adams opened the proceedings, Maclay says, with a new worry over who should sit and stand during the president's address, starting a debate that continued until "all at once, the Secretary, who had been out, whispered to the Chair that the clerk from the Representatives was at the door with a communication. Gentlemen of the Senate, how shall he be received?"

Another debate began, Maclay says, while "repeated accounts came that the Speaker and Representatives were at the door. Confusion ensued; the members left their seats" to rush to open the door for the Speaker and members of the House. Then, "here we sat an hour and ten minutes before the President arrived—this delay was owing to Lee, Izard and Dalton [the Senate half of Washington's congressional escort] who had stayed with us while the Speaker came in, instead of going to attend the President."

When the president finally arrived, Maclay writes, he "advanced between the Senate and Representatives, bowing to each. He was placed in the chair by the Vice-President," who then took his own seat on the right while the Speaker of the House sat in the one on Washington's left. A hush fell.

Adams had prepared a short welcoming speech, but was struck by stage fright as silence lengthened. Finally, Adams "rose and addressed a short sentence to him. The import of it was that he should now take the oath of office as President. He seemed to have forgot half what he was to say, for he made a dead pause and stood for some time, to appearance, in a vacant mood. He finished with a formal bow, and the President was conducted out the middle window into the gallery (balcony)," where there waited an armchair and a small table draped in red bearing a large Bible.

The cheering crowd jammed all the streets that could be seen from the second-floor porch. Washington laid his hand over his heart and bowed several times, then took his seat while more and more dignitaries filed onto the portico until all who could fit had found a place.

When he rose to be sworn, Washington moved near the railing in order to let as many as possible below see him. The crowd became silent. "Small, short" Mr. Otis, secretary of the Senate, held the open Bible while Robert R. Livingston, chancellor of New York, administered the oath prescribed by the Constitution—"Do you swear," Livingston asked, "that you will faithfully execute the office of President of the United States and will, to the best of your ability, preserve, protect and defend the Constitution of the United States?"

"I solemnly swear," Washington replied, repeating the words of the oath.

"It is done," Livingston said. Turning to the crowd, he raised his hand and shouted, "Long live George Washington, President of the United States." They answered with a roar of approval, ending in three lusty cheers.

"The scene," wrote an onlooker, "was solemn and awful beyond description . . . The circumstances of the President's election, the impression of his past services, the concourse of spectators, the devout fervency with which he repeated the oath, and the reverential manner in which he bowed down and kissed the sacred volume, all these conspired to render it one of the most august and interesting spectacles ever exhibited."

The company came back into the Senate chamber, where, Maclay writes, "The President took the chair and the Senators and Representatives their seats. He rose—and all arose also — and addressed them. This great man was agitated and embarrassed more than ever he was by the leveled cannon or pointed musket. He trembled, and several times could scarce make out to read, though it must be supposed he had often read it before. He put the fingers of his left hand into the side of what I think the tailors call the fall of the breeches [side pocket], changing the paper into his right hand. After some time he then did the same with some of the fingers of his right hand. When he came to the words *all the world,* he made a flourish with his right hand, which left rather an ungainly impression. I sincerely, for my part, wished all set ceremony in the hands of the dancing-masters, and that this first of men had read off his address in the plainest manner, without ever taking his eyes from the paper, for I felt hurt that he was not first in everything."

Fisher Ames, as gifted as Maclay in malicious and unsparing writing but not burdened by his resentments, saw Washington's inaugural address differently:

"Time has made havoc upon his face. That, and many other cirumstances not to be reasoned about, conspired to keep up the awe which I brought with me. He addressed the two Houses in the Senate chamber; it was a very touching scene, and quite of the solemn kind. His aspect grave, almost to sadness; his modesty, actually shaking; his voice deep, a little tremulous, and so low as to call for close attention; added to the series of objects presented to the mind and overwhelming it, produced emotions of the most affecting kind upon the members. I, Pilgarlic [a self-mockery on the order of "stupid fool"], sat entranced. It seemed to me an allegory in which virtue was personified."

Addressing the hundred or so lawmakers and dignitaries, Washington dwelt on two themes that had often been in his letters and remarks—his sense of duty to the office he had been asked to fill and his hope for the blessing of divine Providence. As to "particular measures," he chose to be deferential, expressing confidence that the legislative branch would provide the various authorities needed to carry out the purposes of the Constitution. However, he did make a point of Article V, the procedure for amending, declaring his "entire confidence" that the lawmakers would respond to "the objections which have been urged against the system" and the "inquietude which has given birth to them."

He surprised no one when, just before ending, he informed them that he declined the president's salary as he had done the commander-in-chief's. This, he explained, accorded with his personal standard of public service, but—making sure he set no formal precedent—he carefully noted that compensation was "indispensably included in a permanent provision for the executive department."

After congratulatory handshaking all around, the members joined the visiting dignitaries in the inaugural procession—reformed in the same order as before, but this time on foot—which moved on to St. Paul's Chapel where the Episcopal bishop "read prayers suited to the occasion." With that, the first inauguration of an American president was over. "We were then met at the church door by our carriages," Lear wrote, "and we went home."

Inaugural night was for celebrating. After a quiet dinner at the house on Cherry Street, the new president and his two aides, Humphreys and Lear, rode in carriages to the home of the chancellor, Robert Livingston, and from there went on to the residence on Broadway of Washington's old military comrade, Henry Knox, and Knox's wife, Lucy. Although dozens of New York figures might have made a good claim on Washington for the evening, his spending it with Knox was especially fitting.

Called the three-hundred-pound Boston bookseller as often as he was called General Henry Knox, secretary of war, Knox had served with Washington from the beginning of the Revolution. Washington had named him commander of the Continental Artillery—though everything Knox knew about it he had only read in books—and they had corresponded constantly since the war ended. Much of Washington's fear for the country before the constitutional convention he had poured out to Knox in his letters, and, for his part, Knox had worked fervently to promote the Constitution.

Everybody talked about Knox's weight and Lucy's (around two hundred fifty pounds), but they were one of New York's best-liked couples, especially for the gaiety and good conversation at the dinners and teas they gave in their home. On Inauguration night, Washington and a large crowd of other guests gathered on the spacious veranda from where "we had a full view," Lear said, of "a display of most beautiful fireworks and transparent paintings at the Battery." At ten o'clock, the president and his aides said goodnight to the Knoxes and set out for Cherry Street—on foot, because the streets were so full of revelers that a carriage could not get through.

16

"We Are in a Wilderness"

COVERING ABOUT A SQUARE MILE on the lower tip
of Manhattan Island, New York City was America's second
largest and probably its fastest growing city. In twenty years, its
population of thirty thousand persons would double.

When King George III's troops had evacuated the town six
years earlier, refugees (about half the inhabitants) returned to
find the city's best buildings, including many churches, turned
into hospitals, jails, warehouses, barracks, and stables. Beautiful
shade trees had been axed for fuel, the street paving had not
been kept up, and the city's wells had become polluted. Trinity
Church stood a charred ruin—one of seventeen hundred buildings burned in a great fire that swept the city (some suspected
sabotage) shortly after the British seized it in 1776.

The residents had rushed to work rebuilding, and in 1789
not many traces remained of the devastation. Municipal authorities had erected a poorhouse and foundling home—together called City Hospital, a Government House and a House
of Correction. A college, a medical hospital, a lending library,
and the John Street Theater all had been privately established
or reopened and were well patronized.

Piers and wharves had been repaired; public markets and shops were thriving. Throughout the city, coffeehouses and taverns catered to the men's political and eating clubs—the most prestigious being the Tontine coffeehouse at Nassau and Wall, where Alexander Hamilton and the Federalists gathered.

Some things remained raw or, at least, uncosmopolitan. The narrow streets ran so haphazardly that travelers complained of difficulty getting around, and sidewalks, where they existed, were both narrow and gouged by cellar openings which reduced the width even more. The residents were not meticulous about keeping the streets clean, a visitor noticed, and "it is not unusual to see animals of all sorts wandering about, chiefly cows and pigs. Although windowpanes and sidewalks are washed on Saturday, nobody bothers to remove the dead dogs, cats, and rats from the streets."

One section was ahead of the rest: the vicinity of Wall Street and Broad. There, reconstruction of Trinity Church had been finished for about a year, and a business district had sprung up nearby. On these streets were clustered the fashionable homes of leading businessmen, attorneys, and public officials, and on fair Sundays groups of finely attired men and women could be seen strolling along the Battery or picnicking nearby.

Hamilton lived at 57 Wall; another leader at the bar, who was soon to be appointed state attorney general, Aaron Burr, was at No. 4 Broadway near Henry Knox's and the governor's house; United States representatives and senators were packed into the fine boardinghouses on Wall, Maiden Lane (Madison and four other Virginians were at No. 19), Great Dock, and Water streets. William Maclay was housed at Mr. Vandolsom's near (appropriately enough) Bear Market. Washington's house on Cherry Street near the East River was considered "uptown" and not quite as fashionable as the neighborhood of Wall Street; John and Abigail Adams had rented Richmond Hill, an elegant mansion overlooking the Hudson River from Greenwich Road, where Washington had kept the Continental Army headquarters during the winter of seventeen seventy-six to seventeen seventy-seven.

An official Inaugural Ball, canceled as inappropriate with Washington's lady absent, was replaced by a private ball attended by about three hundred a week later at the city Assembly Room on Broadway near Wall. As part of the "very splendid" production, a page met each lady as she entered and presented to her an ivory fan made in Paris that revealed a medallion portrait of Washington in profile when it was opened.

"The collection of ladies," wrote a guest, "was numerous and brilliant and they were dressed with consummate taste and elegance." And elegance—as jewelry was not fashionable in 1789—was stamped by the gowns and headdresses and was achieved with painstaking and time-consuming labor.

"One favorite," wrote a memoirist, Colonel W.L. Stone, who seemed to have a photographic eye, "was a plain celestial blue satin gown with a white satin petticoat. On the neck was worn a very large Italian gauze handkerchief with border stripes of satin. The headdress was a *pouf* of gauze in the form of a globe, the *creneaux,* or headpiece, which was composed of white satin having a double wing in large plaits and trimmed with a wreath of artificial roses, falling from the left at the top to the right at the bottom in front and the reverse behind. The hair was dressed all over in detached curls, four of which, in two ranks, fell on each side of the neck and were relieved behind by a floating *chignon.* "

Unfortunately, Colonel Stone forgot to say who was wearing what, but the costume might well have belonged to beautiful Sarah Livingston Jay, wife of John Jay. Sally Jay never came up in gossip without it being mentioned that while the Jays were in Paris in 1783, a theater audience had risen to its feet, mistaking her for Marie Antoinette. Although criticized as vain and domineering (Jay, the Spanish ambassador said, loved her "blindly,"), she was a leader in New York society.

But she was not *the* leader. Rather she was part of a collegium of about a dozen women, including at least two other Livingstons, all of whose spouses had become prominent during the Revolution. Washington had known many of them since the army's winter encampments when they joined their husbands for the idle months, and he happily danced to the full length of propriety with his favorites.

The civic ball was followed a week later with a grand ball at the residence of the French consul, the Count de Moustier, who "exhausted every resource to produce an entertainment worthy of France," according to the Marchioness de Brehan, the consul's sister-in-law and mistress (a scandal because the society women thought she was old and ugly, Madison told Jefferson).

The highlight of the minister's ball, beginning immediately after Washington entered the ballroom, enraptured even the jaded. "A most curious dance, called *En Ballet*" was performed, a congressman wrote to his wife. "Four of the gentlemen were dressed in French regimentals and four in American uniforms; four of the ladies with blue ribbons round their heads and American flowers, and four with red roses and flowers of France. These danced in a very curious manner, sometimes two and two, sometimes four couple and four couple, and then in a moment all together, which formed great entertainment for the spectators to show the happy union between the two nations."

In another room, a wall-to-wall table cut the room in half. Behind it, "the whole wall . . . was covered with shelves filled with cakes, oranges, apples, wines of all sorts, ice creams, et cetera and highly lighted up. A number of servants from behind the table supplied the guests with everything they wanted . . . as they came in to refresh themselves, which they did as often as a party had done dancing." Showing that he was behaving himself, the congressman added, "we retired about ten o'clock in the height of the jollity."

". . . LIKE AN EASTERN LAMA . . ."

"The paper will only mark out the mode and the form," a member of the Constitutional Convention had observed. "Men are the substance and must do the business." With Washington's inauguration over, the question was: what should come next?

For Congress, the answers were obvious. It must establish a revenue base—a steady, reliable flow of money for operating the government—and it must pass laws creating the executive departments and providing for the judiciary as well. In short, it needed immediately to legislate the organic matter of the government.

The president's situation was different. Washington had to wait for the Congress to create his departments and fund them. The delay was fortunate because it allowed time for consultation on his appointments and for informing him on recent foreign and domestic developments. It also gave Washington a chance to consider the outward appearance of the presidency, a matter of great delicacy and importance.

Washington had not forgotten—despite the fever pitch of his welcome—that the American people were not of one mind about this government. By adopting regal pretensions, he could do great damage to the *political* authority which the Constitution implied for his branch, provoking the Congress to undermine his actual authority at the outset. But if he took careful steps to delineate the executive image, to elevate it in a distinctly American way, the exercise of presidential powers would meet with greater trust and and approval.

At Knox's inauguration-night party or a few evenings after, the president took Alexander Hamilton aside. He had to stop the steady stream of callers. As he put it to someone else later, "by the time I had done breakfast, and thence till dinner, and afterwards till bedtime, I could not get relieved from the ceremony of one visit before I had to attend another. In a word, I had no leisure to read or to answer the dispatches that were pouring in upon me from all quarters."

To conserve his working hours, Washington had decided to fix a time to receive visitors—from two to three o'clock Tuesdays and Fridays. He also felt he should neither return visits nor accept invitations to entertainments. That was not just a matter of time, which would have been tremendous; he did not think it would be appropriate for the president to socialize other than officially. He had arranged to have his policy on visiting published in the newspapers of Saturday, May 2.

But other things needed to be thought out. He was responsible for setting the tone of the office, one that the public would accept as well. What etiquette then, he asked Hamilton, would be proper for the president? Hamilton offered to put his ideas in writing and send them along in a few days.

On May 5, Washington held the first of his newly instituted receiving days, and according to his secretary, Tobias Lear, "we had a numerous and splendid circle between the hours of two and three." But the president was not going to get away un-scathed with his first announced policy. Already noisy grum-bling had started over the advertisement, which had looked like a royal proclamation to the vigilant guardians against monarchy and had alarmed his supporters, too.

The day after the announcement, a former comrade in arms, General Arthur St. Clair, had gone out collecting reaction that he intended to take to Washington. He hunted up Maclay for his opinion, which Maclay, of course, gave. Maclay conceded that a deluge of visitors would make it impossible for Washing-ton to take care of business. "But, on the other hand," he told St. Clair, "for him to be seen only in public on stated times, like an Eastern Lama, would be equally offensive."

If nobody could see Washington privately, it would weaken him; business would be done without him, Maclay predicted. Or, just as bad, he would be accused of favoring those who were allowed to visit, and at the same time, everyone would pay court to those supposed favorites.

If St. Clair did repeat his view to Washington, Maclay added, "best never make any mention of my name . . . my late conduct in the Senate had been such as would render any opinion of mine very ungracious at court." (Maclay had been leading the fight in the Senate against creating a presidential title, which he believed Washington craved.)

As a former president of the Continental Congress, St. Clair did not have to wait for Tuesday or Friday to speak to Washing-ton, which he apparently managed to do. Either wickedly or in ironic coincidence, that same week Washington sent Senator Maclay a ticket inviting him to the president's box at the John Street Theater the following Saturday night—Washington's first attendance at the playhouse since taking office. Maclay confessed to his diary:

"Went. The President, Governor of the State, foreign ministers, Senators from New Hampshire, Connecticut, Pennsylvania, M. and South Carolina, and some ladies in the same box. I am old, and notices or attentions are lost on me. I could have wished some of my dear children in my place. They are young and would have enjoyed it. Long might they live to boast of having been seated in the same box with the first Character in the world. The play was the 'School for Scandal.' I never liked it; indeed, I think it an indecent representation before ladies of character and virtue. Farce: the 'Old Soldier.' The house greatly crowded, and I thought the players acted well; but I wish we had seen the 'Conscious Lovers,' or some one that inculcated more prudential manners."

Maclay's ticket may have been wasted, but Washington had not expected it to solve the problem in any case. Criticism such as the Pennsylvanian's, he knew, could not be treated lightly. He now had received Hamilton's letter on etiquette and he had been mulling it over carefully.

Hamilton thought that an hour just one day a week for receiving visitors was enough, with the president actually being present for about half that time. Formality was not necessary—"he may converse cursorily on indifferent subjects with such persons as shall strike his attention," and, when his half-hour was up, "disappear." *Who* may visit should be controlled; "a mode of introduction through particular officers will be indispensable."

While Hamilton agreed that the president should not return visits or accept invitations, he recommended giving two or four "formal entertainments" each year on the anniversaries of important events in the revolution. If two, the occasions should be Independence Day and the inauguration of the president, "which completed the organization of the Constitution."

If the president wished to make it four times a year, then Hamilton recommended adding the dates of the treaties of alliance with France and of peace with Britain. He did not explain why, but the result of his list would be to commemorate America's milestones in freedom, government, military power, and peace.

The guest list for formal entertainment should be limited to members of the two houses of Congress, principal officers of the government, foreign ministers, and "other distinguished strangers." At that, the list would go well over a hundred, but "separate tables in separate rooms" were acceptable and he saw no other way by which foreign ministers could "with propriety be included in any attentions of the table which the President may think to pay."

Shooting for some informality, Hamilton proposed that on the visiting days the president either personally or through an aide invite up to six or eight legislators or other "official characters" to dine with him that same day.

Others might disagree with the last recommendation, Hamilton said, but "I believe it will be necessary to remove the idea of too immense an inequality, which I fear would excite dissatisfaction and cabal. The thing may be so managed as neither to occasion much waste of time, nor to infringe on dignity."

Interestingly, Hamilton used the opportunity to raise an issue that still bedevils presidents and sometimes gets them into trouble: "It is an important point to consider what persons may have access to Your Excellency on business."

Department heads and certain foreign ministers were entitled to the privilege, Hamilton thought. Members of the Senate should also have "a right of *individual* access on matters relative to the *public administration* . . . I believe that it will be satisfactory to the people to know that there is some body of men in the state who have a right of continual communication with the President. It will be considered as a safeguard against secret combinations to deceive him."

Members of the House of Representatives might be offended, which deserved some thought, Hamilton said, but the Constitution gave a reason for the distinction—it joined the Senate and president in executive functions on treaties and appointments. "This makes them in a degree his constitutional counsellors and gives them a *peculiar* claim to the right of access."

Hamilton's advice was miles away from what would make the hospitable Virginian feel at home or give free play to Washington's political style—the diffuse, random, and numerous private contacts through which he spread his influence and kept himself informed. It was, however, a long stride in the direction Washington wanted to head: a pattern under which official entertaining and official access would help support the dignity of his office and its purposes.

The president was enormously pleased. "I beg you to accept my unfeigned thanks for your friendly communications of this date—and that you will permit me to entreat a continuation of them as occasions may arise," he replied that same day.

He had his secretary rewrite Hamilton's suggestions in the form of a series of questions on private and public etiquette and sent the queries to John Adams, John Jay, and Madison. One question that he added makes clear how badly his published notice had backfired. "What will be the least exceptionable method of bringing any system . . . before the public?" he asked.

After a week of keeping all his associations official, Washington could see that he would not relish doing so for the next four years. Would it be improper for the president to make informal visits, he asked, "that is . . . calling upon his acquaintances or public characters for the purpose of sociability or civility?" If he could, how could it be made evident that the calls were private "so as they may not be construed into visits from the President of the United States?" And lastly, asked the most avid tea-partygoer in America, "in what light would his appearance *rarely* at tea-parties be considered?"

Adams's reply did not differ much from Hamilton's advice except in one striking respect: Adams did not suggest that any official or lawmaker had a *right* to see the president or that the President had a duty to see any, as Hamilton had done. Adams's advice hews more closely to modern practice: "In every case, the name, quality, and—when these are not sufficient to raise a presumption in their favor—their business, ought to be communicated to a chamberlain, or gentleman in waiting, who should judge whom to admit and whom to exclude."

Private visits would definitely not be improper, Adams said. Informal attire and "few" attendants would show that such visits were made as a citizen or a friend. "The President's private life should be at his own discretion and the world should respectfully acquiesce," Adams said. However, he did recommend one exception to the no-visits-in-the-character-of-president rule: The president should return a call by a visiting sovereign.

Washington continued to receive on Tuesdays, but he turned over the Friday "levee"* to his wife when she arrived at the end of May, participating in her receptions as a private guest rather than as president. She soon moved her levees from afternoon to evening, and had them handled as tea-parties at which the ladies were able to be seated—though the men remained on their feet, as they did when visiting the president.

Talk rated his receptions as stiff and dull, but "Lady Washington's" were popular, in part because the president relaxed and enjoyed himself. But the main reason Martha Washington's visitors left happy was that the chubby, grandmotherly Martha—as she has come down to us in history—was, in fact, a consummately graceful hostess.

Abigail Adams, a gifted observer with several years in European courts for reference, was unstinting in her praise of Martha Washington. She found her "plain in her dress, but the plainness is the best of every article . . . Her hair is white, her teeth beautiful" and her figure better than Abigail's own. The president's lady, she said, "is one of those unassuming characters which create love and esteem. A most becoming pleasantness sits upon her countenance and an unaffected deportment which renders her the object of veneration and respect."

Martha and her husband were both happy to adopt John Adams's view on going out privately, but the world at large continued to differ on its interpretation of proper presidential deportment. Within three months, Washington was receiving concerned letters from Virginia about suspiciously high-toned manners in New York.

To an old friend who passed along gibes reportedly made by Patrick Henry at the governor's dinner table, Washington re-

---

*Critics attached the label to Washington's receiving hour. The word was appropriated from the French, 'to raise or elevate,' and was the nomenclature for the British king's visiting hours. The expression adhered, even after criticism died away.

plied with undisguised irritation that the question of titles had been settled ("I hope never to be revived"); that he had never seen the vice-president out with more than two horses drawing his carriage, let alone six, as claimed; that his Tuesday visitors came at their own option, without invitation.

"Gentlemen, often in great numbers, come and go; chat with each other and act as they please. A porter shows them into the room and they retire from it when they choose, without ceremony. At their first entrance, they salute me and I them, and as many as I can, I talk to. What 'pomp' there is in all this I am unable to discover," Washington seethed. If discomfort were the problem, he added, he would have preferred letting everyone be seated, except he did not have enough chairs, and if his bows were thought stiff, had his critics considered his age?

What was worse was the accusation that he refused to dine out: "So strongly had the citizens of this place imbibed an idea of the impropriety of my accepting invitations to dinner that I have not received one from any family (. . . though I have received every civility and attention possible from them) since I came to the city," he wrote. "If this should be adduced as an article of impeachment," he added sarcastically, "there can be at least one good reason adduced for my not dining out—to wit, never having been asked to do so."

"PRIME MINISTER" MADISON

John Jay and James Madison may have answered Washington's etiquette queries orally, because no written replies have been found. However, Madison probably urged Washington to make things as informal as possible. He most likely suggested not requiring invitations or introductions for visitors at the levees but receiving any gentleman who appeared in proper attire, as Washington was doing.

Urging Washington to lower the tone of the levee would have conformed with Madison's simultaneous leadership in the fight in the House against the creation of a presidential title. He wrote triumphantly to Jefferson that "we have pruned the ordinary style of the degrading appendages of Excellency, Esquire, et cetera, and restored it to its naked dignity . . . This, I hope will show to the friends of republicanism that our new government was not meant to substitute either monarchy or aristocracy and that the genius of the people is yet adverse to both."

Twenty-some months more would carry Madison far, far away from his concordance with Washington, but their relationship during the president's first ten months in office was one of the most unusual in the history of relations between presidents and leaders of Congress. In fact, during that time, Madison was (though the Constitution hardly provided such a thing) nothing less than Washington's prime minister.*

Collaboration between them had started with Washington's canal project in 1785 and grew in the months just previous to the Philadelphia convention. It matured rapidly in the convention and was a full-fledged partnership by the time the ratification battles had ended.

Washington's election as president, which had been assumed even as the Constitution was being written, was certain by February, 1789. (It was so widely taken for granted that, by the middle of 1788, he was already receiving letters from job-seekers.) Toward the end of that month, Madison arrived at Mount Vernon, himself newly elected to the House of Representatives, for discussions about what would come next. He stayed a week, becoming in effect Washington's chief political advisor and manager as they worked out their plans.

Washington thought it important to demonstrate his attitude that the legislative initiative belonged to Congress, and he showed Madison a seventy-three-page inaugural address that he intended to embody the idea. While his most specific proposal was that Congress quickly begin work on a bill of rights, the speech went much farther in exhorting Congress in general terms than Washington usually did. It was, Madison said later, a "strange production," which he suspected had been drafted by Washington's aide, David Humphreys, and he readily agreed with Washington's request to help rewrite

---

*Washington might logically have made such a partner of the vice-president who, in the electoral system, was truly the second most highly regarded man in the country. However, Washington and Adams disliked one another, and had since early in the Revolution.

it. Then Madison went on his way to New York.

By the time Washington was inaugurated, Madison was already the clear political leader of the House (though a well-liked Pennsylvanian had been elected Speaker). He had made the first legislative proposal—for import duties on a long list of goods and raw materials—and was fighting hard for its passage against the same web of sectional pressures he had become familiar with at Philadelphia.

After Washington delivered the inaugural address Madison had written,* the House of Representatives, following the British custom, voted to prepare a reply. Madison drafted that, too. Soon came a note from Washington: ". . . as you have begun, so I could wish you to finish the good work in a short reply to the Address of the House of Representatives (which I now enclose) . . ." Madison did. Without a flicker of humor or irony or even revealing that he had written all three, he also mailed off copies to Jefferson.

About ten days after his ghost-writing exercises, Madison moved that three executive departments be created—foreign affairs, treasury, and war—and that the heads of each, or secretaries, appointed by the president be subject to the advice and consent of the Senate.

He also proposed that those officers serve at the pleasure of the president, causing an immediate eruption of opposition. The strongest resistance came from members who insisted that the chief executive also must obtain Senate consent in order to dismiss a secretary. Others felt the Constitution did not give the president power of removal at all, because it specifically provided for impeachment to remove "all civil officers of the United States."

The misinterpretation of the impeachment clause was easy for Madison to answer—having only recourse to impeachment for removal would secure every officer in place during good behavior. That had not been intended.

*Madison was usually a good writer, but Washington's inaugural address was not universally acclaimed. Fisher Ames sent a copy to his "Wednesday night club" and was upset at their "very censorious" reaction, though he granted that "the sentences are rather long and not so simply constructed." Maclay promised himself "I will read it again, but I declare I am inclined to place it under the *heavy* head."

However, giving the president exclusive power of removal stirred up the persistent concern about a too-strong executive. "I think it absolutely necessary," Madison argued back. "It will make him in a peculiar manner responsible for their conduct and subject him to impeachment himself if he suffers them to perpetrate . . . crimes . . . or neglects to superintend their conduct so as to check their excesses."

Fisher Ames of Massachusetts, who had been powerfully battling Madison's revenue proposals,* joined him on the removal battle. "The President is required to see the laws faithfully executed," Ames said. "He cannot do this without he has a control over officers appointed to aid him in the performance of his duty. Take this power out of his hands and you virtually strip him of his authority." Ames also saw the likelihood that, if the Senate were involved, "they will be enabled to hold the person in office," no matter how necessary or proper it might be to dismiss him. "It creates a permanent connection; it will nurse faction; it will promote intrigue to obtain protectors and to shelter tools."

After several weeks, the House approved the resolution the way Madison had proposed.

The James Madison who was emerging had caught everyone's attention, particularly for his avid promotion of tax discrimination in favor of French shipping over English and his battle for the President's removal power. Senator Maclay had been hearing enough about him on those two topics that, on July 1, he had an item he thought interesting for his diary.

"Madison," he wrote, "is charged with having labored for the whole business of discrimination in order to pay court to the French nation through Mr. Jefferson, our Minister to Paris. I feel much readier to believe him guilty of . . . urging the doctrine of taking away the right of removals of officers from

---

*In May, Madison put before the House a proposal to charge duties on foreign shipping that would discriminate against England (which refused to discuss a commercial treaty) in favor of France (with which we had such a treaty). Madison pushed the bill through the House quickly, but the Senate deleted the discrimination for fear of starting a trade war and the loss of import revenues. Madison kept Jefferson minutely informed on the bill's progress, and some complained that Madison was "very Frenchified in his politics." But Washington, too, wanted the discrimination which he thought warranted by "justice and policy."

the Senate in order to pay his court to the President, whom, I am told, he already affects to govern."

Maclay got a fairer appraisal of the Madison-Washington teamwork on August 16 from another senator, who was "clearly of opinion that all the late measures flowed from the President. Mr. Madison, in his opinion, was deep in this business."

Madison was indeed "deep in this business," as deep as anyone cared to imagine. Not only was he originating the legislation to create the departments and consulting with Washington on what to provide, but the president was also asking Madison's opinion on the those he proposed to appoint to operate those same departments.

Maclay's tidbit that Madison "affects to govern" Washington probably did not originate with Madison (though, if it did, Madison would hardly have been the only man in history to inflate his influence). Rather, it rings almost identical to the assertion a dozen years earlier about Hamilton, that Washington was "governed by one of his aides."

The gossiping observers were seeing a trait more visible in Washington's new prominence than it had been in the confines of the military: that he always led without making conspicuous use of his authority to "command." It was never very long before observers got over the idea that anyone "governed" him. As Abigail Adams said of him in a different context: "This same President has so happy a faculty of appearing to accommodate and yet carrying his point that, if he was not really one of the best-intentioned men in the world, he might be a very dangerous one." And right now Washington was extracting from Madison, as he had from Hamilton, every particle of exertion that Washington thought was needed to get the results he wanted.

Taming the Wilderness

At mid-June, Washington was struck down by a dangerous disease—anthrax. His illness began as a high fever and a pain in his upper left thigh near the buttock, which proved to be an ulcer that had to be cut out. The operation revealed infected tissue spread so wide and deep that the incision necessary to remove all of it left a wound that took more than a month to close. The fever from the infection abated after five days, but July was almost gone before Washington could do more than prop himself up, on his side.

Washington was seeing a few people by early July, however, and Madison kept him posted on the progress of the bills for the executive departments and the federal judiciary, all of which had been introduced before the president fell ill. The legislation was proceeding slowly, Madison reported, partly because of mistakes in committee drafts and "prolixity" in the debates, but mostly because of their inherent novelty and complexity.

"We are in a wilderness," Madison said when writing Jefferson, "without a single footstep to guide us. Our successors will have an easier task, and by degrees the way will become smooth, short and certain."

The path Washington blazed through one thicket in the wilderness is now among the system's best known: the way "advice and consent" operates between the president and the Senate. So familiar are news stories about the Senate accepting, resisting or rejecting presidential appointees or treaties, that it is easy to forget that the process could have been much different—and might have been, had Washington really been as deferential to the legislative branch as he wished them to think.

The Constitution did not say whether the President should refer to the Senate *before, during,* or *after* exercising his share of the power to appoint officials or make treaties. Nor did it say where or how he should consult them. It only said he "shall have the power, by and with the advice and consent of the Senate" to make treaties and appointments.

In the appointments of customs officials requiring Senate advice and consent, all had seemed to go well with the first method Washington employed. He made his selections and sent the names to the Senate, which reviewed and approved them. But early in August, Georgia's senators opposed Washington's choice for customs collector at the port of Savannah, and the Senate, in a secret ballot, rejected the nomination. Angry at both the secrecy and the lack of a chance to defend his choice, Washington sent a brusque letter suggesting that the Senate give him that opportunity when a nomination appeared "questionable to you."

With that irritation still prickling, Washington then received a visit from a Senate committee hinting that the Senate would like to manage these matters orally—in other words, actual consultation. With treaties, such consultation was "indispensably necessary," Washington told them, and it might be proper in appointing ambassadors. But was he supposed to call upon the Senate? Would the vice-president let him have the chair? If not, should the president expect to be in an "awkward situation" when he was there? As to appointees, he did not think the president should be on hand to "hear the propriety of his nominations questionned" or the Senate, for that matter, be obliged to debate in front of him. Each might feel forced to make explanations to the other, he pointed out, when both possessed the right not to explain.

Washington sent the committee off to chew over his remarks and summoned Madison post haste. When the committee reappeared by appointment two days later, Washington announced his position as worked out with Madison. When the president exercises his treaty and appointment power, he said, "the Senate . . . is evidently a council only . . . not only the *time,* but the *place* and *manner* of consultation should be with the President."

He expected circumstances and experience to reveal how he would eventually want to do this, but "it would seem not amiss that the Senate should accomodate their rules to the uncertainty of the particular mode and place . . . providing for the reception of either oral or written propositions and for giving their consent and advice in either the *presence* or *absence* of the President, leaving him free to use the mode and place" most convenient for him.

Without baldly saying so, Washington had given himself the right to entirely shut the Senate out of any participation in treaties and appointments until their approval was sought.

However, he was not inclined to go that far yet.

On August 22, Washington and the acting secretary of war, Henry Knox, presented themselves at the Senate, which had been notified the previous day that they would be coming, but not why.

"The President was introduced and took our Vice President's chair," Maclay recounted in his journal. "He rose and told us bluntly that he had called on us for our advice and consent to some propositions respecting the treaty to be held with the southern indians." Knox handed Washington a paper and Washington handed it to Adams to read aloud.

"Carriage were driving past, and such a noise, I could tell it was something about indians, but was not master of one sentence of it. Signs were made to the doorkeeper to shut down the sashes."

The paper summarized proposed treaties which a negotiating commission were to take into talks with the Creek, Chickasaw, and Cherokee tribes. Says Maclay, Adams began to read off the points and asked, " 'Do you advise and consent, etc.? There was a dead pause . . . I rose reluctantly indeed . . . it appeared to me that, if I did not, no other one would and we should have these advices and consents ravished, in a degree, from us.

"Mr. President," Maclay said, addressing Adams as president of the Senate, "the business is new to the Senate. It is of importance. It is our duty to inform ouselves as well as possible on the subject. I therefore call for the reading of the treaties and other documents alluded to in the paper before us.

"I cast an eye at the President of the United States. I saw he wore an aspect of stern displeasure."

The program fell apart. Knox read off some papers he had plucked from his satchel. One senator asked to see one treaty; another asked for a postponement. "The business labored . . . There appeared an evident reluctance to proceed," Maclay said, until finally another senator moved that the papers be turned over to a committee for study, which Maclay supported strenuously.

"As I sat down, the President of the United States started up in a violent fret. *'This defeats every purpose of my coming here'* were the first words that he said. He then went on that he had brought his Secretary of War with him to give every necessary information, that the Secretary knew all about the business and yet he was delayed and could not go on with the matter. He cooled, however, by degrees."

Washington agreed to the postponement and said he would return Monday. "A pause for some time ensued. We waited for him to withdraw. He did so with a discontented air—had it been any other man than the man whom I wish to regard as the first character in the world, I would have said, with sullen dignity."

The Senate used its and Washington's full day Monday to debate the seven treaty items, and, outwardly calm, Washington was able to depart finally, advice and consent in hand. But once outside the chamber, he was overheard muttering that he would "be damned if he ever went there again!" Thereafter, he sent papers and let his department heads meet with Senate committees, but the experience had been enough for him to rule out as impossibly tortuous formally obtaining advice from the Senate prior to making his decisions.

THE PRESIDENT'S MEN

Washington had given careful thought to who should head the three departments that were being provided to him. As early as May, Madison had written to Jefferson reporting that war would remain with Knox, foreign affairs with Jay—if Jay wanted it—and treasury would go to either Jay or Hamilton. And, Madison added, "I have been asked whether any appointment at home would be agreeable to you. Being unacquainted with your mind, I have not ventured on an answer."

The president liked the idea of continuing Jay and Knox because both had served well under the confederation, had strong reputations, and were close friends of his. But, most important, reappointing them under the new government would please those who were perpetually suspicious of his plans. For treasury, Washington had received Madison's view that Hamilton was "perhaps best qualified for that species of business and . . . would be preferred by those who know him personally." But Washington also knew that the New York chancellor, Robert Livingston, wanted the post—and Livingston was both extremely powerful and had been a crucial figure supporting the Federalists in New York.

The Congress had sent Washington authority to appoint an attorney general, a parttime counselor who would serve on a retainer as the president's lawyer. It was the ideal spot for Edmund Randolph, whom Washington preferred from long years of close acquaintance and whose participation in the government, he believed, would be good for it.

In August, Jay told Washington that he would prefer serving as chief justice of the Supreme Court, and Washington, after discussing it with Madison, concurred. At that same discussion, it is probable, but undocumented, that Washington and Madison agreed that only one other man had the right background for head of foreign affairs: Jefferson. However, Jefferson's reply to Madison's May letter could not be expected for several more weeks and there was no point in sending a further inquiry. Before a new letter could reach him, Jefferson would be sailing home on his long-awaited leave. The only thing to do was wait.

As for Hamilton, Washington had barely seen him since the inauguration celebrations nor had they corresponded since their exchange on presidential etiquette. It was just as well: Washington had to remain on good terms with Governor Clinton, and Hamilton had almost managed to retire the governor in elections in May. He had formed a committee for Robert Yates—the same anti-Federalist judge who had fought him in Philadelphia and Poughkeepsie—as a "moderate" alternative, pounding away at Clinton's efforts to organize a national movement for a second convention and his refusal to call the legislature into session after ratification. Because of the delay, New York had not voted in the presidential election nor had the state picked its United States senators, a point Hamilton had harped on in his attacks.

Washington knew that the New York chancellor, Livingston, wanted to be secretary of the treasury. But he may not have

known that when he decided to appoint Hamilton he was dealing the second Hamilton-related blow in six weeks to Livingston's prestige. The first had come in mid-July when Hamilton
ignored his political debt to Livingston for help at Poughkeepsie and pushed through his own two choices for the state's two
United States Senators.

In defeating Livingston's choice for one of the seats, Hamilton won for himself an implacable enemy who from then on
would devote his vast political power to opposing him. The
man whose career Livingston would foster against Hamilton's
would be Aaron Burr, Hamilton's future murderer, and Livingston would throw all of his support into opposing Washington's
policies when the time and the opportunity came.

The next decision Washington made set the stage for that and
much more: he decided to shortcut the sounding-out of Jefferson and simply have a message waiting when Jefferson's ship
docked, offering him the position of secretary of state. Jefferson's reply, when it came in late December, was full of reluctance. He had hoped to go back to France; he did not like the
way the department had been set up; and he could not alter his
plans in Virginia to be in New York any earlier than the end
of March. Knowing this, if the president still wanted him to do
it, would he please ask him again. Washington did.

Bringing both Hamilton and Jefferson into secretaryships,
Washington had put two scorpions in a bottle. Their ability to
work together would not last for more than a few months, and
in just over a year Jefferson would organize a party to destroy
Hamilton. Their battles would spread into the public print, but
the mark most often hit was Washington. In the end, the warfare between them would tear Washington's administration
apart.

17

Promises to Keep

‘ ‘ M Y O W N O P I N I O N has always been in favor of a bill of
rights,” Madison had written Jefferson three months after the
ratification battle in Virginia. “At the same time,” he added, “I
have never thought the omission a material defect, nor been
anxious to supply it even by *subsequent* amendment for any
other reason than that it is anxiously desired by others.”

Madison, in fact, had formulated a lengthy and carefully
reasoned list of arguments against a bill of rights. In theory, he
found it illogical. “A solemn charter of popular rights” was
necessary in a monarchy to act as a standard for measuring
public acts, a “signal for rousing and uniting the superior force
of the community.” In a popular government, the people were
sovereign “and, consequently, the tyrannical will of the sovereign is not to be controlled by the dread of an appeal to any
other force within the community.”

A more concrete objection Madison had was a potent one:
that it might be politically impossible to frame “a positive declaration of the most essential rights.” It was more likely that, in
declaring a right, the drafters would make it narrower than it

should be. He also feared that declaring various rights would imply that the government possessed powers that it had not been given. But when elections for lawmakers in the new government had begun, Madison discovered, to his shock, that he might have no hand whatever in resolving the question.

Madison was a congressman—not the senator that his friends had tried to make him—because Patrick Henry had demonstrated conclusively that Virginia's eventual acquiescence in the unamended Constitution could not be taken for granted. Antifederalists in the legislature had easily defeated Madison for the Senate, electing two of their own, William Grayson and Richard H. Lee. Henry then had applied himself to keeping Madison out of the House of Representatives. First he made sure that Madison's home district was drawn large enough to include a majority of anti-Federalist voters; then he persuaded James Monroe to run for the seat.

Madison's friends' hysteria finally brought him home from New York and to the realization that he would have to campaign to be part of the government he had helped create. To counter "the calumnies of anti-Federal partisans," Madison had spent two months traveling through his district, sometimes appearing with his opponent, Monroe.

Although Madison's margin of victory had been comfortable, he had been grilled relentlessly about why he "had ceased to be a friend to the rights of conscience." He still did not agree that the Constitution threatened them, but the time for debate was past. The voters' fear was tenacious and had to be put to rest. He told them that "I have never seen . . . those serious dangers," but he pledged his support for early amendments.

A few days after Washington's inauguration, Madison took the House floor to announce his intention to offer a bill of rights. It was a flanking maneuver, to hold back action on an application just arrived from the Virginia legislature calling for a general convention to amend the Constitution. He did present his list of amendments in June, but Congress's work on import duties and setting up the government departments prevented any debate on it until mid-August, approaching the close of the session.

Not everyone was impressed. "Mr. Madison has introduced his long expected amendments," Fisher Ames wrote to a friend. "They are the fruit of much labor and research. He has hunted up all the grievances and complaints of newspapers, all the articles of conventions and the small talk of their debates . . . There is too much of it . . . Upon the whole, it may do some good towards quieting men who attend to sounds only, and may get the mover some popularity, which he wishes."

Madison's list of seventeen proposals included the ten amendments that became the bill of rights. He also sought to respond to the anti-Federalist complaint that the Constitution's wording on the ratio of representation did not insure that *every* thirty thousand persons would be represented. ("The number of representatives shall not exceed one for every thirty thousand, but each state shall have at least one representative.") Madison's wording fixed the ratio firmly and set a maximum for the number of representatives in the House, but he left the numbers blank to be arrived at through debate.

As Madison had said in Philadelphia, he thought it "indecent" that Congress should put its hand in the public purse for its own pay. In the conventions, opponents of the Constitution had raised the same point, and Madison had written an amendment that he thought would remedy the indecency, if not removing temptation entirely. The amendment he proposed provided that no law changing congressional salaries would take effect until a new Congress had convened after an election. Theoretically, it would cause a congressman to hesitate to approve a raise that his opponent would collect after the taxpayers punished the spendthrift by voting him out of office.

No law is without someone who can fancy a way of abusing it: Theodore Sedgwick of Massachusetts called for disapproval of the amendment. Congressmen, he thought, would be tempted to lower salaries in order to discourage challengers from running or merely to court popularity. He did not explain why he, or anyone, would go to so much trouble to be reelected at lower pay. The House could not figure it out either, and retained the amendment in the list.

Madison's other amendments included one that barred the

states, in addition to the national government, from violating religious freedom, freedom of the press, and trial by jury —which would have immediately empowered the federal government to do in some cases what it can today as a result of court interpretation: enforce individual civil rights against state violations. That proposal, however, was not approved by the Congress.

Number four on Madison's list said "The freedom of speech and of the press, and the right of the people peaceably to assemble and consult for their common good, and to apply to the government for a redress of grievances, shall not be infringed."

Sedgwick called for deletion of "to assemble," arguing that freedom of speech implied the right of assembly. When another congressman contended they were different, Sedgwick pressed. Separately protecting assembly was the beginning of a long road down to distinguishing among all kinds of conduct that was taken for granted. Why not provide for a man's "right to wear his hat, get up, go to bed and so on, when he pleases?" Sedgwick was being sarcastic, but his point—that free speech applies to more than just talking—is one that keeps courts across the country busy today, often on cases involving such things as nude dance clubs, but also on such laws as those governing campaign contributions.

In his time, however, his contemporaries knew nothing of strip joints and "PACs" (Political Action Committees). They rejected Sedgwick's motion from a conviction that unpopular governing bodies will always try to disperse groups assembled to criticize them.

Madison's original freedom of religion amendment said: "The civil rights of none shall be abridged on account of religious belief or worship, nor shall any national religion be established, nor shall the full and equal rights of conscience be in any manner, or on any pretext, abridged."

His intention, he said was "that Congress should not establish a religion, enforce the legal observation of it by law, nor compel men to worship God in any manner contrary to their conscience."

A Connecticut member foresaw that a church might be unable to use the courts to collect from someone who failed to pay a pledged contribution (which was as good as a contract). Would not the debtor contend that the court had no power to order him to pay, because such an order would amount to "a support of ministers or building of places of worship?"

Madison replied that if the word "national" was inserted before "religion . . . it would satisfy the minds of the honorable gentlemen." His amendment aimed an easing the concern of those who feared that "one sect might obtain a pre-eminence or two combine together" and establish a religion to which they would compel others to conform.

When the anti-Federalist members fought the word "national," Madison withdrew the motion and the House adopted by a vote of fifty-one to twenty a clause offered by a New Hampshire member providing that "Congress shall make no laws touching religion or infringing the rights of conscience." Fisher Ames came back a few days later with a substitute, apparently worked out with Madison, that the House accepted.

The substitute had two interesting changes: no laws "touching" religion was changed to "establishing" and a phrase "or to prevent the free exercise thereof " was added. Madison's great personal concern was to prevent the national government from supporting religion—as far back to his collaboration with Jefferson and into his old age when he would write copiously about it—but the substitute amendment approved that day was not debated before it was voted upon.

Madison had wanted his seventeen amendments imbedded within the text of the Constitution, rather than added at the end. After realizing that the question was going to cause problems, the House had put off resolving it until finishing their review of the amendments. Although the choice seemed simple—as if it was between inserting the changes in suitable spots or tacking them on—the strongest supporters of the Constitution fought hard to prevent the original document from being opened up internally. Making changes within the text would expose the Constitution's essentials—the power of taxation, representation, the president's appointments—and invite a much broader rework of what the people already had ratified.

The House having finished its work on Madison's list in a matter of days, Sherman moved that the amendments be adopted as a block, to follow the body of the Constitution. Vining of Delaware supported Sherman, arguing, as he had when changing the main text was first proposed, "He had seen 'an act entitled an act to amend a supplement to an act entitled an act for altering part of an act entitled an act for certain purposes therein,' " which would be the outcome of trying to perform surgery on the main text. Madison, after seeing in the debate a tendency to spread his amendments into parts of the Constitution he favored, now yielded to Sherman's motion, which passed on a two thirds vote.

All seventeen of Madison's amendments, somewhat shorter but not much changed otherwise, were approved and sent on to the Senate. The Senate reduced the list to fourteen, and in a conference committee headed by Madison for the House and Ellsworth for the Senate, the number was reduced to twelve.

The final list approved by Congress contained twelve amendments: the states ratified ten—today's Bill of Rights—but the first two, affecting congressional salaries and fixing the ratio of representation, were not ratified by the requisite number of states.

Despite the enormity of the fuss made over a bill of rights, once passed, the first ten amendments lay almost dormant for decades. There was one exception: the First Amendment exerted an imperfect restraining influence on the government in 1798, when the nation was convulsed over our undeclared naval war with France and Congress passed the Sedition Act,* empowering President John Adams to prosecute political and newspaper critics.

The amendment's influence was imperfect because, on one hand, fifteen indictments and ten convictions resulted from Adams's energetic use of the power. On the other hand, Adams's use of the Sedition Act cost him his re-election to the

---

*The Sedition Act is always discussed together with the Alien Act, because the political furor prompted both and both were attacked at the time as equally violating the Constitution. However, the Alien Act not only was constitutional, but its descendant, the World War II Enemy Alien Act, is in force today.

presidency and played a major role in the downfall of the Federalist party. The price Adams and the Federalists paid provided an object lesson, and no party again attempted so flagrantly to abridge freedom of the press and speech—in all, fulfilling Madison's description of a bill of rights as "a signal for rousing and uniting the superior force of the community."

Nevertheless, even when Jefferson, the Sedition Act's most influential critic, became president, it was not repealed and was never overturned by the federal courts. Those courts, vigorously partisan at the time and appointed for life, refused to allow constitutional challenges to the Act on the grounds that when Congress debated the First Amendment in 1789, nothing had been said about erasing the English common-law concept of "seditious libel." Jefferson did not avail himself of the opportunity to go after his own critics under it (although state prosecutors appointed by his party did so under similar state laws, which Jefferson's enemies furiously denounced as amounting to the same thing).

In the sense that the Bill of Rights was written in 1789 and ratified by the end of 1791, it was "born" two hundred years ago, but, as a civil list of "thou shalt nots," it was in the wings, off the stage of history, and did not come into the spotlight of national policy through litigation for almost three decades, and then only sporadically. Yet the first ten amendments did draw a line of which the political branches were conscious, one that became ever more important as government grew and increased its role in national life. And that was something "the people"—much more than the Framers—saw, from the instant that the Constitution was unveiled.

18

"Like two fighting-cocks"

''CONGRESS MAY GO HOME. Mr. Hamilton is all-powerful and fails in nothing he attempts," fulminated Senator Maclay in his journal on February 9, 1791, two months into the third session of the First Congress.

Since the opening of the second session a year earlier, and even more clearly in the third, Hamilton, as secretary of the treasury, had supplanted Madison in controlling the direction the national system would take, and—to the discontent of both Madison and Washington's secretary of state, Jefferson—had become the adviser the president most often heeded.

In the short span of his first eighteen months at the helm of the Treasury Department, "the bastard brat of a Scotch peddler" laid the economic foundation of the future American empire. The thirty-three-year-old treasury secretary created, and the Congress passed, the framework of a financial system to manage the national debt, domestic and foreign; to take over and consolidate the states' remaining debts from the Revolution; to institute a revenue base for safeguarding America's creditworthiness; and to establish a national bank.

With the success of Hamilton's financial plan, accolades for his genius were on every federalist's lips, and he could have retired before the summer of 1791 secure in his title of "Founder." But he did not. His power, prestige and nation-building efforts were to go on until the late 1790s, when Jefferson would triumph in a brutal struggle between them—one which was about to break out at the time Maclay penned his complaint in his journal.

For pure passion and, in its later stages, soap opera, the battle between Jefferson and Hamilton has no parallel in American political history. With the two men, in Jefferson's words, "pitted against each other every day in the cabinet, like two fighting-cocks," their war began as a series of ideological skirmishes and ended as a contest for national leadership in which no quarter was given.

Hamilton and Jefferson's confrontations in that struggle not only produced constitutional precedents in force today, but especially important, the extreme heat of their warfare established the sturdiness of the Constitution (an irony since both men were so skeptical of it) and the two philosophical poles between which America's government could safely move.

BEFORE THE STORM

That Jefferson and Hamilton were "born to hate each other," as one of Washington's biographers has put it, was not immediately apparent, though they were obviously different at first sight. Hamilton, fourteen years Jefferson's junior, was brisk, trim; rosy-cheeked, and almost military in his bearing, overflowing with energy and aggressive amiability. And either he had curbed the "tincture of vanity" that William Pierce had noticed in the convention, or it was within bounds for his station, for Senator Maclay not only failed to see it but described Hamilton as having "a very boyish, giddy manner and Scotch-Irish people could well call him a 'skite.' " Jefferson, now forty-seven years old, "transgresses [Maclay said, comparing the cabinet members] on the extreme of stiff gentility or lofty gravity." Seated, the secretary of state, though well-dressed, "has a lounging manner, on one hip commonly, and

with one of his shoulders elevated much above the other
. . . his whole figure has a loose, shackling air. He had a rambling, vacant look, and nothing of that firm, collected deportment which I expected . . ."

But the surface differences between Hamilton and Jefferson
were not the combustible element waiting to be ignited; in
philosophy of government, they were so completely opposite
that barely a policy or approach existed on which there was the
slightest hope that they could agree.

"I . . . proceeded to New York in March, 1790," Jefferson
wrote decades later. "The President received me cordially and
my colleagues and the circle of principal citizens apparently
with welcome. The courtesies of dinner parties given me . . .
placed me at once in their familiar society. But I cannot describe
the wonder and mortification with which the table conversations filled me. Politics were the chief topic, and a preference
of kingly over republican government was evidently the favorite sentiment . . . I found myself, for the most part, the only
advocate on the republican side of the question."

The dinner tables of New York were federalist and Hamil-
tonian—abuzz with plans to give weight and dignity to the
national government, to stimulate commerce and expand manufacturing, and to usher in a golden age of prosperity. For
this was the "can-do" crowd, with its "high-flyers" and "first
characters," all eager to burst forth and amaze a watching world
under the leadership of the majestic Washington and brilliant
Hamilton.

The Federalists' highly-charged expectations carried their
share of predictable baggage: strutting supporters whom Maclay, long before Jefferson arrived, was calling the president's
"court" and castigating as "every one ill at ease in his finances;
every one out at the elbows in his circumstances; every ambitious man, every one desirous of a short-cut to wealth and
honors . . . aiming with all their force to establish a splendid
court with all the pomp of majesty."

When Jefferson appeared in the Federalists' drawing rooms,
the recent ambassador did not look like a mortified dissident.
He had not yet adopted the shabby republican costume for

which he would be noted in later years, and a Philadelphia woman who saw Jefferson on his trip to New York described him wearing "suit of silk, ruffles, and an elegant topaz ring." Another observer called him "conspicuous in red waistcoat and red breeches, the fashion of Versailles." Nor did he overplay the philosopher (as he would infuriate the Federalists by doing later) or shrink from the Federalists' worst vice—gossip. "I looked for gravity," Maclay said, reporting his first exposure to Jefferson, "but a laxity of manner seemed shed about him. He spoke almost without ceasing . . . It was loose and rambling, and yet he scattered information wherever he went and some even brilliant sentiments sparkled from him. The information which he gave us respecting foreign ministers, etc., was all high-spiced. He had been long enough abroad to catch the tone of European folly."

Diplomacy and French *beau monde* may have colored Jefferson's conversation, but they had not sapped his vigilance against incipient kings and aristocrats. Before going abroad in 1784, he had visited Washington one evening and belabored him far into the night about the Society of the Cincinnati, then newly organized, of which Washington was president. Conferring membership only on revolutionary officers and their sons, the society, Jefferson warned, was the fetus of a new aristocracy—one that would eventually try to make Washington king. Though he wanted the group disbanded, he had only convinced Washington to request them to discard the hereditary provision, which they did.

Now Jefferson was back from France even more alert, having long since communicated to Washington his dislike of the president's unlimited reelectability under the new Constitution. The people, he thought, would always reelect the sitting executive, who would soon amass all the unchecked power of a monarch.

"I was much an enemy to monarchy before I came to Europe," he had added in his letter to Washington, "I am ten thousand times more so since I have seen what they are. There is scarcely an evil known in these countries which may not be traced to their king as its source, nor a good which is not derived from the small fibres of republicanism among them."

In New York, the new secretary of state swiftly became sensible of Hamilton's potency—especially as it had touched Jefferson's department, to make Gouverneur Morris an unofficial envoy in London exploring possible improvements in British-American relations. Hamilton had urged Morris's appointment when an unsolicited hint of British interest had come to Washington the previous fall, and, in spite of Madison's plea to wait until Jefferson could be consulted, the president had asked Morris to handle the exploratory mission.

Responding to the British feeler was merely prudence on Washington's part; he did not intend to drop America's demand for compliance with the 1783 peace treaty. But it also meant that the president was listening to Hamilton, a forthright admirer of the British system and an advocate of evenhandedness in relations with England and France. Washington had not retreated from his support of the pugnacious stance Jefferson and Madison advocated—specifically, taxing English shipping more heavily than French—but the decision on the Morris mission was disquieting.

If Jefferson was uneasy about Hamilton's ideas in foreign policy, he was appalled to see how Hamilton's design for rescuing the public credit, being unveiled in stages, had whipped a "mercenary phalanx" into wild anticipation of early profits and long-term commercial expansion. He disbelievingly registered the treasury secretary's view, the creed of the Federalists, that for the national government to possess energy and stability, it must be "high-toned" to command respect and must harness private capital in support of national ends. And he drew the worst possible inferences from Hamilton's advocacy of using men's self-interest to strengthen the government instead of relying on their innate goodness. Visions of the natural aristocracy, the virtuous agrarian society, America's destiny, ravished and disfigured by insatiable "money men" and British-style ministers rose up before Jefferson's eyes, and he decided that Hamilton was "not only a monarchist, but for a monarchy bottomed on corruption."*

*Jefferson was an adherent of the theory of Henry St. John, First Viscount Bolingbroke, an early eighteenth-century British Tory from whose writings Americans had

As Fate would have it, although Hamilton's financial program was both brilliant and sound, its most expensive component, establishing the public credit, actually did result in rewarding both greed and blatant self-dealing by public officials, and compounding the burdens of the innocent—which lent great credence to the attacks on him and the Federalists from then on.

The self-dealing began almost immediately—the most flagrant instance right under Hamilton's nose—when he began preparing his plan to pay off $11.7 million in foreign loans, $42.4 million in old Confederation certificates and another $21 million of the separate states' Revolution debts. William Duer, assistant secretary of the treasury, acting on his insider knowledge of Hamilton's plans, dispatched agents to buy up all the Continental certificates they could locate, made a secret deal with another man to purchase as many state notes as they could obtain for $16,000, and spread the word to select friends to do the same.*

It was bad enough that, over the years, countless original holders of the certificates—many of them revolutionary soldiers

---

drawn part of their scripture of republicanism. Bolingbroke contended that "artificial money"—public debt, stocks and bank notes—and the men who traded in them were instruments of corruption in Parliament that allowed the monarch to defeat the check on him. In Bolingbroke's theory "corruption" was not a condition of general depravity (although that was considered an effect), but the systematic creation of a dominant, bought-off faction in government which would hold liberty to no account and under which liberty would vanish. The agrarian republic, which had no use for artificial money, was less susceptible to this danger.

*Duer was not breaking any law. In fact, public officials were not expected to give up their financial interest in matters they handled in the course of their duties. A man's honor was expected to keep him from exploiting his position, and the censure that flowed from betraying a public trust was a sufficient deterrent for most. Propriety was sometimes as fuzzy then as now, and wise public men (unlike Duer) made sure they erred on the side of caution. For example, soon after Hamilton's appointment, he received a letter from the revolutionary hero, Gen. Henry "Light Horse Harry" Lee, one of his closest friends. Lee asked how "speedily" the value of debt certificates would rise and how the interest payments would be made. "These queries are asked for my private information; perhaps they may be improper," Lee said. "I do not think them so, or I would not propound them. Of this you will decide and act." Hamilton replied that he was not sure if Lee's questions were improper, "but you remember the saying with regard to Caesar's wife. I think the spirit of it applicable to every man concerned in the administration of the finances of a country. With respect to the conduct of such men, *suspicion* is ever eagle-eyed." Hamilton did not impose his personal standard on Duer and fire him. Today, he would have little choice, but, in his own time, the decision was his to make—as the hard consequences to his reputation were his to live with.

who had accepted them in lieu of pay—had been forced by hardship to sell the paper at a fraction of its value. Duer's insider tip that Hamilton would propose redemption at full face value from the *current* owners spread far and wide, setting off a rampage of speculators trying to find and buy up certificates before their holders learned that the government would meet its obligation.

As Jefferson, who had not yet reached New York, heard it: "Couriers and relay horses by land and swift sailing pilot boats by sea were flying in all directions. Active partners and agents were associated and employed in every state, town, and country neighborhood, and this paper was bought up . . . Immense sums were thus filched from the poor and ignorant and fortunes accumulated . . ."

Madison, witnessing the shameful spectacle, tried to change the outcome. He introduced an amendment to Hamilton's plan so as to deny full payment to nonoriginal holders and return the difference to original holders who had sold off. "The transfers extend to a vast proportion of the whole debt and the loss to the original holders has been immense," Madison said. "The injustice which has taken place has been enormous and flagrant and makes redress a great national object."

However, in congressional debate, much embittered by the fact that some lawmakers were also speculating in certificates, Madison was trounced—thirteen to thirty-six. But the whole Federalist position had been tainted and the rafters at Federal Hall rang with anti-Federalist denunciations of the greed and self-dealing and cries of compassion for the veterans and their families injured by the hard-hearted secretary of the treasury. "Folly and wickedness," lamented the *Pennsylvania Gazette*. The Federalists had gained character with "speculators and British and Dutch brokers" but lost it "with their army, with the best Whigs [republicans] in the union, and with half the widows and orphans in the United States."

In truth, as the Federalists pointed out, Madison's idea was unworkable. Should every original holder who had disposed of his certificates at a discount be compensated? What of those who sold not from need, but because they had no confidence in ever getting full value? What of those who sold from necessity, but later flourished and bought more certificates as speculation? And those who had sold merely to finance investments in land and other ventures? Nor was every subsequent certificate-owner a speculator; many were merely ordinary people trying to make a sound investment. As Hamilton wrote in submitting his plan, "questions of this sort . . . multiply themselves without end."

Moreover, tracing original holders or just verifying their claims would be a monumental and fantastically expensive task under the best of circumstances, and the circumstances were not even promising for such an undertaking. For convenience, the Army had often issued the certificates in bulk, payable to individual pay clerks or commanders. Those men (and there had been thousands over the eight-year war) then simply signed them over to the soldiers in their units, the farmers and the tradesmen who supplied the army as it moved through the country. In making his redemption plan, Hamilton, who had been captain of an artillery company for six months in 1776, needed to look no farther than his own desk drawer, where his chaotic army paybook gave testimony that the pay records were unreliable—if, indeed, they had been returned to the government at all.

Despite the excited debate over practicality, justice, and greed, the determining factor in the vote was Hamilton's fundamental argument that "every breach of the public engagements, whether from choice or necessity, is . . . hurtful." The United States could not found its credit standing on a "capricious" idea. "That the case . . . is a hard one cannot be denied," Hamilton said, but trying to make reparations to original holders and punish later ones would be "ruinous to public credit . . . The nature of the contract in its origin is that the public will pay the sum expressed in the security." Spurning that obligation would amount to welshing on a debt and destroying the United States' ability to borrow again.

So decisive a victory for the first step in Hamilton's financial plan should have been sweet to him, but it was not. He had been shaken when, shortly before the debate, Madison had informed him that he would oppose it. Ever since beginning to work together in 1782, they had agreed on full payment of the debt without discriminating among creditors and, Hamilton said later, "down to the commencement of the new government," Madison had never "glanced at the idea of a change of opinion. I wrote him a letter after my appointment, in the recess of Congress, to obtain his sentiments on the subject of the finances. In his answer, there is not a lisp of his new system."

And that was not all: when the debate began "and afterwards, repeated intimations were given to me that Mr. Madison . . . had become personally unfriendly to me; and one gentleman in particular, whose honor I have no reason to doubt, assured me that Mr. Madison, in a conversation with him, had made a pretty direct attempt to insinuate unfavorable impressions of me." In a word—although Hamilton did not immediately come to that conclusion—Madison had defected from the Federalists and assumed leadership in opposition to them and to their chief. Henceforth, Federalists in the House would be led by Fisher Ames of Massachusetts.

To sell his plan for taking over the individual states' outstanding Revolution debt, Hamilton and Ames had one argument with a nice ring of justice: "Expenses for the particular defense of a part in a common war" should be "a common charge." However, lawmakers representing states that had already extinguished most of their debts had another: their constituents had paid their obligations; the national government had no right to tax them again to bail out less responsible states.

Again, Hamilton's fundamental objective was sound: from state to state, various repayment schemes and the taxes to fund them would produce "collision and confusion"—not just between states, but between the states and the national government. Such jarring and competing had been a principal evil of the Confederation and Hamilton was determined to remove the chance for history to repeat itself.

This time, however, Madison proved a formidable opponent. He "hangs heavy upon us," Ames wrote, bewildered. "If he is a friend, he is more troublesome than a declared foe. He is so much a Virginian, so afraid that the mob will cry out *'crucify him'*, sees Patrick Henry's shade at his bedside every night, fears so much the eastern confederacy . . . that he has kept himself wrapped up in mystery and starts new objections daily."

Quietly, meticulously, Madison was forging a coalition of lawmakers disgusted at a renewed orgy of speculation (now in state certificates), those from the states that had paid most of their debts, plus a handful of unreconciled anti-Federalists who recognized the strong tendency toward national consolidation inherent in the assumption bill. Debate raged for weeks—the bitterest contest yet seen in the year-old House of Representatives, complete with threats of secession. When the tide clearly turned against the Federalists, even Duer's quiet resignation from the treasury failed to stem it, and Madison's forces defeated the assumption plan by just two votes.

The Federalists were down but not out: the second leg of Hamilton's program, a revenue (funding) system, was before the Congress, and the friends of assumption breathed new life into that plan by inserting assumption in the funding bill. Their position hardened—funding with assumption, or no funding at all—in effect taking hostage the continental and foreign debt repayment plan already passed. A new battle was on, and Jefferson was drawn in, "duped into it by the Secretary of the Treasury," he untruthfully told Washington a year later, "and made a tool for forwarding his schemes, not then sufficiently understood by me."

To the embarrassment of Jefferson's admirers, he insisted on his story of violated innocence all his life, because he bitterly regretted his role in passing the assumption bill. Not only did the legislation nourish the strong national government he despised, but his aid contributed mightily to Hamilton's march to the zenith of his power. The truth was, however, that, at the time, Jefferson thought the assumption bill valid, and neither another plague of speculators nor the unavoidable retaxation of some citizens outweighed in his mind its probable benefits.

"In the present instance," he wrote to James Monroe within days of lending his assistance, "I see the necessity of yielding to the cries of creditors in certain parts of the union, for the sake of union and to save us from the greatest of all calamities, the total extinction of our credit in Europe."

Jefferson thought it should pass and would pass, and when he heard that Hamilton was trying to trade votes for the site of the national capital to get the votes he needed on assumption, Jefferson seized the opportunity to engage in the unphilosophical practice of political backscratching. Specifically, he helped Hamilton in order to place the permanent capital of the United States on the Potomac River opposite Virginia. But let Jefferson tell it:

"Hamilton was in despair. As I was going to the President's one day, I met him in the street. He walked me backwards and forwards before the President's door for half an hour." Hamilton looked "somber, haggard, and dejected beyond description," Jefferson noticed, his usually immaculate clothes "uncouth and neglected." The secretary of the treasury "painted pathetically the temper into which the legislature had been wrought, the disgust of those who were called the creditor states, the danger of the *secession* of their members and the separation of the states."

Members of the administration should stick together, Jefferson quotes Hamilton as pleading. "Though this question was not of my department, yet a common duty should make it a common concern . . . the President was the center on which all administrative questions ultimately rested and all of us should rally around him and support . . . measures approved by him."

Jefferson played dumb. "I told him that I was really a stranger to the whole subject" but, then, "if its rejection endangered a dissolution of our Union at this incipient stage, I should deem that the most unfortunate of all consequences." The secretary of state proposed that Hamilton "dine with me the next day, and I would invite another friend or two . . . I thought it impossible that reasonable men consulting together coolly could fail, by some mutual sacrifices of opinion to form a compromise."

The friend Jefferson invited to dine and reason together coolly with Hamilton was Madison. Joylessly aware, too, of the need for a solution, the opposition leader allowed himself to be talked out of his fight and ended by agreeing not to try to hold his ranks, though he himself refused to change his vote.

"But it was observed," Jefferson says, "that this pill would be peculiarly bitter to the southern states and that some concomitant measure should be adopted to sweeten it a little to them." If the seat of government went to Philadelphia for ten years and the Potomac permanently afterward, "this might, as an anodyne, calm in some degree the ferment . . . So two of the Potomac members (White and Lee, but White with a revulsion of stomach almost convulsive) agreed to change their votes, and Hamilton undertook to carry the other part.

"And so," Jefferson says, his innocence suitably outraged, "the assumption was passed and twenty millions of stock divided among favored states and thrown in as a pabulum to the stock-jobbing herd. This added to the number of votaries to the Treasury and made its chief the master of every vote in the legislature which might give to the government the direction suited to his political views."*

A few weeks later, the second session of the First Congress adjourned for the summer, never again to sit in New York. When the third session began in December, the government would be in the new temporary capital, Philadelphia.

THE "REPUBLICAN COURT"

Fisher Ames had worked to keep the seat of government in New York, and, upon his arrival in Philadelphia, fate seemed eager to vindicate his resistance. "I arrived in the city last Sunday evening and lodged at the Indian Queen," he reported to a friend on December 12, "where I found it difficult to write you. We had no sooner landed our baggage in the stage office . . . taken a dish of tea, etc., than we learned that the room

---

*And Virginia had won a hot contest in which the north, south and middle states—in the old Continental Congress and the new—had deadlocked time and again. Proximity to the capital meant, besides prestige and economic benefits, more influence on national measures than more distant states would have.

where it was left was robbed . . . We were disturbed by this misfortune, as you may suppose, and kept up almost all night."

Ames thought his own trunk had been saved because his name was on it; other travelers lost luggage that was found the next day in a field. The owners' linens, shirts, and other possessions were gone, but the thieves had overlooked nearly thirty thousand dollars in securities mixed among the papers in one trunk. The safe recovery of the securities came as a minor reprieve from disaster for two men already in deep trouble, one of them a Framer of the Constitution.

Almost ten thousand dollars of the securities belonged to Oliver Phelps of Massachusetts, and the balance very possibly to Nathaniel Gorham, the Boston merchant who had chaired the Committee of the Whole in the Constitutional Convention. Phelps and Gorham were the principals in one of the largest land speculations of the time, having contracted in 1788 to purchase six million acres in western New York. At first, the price—$1 million in Massachusetts debt certificates—had been a bargain; the scrip was on the market for a tiny fraction of face value.

By the end of 1790, however, Hamilton's assumption plan had driven the price of state paper so high that the two men were no longer able to meet their payments. They were fighting insolvency when Phelps's trunk was purloined and, soon after, were obliged to surrender the land. Gorham was ruined and died in 1796 of stroke brought on by his unending financial crisis.

Apart from the politics of siting the capital, many members of the government were pleased with the move to Philadelphia, feeling like Ames, that it was "a magnificent city" (not Maclay, of course, who grumped that New York's "allurements are more than ten to two" by comparison and that "I know no such unsocial city as Philadelphia"). Washington, of course, was completely at home in the great city, and it did not hurt that it was a day's or two ride closer to Mount Vernon.

On its side, Philadelphia reacted to the return of its stature as the national capital with wild joy. Convinced that the government could be made to forget its commitment to move on to the Potomac, the elite of the city turned on an astounding performance of elegance and luxury as persuasion. "You have never seen anything like the frenzy which has seized upon the inhabitants here," an observer wrote,—"They have been half mad ever since this city became the seat of government and there is no limit to their prodigality."

Abigail Adams, who had dreaded Philadelphia's climate and high cost of living, was delighted. She soon was writing to her sister, "there is much more society here than in New York, and I am much better pleased and satisfied than I expected to be." The city was providing "one continued scene of parties upon parties, balls and entertainments equal to any European city." She praised the friendliness she found, which was "kept up with all the principal families, who appear to live in great harmony, and we meet at all the parties nearly the same company."

For Jefferson, the change was an improvement in every way. He had spent more time in Philadelphia, had a half-dozen old and particularly valued friends there, and was able to rent a fine house on terms that allowed him to alter extensively and add to it to suit his taste and interests. Even Philadelphia's high society was more to his liking, especially because its leading lady, lovely Anne Bingham, had been part of what Jefferson called "our charming coterie in Paris" in 1785.

Just turned twenty-seven, Anne Bingham was reaching the peak of her powers. Graceful, vivacious, intelligent, and light-hearted, she managed her home, her entertainments, and her social position with a skill that surpassed all others. Even Senator Maclay—who had found fault with every fine table to which he had been invited, including the President's—had only praise after dining at the Binghams. They "entertain in a style beyond everything in this place or perhaps in America," he wrote. "There is a propriety, a neatness, a cleanliness that adds to the splendor."

Jefferson, who liked women of a softer style than the sparkling Anne, treated her with a kind of hectoring affection. It showed vividly in an exchange of letters between them starting in the summer of 1787, while he was still in Paris and she had been back in America less than a year.

". . . tell me, truly and honestly," he had written, "whether you do not find the tranquil pleasures of America preferable to the empty bustle of Paris?" To make clear what empty bustle he meant, he had launched into a mocking description of a day in the life of a typical Parisian society woman "propped on bolsters and pillows, and her head scratched into a little order . . . If the morning is not very thronged, she is able to get out and hobble round the cage of the Palais Royal . . . she flutters half an hour through the streets by way of paying visits . . ." On and on he had gone, concluding "this is the picture in the light it is presented to my mind. Now let me have it in yours."

Mrs. Bingham did. "I am too much flattered by the honor of your letter," she began politely. "The candor with which you express your sentiments merits a sincere declaration of mine.

"I agree with you that many of the fashionable pursuits of the Parisian ladies are rather frivolous . . . but the picture you have exhibited is rather overcharged. You have thrown a strong light upon all that is ridiculous in their characters and you have buried their good qualities in the shade . . .

"The state of society," she lectured the philosopher, "in different countries requires corresponding manners and qualifications; those of the French women are by no means calculated for the meridian of America . . . But you must confess that they are more accomplished and understand the intercourse of society better than in any other country. We are irresistibly pleased with them because they possess the happy art of making us pleased with ourselves, their education is of a higher cast, and by great cultivation they procure a happy variety of genius which forms their conversation . . .

"The women of France interfere in the politics of the country, and often give a decided turn to the fate of empires. Either by the gentle arts of persuasion or by the commanding force of superior attractions and address, they have obtained that rank and consideration in society, which the sex are entitled to, and which they in vain contend for in other countries. We are therefore bound in gratitude to admire and revere them, for asserting our privileges as much as the friends of the liberties of mankind reverence the successful struggles of the American patriots."

Jefferson had been unabashed; in his next letter, he tried to stir her up again: "All the world is now politically mad . . . You, too, have had your political fever. But our good ladies, I trust, have been too wise to wrinkle their foreheads with politics. They are contented to soothe and calm the minds of their husbands returning ruffled from political debate . . . You will change your opinion, my dear madam, and come over to mine in the end." Comparing French and American women again, he demanded: "confess that it is a comparison of Amazons and Angels."

Anne, however, had ignored him, happily Americanizing the qualities she admired in French women, adding them to the "amiability, ease and sprightliness" her admirers so highly praised. In the same enthusiasm, she and her husband led a change of fashion to styles *à la republicaine,* making chic the leveling spirit of the French Revolution (midway through its second year when the government moved to Philadelphia).

Anne's towering headdresses tumbled in favor of her natural tresses cascading in ringlets to the shoulders; low-heeled slippers replaced high; her huge hats shrank to small bonnets; her silk brocade gowns she abandoned for muslin and dimity. For men, "republican" attire wrought an even more dramatic change. Powdered queues were lopped off and the hair worn short and unadorned; richly colored velvet, silk, and satin suits gave way to dark-toned cloth; long coats became short and ruffles and shoe buckles disappeared. Long pants replaced knee breeches, and when knee breeches were worn it was with striped yarn stockings instead of black or white silk.

The heyday of the "Republican Court," as it came to be called, with Anne Bingham the uncrowned queen, lasted about two years. Although Anne and the rest of Philadelphia's fashionable society flourished through the Federalist decade of the 1790s, starting in 1793, their high-living style became the target of angry public reproach as evidence of creeping monarchism in America. In sad coincidence, two months after Jefferson became president as the leader of the forces against the evil trend, the celebrated Philadelphia beauty died of tuberculosis, at age thirty-seven.

But as the third session of the First Congress got under way in the winter of 1790–91, not even a small cloud on the horizon gave a clue to the tempests and strains on the ship of state that lay a few years ahead.

THE STRUGGLE BEGINS

On December 13, 1790, Hamilton sent to Congress his third great report, calling for a national bank to be established as a profit-making public corporation. The government would use this institution to receive taxes collected, borrow money, service the national debt obligations, and issue paper that would circulate in the absence of a national currency. The Senate moved first, in early January, to act on his recommendation.

From amid the familiar heaps of snuff, Constitution Framer Oliver Ellsworth, now a senator from Connecticut, introduced the bank legislation, and, said Senator Maclay, "of course, he hung like a bat to every particle of it . . . All-powerful and eloquent in debate, he is, notwithstanding, a miserable draftsman."

Perplexity and Ellsworth's draftsmanship seemed to stymie the Senate, which debated the bill in a "desultory" way for several days, until Maclay moved for putting it off in order to seek more information from Hamilton. That prodded the Federalists, who were supposed to know what they were doing, and "such a scene of confused speeches followed as I have seldom heard before," Maclay wrote. "Everyone affected to understand the subject and undervalue the capacities of those who differed." Once started, the senators snipped and pruned for about a week, passed the bill on a voice vote January 20, and sent it along to the House of Representatives.

In the House, Madison's weapon of choice was his famous logic and reasoning, and he called for rejection of the bank as unconstitutional. This was "a potent attack on the bill," Ames realized, because of the "peculiar weight" Congress felt was due Madison's opinions from his by then well-known leadership both in the convention and in ratification.

The main thrust of Madison's attack was that the bill was a

Pandora's box—that Hamilton was stretching the Constitution's "necessary and proper" clause so far as to justify the government doing anything it pleased. Madison was not saying that the Constitution left no discretion to Congress; he himself had asserted—in earlier debate over an article in the Bill of Rights*—that "there must necessarily be admitted powers by implication, unless the Constitution descended to recount every minutia." But Hamilton's bank went dangerously beyond the strict construction demanded to make an act "necessary and proper."

The bank was "founded on remote implications," not on any "safe reasoning" that a national bank must inevitably result from any of the expressed powers, Madison said. It would subvert the whole reason for having a Constitution: to erect a government "composed of limited and enumerated powers." That the bank might be convenient for the government in carrying out its financial powers, he did not doubt—but that did not make it "necessary" in the constitutional sense.

For all its importance and the implications for future constitutional interpretation, the bank bill debate was short—consisting essentially of Madison's "potent attack" and Fisher Ames's eloquent, hastily improvised reply. Then the House approved the measure by a lopsided vote of 39 to 20—dramatic proof of the near prostration of the opposition by the triumphant Federalists.

Despite the overwhelming congressional approval that sent the bank bill to his desk, Washington was deeply troubled by Madison's challenge to its constitutionality and hesitated to sign it. The president had never exercised the veto power, but he believed that if any instance called upon him to check the legislative branch, it assuredly was when a bill was unconstitutional.

Washington asked Jefferson and Attorney General Edmund Randolph to submit written opinions. Both did, supporting Madison. In his short paper, Jefferson repeated Madison's arguments in the House, but then went far beyond them: the Consti-

---

*The Tenth Amendment, reserving to the states powers not delegated to Congress

tution's necessary and proper clause, Jefferson declared, restricted Congress to creating only "those means without which the grant of power would be nugatory [worthless]." Further, he made clear, the proposed activities of the bank would impinge on the statutes of and the powers reserved to the states. The national financial business, he argued in effect, must suffer itself to be conducted *through* state institutions despite the inconvenience.

Reading Jefferson's opinion, Washington might well have heard a distant echo of Luther Martin and the small-states men at Philadelphia clamoring for state sovereignty. If he did, Hamilton capitalized on it when the president sent him the Randolph and Jefferson papers and asked him to respond.

In his answer, Hamilton rested his argument on a principle so simple and clear that it was almost as if he had settled his own dispute with the Constitution (that it was too weak). He based his argument on national sovereignty—not sweeping or unlimited, but total sovereignty in the enumerated powers that the Constitution vested in the national government.

If a power such as taxation was granted to the national government, he said firmly, the government was sovereign in that power. It had "a right to employ all the means requisite and fairly applicable to the attainment of the ends of such power . . . It is unquestionably incident to *sovereign power* to erect corporations, and consequently to *that* of the United States in *relation* to the *objects* intrusted to the management of the government."

Hamilton then reduced the Jefferson-Madison distinction between "necessary" and "convenient" to a dangerous bogus argument. The secretary of state's definition of "necessary," Hamilton wrote, would "give it the same force as if the word *absolutely* or *indispensably* had been prefixed to it . . . There are few measures of any government which would stand so severe a test. To insist upon it would be to make the criterion of the exercise of any implied power a *case of extreme necessity.*" In a word, Jefferson's construction would have the government perpetually operating on the brink of collapse.

As bad or worse, every change of opinion or circumstance

would lead to dispute over the necessity of any action. The only rational interpretation of the necessary-and-proper clause was to take the word *necessary* in its "common mode of expression . . . *needful, requisite, incidental, useful,* or *conducive to,"* Hamilton said.

The Constitution had given "explicit sanction to the doctrine of *implied powers,"* but not the behemoth that Jefferson claimed would "take possession of a boundless field of power, no longer susceptible to any definition." Rather, Hamilton said, the government is "sovereign to a certain extent—that is, to the extent of the objects of its specified powers . . . If the *end* be clearly comprehended within any of the specified powers, and if the measure have an obvious relation to that end and is not forbidden by any particular provision of the Constitution, it may safely be deemed to come within the compass of the national authority."

Considered one of America's great state papers, Hamilton's exposition of the doctrine of implied powers, written in a matter of days, runs more than twenty thousand words. It was the forerunner to (and is thought to have been the principal reference for) Chief Justice John Marshall's 1819 ruling by which the doctrine of implied powers acquired the sanction of constitutional law *(McCullouch v. Maryland).*

While Washington waited anxiously to hear from Hamilton before the expiration of the ten days allowed for him to veto the bill, he had several conversations with Madison about it. In their talks, Madison thought, the president seemed to agree with him, though making no commitment. Madison was sure he and Jefferson had won when, a few days before the deadline, Washington "desired me to reduce into form the objections to the bill, that he might be prepared in case he should return it without his signature."

Madison drafted the requested veto message for the president, but it was never used. When Washington had digested Hamilton's opinion, his hesitation vanished. He signed the bill creating the bank on February 23, 1791.

The historic First Congress adjourned *sine die* on March 3. The fireworks over Hamilton's financial plans had created high drama, but they were by no means the sole focus of attention. The government had truly come to life during the First Congress; an astonishing amount of work had been done.

Besides begetting the executive departments and the Bill of Rights, the Congress had approved revenue measures (import tariffs, tonnage taxes on shipping, and a trouble-promising excise tax on whiskey), maritime regulations, lighthouses, customs offices, post offices and post roads, and a mint. It had established the federal court system, with six justices serving as the Supreme Court, thirteen district courts, and three circuit courts. It had provided for army and militia requirements, for naturalization of foreign-born citizens, for copyrights and patents, for federal salaries, and for the first national census. And it had voted to accept into the union two new states, Vermont and Kentucky.

Feeling its way along under the new Constitution, Congress found that some things came easier than others. The reunion of all thirteen original states under the new government was a case in point. All North Carolina had been waiting for was assurance of a Bill of Rights, and she scheduled a ratifying convention immediately, joining the union on November 21, 1789 (arrival of her representatives in Congress in March gave Madison the votes he needed to beat Hamilton in the first round of the assumption fight). Not so Rhode Island; she seemed sure to stay out forever. But on May 26, 1790, she ratified—under a threat damned by Maclay as unjustified "on the principles of freedom, law, the Constitution or any other mode whatever."

Maclay's wrath was directed at a bill passed by the Senate, a week before Rhode Island's ratification convention opened, breaking off commercial relations between the United States and the tiny state. An "arbitrary and tyrannical" stroke, its sponsors freely admitted, said Maclay, "meant to force her into an adoption of the Constitution." Though the extortion worked, it was close: the vote of Rhode Island's convention to ratify was only 34 to 32.

The patent and copyright bills activated the constitutional power of Congress "to promote the progress of science and useful arts by securing for limited times to authors and inventors the exclusive right to their respective writings and discoveries." Copyright administration was put under the clerks of the federal district courts, but the Department of State, then having charge of most domestic affairs that were not military, financial or judicial, administered America's first patent act.

Jefferson, as the first administrator of the U.S. Patent system, took seriously, and perhaps too literally, the act's charge to "examine" patent applications (this was catnip to the compulsive tinkerer in him). But after a few adventures with inventors reproducing their experiments in his office, he soon found himself "oppressed beyond measure" by the duty, and appealed to Congress for relief.

Under another section of the Constitution, the power to "fix the standard of weights and measures," Congress also sent Jefferson the one-time chore of reporting his ideas on the subject, one as fascinating to him as inventions. His resulting paper was well received (even by Hamilton to whom Jefferson sent a draft because of its section on coinage), but Congress took no action. Had they adopted his preference—a decimal system—the foot today would be ten inches, an inch would be slightly longer than it now is, and a mile would be almost twice as long a distance.

On the negative side of the ledger, the First Congress set a tragic precedent by refusing to go through the door on slavery that the Constitution left open. Very early in the first session, during debate on Madison's import tax bill, Josiah Parker of Virginia had proposed including a ten-dollar duty on every slave imported, the maximum tax the Constitution allowed. A Georgia member replied for the deep South, accusing Virginia of seeking to monopolize the trade with her slave surplus. Madison came to Parker's aid, but urged his colleague to make the proposal a separate bill, to avoid delaying the tax legislation. Parker agreed and the subject had been dropped.

In the second session, amid the fight over assumption, Quaker delegations from New York and Philadelphia appeared with petitions on the same day that a memorial was presented by Benjamin Franklin's Pennsylvania abolition society—all asking Congress to take steps toward complete abolition of slavery and to discourage the trade. "It is a question," Fisher Ames wrote a friend in Boston after debate began, "that makes the two southern states mad and furious."

South Carolina and Georgia members warned that, if the House sent the petitions to committee, it would "blow the trumpet of sedition in the southern states," but the House did so anyway. The committee report was innocuous—stating that Congress could not end the slave trade for another eighteen years, though it had the power to tax it and impose some regulations—but an ugly confrontation exploded anyway, pushing assumption aside for days.

"The Quakers have been abused, the eastern states inveighed against, the chairman rudely charged with partiality," Ames wrote. "Language low, indecent and profane has been used. Wit equally stale and wretched has been attempted." A twenty-five to twenty-nine vote ordered the committee report to be entered in the House journal—in effect, asserting the power of the House to act against slavery, but not exercising it in any way.

The third branch of America's government came to life on Monday, February 1, 1790 when the Supreme Court of the United States met for the first time. The courtroom, on the second floor of the three-story Royal Exchange, was "uncommonly crowded," with local officials and attorneys, the *New York Daily Advertiser* reported, "but a sufficient number of the judges not being present to form a quorum, the same was adjourned" until the next day when another justice arrived.

Besides appointing John Jay chief justice, Washington had named to the court three Framers of the Constitution—James Wilson of Pennsylvania, John Blair of Virginia, and John Rutledge of South Carolina. However, the district courts (established only four months earlier) were barely in operation, so no cases requiring Constitutional interpretation or otherwise would come to the high court for another three years.

Jay, who was pronounced "elegant" in a black silk robe with white and salmon-colored facings, eschewed the professional wig of English judges (which Jefferson said made them look "like rats peeping through bunches of oakum"). Associate Justice William Cushing, not as wise, walked along New York streets so adorned—but only once. "Little boys trailed after him and a sailor called 'My eye! What a wig!,' " according to Supreme Court historians, and Cushing's wig was seen no more.

The justices used the ten-day session to formulate the first court rules, appoint a crier and clerk, and admit nineteen attorneys to practice before the court. They opened their second session on August 2 (two sessions a year were required by the Judiciary Act), completed the business in one day, and adjourned.

DELENDA EST CARTHAGO

"There was a passionate courtship between the chancellor, Burr, Jefferson and Madison when the two latter were in town. *Delenda est Carthago* is the maxim adopted with respect to you," wrote Robert Troup, Hamilton's former law partner, on June 25, 1791, to the secretary of the treasury.

Federalists from Philadelphia to Boston were buzzing about what Jefferson and Madison were up to: the pair met in New York in mid-May, had stayed for some time, and then departed for a trip through New England that was billed as a botanical expedition to study the habits of the Hessian fly for the American Philosophical Society. Nobody believed them; testing the water for an anti-Federal resurgence seemed a much more likely explanation.

Madison's leadership against Hamilton's measures in Congress had left no doubt that he stood in opposition. That Jefferson agreed with Madison had been surmised—his closeness to Madison and his well-known ideas of government certainly did not make him a Federalist. But Washington considered his cabinet a team, men of measures and policies, not of parties, leading the government along its new path. And so it had seemed until a few weeks before Troup's letter. Then Jefferson's true feelings had suddenly become a matter of national public knowledge. The world had been informed that the author of the Declaration of Independence thought the time had come to "rally a second time round the standard of Common Sense." And, if Troup was to be believed, the chosen way to do it was by toppling Hamilton.

The debt repayment plan, the assumption bill, the national bank, the excise tax on whiskey—all the measures that Hamilton devised to give energy and stability to the national government represented to Jefferson a scheme of subversion. The Federalists—like those against whom Bolingbroke had warred in the 1730s in England—planned for "the Constitution to be construed into a monarchy and to be warped in practice into all the principles and pollutions of their favorite English model."

Adding to Jefferson's fear and loathing, Vice-President John Adams had begun a series of newspaper essays, *Discourses on Davila,* that seemed designed to poison the public's mind against republicanism. Adams had a mixture of motives for the *Discourses,* of which a major one was to defend his advocacy of formal titles and forms in government. Another was to disabuse his countrymen of the romantic notion that the French Revolution was like the American and to warn Americans against applying French revolutionary yardsticks to more than just the muslin for Anne Bingham's gowns.

The fatal flaw Adams saw in the French Revolution was that its new "national assemblies," by which rank and privilege had been abolished and equality among all citizens established, were a dangerous fiction. Men naturally seek fame and distinction over one another, Adams asserted. It is a human hunger. The only safe system is one that recognizes that passion, provides for it, and regulates it—a balanced government.

The French "will fail of their desired liberty,"* Adams predicted. "It is a sacred truth . . . a sovereignty in a single assembly

---

*Adams was right. The French people, wound up for reform, were adrift in their equality and unable to deal with the economic misery and deprivation that had awakened their revolt. Intrigues flourished and the largest figure in the French Revolution from 1789 to 1791, Lafayette, proved to be an ineffectual leader. As Gouverneur Morris reported in a December, 1790 letter that must have given great pain to Washington (who loved Lafayette like a son), "Unfortunately both for himself and his country, he has not the talents which his situation requires. This important truth, known to the few from the very beginning, is now but too well understood by the people in general. His authority depends on incidents, and sinks to nothing in a moment of calm." Lafayette would be forced to flee; and each successive group of leaders would be worse than the last.

will certainly be exercised by a majority as tyrannically as any sovereigny was ever exercised by Kings or nobles. And if a balance of passions and interests is not scientifically concerted, the present struggle in Europe will be little beneficial to mankind and produce nothing but another thousand years of feudal fanaticism under new and strange names."

Hardly anything could be better calculated to madden Jefferson. "I had left France in the first year of her revolution in the fervor of natural rights and zeal for reformation," he wrote years later. "My conscientious devotion to these rights could not be heightened, but it had been aroused and excited by daily exercise." And now his longtime friend was the dupe of "these *energumeni* of royalism," the Federalists, and "by them made to believe that the general disposition of our citizens was favorable to monarchy."

In vain did Washington object to Jefferson that "he did not believe there were ten men in the United States whose opinions were worth attention who entertained such a thought." Jefferson took the president's protest as evidence of his unawareness of "the drift or of the effect of Hamilton's schemes," because Washington was "unversed" in finance. And when Washington still would not buy Jefferson's view, it was because "the Federalists got unchecked hold" of him. "His memory was already sensibly impaired by age, the firm tone of mind for which he had been remarkable was beginning to relax, its energy was abated, a listlessness of labor, a desire for tranquility had crept on him and a willingness to let others act and even think for him."

By the time Washington had to talk to Jefferson about it in 1792, though, the secretary of state's campaign of opposition to the administration in which he served was already eighteen months old. He had taken the first step on February 28, 1791, five days after Washington had signed the bank bill. Jefferson set out that day to recruit an editor to launch a national anti-Federalist newspaper.

The man he hoped to get was Phillip Freneau, the "poet of the Revolution" (the American, not the French), to whom he offered a job as a translator in the State Department. The job, he assured Freneau, would not interfere with any other work that he might wish to do. Freneau declined at first and had to be coaxed into accepting, but when he did, he threw himself into the project—as did Jefferson and Madison, who solicited subscriptions for the newspaper from anti-Federalist friends around the country.

In late April or early May, Jefferson received a pamphlet that he and other agitated republicans had been awaiting, Thomas Paine's famous *Rights of Man,* which had been published in London in February and had created an immediate sensation. Paine had followed the trumpet of rebellion and moved back to Europe, living in England and supporting the French Revolution. Now, in answer to a distinguished English writer attacking the principles of the French Revolution, Paine penned a reply lambasting the British constitution and lauding the upheaval in France.

By mere chance, Jefferson said later, the copy of Paine's pamphlet that came to him was one intended for a Philadelphia printer to use in producing an American edition. Jefferson was asked to forward it to the printer when he had finished with it. The Secretary of State complied, attaching a note to the printer, a man he did not know, saying of Paine's pamphlet, "I am extremely pleased to find it will be reprinted here and that something is at length to be publicly said against the political heresies which have sprung up among us. I have no doubt our citizens will rally a second time round the standard of Common Sense."

When the Philadelphia edition of *The Rights of Man* rolled off the press, Jefferson's note was prominently displayed as an introduction. The printer, though he hardly needed to do so, pointed out that the note did honor to the secretary of state "by directing the mind to a contemplation of that republican firmness and democratic simplicity which endear their possessor [Jefferson] to every friend of the rights of man."

Adams's *Discourses on Davila* were "the heresies" Jefferson meant, and everyone knew it. "The pamphlet—with your name to it so striking a recommendation to it—was not only industriously propagated in New York and Boston, but, that the recommendation might be known to everyone, was reprinted with great care in the newspapers and was generally considered as a direct and open personal attack upon me," Adams wrote Jefferson after Jefferson finally, two months after the publication, sent a letter saying he had been "thunderstruck with seeing it come out at the head of the pamphlet."

Whatever the truth of Jefferson's insistence that he had unburdened himself to "an utter stranger to me" about his disaffection with the administration in which he served—in order, he said, "to take off a little of the dryness of the note" forwarding the pamphlet—the publication served admirably to announce far and wide that the author of the Declaration of Independence believed the time had come to "rally a second time."

A few days after *The Rights of Man* appeared, Jefferson rode out of Philadelphia to meet Madison in New York. It was there that Hamilton's former law partner, Troup, saw and heard of the consultations with the chancellor, Robert Livingston, who had been Hamilton's valuable ally in the adoption of the Constitution. Livingston was now a committed enemy to Hamilton, thanks to Hamilton's crowding him and the rest of the political aspirants in the huge Livingston dynasty out of every possible role they might have played in the new government—one of three or four colossal mistakes Hamilton made in his career for which he paid again and again. When Jefferson's party took shape, Livingston would be among its New York leaders.

It was always the Federalists who insisted that the Hessian fly trip was a cover for a political agenda; the two men's admirers insisted it was purely a vacation. Jefferson and Madison actually spent most of their time observing nature—without spotting the fly. But they also paid numerous political courtesy calls which would have accomplished an essential purpose—to make sure the potential opposition was, in fact, really there. Considering the magnitude of what they were about to do, they would have been foolish to skip such a step.

And it becomes even more probable in view of the fact that their most valuable political operative preceded them. John Beckley (last seen loitering in Philadelphia after losing the secretaryship of the Constitutional Convention to Hamilton's nominee) had just been visiting the same cities to which Jefferson and Madison went. The first clerk of the House of Representatives, elected with Madison's sponsorship, the fanatically republican Beckley, with "the keenest pair of ears in the country," was now the two men's chief source of political intelligence.

Once Jefferson moved into full, open opposition, Beckley became steadily more valuable. He hunted down rumors and discontents to bring back to his leaders and carried out messages and chores unsuitable for Jefferson or Madison to handle. He identified supporters and helped those supporters plan their strategies. He knew who was up and who was down everywhere; he had an uncanny knack for counting votes. He seemed always to show up with what Jefferson needed almost before he knew he needed it. (Beckley had obtained the copy of *The Rights of Man* that Jefferson had then sent on to the printer.) His name crops up repeatedly in Jefferson's papers—"Beckley tells me," "Beckley brings me," "Beckley knows."

To top it off, Beckley had luck in his favor as well: by chance, his young bride was the niece of Hamilton's oldest friend in America, Hercules Mulligan, a well-to-do haberdasher in New York, who had been Washington's favorite spy during the British occupation and who was still the president's friend and tailor.

When the time came to make a noose of Hamilton's libido, it would be Beckley who would see to it that an anti-Federal newspaper editor, James T. Callender (whose poverty had touched Jefferson's sympathy and purse), obtained the requisite documentation.

Beckley was a hard character, but not a political goon. He was an original member of the Phi Beta Kappa society, a former mayor of Richmond, and a knowledgeable, if radical, politician. His entire official career consisted of clerking for important bodies, fourteen altogether in his lifetime. For Beckley's services to the republic, a grateful President Jefferson appointed him the first Librarian of Congress.

Besides courting Livingston in New York, Jefferson met with

Freneau who still hesitated to come to Philadelphia. Freneau finally changed his mind after Jefferson made it plain that, in addition to a $250 State Department salary and responsibilities that would "not interfere with any other calling," Freneau would have "perusal of all my letters of foreign intelligence" and "the publication of all proclamations and other public notices within my department and the printing of the laws."

Freneau arrived in Philadelphia in late August, 1791, and the first issue of his *National Gazette* appeared on October 24, with columnist James Madison writing under various pen names. For about three months, Freneau and Madison walked softly, then Madison opened up on Hamilton early in 1792. Freneau's own favorite target was the president, on whose doorstep the editor deposited three copies of his *National Gazette* every day. The barrage continued through the summer of 1792.

In the Federalist newspaper, an angry Hamilton, writing as "T.L." exposed the secretary of state's sponsorship of Freneau, and Washington, "evidently sore and warm," raised it with Jefferson, who jotted a note for his memoirs that day. "I took his intention to be that I should interpose in some way with Freneau, perhaps withdraw his appointment of translating clerk to my office. But I will not do it. His paper has saved our constitution."

Once Hamilton started writing rebuttals, he could not stop, and the two sides blasted each other in every issue of their respective journals. Pseudonyms notwithstanding, the identities of the warring parties were plain, if not the names of those who were brandishing the quills. The whole country was agog; it was utterly inconceivable that the two leading men in Washington's government were tearing each other apart like this. The president finally demanded explanations, received a denial of any responsibility from Jefferson and an acknowledgement of his role with a refusal to stop from Hamilton—and the war went on.

Washington put up with it for two months more, but he was getting tired of being hit. When Freneau published what Jefferson called a "pasquinade" (a libelous satire) that ended with the president on the guillotine, "The President was much inflamed," Jefferson wrote after that day's cabinet meeting, "got into one of those passions when he cannot command himself; ran on much on the personal abuse which had been bestowed on him . . . *by God,* he had rather be in his grave than in his present situation; that he had rather be on his farm than to be made *Emperor of the world;* and yet that they were charging him with wanting to be a King. That that *rascal Freneau* sent him three of his papers every day, as if he thought he would become the distributor of his papers, that he could see in this nothing but an impudent design to insult him. He ended in this high tone. There was a pause. Some difficulty in resuming our question . . ."

In context, Jefferson's equanimity about Washington's fury shows the philosopher-founder at just about his worst. It was very much attributable to him that, from Massachusetts to Georgia, anti-Federalists were in full cry for the first time since the year of ratification.

Only now there was a new, bloodthirsty tenor to which Jefferson was all too indifferent: the standard they carried was that of the Jacobins, who were perverting the French Revolution into the Reign of Terror, had guillotined Louis XVI and were about to do the same to Marie Antoinette and her child, the 14-year-old dauphin. The reheated American republicans were singing the French marching song, *"Ça ira! Ça ira!,"* organizing democratic societies modelled on the French Jacobin clubs to protect America's "endangered" liberties and demanding that America join France in its shooting war with England. A mob that John Adams estimated at ten thousand had swarmed through the streets threatening to "drag Washington out of his house."

But Jefferson went on believing. Even in 1793, when France would be awash in blood and war, he would reproach his disillusioned protege, William Short, still serving in the Paris embassy, "my own affections have been deeply wounded by some of the martyrs to this cause, but rather than it should have failed, I would have seen half the earth desolated."

If Jefferson had been as bloodthirsty as he liked to sound, or if his ambition had exceeded his principles, or had military men been numerous in the ranks of his followers, he might have brought the Constitution to an early demise in the late 1790s. But he was not trying to overthrow the system; his reservations about the Constitution were very nearly gone by the time he began his campaign.

He feared the leading principles of Federalism—vigorous, capitalist, "high-toned" government—for precisely the reason he had stated to Madison in 1788: "I am not a friend to very energetic government; it is always oppressive." He was convinced that the Federalists would do, and were doing, everything in their power to break out of the constraints of the Constitution, but he no longer feared the Constitution itself, as he had when he had first seen it.

Jefferson therefore submitted his fiery radicalism to constitutional processes for vindication. He directed the rise of republicans into the Congress and himself into the presidency propounding a view of the national authority vastly different from that of the men under whom the Constitution had begun. He needed no guns, bloodshed, martyrs or prisoners. The course was charted in the Constitution and he followed it.

The test to which Jefferson put the Constitution came early—certainly too early for Washington or Hamilton to appreciate—but it answered questions that could not safely be ignored too long: did the Constitution provide a government resting workably on the whole people, or was it tailored for the men who had participated in designing it. Was it a system which held out hope for different aspirations or would deep differences require the age-old recourse to the sword? Those questions were asked in the Constitutional Convention and more loudly and more often in the ratification. Almost half the people doubted that they had been answered—until Jefferson established his party.

Washington died in 1799 troubled and bitter about the turmoil of his second term and alienated from Jefferson. Adams left office simply bitter and the breach between him and Jefferson did not heal for thirteen years.

Hamilton, while he considered Jefferson "a man of profound ambition and violent passions," was younger and still looking ahead. In 1801, pointing out that "if there be a man in the world I ought to hate, it is Jefferson," he threw his influence on Jefferson's side to break the deadlock in the House of Representatives' presidential vote after the Jefferson-Burr electoral tie.

Referring to himself as a "disappointed politician," Hamilton then withdrew to private life, staying out of national politics until 1804 when he intervened in a secession scheme being hatched by New England Federalists with the cooperation of Vice-President Aaron Burr. That was Hamilton's last attempt to prop "that frail and worthless fabric." Burr challenged him to a duel that took place on July 11, 1804, Burr's shot inflicting a mortal wound of which Hamilton died thirty-six hours later. He was forty-six years old.

19

" . . . But then your feet are always in water"

"A MONARCHY," said Fisher Ames during a 1795 speech in the House, "is a merchantman which sails well, but will sometimes strike on a rock and go to the bottom; a republic is a raft which will never sink, but then your feet are always in water."

America's raft, though, was a strange piece of business: it had a tendency to a centrifugal spin, and as the craft proceeded on its journey, the spin grew ever faster.

The first twenty-five years of the republic seemed to many Americans a failed experiment. Defeat of the Federalists had smothered the fire of nationalism, eliminating the specter of a government "vibrating between monarchy and a corrupt aristocracy" that George Mason had predicted. But if nationalism tended toward monarchism, the federal part of the "partly national, partly federal" system harbored evils of its own. Under the limited government policies of Jefferson and then Madison, the localist tendencies that had been preserved in the Constitution were given free play, and the devil of disunion waited at the end of that road.

In Jefferson's first term, the Louisiana Purchase negotiated by the president's anti-Federalist protege and fellow Virginian, James Monroe, awakened New England sectionalism, as horrified Federalists there predicted annihilation of their economic interests by a gigantic, slave-owning South wrought from the acquisition. Secessionist intrigues sprang up from Boston to New York, gaining little support at first. Then Jefferson withdrew American shipping from the seas, trying through trade pressure to stop the warring British and French from interfering with neutral American ships. As vessels and cargo rotted in American harbors for more than a year, a cry for separation spread through the North and ended only with repeal of the embargo.

By the 1830s, a pebble Jefferson had sent tumbling down the hill in the 1790s became an avalanche. The Kentucky and Virginia resolutions—which came from his pen against Adams's Alien and Sedition acts in 1798—had been official claims by states to a right to interpret the constitutionality of national laws and reject them if they chose. More than thirty years later, that doctrine became the basis for the "nullification movement." It culminated in South Carolina, where a state convention called for the purpose declared null and void a federal tariff law that favored New England and hurt the South. Although the constitutional crisis was resolved by compromise (Congress amended the tariff), the strains in the young Union were now transformed from republicans versus "monocrats" to national supremacy versus states rights.

The tortured fabric of nationalism burst when the strain became too great at the point where the convention had only stitched a compromise—the preservation of slavery. The failure did not come suddenly; a rending sound had been heard, and compromises made, again and again: in Congress in 1790 when the Quakers' and Franklin's abolition society petitions had been received; again in 1820 with the Missouri Compromise, which prohibited slavery in new territories and fenced the institution into the South; in 1850 with a four-part compromise devised by Daniel Webster and Henry Clay to defeat the "Wilmot Proviso" that had sought to prohibit slavery in southwest lands that had been won in 1848 in the Mexican War.

Nationalism had never grown strong in the South, even in the best days of the Federalists. Now it was a feeble shadow there, and the industrial-commercial North seemed to many southerners almost a foreign oppressor living up to the worst fears of George Mason, Patrick Henry, and Thomas Jefferson. With slavery bottled up by free territories, the slave states began to realize that abolition—and destruction of their agrarian way of life—was only a matter of time if they could not undo these Federal acts and extend slavery into the new territories. Their right to carry slaves into other regions and the right of the territories to accept slavery—states' rights (and its theoretical equivalent in the territories, "popular sovereignty")—was the principle; they would assert it to the nation that was isolating them.

Strength in Congress and skillful political bargaining brought the South partial success in 1854; the Kansas-Nebraska Act repealed the Missouri Compromise and granted settlers the choice of free-or-slave. But in 1857, the Supreme Court, under Chief Justice Roger Taney, gave states' rights and "pop sov" a total victory, ruling in *Dred Scott* v. *Sandford* that Congress could not regulate slavery—the Constitution left that power to the states; the South was free to carry slavery to new states.

The nation, having pushed incrementally to curtail slavery, seemed unsure whether to let the minority push the majority back. In the 1860 election, it gave sixty percent of the popular vote to three candidates who would have allowed "pop sov," though only one, receiving fifteen percent, ran on a platform so firmly pledged.* The electoral college, however, reflecting the people as states, showed no retreat from the isolation of slavery. The electors cast sixty percent of their votes for Abraham Lincoln, electing a president who unalterably opposed allowing slavery into the territories, but promised not to interfere where it existed and even endorsed a constitutional amendment securing that pledge.

But the slave states were beyond compromise. They se-

---

*None of the four candidates, including Lincoln, campaigned on a platform to abolish slavery.

ceded—the last line of defense and logical endpoint of their doctrine of states' rights.

And the last line of defense for the nation was not to recognize the secession. Allowing states to withdraw spelled ultimate national disintegration, the very fate that fifty-five men had gone to Philadelphia to prevent. Whatever constitutional rights the slave states believed those men had provided them, secession was not among them. A union was now to be preserved, and, four years and six hundred thousand dead Americans later, the principle of one American nation prevailed.

The greatest danger to the Constitution might be said to have come *after* the Civil War, when the victorious political leaders might well have tried to radically redesign the vessel to deal with such parts of it as had appeared faulty before or during the strife. The temptations were plain—the Supreme Court that handed down the *Dred Scott* decision and the chief executive's usurpation of congressional prerogatives (if not constitutional powers), to name just two. But America did not yield to those temptations, and the republic—three branches, checks and balances, enumerated powers, elected representatives, and even states' influence—remained almost as it had been before. It was as if Americans had concluded that, when the blood faded from the water, it would be better if their feet were still wet. They had gotten used to their raft—and it had not sunk.

The letter of the Constitution has changed very little in the last two hundred years. Since the Bill of Rights was ratified in December, 1791, only sixteen amendments have been added.

Seven amendments spread political equality throughout the land, aligning the country's political life more closely with the principles of the Declaration of Independence, which would have pleased Jefferson, its author.

Articles Thirteen, Fourteen and Fifteen were post-Civil War amendments abolishing slavery and establishing full political rights for all men. Article Nineteen extended suffrage to women—not Jefferson's cup of tea in his lifetime, but perhaps it would have been had he lived in 1920. Article Twenty-three, ratified in 1961, enabled District of Columbia residents to vote in presidential elections.* In 1964, the twenty-fourth amendment killed the poll tax, a subterfuge of the unrepentant South to circumvent the fifteenth amendment and disenfranchise black voters once more. The twenty-sixth amendment, ratified in 1971, lowered the voting age to eighteen.

Two early twentieth-century amendments tightened the tie between the people and the government. Article Sixteen permitted Congress to pass an income tax without apportioning the levy among states or linking it to the census. Article Seventeen provided for popular election of senators, transferring that power from state legislatures to the people.

The Twenty-second Amendment, ratified in 1951, was a reaction to Franklin D. Roosevelt's election to four terms as president. Jeffersonian in impulse and reflecting his distrust of holders of power, it is, however, undemocratic in that (as some delegates in Philadelphia said) if the people are happy with the incumbent, they should be able to elect him again. In 1987, other observations from 1787—mainly about ineligibility producing weakness or misconduct—were being heard, and if second-term failures become the rule, they may one day convince.

Three amendments—the Twelfth, Twentieth, and Twenty-fifth—did not affect the relationship between the people and the government. They fixed procedures for some situations which the framers had left to chance affecting the office of president:

Amendment Twelve resulted from the Jefferson-Burr electoral tie† of 1800 which produced six days of suspense and

---

*The Framers assumed that the government would be heavily influenced by those living in the capital, giving a double advantage to the host state. The solution was to provide a "district (not exceeding ten miles square)" that would not be a state. They supposed that anyone residing in the federal district would not expect to vote. The Twenty-third Amendment was a goal of the civil rights movement because the city of Washington (which did not exist in 1787) was about three-quarters black. Even then, the amendment did not provide voting representation in Congress. A new amendment, providing full representation by permitting the city to become a state, was before the Congress in 1987. With both houses controlled by Democrats (whose numbers would increase because the city votes Democratic in a ratio of nearly ninety percent), the statehood amendment was thought to have a fair prospect for passing.

†The tie was not quite by chance. Jefferson's party was so disciplined that the Republicans (as his followers were by then known) obediently cast their votes only for Jefferson and Burr, it being understood that the vice-presidency was to be Burr's reward for delivering the North for Jefferson. In the very first presidential election,

partisan struggle while the House of Representatives decided the winner. The amendment directs presidential electors to distinguish between their votes for president and vice-president.

The Twentieth Amendment provides for executive succession in the event a president-elect dies before inauguration, and the Twenty-fifth establishes the manner in which presidential power may be transferred to the vice-president in case the chief executive becomes temporarily unable to discharge his duties.*

Prohibition (Article Eighteen) was the idea and victory of the women's suffrage movement. An attempt at moral regulation in the spirit of sumptuary legislation, it would have gratified George Mason, but it created a nation of scofflaws consorting with gangsters—which would have depressed him. To repeal it, since it was a constitutional amendment, the constitution had to be amended again, by the Twenty-first Amendment. To the extent that a crusading populism had produced a constitutional mistake and correction, the two amendments were at least instructive.

"IT IS A *CONSTITUTION* THAT WE ARE EXPOUNDING"

"We must never forget," said Chief Justice John Marshall, "that it is a *constitution* that we are expounding."

The courtroom was almost empty that day, March 6, 1819, and perhaps the great jurist paused in reading his ruling to allow himself a smile at the attorney representing Maryland, in

---

Hamilton warded off a potential tie between Washington and John Adams by urging some of the Federalist electors to "throw away" their votes on local figures. The idea worked too well. Adams got an embarrassingly low number of votes and briefly considered declining.

*The serious illnesses of three modern presidents—Woodrow Wilson, Franklin Roosevelt, and Dwight Eisenhower—created the concern that led to the Twenty-fifth Amendment in 1964. When Ronald Reagan underwent emergency surgery as a result of an attempted assassination only weeks after taking office in 1981, his aides did not take the preparatory steps in the amendment. Reagan's time under anesthesia was short and no complications arose, but congressional and press criticism was pointed. When the dilemma again presented itself before Reagan's cancer surgery in 1983, the president ordered the required papers to be prepared and held in case they were needed.

the matter of *McCullouch* v. *Maryland*. The lawyer was a converted supporter of the Constitution, but not to the part that had been his most valuable contribution to it—its supremacy clause. And national supremacy was the principal issue of the case.

At age seventy-five, after fifty years of hard drinking, Luther Martin, Constitution Framer, was still on his feet. His mind was much wasted, but still among the best—good enough for his home state to dispatch him against the Second Bank of the United States* and its attorneys, Daniel Webster, the most splendid lawyer-orator of the day, and William Pinkney (not a South Carolina Pinckney), whom Marshall called "the greatest man he had ever seen in a court of justice." And Martin was as long-winded as ever; "Our bank argument," Webster wrote to a friend, "threatens to be long . . . Martin has been *talking three days*."

If the lawyer and jurist smiled at each other, it was only because Martin would have liked the chance to bare his teeth at the chief justice. Detesting Thomas Jefferson was the only thing they had in common (and with Martin it was purely a personal grudge—he thought Jefferson had insulted his wife's family). Marshall was an ardent nationalist, a passionate admirer of Washington and Hamilton, an appointee of John Adams. He headed the last place in government where a good number of Federalists could be found, and was the last Federalist with the stature of the originals.

Hamilton, in *The Federalist,* had assured the public that the judiciary was the weakest branch, having neither the power of the sword nor the power of the purse, but Marshall had shown in 1803 that he was willing to use what he had. In a legal faceoff with the Jefferson administration, Marshall had ruled a portion of a law unconstitutional—the first time the court had taken that step. He had cleverly ruled in favor of the administration, but a constitutional declaration had not been asked for. In fact, the ruling disappointed the Jeffersonians, who had been hoping the

---

*The charter of Hamilton's Bank of the United States expired in 1811. Congress refused to recharter it, but after the lack of it caused financial disarray in the War of 1812, President Madison accepted its renewal.

court would issue an order it could not enforce.

After that, Marshall started overturning *state* laws, and not because they interfered with federal laws or treaties. By adding new dimensions to familiar and already well-defined concepts such as the nature of a contract, he had been finding violations of the Constitution in all kinds of state legislation. It was all part of his Federalist ideology; now that Martin would like Marshall to overturn a congressional act for the sake of a state, the Marylander could be pretty sure it would not happen.

In the case on which Marshall was ruling, Martin had presented the state sovereignty argument at which he had had so much practice. And he had tried, as Jefferson and Madison had years earlier, to prove the Second Bank of the United States unconstitutional by a rigid interpretation of the Constitution's "necessary and proper" clause. He also had sought to bolster his side by adding that the men in the Philadelphia convention "disclaimed" any intent for the government to exercise powers not enumerated—opponents' suspicions had been called "a dream of distempered jealousy." The Constitution, he added, would not have been adopted if the Framers had "fairly avowed" such intent.

The unanimous ruling, written by the chief justice himself, rebuffed Martin's attack on national sovereignty and drew different conclusions about the Framers' intent.* Marshall then declared that national sovereignty extended to the means by which the government carried out its enumerated powers—and ruled that both the means and the sovereignty were implicit in the necessary-and-proper clause of the Constitution.

"This provision," said Marshall, "is made in a constitution intended to endure for ages to come and consequently to be adapted to the various *crises* of human affairs."

With that ruling, Marshall opened the door to enlarged government under the section of the Constitution enumerating the powers of Congress—most especially the first and third para-

---

*Marshall knew many of the Framers and had read *The Federalist,* as well as all of George Washington's papers, which he had been allowed to use in writing his five-volume biography of the first president. Still, he confined his references to construing their intent from the Constitution's text.

graphs: to "lay and collect taxes . . . and provide for the common defence and general welfare of the United States" and "to regulate commerce . . . among the several states."

And because he ruled that the Constitution was intended to "be adapted," he also finished setting the stage for today's most vigorously disputed question on the Constitution: the role of the Supreme Court.

"The judiciary of Aragon became by degrees the lawgiver," John Dickinson had remarked in the Constitutional Convention, but as an observation, not a prediction. In fact, neither he nor his colleagues analyzed the future development of the judiciary as they did the legislature and executive branch they created. Rather, the Framers established the judiciary branch almost casually, with little argument, because they agreed in general on its function. They laid down the jurisdiction the court would have in "cases" and "controversies" under the Constitution and federal law, but did not explicitly give it the power to set aside laws as unconstitutional. A few delegates thought the court should not do so, but that was a minority view.

Although the delegates saw the importance of judicial independence, they did not think of the judiciary as superior in authority to the other branches of government; they left to Congress the entire organization of the judiciary, including the number of Supreme Court justices and what lower courts to establish. Nor, at the outset of the government, was the Supreme Court regarded as "co-equal" with the legislative and executive. As Hamilton had said in his etiquette letter to Washington, the inauguration of the president "completed the organization of the Constitution."

And Marshall, though aggressive and independent, did not greatly change that relative position of the judiciary. In the thirty-four years during which he was chief justice, the Supreme Court actually overturned an act of Congress only once and state laws about a dozen times. His successor, Taney, although as ardent a states' rights man as Marshall had been a nationalist, was just as careful. By the opening of the Civil War, when the Constitution was seventy years old, the high court in total had invalidated just two congressional acts and twenty state laws.

For about twenty years after the Civil War, the Supreme Court remained slow to overturn legislation. But from 1890 to 1937—from the Gilded Age of commercial and industrial prosperity through the Great Depression—the Court struck down 69 federal laws and 228 state statutes. Those years were no romp for "levelling" ideas; it was the Court's era of property rights. Most of the invalidated laws either had been fought for by the reform movement that swept the country against great industrial and transportation combinations or were the most ambitious of Franklin D. Roosevelt's Depression recovery programs. The Court had become a "super-legislature," complained Justice Louis Brandeis; its self-aggrandizement knew "hardly any limit but the sky," said Justice Oliver Wendell Holmes. It was not accepting the popular will.

By the end of the 1970s, the Court had become egalitarian in philosophy, striking down laws that interfered with integration, civil rights, due process, privacy, women's rights. It also had moved from ruling on laws to ruling on the administration of federal, state, and local governments and agencies as well as private entities where egalitarian precepts might be violated.

The high-water mark of Court liberalism had been the reign of Chief Justice Earl Warren. His successor, Warren Burger, and President Richard Nixon's two other conservative appointees restrained but did not reverse the ideological trend. With the appointment of Burger's successor in 1986, William Rehnquist, and a new conservative associate justice, Antonin Scalia, liberals and conservatives alike were predicting a complete ideological turnaround, but rulings from the new court's first cases in the spring of 1987 did not augur so sharp a difference.

Nevertheless, the clap-of-doom tone of liberals, the profound glee of conservatives, and the avid analysis that continued to fill the press rang with the excitement that attended congressional elections and debate from the beginning of the government and through the nineteenth century.

The Court had reached the point where, in 1986, it reviewed some legislation before it could go into operation and heard a case in which it was asked to regulate the presidential "pocket veto" by defining it. On social policy, it was so thoroughly in command that, in a front-page analysis of Justice Lewis Powell (who had often cast the fifth vote in the Court's five-to-four majorities), *The New York Times* could declare him to have "as powerful an influence as anyone alive today in setting the law of the land on a stunning array of social issues—more than Chief Justice William H. Rehnquist, more than Chief Justice Rehnquist's predecessor, Warren E. Burger, more in a sense than even Ronald Reagan."

Conservatives and liberals agree that the Court has been writing the law of the land—especially surmising social principles from the Declaration of Independence and Bill of Rights and adding them to the Constitution the way wider suffrage, political equality, the income tax and democratic control of the Senate were added by overt amendment. The public agrees as well: the new constitutional requirements have been ratified informally by America's institutions, public and private, which adjust to them as they would to a new law. The process resembles that of the British constitution, which is unwritten and changes from generation to generation, the difference being that Parliament makes the changes while the American document is being amended by decree.

Liberals call the Court's modern role the manifestation of the "living Constitution," which infuriates conservatives who do not like being put in the position of calling it a dead Constitution. In reply, they label the Court's history a "usurpation" of legislative and executive prerogative by nine unelected men, and call for "jurisprudence of original intention"—in other words, rule as the Framers intended and quit the field of policy.

While rejecting the label of usurper, two members of the Burger Court, and possibly others whose views have not been publicized, admit concern about an over-reliance on the Court. One, Associate Justice Harry Blackmun, pointed out during an interview with the journalist, Bill Moyers, that Congress now often legislates with the expectation that the Court will redeem its errors. The most striking example of Congress doing so came in 1986, when the Court sorted out the permissible from the impermissible in the national deficit reduction program, the

Gramm-Rudman-Hollings bill—which had been written by the Congress, signed by the president, and carried to the marble courthouse behind the Capitol as if the bill were a draft.

The other, former Chief Justice Warren Burger, now chairman of the national commission for the Constitution Bicentennial, has for several years called for a new look at the way the great branches of the government are functioning. "The authors of the Constitution," he has said, "did not contemplate that the judiciary would be an overseer of the other two branches. At most, they expected that the judicial function would be confined to interpreting the laws before them and deciding whether particular acts of the Congress, the Executive, or the states were in conflict with the Constitution."

As the two-hundredth birthday of the Constitution neared, the leader of the conservative attack on the Court's modern role was Attorney General Edwin Meese III, who all but laid siege to the Court's most ideological liberal, Justice William Brennan, in an effort to provoke a nationwide debate on the subject. Shocked, Brennan contributed a few angry speeches to the cause, but the political fire appeared to flicker out on both sides. One reason was that perhaps, as a *New York Times* analysis observed, Meese "often makes potentially far-reaching but fundamentally ambiguous statements about issues of great profundity and complexity without spelling out what he means."

Meese chose to attack on terrain mystifying to interested lay observers: whether the Court had the power to require states to comply with the Constitution. His critics immediately shelled his position with mockery, and withdrew to wait. The attorney general then asserted the more defensible view that both the Congress and the president have an obligation to interpret the Constitution and decide for themselves what its principles are. That fusillade landed in the bushes of scholarship, from where some experts shot back that Meese had issued an "invitation to lawlessness." The battlefield fell silent a few weeks later, when the Reagan administration's arms dealings with Iran and, subsequently, the diversion of funds to Nicaraguan *contras* were disclosed.

Whether Meese meant to or not, in his second foray, he had

found a point of agreement with the two concerned Supreme Court justices: the striking difference between eighteenth- and nineteenth-century congressmen and their modern successors in their view of lawmaking relative to the Constitution. In congressional debate in the first century of the government, no lawmaker failed to justify himself on constitutional principle. His modern successor rarely has such an impulse—he no longer sees that as his job. And it is into that vacuum that the Supreme Court has moved.

In early summer, 1987, Meese told reporters that the Supreme Court would probably decide if the president had the power to defy the congressional ban on aid to the Nicaraguan rebels. It seemed a shriek of surrender. For the more than fifty years of controversy about the Court, "judicial review" (an American creation at the time of the Revolution) had stuck closely to its roots in English common law and theories of natural rights—individual rights. Whether "conservative" or "liberal," the Court had made most of its disputed decisions in this area. However, Meese's unexpected concession made concrete a threat that was only implicit in the Court's earlier forays on the deficit bill and the pocket veto: that the nine justices would begin defining the powers of the other branches that had been left ambiguous in the Constitution. It seemed at last "agreed on all hands," as Madison would say, that the Court was above its "co-equal" branches and could end any contention between them. In Fisher Ames's simile, the Court stood ready to bail the last of the water out of the republician raft and rebuild the vessel to leave America's feet comfortably dry.

Or so it seemed. Soon after Meese's remark, Justice Powell, often the fifth vote in the court's five-to-four majorities, announced his retirement. President Reagan had his chance to end the Court's liberal era and enshrine the conservative idea that (in the words of his nominee, Judge Robert H. Bork) "abstinence from giving his own desires free play . . . continuing and self-conscious renunciation of power . . . is the morality of the jurist." Suddenly, a descent by the Court was just as possible.

The prospect of dethroning the benevolent oligarchy that

had written so many popular ideals into the law was dramatic and ripe with implications. Unless the nation plunged into war or economic collapse, it was to be the important business opening the Constitution's third century—to be worked out in terms of years and by answering other questions. Would a majority of the justices decide to renounce a power? Or would the fifty-year egalitarian era of the Court give way to a similarly activist era of property rights and other nonlevelling concepts both bedrock in democratic theory and grist for demagogues? Either way, would the legislative and executive branches feel compelled to reclaim their constitutional berths? Would they exercise their powers if the Court refused to act for them? Would they continue to pass laws inviting judicial rejection or revision? And, having known smoother sailing and drier feet by depending on the Court, would Americans demand that the merchantman sail on?

In May, 1796, the end of his time in office approaching, George Washington sat down and wrote a passionate farewell to the nation, an address which he summoned Hamilton to cool off. When the work was done, one of America's greatest state papers had been written, breathing the first presidents's faith in the people of America and in "the free constitution which is the work of your own hands." And flowing from he called the "most ardent wishes of my heart" were these thoughts:

"The basis of our political system is the right of the people to make and to alter their constitutions of government. But the constitution which at any time exists, until changed by an implicit and authentic act of the whole people, is sacredly obligatory upon all . . . Toward the preservation of your government and the permanency of your present happy state, it is requisite . . . that you resist with care the spirit of innovation upon its principles, however specious [pleasing] the pretext . . . Changes upon the credit of mere hypothesis and opinion exposes to perpetual change from the endless variety of hypothesis and opinion . . . It is important, likewise, that the habits of thinking in a free country should inspire caution in those entrusted with its administration to confine themselves within their respective constitutional spheres . . . The spirit of encroachment tends to consolidate the powers of all the departments in one and thus to create, whatever the form of government, a real despotism . . . If in the opinion of the people, the distribution or modification of the constitutional powers be in any particular wrong, let it be corrected by an amendment in the way which the constitution designates. But let there be no change by usurpation, for though this, in one instance, may be the instrument of good, it is the customary weapon by which free governments are destroyed. The precedent must always greatly overbalance in permanent evil any partial or transient benefit which the use can at any time yield."

And, as the Constitution turned two hundred in 1987, that fundamental excercise of constitutional power was what Americans of every belief were thinking and arguing about.